Music in Black American Life,
1945–2020

MUSIC IN AMERICAN LIFE

A list of books in the series appears at the end of this book.

MUSIC IN
BLACK AMERICAN LIFE,
1945–2020

A University of Illinois Press Anthology

Compiled by
LAURIE MATHESON

Introduction by
TAMMY L. KERNODLE

**UNIVERSITY OF
ILLINOIS PRESS**
Urbana, Chicago, and Springfield

Library of Congress Cataloging-in-Publication Data
Names: Matheson, Laurie Christine, compiler. |
    Kernodle, Tammy L., writer of introduction.
Title: Music in black American life, 1945-2020 : a University of
    Illinois Press anthology / compiled by Laurie Matheson.
Description: Urbana : University of Illinois Press, 2022. | Series:
    Music in American life | Introduction by Tammy L. Kernodle.
    | Includes bibliographical references and index.
Identifiers: LCCN 2022005995 (print) | LCCN 2022005996
    (ebook) | ISBN 9780252044588 (cloth) | ISBN 9780252086663
    (paperback) | ISBN 9780252053597 (ebook)
Subjects: LCSH: African Americans—Music—History and
    criticism. | Blacks--United States—Music—History and
    criticism. | Music—United States—History and criticism.
Classification: LCC ML200 .M88 2022 (print) | LCC ML200
    (ebook) | DDC 780.89/96073—dc23/eng/20220302
LC record available at https://lccn.loc.gov/2022005995
LC ebook record available at https://lccn.loc.gov/2022005996

Contents

Preface

The two volumes of *Music in Black American Life* highlight the richness and variety of Black music-making, from enslavement to *Hamilton*, representing a broad spectrum of genres: from Black folk music and rural string band practices to spirituals; classical to blues and gospel; and jazz to R&B and hip-hop. Featuring new introductions from Sandra Jean Graham and Tammy L. Kernodle, this project celebrates several milestones in the music list of the University of Illinois Press. The year 2022 marks the fiftieth anniversary of the Music in American Life series and the fifteenth anniversary of the series African American Music in Global Perspective. The journal *American Music* celebrates forty years in 2023; and 2023 also marks the fortieth anniversary of the establishment of *Black Music Research Journal* as the flagship publication of the Center for Black Music Research, as well as the fifteenth anniversary of the start of the publishing partnership between *BMRJ* and the University of Illinois Press.

But beyond these anniversaries, these volumes celebrate the influential work of scholars devoted to illuminating and understanding the Black musical experience. The emphasis here is on Black music-making in a material sense, and in a range of contexts (composition, pedagogy, performance) and venues (streets, dance halls, churches, concert halls). I have striven to prioritize Black authors and to represent as broad a gamut of styles and regions as possible.

Like American music itself, these four publication streams are the result of meaningful collaborations. Both the book series Music in American Life and the journal *American Music* were ideas seeded by Press director Richard Wentworth. Music in American Life was carried forward with tremendous passion and intellectual rigor by editor Judith McCulloh, in consultation with folklorist and polymath Archie Green (who reportedly named the series), among many others. Archie Green's book *Only a Miner* was the first book published in the series, which crosses the threshold of 250 titles as of the end of calendar 2021. It has been my great pleasure to shepherd the Music in American Life and the African American Music in Global Perspective series since becoming music editor in 2005.

Issue 1 of the journal *American Music* features a mission statement that also resonates with the series, pledging to "deal with all aspects of American music and music in America: genres and forms; geographical and historical patterns; composers, performers, and audiences; sacred and secular traditions; cultural, social, and ethnic diversity; the impact and role of the media; the reflection of social, political, and economic issues; problems of research, analysis, and archiving; criticism and aesthetics; and more." Editor Alan Britton continued, "My hope is that *American Music* can begin to open doors in the walls of the compartments into which students of the multiple musics of America still remain isolated—each unaware or only vaguely aware of the others—so that the full scope of the American musical enterprise can become known and understood here and everywhere." From its founding through 2006, *American Music* was the journal of the Society for American Music (formerly the Sonneck Society).

The first issue of the *Black Music Research Journal* was published in 1980, with a dedication to John W. Work II (1872–1925), a collector and arranger of folksongs and spirituals and professor of history and Latin at Fisk University, and his son, John Wesley Work III, a highly productive composer and professor of music at Fisk from 1926 to 1966. The pioneering musicologist Samuel A. Floyd founded and oversaw the journal, first at Fisk and then at Columbia College in Chicago. The journal became the flagship publication of the Center for Black Music Research, which Floyd directed from 1983 to 1990 and 1993 to 2002. Volume 28, No. 1 (Spring 2008) was the first to be published by the University of Illinois Press. Sadly, the journal ceased publication in 2016.

The series African American Music in Global Perspective is published in collaboration with the Archives of African American Music and Culture at Indiana University. Indiana University faculty Portia K. Maultsby and Mellonee V. Burnim worked with editor in chief Joan Catapano in establishing the series at Illinois, and the first volume was published in 2007. Eileen M. Hayes has recently replaced Burnim as coeditor. The series seeks to foreground the cultural perspectives of the primary creators and performers of the musics, highlighting the voices of African Americans themselves.

Working with many of the scholars represented in these volumes, and being part of the larger community of American music scholars, is an enormous privilege, and assembling these anthologies out of the immense wealth of University of Illinois Press publications in Black music has been a joy.

Acknowledgments

It would be difficult to overstate my delight when Sandra Graham and Tammy Kernodle accepted my invitation to contribute introductions to these volumes. I gratefully acknowledge the indispensable assistance of Angela Burton and Mariah Schaefer at the University of Illinois Press in screening and clearing permissions and carrying out many administrative pre-production details. I also acknowledge Dawn Durante, who established the Press's Anthology series, and Alexa Colella, whose Common Threads series is also a model.

In my work at the Press, I stand on the shoulders of mentors Judy McCulloh, Joan Catapano, and Richard Wentworth. Most of all, I am grateful to the musicians and the scholars whose work fills these volumes. In the language of our current historical moment, Black lives matter to American music, and to American music scholarship.

Laurie Matheson
Director, University of Illinois Press

Music in Black American Life,
1945–2020

Introduction

TAMMY L. KERNODLE

"It is because the past is a guide with roads pointing in many directions that each generation and epoch must make its own studies of history."
—Earl E. Thorpe[1]

During the last quarter of the twentieth century, the historiography of black music-making in America grew exponentially and black music studies gained firmer footing as a disciplinary field. The intellectual labor that precipitated these phenomena was connected fundamentally to the ideological aims of the Black Power and Black Nationalism movements that established the study of black culture in institutional settings in the years immediately following the assassination of Dr. Martin Luther King, Jr. It also connected with the emergence of what I call the black music intelligentsia and their construction of intellectual infrastructure that advanced their challenges to the exclusionary frameworks of American music scholarship. This anthology represents how their work in the 1970s and 1980s spawned new methodologies and modes of inquiry that frame contemporary black music scholarship.

To best understand the connection between the intellectual work advanced by this black music intelligentsia and the scholarly voices represented in this anthology, we must go back to the beginning. In this case, back to 1971, when the first definitive musicological study of the development and evolution of black music in America was published. Eileen Southern's *The Music of Black Americans—A History* signified the beginning of an important epoch in black music studies. It advanced a framework that demonstrated the role black music played in the development of American culture and identity and centered Southern as one of the primary figures advancing new methodologies of research. She was part of a larger community of historians, musicians, librarians, and composers whose work precipitated the expansion of the black music historiography over the next thirty years. The work of black music intelligentsia, much like the essays contained in this volume, blurred the disciplinary lines that existed between ethnomusicology, musicology, music theory, black studies, composition, and performance studies. They were also not content to wait for the existing intellectual infrastructure to recognize the importance of their work. Drawing on the ideology of "institution-building" that was promoted through the black liberation movement, they created a multi-tiered, multi-faceted mechanism to disseminate their work.

This intellectual infrastructure supported not only the publication of scholarship, but also the performances of works by black composers, and the curation of black music ephemera. A significant and important part of this mechanism was scholarly journals, which elevated the voices of scholars, composers, and musicians during the latter part of the twentieth century. *The Black Perspective in Music* (*BPIC*) was the first journal solely devoted to the study of black music. Launched by Eileen Southern and her husband, Joseph Southern, in 1973, the journal filled a significant void and featured an array of content from scholarly articles to interviews with composers and musicians to news that documented the activities of the black music community. *BPIC* was followed in 1983 by *American Music*, the first journal associated with the Sonneck Society for Music (now called the Society for American Music), a professional organization devoted to the study of the musics of the Americas. Although there was no direct connection with the black music intelligentsia, *American Music* was important in terms of promoting scholarship on black music. Two years later, Samuel Floyd launched the *Black Music Research Journal*, which significantly shaped the framework of black music scholarship. The continued legacy of these journals is evident in that sources drawn from them pepper the bibliographies of some of these essays, and also in that some of the essays are drawn directly from them.

The full scope of the impact and importance of the black music intelligentsia can't be fully discussed in this space, but it bears noting that their voices echo in this volume. This anthology, although not comprehensive in its coverage, embodies what Samuel A. Floyd, Jr. advanced throughout his life and work as a philosophy on black music. Each of these chapters unearths, explores, and explains ideas, facts, events, phenomena, and records that have been neglected, forgotten, ignored, falsified, or were unknown.[2] They invoke musicological contexts that are grounded in archival and ethnographic research that illuminates the evolution of black music-making as it shifts from the insularity of communal spaces to the public medium of popular culture. They mark how black music precipitated the aberration of racial, social, and gender norms.

This anthology explores black expressive culture in key moments of liminality where it challenged genre categorization and the exclusionary definitions of what constituted American music. The "between and betwixt" nature of jazz, blues, gospel, R&B, and hip-hop that is chronicled here was created by a number of factors including the changing nature of black labor and identity during the early twentieth century and how this intertwined with waves of black music entrepreneurship, the expansion of the cultural industry, and white America's growing appetite for black culture. This volume centers on five epochs that span black life and black music-making in America from 1945 until the present. They are the Negro Renaissance/postwar era (up to 1953); the civil rights era (1954–1964); the Black Power/Black Consciousness era (1965–1979); the post–civil rights years (1980–2000); and the new millennium (2001–Present).

The first epoch is defined by the music-making that evolved out of the uncertainty of the Great Depression coupled with America's impending entrance into World War II. The exodus of thousands of blacks from the interiority of the South to urban cities in the North and West shaped the cultural life of major cities like Pittsburgh, Chicago, Detroit, Cincinnati, Oakland, and Los Angeles. The porous nature of the geographical boundaries that separated North from South and East from West mirrored the cultural porosity that expanded the Negro Renaissance movement beyond the spatial borders of Harlem. Historians posit that the Harlem Renaissance was over by 1935. However, the music arm of this cultural movement was just beginning to blossom in spaces like Washington, DC, Chicago, Philadelphia, and Los Angeles by that time. It was in these spaces that the ideological scope of the movement extended beyond the Eurocentric conventions and artistic forms promoted by its leadership and came to include the black vernacular forms that mirrored the shifting identity and consciousness of southern migrants and the communities to which they migrated. The liminal nature of these sounds, insulated in the geographic segregation that framed black life in these cities, was resolved by their encounters with a cultural industry whose appetite for black music was buoyed by the entrepreneurial dreams of individuals whose engagement with and access to technology in the form of magnetic tape, microphones, radio, and vinyl records gave birth to a generation of independent labels that captured these sounds of migration. Wayne Everett Goins's "Chess Moves" provides insight into this sound world through his study of the evolving musical life of Black Chicago during the height of the second wave of the Great Migration (ca. 1942–1960). Using the experiences of singer/guitarist Jimmy Rogers as an entry point, Goins takes the reader into the musical life of Maxwell Street, the main cultural artery of Black Chicago, and the frenetic energy of the studios of small labels like Harlem Records, Chicago Records, and Aristocrat, the predecessor to the famed Chess label. Rogers's recollections remind us that the freedom dreams that propelled black migration during World War II often resulted in disappointment and disillusionment, as those promises of sanctuary from poverty, exploitation, and racialized violence rarely materialized. The promises of wealth and fame that prompted musicians to fill recording studios with the sounds of the Mississippi Delta may have birthed American and transatlantic rock culture, but Goins's work illuminates how the originators of this music struggled to survive and thrive in the rapidly changing world of postwar popular music.

Sherrie Tucker's "Nobody's Sweethearts: Gender, Race, Jazz, and the Darlings of Rhythm" explores the exploitive nature of the wartime jazz scene. Her work expands the historical narratives written on the jazz boom of the 1940s by raising questions about how black all-girl bands navigated the commercialization of jazz culture. Tucker's analysis of recording discographies, filmographies, and jazz criticism drawn from black newspapers and jazz periodicals takes the reader deep into the infrastructure and cultural politics that precipitated the ascendance and documentation of certain bands. Using the International Sweethearts of Rhythm and the Darlings of Rhythm as the focus, Tucker illuminates how the wide divergence that often existed between black and white audiences' reception of these groups, especially their displays of sonic and physical femininity, figured into their professional trajectory. Most importantly, Tucker points to how this determined how they were integrated into the white-centered spaces of radio, film, and the recording studio.

Mark Tucker's essay provides us another perspective of the World War II jazz scene. His exegesis on the genesis of *Black, Brown and Beige* details how Duke Ellington challenged America's cultural hierarchy through the advancement of extended musical forms that attempted to widen the sphere of America's symphonic aesthetic. Tucker contextualizes Ellington's musical experimentations in the cultural milieu that framed his post–Cotton Club years and links this evolutionary period and the work *Black, Brown and Beige* to a larger continuum of repertory that drew on both jazz and classical idioms. In addition to emphasizing the musical importance of *Black, Brown and Beige*, this essay analyzes what this work reflected in terms of the development of Ellington's consciousness about blackness and black art. The intellectual narratives of black life Ellington promoted through his jazz suites and large-scale works were significant in bridging the ideological tenets and music of the Renaissance movement with that of the impending black civil rights movement.

The wave of activism that defined the first two chapters of the movement for social change correlated with America's entrance into the Cold War with Russia. Black music and musicians factored significantly into the waves of cultural propaganda that the U.S. State Department shepherded throughout the Middle East, Caribbean, Africa, Europe, and South America throughout the 1950s and 1960s. The roster of black musicians, artisans, and intellectuals who traversed the world included concert artists and composers like Marian Anderson and Julia Perry, and jazz musicians Melba Liston, Dizzy Gillespie, Quincy Jones, and Louis Armstrong. This history serves as the backdrop for understanding how black women musicians navigated the cultural politics of this time. "Black Women Working Together: Jazz, Gender, and the Politics of Validation in Jazz" analyzes how trombonist/arranger Melba Liston figured into this phenomenon through her work with Dizzy Gillespie's State Department band and her collaborations with pianist/arranger Mary Lou Williams. Through an examination of the triangular relationship that existed between Gillespie, Liston, and Williams, I examine how black women navigated the gendered politics of the postwar jazz scene whose promotion of reclaimed masculinity pushed them into the margins. This essay discusses how Liston's arrangements of Williams's *Zodiac Suite* and her early religious compositions contributed to the widening of jazz's cultural imprint. It also explores how their collaborative work led to the establishment of cultural institutions like the Pittsburgh Jazz Festival, which has been significant in celebrating the city's musical history while simultaneously nurturing new generations of jazz musicians and listeners.

The progressive political and cultural consciousness that underscored the music of Mary Lou Williams, Melba Liston, and other black jazz musicians during the late 1950s and early 1960s extended back to the Double V campaign, which championed the fight for democracy abroad and at home. In time, the hypocrisy of America's advancement of democracy abroad became more evident, especially as it became apparent that the federal programs that spurred American growth and consumerism after World War II did not extend to Black America. As a result, the gradualism that previously framed approaches to social change shifted to direct social action. For the generation of young blacks coming of age during the 1950s and 1960s, the need for social change was urgent. They organized under the banners of the Student Non-Violent Coordinating Committee (SNCC) and the Congress on Racial Equality (CORE), which formed the more radical arm of the civil rights movement organizations. Their emergence on America's political terrain coincided with the emergence of a new generation of jazz musicians, who precipitated their own cultural revolution that was equally as transgressive and polarizing.

Just as SNCC and CORE advanced the black liberation movement through their rejection of the assimilation politics of their mothers and fathers, the jazz avant-garde pushed the sonic and cultural dimensions of jazz through their rejection of social and musical conventions of their musical "forefathers" and "foremothers." Robin D. G. Kelley's "New Monastery: Monk and the Jazz Avant-Garde" explores these intra-generational tensions through an examination of Thelonious Monk's positionality to the jazz avant-garde. As one of the musicians who ignited a cultural revolution with his musical experimentations and rejection of social norms, Thelonious Monk spent most of the 1940s and early 1950s in the margins of the jazz scene. Kelley's work illustrates how the rebranding of Monk during the late 1950s was in part emblematic of the efforts of white jazz critics and promoters to discredit avant-garde music and dampen the growing influence of black liberation ideology and the civil rights movement on jazz musicians.

The expansion of the black civil rights movement beyond the economic boycotts, legal challenges, and marches that marked the ascendance of Dr. Martin Luther King, Jr. in the late 1950s represented the emergence of two new strategies for engaging in non-violent protest: embodied resistance and vocalized resistance. Embodied resistance encompassed volunteers using their physical bodies to disrupt the energy or function of a particular space or entity. Examples of this included the sit-ins, pray-ins, wade-ins, and the Freedom Rides that erupted throughout the South during the early 1960s and challenged the Jim Crow policies that defined segregated spaces in bus stations, public parks, pools, and interstate and local transit systems. Vocalized resistance included not only speeches and chanting, but also the singing of freedom songs. The latter became one of the central tools used to mass-mobilize communities, bridge ideological and generational gaps between activists and community members, and resist the physical violence inflicted upon protesters. The growing importance of the freedom song in this strategy of non-violent protest gave rise to the song leader within the ranks of movement organizations and movement culture. These song leaders curated song repertories that consisted of original songs, recomposed Negro spirituals, gospel hymns, and R&B songs. As the direct-action campaigns spread throughout the South, song leaders and song repertories accompanied them. Out of the Albany (Georgia) campaign, three significant voices of the movement emerged: Bernice Johnson, Bertha Gober, and Rutha Mae Harris. Together they and other song leaders from other southern campaigns formed the SNCC Freedom Singers, one of many professional ensembles that toured the country raising money for the movement during the early 1960s. Bernice Johnson Reagon takes readers into the milieu of the mass meetings that incubated the direct-action campaigns in "Let the Church Sing Freedom." Her work sheds light on the resistance narratives that permeate much of black expressive culture even when not referenced explicitly.

The integration of these freedom songs into the performing repertory of white artists like Bob Dylan and Joan Baez during this period represented just how much black music informed the sound world of young, white, middle America during the postwar years. This was accelerated during the 1950s by the expansive programming of black music on radio and the ability to curate musical culture through the technology of hand-held transistor radios. This furthered the blurring of the cultural fault line that attempted to separate black and white popular culture. Although this crossover was slowed for a period as major labels began purchasing the rights to songs made popular by black performers and re-recording them with white artists, it did not stop white listeners from searching for the original recordings.

Nelson George's historicizing of the rise of Motown Records outlines how the record company continued the blurring of these cultural lines. His work illuminates how King's integrationist ideology underscored Berry Gordy's vision of creating a soundtrack that would accompany the promoted visions of an integrated America. "Production Line" unmasks the mechanism that constructed the Motown Sound and promoted a new black consciousness through The Supremes, The Temptations, and Marvin Gaye. However, just as Motown was ascending to the rank of cultural powerhouse in the mid-1960s, the black liberation movement took a radical shift in focus, and the sound and image of black popular music would reflect this change.

The escalating violence directed at the movement in the mid-1960s led many to question their allegiance to non-violent resistance. Despite the passage of key civil rights legislation in 1964 and 1965, racial tensions continued to boil over. In 1965, the southern California neighborhood of Watts erupted in what would be the first in a series of uprisings in cities throughout the late 1960s. Cleveland's Hough neighborhood exploded in 1966, and during the summer of 1967 (between May and September) more than 170 cities in 34 states and the District of Columbia were the site of some type of uprising or riot. It was a sign that the movement had expanded beyond the geographical borders of the South, and that non-violent resistance had given way to social unrest in the form of rioting. The destabilization of the black community was magnified further by the escalation of America's involvement in the Vietnam War in 1967 and with the assassinations of Robert Kennedy and Martin Luther King, Jr. in 1968.

Of the variant social movements that emerged during this period (1965–1979), the imprint of the women's liberation movement and the Black Nationalism movement was most evident on popular culture.

This was heard and seen in the widening of the girl culture. The singer-songwriter aesthetic became one of the ways in which mature representations of womanhood and women's sexuality outside of objectivity were promoted. While this was evident in the music of Aretha Franklin, Roberta Flack, Joni Mitchell, and Carole King, this also extended to the women's music scene, which provided another platform for female singer-songwriters outside of the mainstream cultural industry. A subculture that points to the intersection of the feminist movement and the gay liberation movement, the women's music festival circuit bore the imprint of the type of institution building that underscored the black civil rights movement. "After the Golden Age: Negotiating Perspective" explores how black women musicians like Linda Tillery navigated the racial politics of this music scene. This work illuminates one of the lost narratives of black popular music that surrounds the place that black queer musicians occupy within the spectrum of black communal identity and black music-making. The exclusionary practices of the women's movement mirrored those of the Black Nationalism movement forcing black women to be caught in the nexus established by the racism of white women and the misogyny of black and white men.

In addition to mediating the interpersonal tensions that existed between black men and women, black popular music during the height of the Black Power era also began to script and promote a new consciousness surrounding black identity and blackness. This was represented in the terminology used to characterize the music during this period. Examples include "soul" replacing rhythm and blues as the marker for the gospel-inflected blues sound associated with artists like Aretha Franklin, Otis Redding, and Booker T. and the MGs. Funk shifted from being about description of a state of being or to characterize a bad odor to terminology branding James Brown's rhythmic, riff-centered band aesthetic. The expansion of gospel music's sound to include elements drawn from rock, soul, funk, and country music during the 1970s came to be categorized as contemporary gospel.

More than just a sound, contemporary gospel and the generation of songwriters and artists that purveyed it spoke to and reflected the shifting consciousness of black America, the black church, and America's political terrain. "Hold My Mule: Shirley Caesar and the Gospel of the New South" widens the gender scope of the study of contemporary gospel, which tends to be male-centered and songwriter-centric. It discusses how Caesar's musical trajectory following her departure from the celebrated gospel group The Caravans aligned her with this emergence of the contemporary gospel aesthetic. Claudrena Harold's work on gospel music draws us into the expanding geographic and sonic diaspora that framed black sacred music during the late twentieth century. Where Chicago, Philadelphia, and Detroit dominated historical narratives about postwar gospel music, late-twentieth-century gospel music culture was deeply shaped by the cultural and musical environments of the West Coast and the "New South." In positioning Caesar's musical experimentation within the cultural environment of her hometown of Durham, NC, Harold reminds us of black music's continuous role in chronicling the shifting geopolitics of black America.

This is strongly seen in relation to how soul, funk, and eventually rap documented the decline of black urban communities. The shift into the 1980s marked the declining influence of liberation movements and organizations, economic decline of urban areas due to white and black middle-class flight, and the beginnings of the deindustrialization of America. The post–civil rights age, as it is commonly referred to, also came to be marked socially by the rise of conservative evangelicalism, the AIDS crisis, the crack epidemic, a war on drugs that ballooned the prison population, and gratuitous wealth and greed. The ascendance of black leaders in key cities in the North and South, and the re-industrialization of major cities like Atlanta, Charlotte, Houston, and Dallas, inspired a wave of reverse migration and the emergence of new forms of black popular culture, the most influential being hip-hop.

The last three chapters of this anthology map the growing influence of hip-hop and rap music during the last thirty years. Cheryl Keyes's "The Development of the Rap Music Tradition" surveys the beginnings of this cultural movement by transporting readers back to the South Bronx in the 1970s. It contextualizes how hip-hop was a nexus of many forms of black expressive culture that provided disenfranchised black and Latinx youth the means to give voice to their experiences and transcend the desolation and absence of hope that surrounded them. It also outlines the cultural and musical link between early hip-hop and funk, soul, and Afro-Caribbean musical practices and underscores the grass-roots infrastructure that supported the subculture before it was subsumed by the mainstream cultural industry and mass commercialized.

Hip-hop incubated the consciousness of a generation of latchkey children navigating their way through the social politics of post–civil rights era America. It also framed and promoted new representations of masculinity and femininity that brought to light tensions that developed between black women and men. Gwendolyn Pough's "Hip-Hop Soul Divas and Rap Music: Critiquing the Love That Hate Produced" provides a window into understanding how artists like Mary J. Blige and Lil' Kim gave voice to these tensions and attempted to reconcile them while simultaneously reclaiming and rescripting their sexuality and lived experiences. Pough situates hip-hop, soul, and the rap performances of female MCs within the budding of third wave feminism that transformed the narratives of pop music during the 1990s and 2000s.

The accelerated crossover of black music that took place in the 1960s and 1970s was slowed by the corporate takeover of small indie labels, launching of black music divisions at major labels, and re-formatting of radio stations according to audience demographics and geography. This was further exacerbated by the emergence of cable television, the music video, and network channels such as MTV, which initially refused to program the music videos of black artists. However, by the mid-1980s MTV could no longer ignore the growing cultural currency of Michael Jackson, Whitney Houston, Prince, or Run-DMC. Artists unable or unwilling to wade through the politics of sound and image that equated with crossover success during this period either fell into obscurity or transitioned into the sphere of maintaining a fan base primarily within the black community.[3]

The decentralization of the recording industry and the music video was precipitated by the emergence of digital platforms such as MySpace, Spotify, YouTube, SoundCloud, and Bandcamp in the early to mid-2000s. These mediums have given musicians agency over their sound and the dissemination of their music. They have also significantly reshaped the culture of music consumption and broadened the audience for black music. As a result, the Millennial generation and Generation Z experience music devoid of the cultural and racial politics that framed the sound worlds of their parents and grandparents. This is not without its own issues, especially as the appetite for black culture continues to grow and debates surrounding cultural appropriation erupt. It should be noted, however, that the seeming "post-racial" aspects of the contemporary popular music scene does mirror much of the political and social climate that surrounded the campaign and eventual election of President Barack Obama. Post-racialism first appeared in the 1980s as a strategy to counter the multiculturalism and inclusivity championed by the social movements. It was rooted in problematizing the recognition of racial difference more so than the institutions that promoted white supremacy and patriarchy. It reentered public and political conversations during the Obama years and came to define the sound world that surrounded his presidency. This was due in part to his curation of playlists, first through the technology of the iPod and later through Spotify. The eclecticism of those playlists was significant in further blurring the racialized contexts of American popular music. The de-racializing or re-racializing of rap culture is emblematic of this and has fueled its crossover into other forms of expressive culture. Loren Kajikawa's work points to this through his study of the hit Broadway musical *Hamilton* and its re-interpretation of American history through its use of hip-hop as the performance medium and the casting of multi-ethnic performers. It points squarely at how the "tanning" of American culture that began when black music first entered the mainstream consciousness has now extended to other points around the world.

This introduction begins with a quote from historian Earl E. Thorpe that points to the responsibility each generation has in facilitating understanding of their lived experiences and the surrounding epoch through the writing of history. This anthology represents how two generations of scholars have engaged in this work. The many different methodologies and modes of inquiry advanced through these essays has charted new theoretical pathways that hopefully will serve as a guide to the next generation. After all, they will be the ones expected to frame how black music figures into our current sound world, which is shaped by our navigation of a global pandemic; our negotiation of awareness created by the murders of Ahmaud Arbery, Breonna Taylor, and George Floyd; and a desire to eradicate patriarchy and systemic racism.

Notes

1. Earl E. Thorpe, "Philosophy of History: Sources, Truths, and Limitations," *Quarterly Review of Higher Education Among Negroes* 25:3 (July, 1957) 183.

2. Samuel A. Floyd, Jr., "On Black Music Research," *Black Music Research Journal* 3 (1983): 46.

3. Panama Jackson, "The Black Mainstream," https://www.theroot.com/the-black-mainstream-black-famous-1847326958.

1

Chess Moves

WAYNE EVERETT GOINS

From *Blues All Day Long: The Jimmy Rogers Story*,
by Wayne Everett Goins (2014)

I was livin' in the Maxwell Street area durin' '45 and '46. That's where I'd see
so many musicians and things, by bein' there down in that area. And I started
joinin' in with 'em too, playin' on the street.
—Jimmy Rogers

The blues carnival atmosphere on Maxwell Street really appealed to Little
Walter, so much so that he became a regular fixture there on weekends, even
after he became part of an official, unionized band. Although the money-making
opportunities there were well received by musicians, being part of that scene
was seriously frowned upon, as Jimmy observed during an interview.

The union didn't want us to play down on Maxwell Street. The hardest job
for us was to keep Walter out from down there. If they had found out about
it, they would have stuck a fine on him or blackballed him—like they done
to Baby Face [Leroy Foster]. But on Saturdays, maybe Sunday evenings, he'd
be around there makin' him quarters and things. He could really make more
money on the street than he could at a gig 'cause you'd have a thousand people
durin' the day walkin' up and down Maxwell Street. When you belong to a
union, they don't want you to be doin' that 'cause it's scabbin'. They can't get
any money out of it. It's just like the government is about bootleggin' whiskey.
They wanna have their hands in everything.[1]

Unbeknownst to many of the performers, there would even be spies strategically located on the more popular corners of Jewtown, laying low until they
thought they spotted a culprit. Sometimes they'd get made by members of the
blues crew, who never hesitated to send up a flare and notify all others in a coded
verbal warning. Eventually Jimmy would look out for Little Walter in this way.
"We'd quick run down and tell him, 'The Hawk is out,'" Rogers said.[2]

Cousins Floyd and Moody Jones also hung out with Jimmy and Snooky Pryor on Maxwell Street.[3] The atmosphere there remained attractive to musicians, both because they made substantially more money than they ever could have made in the clubs and because the club gigs were all sewn up by the leading Chicago blues stars who had been situated before the youngsters ever arrived. Out of necessity Jimmy and his boyhood pals found a different route: they hustled on the street, their egos bolstered and their pockets lined by their weekend take. Snooky, who had teamed up with Floyd Jones, said, "Man, we used to make shoeboxes of money, me and Floyd . . . We used to have to dump that shoebox about three or four times . . . I used to make so much money down there in Jewtown, I used to go home walkin' sideways!"[4]

Snooky was always down on Maxwell Street, hanging out with his buddies in pursuit of both music and money. "It was me and Floyd Jones and Stovepipe [Watson] and One-Legged Sam Norwood and a guy we used to call 'Milk Finger,' Othum Brown, who was from Marks, Mississippi." About the environment on Maxwell Street, Pryor said, "It was real nice for a beginner to learn." He described the atmosphere as "booming every day. It was like every day was Sunday . . . Just name anything in this world that you wanted, you could get it off Maxwell Street. They had fortune tellers, magicians, food, shoes . . . I think people used to steal stuff, bring it down there and sell it cheap."[5]

The musicians who entertained the throngs made less than ten dollars on average for playing all night long. With the free-spending, oversized crowds wandering up and down the streets in either direction, a few quarters here and there from several hundred patrons quickly turned into some real cash for the performers. The money served as encouragement for them to play even harder and longer in order to entice those who stood all around them to remain and drop a few more coins. In spite of the hassles, playing down on Maxwell Street was definitely worth the trouble, even if the club owners and other musicians in town frowned upon it because they thought it was "beneath them." In reality some of the greatest ideas for the lively music delivered in the blues clubs at night were born during the day on the corners along Maxwell Street. Jimmy Rogers described the musical atmosphere this way: "We were doin' [the song] 'Caldonia,' boogie woogies, all kinds of stuff. That's where I made up 'That's All Right' and all that stuff. I was building those songs up. We did that on the street. You don't worry about nobody trying to steal your stuff back then during that time. Later years they started that. Man, we'd just get some ideas and go on and do 'em."[6]

And there were dozens of other artists making their money down there too, including upright bassist Ed Newman, washboard player "Porkchop" Eddie Hines, and guitarist/singer/harp player Johnny Watson—better known as "Daddy Stovepipe." Watson, whom Jimmy described as a well-traveled "short little dude" in his forties, who wore funny striped suits, was the quintessential type of guy you'd run into on the weekend at Jewtown. He was a street-hustler type, a fast-talking entertainer who could grab your attention and hold it until both artist and observer got something out of the deal. Washboard player, jester, jokester, tap dancer, kitty collector. That's what it took to "get over" when you were laying it down on the Near West Side of town.

Since he'd arrived in 1945, Jimmy had had the fortune of placing himself at the beginning of a slowly emerging underground recording scene that took place right in the heart of Maxwell Street. By 1946 several aspiring entrepreneurs emerged to encourage the various street musicians to hitch their wagons to an independent little machine that could make them a star. These rookie producers often doubled as engineers as well, using their own rogue equipment to fashion primitive shellac recordings that, while not very not high in quality or quantity, still served as immediate feedback for local artists who wanted so badly to break through the airwaves by any means necessary. Jimmy, whether willing to admit it or not, was as eager as the rest of them to find anyone who could help further his career. Certainly to have bragging rights—to be able to say, "Hey, look at me; I have a record out!"—was of prime importance to all those blues people who aspired to someday be as big as the likes of Sonny Boy, Tampa Red, Big Maceo, Memphis Minnie, or Memphis Slim. The way Jimmy figured it, if he couldn't make it on an important label under his own steam, he'd try his best to cut sides with whatever smaller outfit he could until he could grow some funk of his own.

Jimmy got his first taste of session work in September 1946 when he managed to do a little work as a sideman. By that time J. Mayo Williams, a young entrepreneur from Pine Bluff, Arkansas (although he publicly claimed Monmouth, Illinois, as his hometown), had been in the record business for more than twenty years, serving as a producer and talent scout for "race records," or music recorded by and tailored to the black community. Williams, who worked between New York and Chicago, had started up two small labels: Chicago and Harlem (and eventually two more: Southern and Ebony Records). This former NFL pro football player (one of the first three African Americans in the history of the league) was trying to convince local blues artists like Jimmy, Muddy, Sunnyland, and several others to lay down tracks for his fledgling label, one of a small handful of independent recording companies in Chicago at the time.

Years later, when asked if he remembered recording at the label for J. Mayo Williams, Jimmy thought for a minute, then said, "Mayo Williams . . . yes, I did. I cut with Sunnyland Slim and I cut with Lee Brown," he said of his early stint with Harlem Records.[7] "We did that stuff down at 20 North Wacker Drive. Me, Sunnyland Slim, Memphis Slim, Othum Brown, Lee Brown and Leroy Foster. 'Cause I worked for that label then—Harlem Records."[8] Jimmy even recalled a few of the details regarding the circumstances surrounding how the music went down once they were in the studio: "At the time, Memphis Slim was playing the piano for Sunnyland. He could play, he could play like he do now, but he was studio-shy and he was afraid he would make a mistake. Slim was at the microphone and James Mayo Williams had to tell him to back off because they couldn't balance his voice." Jimmy tried to probe even deeper to yield more memories of the session. "I'm trying to remember the titles of the songs, it's been so long. All of us was down there. We had Big Crawford on the bass. I can't think now who was [on] drums. It was around 1946 or '47. This was around the same year that I recorded for Bernard [Abrams]. It was in the fall, maybe September or October."[9]

Jimmy's relationship with Lee Brown—a local piano player who, at the time, was working diligently at establishing his own legacy as one of the most important movers and shakers in the field—was sometimes tenuous at best. Even if Brown's musical skills met with Jimmy's approval, it wasn't by a huge margin, as Jimmy never actually gave Brown what might be called a ringing endorsement. When commenting about Lee's performance level or his personality, Jimmy mused:

> Lee Brown, he used to talk a lot. He was a little jive piano player. He couldn't play too much but he could play a little bit. And he'd run around and he'd talk a lots. He never could work with nobody too much. He's kind hard to get along with. Lee Brown was something else, man . . . He'd have to argue with himself! We'd always get along, but he had something—inferiority complex or somethin'. When you come around, he'd figure out somebody was tryin' to take advantage of him all the time or somethin'. So I just treat him nice, and we'd have a few laughs and have a few drinks and I'm gone.[10]

Jimmy, still trying to put together his own recording band while working in conjunction with Muddy Waters, had asked Brown to back him on some gigs, hoping they might create some kind of chemistry that would be worthy of capturing on tape. "Lee Brown was playing the piano with me and if I'm not mistaken, he played behind Muddy too . . . [Bobbie Town] Boogie—he made that before this particular date," Jimmy said. "It came out that year."[11]

"Him and Leroy Foster were playing little local gigs together. Lee Brown would run by the office and if he could catch John [J.] Mayo Williams or something, he'd give him $10.00."[12] The original recording of "Bobbie Town Boogie" that Jimmy is referring to was recorded a year earlier in 1945 by Lee Brown on Mayo's Harlem label. This time around there would be two more recordings that would confuse things exponentially.[13]

Under Mayo's leadership Jimmy recorded his first side as a leader with "Round About Boogie," recorded in Chicago, but, to his great misfortune, when the tune was released, the credit went not to Jimmy Rogers but to Memphis Slim.[14]

To make matters worse, Mayo's Harlem label identified Sunnyland Slim as the lead singer and leader of the combo.[15] Essentially there was no visible trace of Jimmy Rogers on the record; one had to recognize his voice or his harp playing. Jimmy's backing band for that session had Lee Brown on piano, Alex Atkins on alto sax, probably Big Crawford on bass, and possibly Leroy Foster on drums. To complicate matters even further, the flip side listed another title that had a familiar ring, called "Bobbie Town Woogie," which featured Lee Brown, who had already recorded a tune called "Bobbie Town Boogie" just the year before![16]

Evidently Jimmy also worked on the side as a salesman, selling discs for Mayo. According to Rogers, "I was like a traveling record salesman around for different record companies like RCA, Victor, Decca. and different labels around . . . I had like a satchel and you'd pack them, those little 78s." Jimmy was obviously proud of his power of persuasion, as he told writer Norman Darwen, "If a good hit record came out and they could get ahold to it, I was on it, man, I could push it."[17]

Meanwhile, Bernard Abrams, an enterprising blues entrepreneur, owned and operated Maxwell Radio Record Company at 831 West Maxwell, a radio and TV repair store that housed Ora Nelle Records, where he managed to produce several artists over a short span and cut as many sides as he could with the limited resources he had. Abrams was a young Jewish producer who wanted to cash in on all the talent that was flowing through the Maxwell Street area on the weekends. Ultimately he succeeded in becoming the catalyst behind some of the earliest recorded works of the street musicians of the late 1940s. "These fellas that were down here, they used to come into my store," Abrams said. "I used to have a little disc recorder and a mike, they'd sit on a box or something and sing. Well, one day I thought this might sell. I took it to a pressing plant and had records made, a thousand or so."[18]

Another recording opportunity sprang up that same year when Little Walter, along with frequent Maxwell Street visitor Floyd Jones, was called in by Bernard Abrams, who said, "Whyn't y'all come on. I want to make a dub of y'all."[19] Since none of them had contracts at the time, it didn't take much to convince Jones or many others then—Jimmy, Walter, Baby Face, Muddy, or Sunnyland—to wait for a chance to lay down some sides for the small company. Abrams briskly sold copies of the vanity discs for a dollar. Called "dubs," the early batches of recordings were eventually used to form the foundation of what became known as the Ora Nelle label.[20]

The next year, 1947, Abrams convinced Jimmy to lay down a few tracks for him. Jimmy was excited about the opportunity. He might finally have the opportunity to record songs under his own name and hoped the results would come out correctly this time. Jimmy teamed up with Little Walter and Othum Brown to record "Little Store Blues" for Ora Nelle Records.[21] "Muscadine Wine" was another tune that Jimmy and Little Walter recorded, although very few copies were pressed during this time. In the end Jimmy was a bit disappointed that the tune he'd led didn't fare very well: "I made 'Little Store Blues' for a little small label, didn't amount to very much."[22] It turned out that this performance would serve as a foreshadowing of things to come, as it represented one of the earliest cases of—for lack of a better term—"musical incest" regarding tunes connected to his career. When Jimmy and Walter recorded the sprightly jump-blues boogie tune "Little Store Blues," they used an arrangement during the Ora Nelle session that borrowed heavily from the Sleepy John Estes tune of the same key and tempo, titled "Liquor Store Blues."

About this same time period, Abrams also managed to convince singer and guitarist "Bow-Legged" Othum Brown to lay down a few tracks. Abrams had an original tune he wanted recorded that was dedicated to his wife. Brown, therefore, recorded a tune called "Ora Nelle Blues" (Ora Nelle 711), the song title chosen for the small independent label located in the heart of Maxwell Street. Little Walter first played a second guitar line with Floyd Jones behind Othum Brown's vocals. Yet again, another case of mistaken identity would rear its ugly head. Just as there was controversy surrounding "Little Store Blues," a similar situation occurred when Jimmy Rogers recorded "That's All Right," a song that had a chord progression and verse structure that were identical to Brown's version of "Ora Nelle Blues," with the exception of the hook in the lyrics identifying Ora Nelle as the woman in question.[23]

The eerily similar lyrics and arrangement created a situation that could be viewed as a "chicken or the egg" question with regard to which artist—Othum Brown or Jimmy Rogers—had the right to claim the tune as his own. It was an irrefutable fact that even though the titles were different, the lyrics were the same. Although Jimmy won out by receiving credit for the ultimate version of the tune, he did acknowledge that Brown recorded it first, even if the earlier Brown version fell on deaf ears. At one point Jimmy downplayed the significance not only of Brown's role in the tune but also of his place in the blues pantheon altogether, saying, "Othum Brown, he was a drunk, and tried to do somethin' with his 'Ora Nelle Blues.' He tried, but it didn't work."[24]

Later Jimmy's stance regarding the events surrounding the controversy softened somewhat, although he still was reluctant to give too much credit to Brown when it came to the tune he believed was rightfully his. "He [Brown] tried after we were here in Chicago . . . He cut it for some little label, couldn't get anything out of it."[25] Jimmy would say later, "Othum was a pretty good guitar player."[26] Jimmy says the song came from observing a man and a woman who got into a fight, and the guy was telling this woman that although she had mistreated him, it was all right. After he'd experienced his own personal problems, Jimmy said he developed the song from there.[27] Truth be told, the tune, which more than likely had its origins in West Memphis or Helena, Arkansas, was neither Jimmy's nor Othum's to claim. Both had probably picked up the song from Robert Junior Lockwood, who performed the tune on a regular basis as far back as the West Memphis/Helena days. Even Muddy Waters was overheard to say about the tune, "That's Robert Jr.'s song."[28]

Jimmy was clear about his affinity toward the song: "You have to feel a song. I don't think Robert or none of those guys even felt 'That's All Right.' The words that we were usin', they didn't feel it . . . I built it, put it together and lined it out with harmony and built the music around it, and then we recorded it." Still he did not deny the outside influences of a pair of artists who might claim portions of the tune for themselves. According to Rogers, "It was in between Robert Lockwood, Willie Love ideas comin' in and verses like I put some verses with it and built it that way. I built the song. Nobody wasn't doin' anything with it. We would all toss it around . . . and so I put it to work."[29]

Muddy was making his moves too, hooking up with James "Sweet Lucy" Carter, yet another performer who was mingling among the same crowd, trying to make a name for himself. Muddy and Carter both were being courted by Mayo Williams. Jimmy remembered Carter and the session, saying, "James 'Sweet Lucy' Carter—he was a friend of Lee Brown's. They all was south side boys . . . There was a joint on 31st where you could meet anybody you wanted to meet."[30] Muddy also recalled a few details about the Mayo Williams session, saying, "We got half sideman [meaning half the going rate that sidemen were entitled to under legal union rules]." None of the players who recorded that day got the full $82.50, the amount usually given to the leader of the session. Since the restricted union fee at the time was $41.25, Muddy calculated, "I musta got twenty-something dollars out of it."[31]

In a cruel twist of fate, yet another Mayo mishap occurred on the Harlem label. When the recording of "Mean Red Spider" came out, the label on the 78 disc did not identify Muddy and his boys. Instead, "Sweet Lucy" Carter's name was identified; there was no trace of Muddy's name anywhere. Jimmy knew it was another mistake made by Mayo and his careless pressing plant. According to Rogers, "I remember James Carter back in that time, he didn't record [on the session that day]. He [Muddy] had already cut when me and Lee Brown and Leroy recorded [my September '46 sides for Harlem]. James, and it was another guy—an alcoholic dude—Dr. Clayton—hooked him in there. I met a lot of guys back during that time."[32] Clayton was a man who was known as a real character. "He was just a vocal, he didn't play an instrument, but he had a pair of lungs on him there," Jimmy said. "Man, he sounded like a train blowin'. He really could holler."[33]

The botched labeling of the Mayo Williams session was a missed opportunity for Muddy and Jimmy to claim rights to one of their earliest shellac pressings.

Still some good did come out of it, for on the day of their recording, Muddy was introduced to Jimmy's friend Baby Face Leroy Foster, a multitalented musician who played guitar, harp, and drums, and sang too. Baby Face was a real charismatic figure whose wealth of talent, combined with his young looks, made him popular with women and envied by men. He became a permanent fixture with Muddy and Jimmy, the group now forming a triple threat. Foster, one of the more lively characters in the band, was a first cousin to blues piano player Johnny Jones, another hopeful young artist on the Chicago scene. Jimmy remembered when Baby Face entered the picture:

> Leroy started comin' around where we was playin' with Muddy Waters and myself . . . That was [before] Little Walter came in. He started playin' with us. Played drums for a while, he was a pretty good drummer and guitarist, and he could sing good, too. And so he just got with us like that. Year in, year out, we'd be together, it'd be a lot of fun . . . He was a very fine fellow. He just liked to talk a lot and would punch your chest with his fingers when he's talkin' to you, tryin' to get his point over to you. And when you'd be talkin' to him—everybody know Leroy—they would be turnin' away from him because when he'd get down he get carried away in his conversation, so he'd punch your chest out with his fingers.[34]

The union of these four men—Jimmy, Muddy, Baby Face, and Little Walter—marked the beginning of what would become the first phase of Jimmy's participation in one of the greatest blues bands ever assembled. Their musical versatility would prove to be a great asset as they developed a routine and repertoire that represented the arrival of the next generation of young black men who wanted to propel the uniquely American art form farther than it had ever been before.

In 1948 Snooky Pryor was making his own plans for stardom on Maxwell Street, coming up with a couple of catchy tunes, one of which was strikingly similar to a tune John Lee Hooker had recently recorded. According to Snooky, "When I recorded my first record, 'Snooky and Moody Boogie' and 'Telephone Blues,' I was over on the North Side, over there playin' the harp. Hooked up out there in the street. A guy named Chester Scales heard me playin' through that amplifier." He added, "Floyd was supposed to go into the studio with me and Moody to cut the record. It was somewhere on Wacker Drive. And Floyd showed up about week later. I guess he was off somewhere 'juicin'' as we called it back then."[35]

He used the "Boogie" tune he recorded as his theme song well before Jimmy, Muddy, Big Walter, or Little Walter had arrived in town. After Muddy arrived, he and Snooky played at the 444 West Chicago Avenue at the Ebony Lounge and then talked their way into landing a gig that gave them an opportunity to play on Big Bill Hill's radio show every Sunday evening at 4:20 p.m. over the airwaves on the WOPA channel. They also had a regular gig at the Zanzibar (located at Thirteenth and Ashland Avenue), where Snooky always played his signature "Boogie" tune.

The tune obviously had some kind of impact on the local level, because a few suitors came calling once Snooky's reputation grew as a result of the song. After hearing "Snooky and Moody Boogie," Bernard Abrams managed to corner Snooky Pryor, trying to entice him with an opportunity to affiliate himself with the Ora Nelle label. "Yeah," Snooky said, "I remember when Bernard set up that thing, for he tried to get me to record on it . . . after I had done made 'Snooky and Moody Boogie' and 'Telephone Blues' . . . He was a real nice guy, but he just drank heavy. He was all the fun you want to meet. There wasn't a dull moment around him."[36]

Clearly both Jimmy and Muddy were also searching for suitable material to record in hopes that the demos would be suitable enough to get them a little play on turntables, jukeboxes, and maybe a bit of radio airplay. At the same time, they were constantly hitting the streets in search of the next gig. They could always count on one particular person to help make things happen for them: Sunnyland Slim, one of the great patriarchs and benefactors of the blues. "Sunnyland was actually in the business before any of us," said Jimmy. "He was a nice piano player but couldn't get no record out that would do anything. But he opened the door for us, man! One guy I'll always admire is Sunnyland. And he don't regret doing things for you. It's nothing he'll want you to pat him on the back for. It just makes him feel good to do things for people. He may outlive me and he may not, but he's a father of the blues."[37]

Sunnyland had already used his considerable influence to broker the deal that set up the session for Muddy for Aristocrat, a label originally owned by Charles and Evelyn Aron and Fred and Mildred Blount. About the early sessions for Leonard Chess, Jimmy told one interviewer, "We'd cut li'l records for companies that wasn't doing anything. Aristocrat wasn't big but it had big intentions. I wasn't too interested in recording at the time—wasn't any of us too interested in doing it—we just wanted to play, man! Few dollars here, few dollars there."[38]

Jimmy credits Sunnyland for connecting him with the movers and shakers in the business and encouraging them to give him a shot at a career on wax. When he and Muddy finally broke through with Leonard Chess (who was now the co-owner with Evelyn Aron), it was Sunnyland who made it happen. At the time, the company was still under the Aristocrat label, which was how Muddy's first sides were cut (the label name would change soon thereafter). Sunnyland's career was peaking then, and his reputation and word carried a lot of weight with the record executives who looked to him as an unofficial talent scout to keep the Aristocrat roster full.

On one particular day Sunnyland really promoted Muddy's talents to Leonard, who was in search of a musician who could capture the genuine Southern folk sound, something along the lines of John Lee Hooker's or Lightnin' Hopkins's style of authentic rural blues singing and guitar playing. Sunnyland told Chess he knew just the guy to fill the role, bragging that it would only take one phone call to Muddy's house and he'd be there promptly. Sunnyland first brought Muddy along with him on his own recording session when he made "Johnson Machine Gun." When the producer casually asked about Muddy's ability to sing, Sunnyland responded enthusiastically, "Like a bird!"[39]

Sunnyland proudly dialed the number and called Muddy's house to tell him the good news about his presence being required at the record company—and that it would represent his first big break. When Muddy's wife, Geneva, answered the phone to say that Muddy wasn't home, Leonard, who was not one to take no for an answer, barked, "Hell, man, go get him—tell him his mama died, anything!"[40] Leonard demanded that Sunnyland go find him immediately. Muddy was still driving a truck for Westerngrade Venetian Blind Company, the job he'd gotten through his uncle. Jimmy remembered the cushy job that Muddy had at the time: "He'd deliver them, then he'd go home, play around, then go back to the factory . . . You'd see the doggone truck sitting in front of Muddy's place a lot of the time. He'd be in there eating or something. He had a good gig like that."[41]

Muddy was out on his route at the time, and Sunnyland knew the boss at Westerngrade would be highly reluctant to let Muddy take time off for such a project. He also thought Muddy might not believe that such a big opportunity would really take place. He carried out Leonard's scheme to get Muddy's attention. Using the work number that Geneva gave him, he phoned the business office and got through to the secretary, who was then told by Sunnyland that Muddy's mother was gravely ill and that he should come home immediately. Being none the wiser, the secretary passed the message on to Muddy, who, upon receiving the cryptic message, knew immediately that something was afoot, as his mother was already dead, and the grandmother who had raised him was still living in Mississippi. Still, it sounded serious enough that it warranted attention, so some personal time off was granted. By the time Muddy made it home, Sunnyland was there to greet him, and the truth was revealed about the recording session with Aristocrat. They hopped into Muddy's Chevy and headed straight to the studio to speak with Leonard, who was eagerly waiting to meet this unknown artist whom Sunnyland just raved about.

When Leonard finally directed Muddy to record a series of sparse arrangements of country folk blues based around his voice and his guitar, Muddy was more than a bit skeptical about his ability to pull it off. Then again, Muddy thought, this was the same way guitarists Lightnin' Hopkins and John Lee Hooker performed for their respective labels, and they were scoring hits on the charts. Leonard Chess, never one to ignore a current trend in the record industry, wanted to catch the wave while it was still riding high. Muddy had his doubts, though. His interests still lay in developing the sound of the quartet he'd been building with Little Walter, Jimmy, and Baby Face Leroy. Jimmy encouraged him, saying, "Go back to the way you did it down South. Just think back . . . go on and do it!"[42]

Over the next few days they refocused their musical efforts away from the quartet format and concentrated on developing a minimalist sound that would capture what Leonard was after. They ran through several pieces they thought would be appropriate selections to accent Muddy's organic approach to singing and playing. A few songs, like Robert Johnson's "Walkin' Blues," seemed like a perfect fit for the task at hand. After sketching out a few more original arrangements, they felt they were ready. Muddy returned to the studio and delivered his best rendition of the original arrangements he and Jimmy had developed for the occasion. He laid down the superstitious fortune-telling tale of "Gypsy Woman," which went over fairly well, but not well enough to get Leonard to release it right away.

When Sunnyland added his ticklish piano phrases underneath the vocals, the tunes carried a bit more momentum, and Leonard seemed to be satisfied with the results of the session. "Gypsy Woman" (Aristocrat 1302) was recorded in 1947 with Muddy on vocals and guitar, Sunnyland Slim on piano, and Ernest "Big" Crawford on bass. "Two or three days after the session, Muddy told me he done made a tape for Chess," Jimmy said. "Muddy said, 'man, I don't know how it's gonna sound but I got my foot in the door, I think.' Finally we got hold of a disc and we played it."[43]

Still, things weren't all peaches and cream with Muddy and Leonard Chess just yet, as Muddy soon learned how hard it was to collect on the musical installment he had delivered. According to Jimmy, "Muddy couldn't pay his car note. We used to hide the old car to keep the finance company from takin' it. He'd stay in it, send somebody in the store to get what he wanted. Then he'd come back over to my house and hide it in my garage. Chess would dodge him, say he's not in or something, 'cause Chess was scufflin' himself. But Muddy had to pay rent. He'd say, 'damn! It's a wild-goose chase there with Chess.'"[44] Leonard Chess was reluctant to invest too much time and energy in Muddy because of his good, but not stellar, performance on the recent session. As far as Leonard was concerned, Sunnyland hadn't delivered on his promise. Muddy's style wouldn't fully move Chess until 1948, when he recorded two sides that put him over the top once and for all.

In the latter months of 1948 Muddy suggested to Leonard that he should sign and record Robert Nighthawk on Aristocrat. Chess took Muddy's advice and scheduled a session. Nighthawk brought along with him a robust bassist,

Willie Dixon, who eventually impressed Leonard so much that he became a regular session player and producer of numerous sessions.[45] Although it is a well-known fact that Dixon eventually got the main gig as talent scout, arranger, and performer for the Aristocrat label, Jimmy provides a rare glimpse into what might have been had things fallen to Sunnyland, the one who was there first: "Sunnyland, in my opinion, about the whole deal, really was supposed to have the position Willie Dixon got. But he didn't. Dixon had a little more school trainin' than Sunny did, so he got on in there, and that knocked Sunnyland out."[46]

Still, Muddy had gotten his foot in the door, and, whether Leonard Chess wanted to admit it or not, Muddy did leave a lasting impression. How was it that Muddy got the jump on so many musicians who were already in Chicago? According to Jimmy, it was more than just talent; it was also being in the right place at the right time. "Chess was looking for a rough blues singer," Rogers recalled. "Sunnyland had tried; he couldn't make it. Eddie Boyd was playin' blues, but it was a soft, Memphis Slim–type blues, and Chess wanted a rough, Delta sound of blues. And, at the time, Johnny Shines was doin' a stretch in the pen. So Muddy was his next stop."[47] Jimmy felt that Muddy was the most logical choice, and it was the smart move for Chess to capitalize on the uniquely rural sound that Leonard was trying to capture. Muddy's unwavering dedication to the Delta style inherited from birth made him a clear front-runner, a natural. "Muddy was closer to it than Shines were," Jimmy said. "So we just pitched in and put it on the beat, really."[48]

Leonard's label—any label, for that matter—could have benefited from a sound as classic as Robert Johnson's. Jimmy understood that as well as anyone and was willing to do his part to help nurture Muddy's efforts. "If you notice in Robert Johnson's music," Jimmy pointed out, "regardless to the turnarounds and changes of his own style of playing, it had a beat . . . and Muddy was comin' close to that. We just added the beat that Robert Johnson was lookin' for by hisself. Two can do better than one, let's put it that way. So we added to it. It wasn't too hard to just drive Muddy on across the fence, there, you know? We was groovin' together with the stuff, *communicatin'*."[49]

What Jimmy is describing here is actually profound in its simplicity: if Robert Johnson had a full band, this is what his music would have sounded like had he recorded and performed live with a quartet who understood and complemented his musical sensibilities as perfectly as Muddy's band. Rogers obviously felt that Robert Johnson was the single most important influence and ingredient to the Muddy Waters sound and to the legendary Chicago sound as a whole.

With Leonard Chess smelling a potential new star in his stable, his label produced "Good Lookin' Woman" and "Mean Disposition" with the same lineup of Muddy, Sunnyland, and Big Crawford, plus an alto saxophone added for extra measure. This same April 1948 session yielded Muddy's earliest recorded versions of "I Can't Be Satisfied" and "Feel Like Going Home," two of the choices Muddy thought would best depict rural images as he did his best to conjure up the spirits of Robert Johnson and Son House simultaneously. These were all the same tunes that Jimmy rehearsed with Muddy on a regular basis as a duo, and Muddy was none too pleased with having made his debut without his wingman. Still, Jimmy understood that business was business, and their friendship was no worse for the wear because of unexpected circumstances. "He didn't wanna play it by himself," Rogers stated. "Sunnyland kept urgin' him. At that time his bills were gettin' high, his car note and he had to pay his rent."[50]

Indeed, both men were doing their best to hang on to the money generated from the late-night gigs on the weekends. "Muddy was kind of tight with them pennies, man," Jimmy later recalled when describing the frugal manner with which the two men managed to survive during the early days. In light of that, Muddy most likely would have welcomed some form of compensation for his time and efforts for his first session, but none was forthcoming, at least for now. This was partly due to the fact that Muddy had never officially signed a contract. Leonard's brother, Phil Chess, who was in the military service at the time, recalled, "He didn't have a contract with us [Aristocrat] for a long time, it was just a mutual agreement."[51] Muddy never denied this fact, stating, "I thought Leonard Chess was the best man in the business. He did a lot for me, putting out that first record and everything, and we had a good relationship with one another. I didn't even sign no contract with him, no nothing. It was just, 'I belong to the Chess family.'"[52] In truth, Leonard was initially quite reluctant to release the material. It was his business partner, Evelyn Aron, along with talent scout Samuel Goldberg who convinced Leonard that he should support Muddy's work.[53]

Chess recording engineer Malcolm Chisholm remembered Leonard Chess's superstitious nature and how Leonard allowed his personal beliefs to dictate the proceedings of his record label, unbeknownst to the musicians who were directly affected by it: "You would find him acting irrationally in odd ways. He didn't like to record on Fridays, and he'd never record on the 13th, but the seventh and eleventh were nice."[54] Chisholm also reported, "On Muddy's first successful session, the bass player wore a red shirt. The record sold. The next session Leonard said, 'get that bass man. And have him wear a red shirt.'"[55]

"Leonard had an extraordinarily coarse outer manner," Chisholm said. "I always wanted to send him a Mother's Day card because he answered the phone that way—'Hello, Mother!' "[56] Indeed, at least one Chess Records outtake has surfaced where Leonard, speaking to Jimmy during a recording session, can be clearly identified using the "mother" phrase. Apparently it was his ultra-hip Jewish way of using black vernacular as a truncated version of "motherfucker."

After Muddy's breakthrough with the two Aristocrat sides of "I Can't Be Satisfied" and "Feel Like Going Home," his career took flight. "The little joint I was playing in doubled its business when the record came out," Muddy bragged. "Bigger joints started looking for me."[57] Meanwhile, he and his now regular crew—Jimmy, Little Walter, and Baby Face Leroy—were still hitting the late-night streets, making ends meet. They had several regular spots they'd visit, rotating from one club to another and passing the gig to the next guy when they moved on to a better one. They played at Lowell King's at 3609 South Wentworth Street, located near Comiskey Park, where the White Sox continually struggled for World Series contention. The band also had the 708 Club on Forty-seventh Street. They held court at Docie's Lounge, 5114 South Prairie Street, on the South Side. And on the West Side there was Silvio's at 2254 West Lake Street, one of the favorite blues houses among them all. Gaining popularity at an exponential rate, Jimmy and Muddy were working almost seven nights a week on a consistent basis.

The group always traveled as a unit when they roamed from club to club, and between the four of them there was little besides music, whiskey, and women that they were interested in, choosing not to spend any more time on the street than was necessary. After all, it was Chicago, a place that was about as rough as it gets. "Muddy was just a quiet type of guy, he didn't mix too much with people . . . didn't really run around too much to different clubs less'n he had us with him. We went as a group, otherwise Muddy would be someplace at home or somethin," Jimmy revealed.[58]

They were putting in long hours, even though their pockets weren't exactly bulging with wads of bills. Every bar had a policy that restricted the amount of money a blues band could make on any given night. After all, the clubs were open to make money, and the less they spent on overhead, the more lucrative their business would be. Each club owner played by the rules of the day and paid band members under the guidelines that represented the accepted practice of an unspoken three-way agreement between all parties involved. Jimmy knew the routine all too well.

> They had a union scale but most places at that time, they would get a contract but the club would pay this union scale off for you and then they'd pay you *under* scale to have you in the place. We'd just go along with it, you know, 'cause if you'd make ten, fifteen bucks a night—for three nights, forty-five bucks—and you'd get free whiskey and he'd take care of the union tax for you, that wasn't bad . . . You gotta crawl before you walk is the old sayin'. And that's what we were doin'.[59]

By now the Waters-Rogers sound was catching on in clubs, with Muddy leading the way on live sessions. Jimmy described the telepathic relationship that he and Muddy had on the bandstand in a manner that made it sound as easy as drinking a glass of water: "We could play together so easy, I could be talkin' to somebody at the end of bandstand and playin' with the band all at the same time, 'cause it wasn't any problem, 'cause I knowed the changes and the beat. We could just do it. It was simple to us."[60]

Little Walter and John Lee Williamson (Sonny Boy I) were the undisputed kings of the harp. Everything changed on the night of June 1, 1948, however, when Sonny Boy was attacked by several men who stole his personal belongings and left him for dead with a head injury. He managed to stagger home, where he collapsed against the door. In front of his wife, gasping his last breath, he passed away. After the death of Sonny Boy I, Billy Boy Arnold, who was quickly becoming known as Williamson's disciple, would begin trying to fill his shoes, as would another youngster, Amos Blakemore, better known as Junior Wells, who had recently gotten his big break when he was allowed to sit in for Little Walter on a number with Muddy Waters at the Ebony Lounge. Wells eventually became a regular at the club where the group known as the Three Deuces (later renamed the Three Aces) performed. Two of the trio's members, Louis and David Myers, had emerged on the Chicago scene from Mississippi in 1941. Louis played lead guitar while Dave tuned his strings down and played bass on the guitar.

Meanwhile, Little Walter was still sneaking down on Maxwell Street to jam, which was really breaking the rules, because the guys were trying to go "legit" by joining the union.

> He would sneak off down there on Sunday morning. We played Saturday night, man, and somebody would come to us, said, "Hey, man, get your boy down there—go get him, man." We'd go get him, he'd get mad when he see you comin' 'cause he knows you don't want him down there, man. He's makin' more money than on the gig, but I knew about it. After you join the union they had so many rules, at that time, and we was new in the field, we was tryin' to—you know—abide by the rules, because they fine you.[61]

Jimmy, Muddy, and Little Walter were getting closer to perfecting their sound. "We'd do a lot of rehearsin' durin' that time, the three of us," Jimmy said. "And Walter wanted to learn. His ears were open, but he just didn't have nobody to sit down and really teach him. He was mostly playing between Rice Miller and that saxophone sound of Louis Jordan; after he came with us, we developed him mostly into a harder sound."[62]

Sunnyland Slim was still calling many of the shots when it came to controlling the musical events in the blues world of Chicago. He had already used his considerable influence to broker the deal for Muddy's session at Aristocrat. And he'd taken over the gig when Eddie Boyd left the Blue Flame (formerly known as the Flame). Now, in December 1948, it was Sunnyland again who had suggested that the band record a few sides for Tempo-Tone, a small, independent label run by Irving Taman, an entrepreneur who owned a bar called Irv's Boulevard Lounge located at 301 North Sacramento at Fulton Street, the urban part of the Northwest Side. Irv, a former World War II veteran, liked to record the musicians he had performing at his bar, and Sunnyland was his main man. Taman relied on him to recruit all the heavyweights for a marathon session that eventually yielded ten sides for his Tempo-Tone label. The participants included Sunnyland, Muddy Waters, Little Walter, Jimmy Rogers, Baby Face Leroy, Elga Edmonds, Floyd Jones, and Ernest "Big" Crawford.[63] According to the notes in the ledger, Jimmy took the lead vocals (and most likely guitar work) on December 22 and cut two sides: "You Don't Have to Go," and "I'm in Love with a Woman." As fate would have it, however, the X that marked the spot next to the calendar date in the recording ledger revealed that his contribution was not released, thus his music never saw the light of day.[64]

For more than a year now, Baby Face had become such a regular fixture with the Waters/Rogers/Walter trio that the band was now a quartet at their regular roster of clubs. And as they made their rounds, the foursome increased their visibility as well as their reputation as the gold standard for authentic blues from the Deep South. Their inner-city tour still included their regular stops at the 708 Club on East Forty-seventh Street, Docie's Lounge on Fifty-first Street and Prairie, and Silvio's on West Lake Street. And they added the Zanzibar on Thirteenth and Ashland Avenue, the Boogie Woogie Inn, and the Du Drop Inn on Thirty-sixth and Wentworth Street.[65]

Now that they were a well-established quartet, their assault on the public was really beginning to take hold as the band gradually worked their way across the city, spreading the blues. On an average night Jimmy and Muddy would make about eight dollars apiece, plus drinks and a few decent tips thrown in from appreciative patrons. One in particular, Bob Ross, was a serious blues fan who owned a construction firm. Serving as a benefactor of sorts, Ross would call down to whatever club Jimmy might be performing in to make sure the band had several fifths of whiskey on the table when they arrived to play.[66] This kind of special attention pleased the men and gave them encouragement as they continually pushed the envelope to get their sound across.

Sunnyland Slim had also played a vital role in pulling them in at the 708 Club, one of the more popular night hangouts in Chicago. Most nights when they finished their sets there, Muddy, Baby Face, Jimmy, and Walter paid visits to other blues clubs for the dual purpose of sizing up the competition and spreading their own name around. Soon everyone wanted them to be guest performers on the bandstand the moment they arrived. They had become blues royalty among their peers. Jimmy and Muddy would run out to the car, grab a couple of small amps, and they'd quickly launch into a few hot numbers. Walter would coolly ease into the bar, harps neatly tucked away in his pockets. Once they cranked up, they actually *moved* the audience: "When we leave, the crowd would leave too," Jimmy bragged. "So then they called us 'the Headcutters.'"[67]

This became the second and more potent version of the Muddy Waters band.[68] "There were four of us, and that's when we began hitting heavy," Muddy said.[69] "We used to call ourselves 'The Headhunters' [used synonymously and thus interchangeable with "Headcutters"]. We'd go from club to club looking for bands that are playing and cut their heads. 'Here come those boys,' they'd say." Jimmy acknowledged the band's overwhelming presence during those exciting times, saying, "Well, they called us that for a while around. We used to go around and shoot guys down like that. We never blew a gig for that particular thing, but if we were off, to keep from sitting around at home—." You knew what came next: "They'd call us on and then that's it. We could take the gig if we wanted it, but it wasn't payin' nothin' so we just drink and have some fun. That would be a bigger crowd for us on the place we were playing' on weekends, because we'd announce where we were. That's free publicity, that's the way it was. Lots of fun." When asked if others resented their headhunting approach, Jimmy said, "No. If they did, they didn't show it. They would be glad for us to come around, because they were trying to get into the beat that we had, see, and they would like to hear it."[70]

Thus was born the reputation of four of the most dangerous men who ever walked the West Side. This was the new quartet that terrorized the town with a torrential rain of fried country blues unlike anything Chicago had heard before. Indeed, the dual-guitar interaction of Jimmy and Baby Face, with Little Walter's squallin' harmonica over the top—not to mention the powerful vocal delivery of Muddy—was a unique event to witness among those who frequented the nightspots. Furthermore, any member could take the lead vocals at any point during the show. Their show had a sound and a presence that were never captured in the band's studio recordings to such an extent.

Then there was the fact that Baby Face doubled on guitar and drums, Jimmy doubled on guitar and harmonica, and Little Walter doubled on harmonica and guitar, thus adding even more depth and versatility. The band typically would casually stroll up to the stage and make themselves comfortable before firing up a tune. Jimmy explained, "We didn't stand up in those days . . . We sat down when we played. We'd have chairs lined around . . . put the mike up in front of you and you'd sing sitting down. You could keep your time that way, tappin' your foot." Jimmy observed that Baby Face had the loudest taps of all. "Oh, man, he'd click 'em both—*clap, clap, clap!*"[71]

Jimmy was still trying to shake off the disappointment of the Tempo-Tone session when Sunnyland Slim once again lent him a hand. Sunnyland was one of the main artists who recorded for Joe Brown and James Burke Oden (better known as "St. Louis Jimmy"), two entrepreneurs who co-owned the JOB label, a recent start-up in July 1949. Brown had booked a session on August 26, a sort of a variety session that featured Sunnyland, St. Louis Jimmy, Willie Mabon (vocalist, pianist, and harmonica player), and Jimmy Rogers. Under Sunnyland's auspices, Jimmy was allowed to cut two sides as a leader: "I'm in Love" (the same tune he tried to get released on the Tempo-Tone session a little more than ago in December) along with "That's All Right." Sunnyland backed him on piano.[72] Jimmy's bad luck with recording continued, as the two tracks he laid were not released at the time. In fact the six sides that were recorded by Sunnyland (including Jimmy's) would be passed around several times before eventually winding up in the hands of several labels, including Regal, Apollo, and Delmark.[73]

Leonard Chess was finally willing to give in to the pressure from Muddy to allow at least one or two of Muddy's own men to play with him. The session marked Jimmy's first official recording with Muddy for the Chess family.[74] Jimmy was on guitar (along with Muddy) and Baby Face was on drums at the September 1949 Aristocrat date, playing the role of backup band for vocalist and pianist Little Johnny Jones on two tunes, "Big Town Playboy" and "Shelby County Blues" (Aristocrat 405),[75] a tune that Jimmy would record at a later date. On "Shelby County Blues" Jimmy's second guitar part is not very prominent, but on "Big Town Playboy" his unmistakable style cuts right through, and the solo on the recording reveals his identity, with Muddy on second guitar. Muddy then took the lead as they recorded "Screamin' and Cryin'" and "Where's My Woman Been," eventually released as a single (Aristocrat 406).[76] Muddy's fifth and final tune, "Last Time I Fool Around with You," had Muddy on vocals and second guitar, Tampa Red on lead guitar, Ransom Knowling on bass, and Odie Payne on drums. (Red, Knowling, and Payne regularly performed as a unit with Jones during this time.)[77] Upon listening to the tune, one can hear the typical Tampa-style guitar riffs (unlike Muddy's "keen" sound), as well as the choice of key for this song, also common with Tampa's preference. Although this particular recording went unreleased for decades (causing much confusion about Tampa Red's presence), Jimmy confirmed to producer and friend Dick Shurman that it was indeed Tampa Red on the Aristocrat session.[78]

Jimmy began traveling with the Muddy Waters band beginning in October 1949 on a series of on-and-off gigs that would lead them out of town on an increasingly frequent basis. They went through the Southern states, covering Alabama, Louisiana, Arkansas, Tennessee, and North Carolina. Jimmy admitted that the long, late hours proved to be exhausting for some of them: "Man, we'd be sleepy. We played all till maybe 1:00 and then we'd leave out of Mississippi and take the ferry, go over to Helena and go to bed. And at 5:00 you gotta be up and gettin' ready to go to the studio, man."[79]

On Sunday, November 6, 1949, the 708 Club had a "battle of the bands" contest between Memphis Minnie and Big Bill Broonzy, with Jimmy, Muddy, and Sunnyland serving as judges.[80] In December the Headhunters traveled to Helena, Arkansas, to do the KKFA radio show, sponsored by Katz Clothing. The humorous story about Jimmy and Walter oversleeping and leaving Muddy and Baby Face to fend for themselves is now legendary. The latter two found themselves awakened to the sounds of the radio show they were supposed to be on. They were staying in a different hotel and had no way of contacting Jimmy and Walter. So they went on ahead to the radio studio and played guitars over the airwaves, and as they finished the tune, Jimmy later recounted, he heard the radio announcer say, "'Well, Jimmy Rogers and Little Walter is somewhere sleepin' it off. If they hear us, come on in.'" Jimmy and Walter frantically rushed to the station and arrived twenty minutes late (for a show that typically lasted only fifteen minutes); by then Muddy and Baby Face had performed three or four numbers. Muddy gave them both a glare that let them know how angry he was. "He was lookin' right in my face, man," Jimmy remembered. Muddy waved them in, they quickly grabbed instruments that were already set up and waiting, and, according to Jimmy, "They [the listening audience] didn't know whether we were there or not."[81]

The Chess brothers had come to appreciate the special chemistry that the Headhunters created when they performed live. Both Phil and Leonard had an acute level of business acumen that allowed them to parlay various ideas and instincts into lucrative payoffs for their enterprises, though not for their recording artists. They made the smart move, for instance, in the 1940s of buying a few bars where they could not only install the live entertainment lineup (those who happened to be on their Aristocrat label roster) but also dictate what tunes could be played on the jukebox inside in each joint. They were sometimes even smart enough to acknowledge someone else's talents in areas that lay outside of their expertise. Inevitably such acumen created an audience interested in buying the records they played and produced, resulting in expansion of their company.

The success of Chess Records was built on the shoulders of the company's top performers. Jimmy Rogers was therefore an important ingredient for Leonard, who clearly had the means to make him famous. Although it had taken awhile to achieve the bandleader status necessary to cut a deal and move out of the position of a mere sideman, Jimmy would ultimately make himself inseparable from the success of Muddy Waters. About the major impact of Jimmy's musical contribution, Dan Forte—longtime editor, author, and leading authority for *Guitar Player* magazine—once declared unequivocally, "One can't play the Chicago style without borrowing heavily from Jimmy Rogers."[82]

The significance of Jimmy's pioneering of the contrapuntal/supportive second guitar role is considered by serious musicians to be on par with the permanent, mold-shattering technique of Chuck Berry's mastery of the double-stop guitar riffs made so popular on classic R & B hits like "Carol" and "Johnny B. Goode." It's practically impossible to play old-fashioned rock 'n' roll on guitar without using Berry's technique. In similar fashion, authentic Chicago blues cannot be delivered in its pristine form without the liquid formula of harp and two guitars poured over a bed of rhythmic bass and drums. Basic to that formula is Jimmy's always steady *lumpty-lump*—the double-stop rhythmic groove he consistently applied as underpinning for Muddy's mercurial lines of slide guitar—as well as the deft melodic phrases he wove around Muddy's steady groove.

Jimmy's impact on the Muddy Waters band went far beyond his guitar technique, however. While his natural reticence and genuine affection kept him from questioning Muddy's ultimate authority, Jimmy assumed more and more responsibility in shaping the sound of the band, including having a major voice when it came to song selection, personnel, and arrangements. "I built that band," he once said matter-of-factly. "Muddy was the leader but I was leadin' the band . . . I would tell him on the side what he should do, how he should work it. And it worked." Evidently Muddy wanted Jimmy to take an even greater role in the band, because according to Jimmy, "Muddy worried about me singin' all the time. He wanted me to sing. Muddy he said he didn't like his own voice. I don't know why. He sounded all right to me."[83] Jimmy apparently enjoyed his role as behind-the-scenes leader. He always felt more comfortable just seeming to fulfill the role he believed he was meant to play in the group—the ideal supplement to the musical meanderings of Muddy Waters. Over time, he learned how to fly flawlessly in tandem with Muddy to achieve an unsurpassed level of excellence. Listen to how Jimmy obviously relished his role of being the perfect foil to Muddy's every move: "I could understand where he was goin' and lay there, and get under him and ride him in them curves and things. I knew how he was gonna come up there and come down. Drive, then lay under him. You call that *feed*. I knew how to feed him real good."[84]

Even more important was the ability to master the elusive time and feel of the chord progression in Muddy's music. Developing an innate sense for the irregular pace and direction of the band was one of the elements that usually threw the average accompanist off the bucking bronco that was the blues. Jimmy had tamed the wildest aspects of the music some time ago, although he always understood how others could easily get tossed. "Peoples didn't understand the count or how we's doin' that," Jimmy remembered. "That's hard for a straight guy to learn that stuff. We done hit it and gone to something else. We wouldn't stay in one place. You got a lotta different phrases and turnovers and channels. It's like puttin' up a buildin'. You try to explain that to 'em, you disencourage 'em real quick."[85] Muddy had a more specific way of describing his music: "It may have thirteen beats in some song, and the average man, he not used to that kind of thing. He got to follow me, not himself, because I make the blues different. Do that change when I change, just the way I feel, that's the way it went . . . I got just about as good time in the blues as anyone."[86]

Rather than explain, Jimmy and Muddy simply played, and the band built up a following through the gigs they played. Money, however, was always tight. The Headhunters played with some regularity at clubs that included the Boogie Woogie Inn, Lowell King's club, Romeo's Place, the Squeeze Club, and Brown's Village. One income source they could count on was their regular gig at the Zanzibar. On one particular Friday night in 1949 they had unexpected visitors: Leonard Chess, along with a few of his business associates. "Muddy said, 'Leonard's here. He wants to hear us play some of the stuff that we do,'" Jimmy recalled.[87] Those casual words probably hid some powerful emotions—a record producer wanted to hear the band's unique brand of blues. Then and there Leonard first heard the raw effect of Muddy Waters, and he no doubt realized immediately the true potential of what Muddy could sound like back at the studio if they'd allow him to play with his own group of musicians.

Jimmy Rogers observed the natural transition from the old to the new during the late 1940s and the early 1950s, and he suddenly realized that his past, present, and future were all linked together, forming a crossroads in his musical life. Indeed, those blues heroes he worshipped in his teens were now gradually becoming relics in real time, and the future was something that Jimmy and his peers—Muddy, Little Walter, brothers Louis and Dave Myers, Baby Face, and others—held in their hands like a precious pearl that was ready to shine brighter than the gemstones of the past. "Memphis Minnie, Tampa Red and Memphis Slim and fellows of that nature, they had been real hot with the blues—but they were dying off," Jimmy recalled. "They got real common—that type of blues at that time. And we came right in at that time and grabbed the blues again and put fire behind them and started livenin' it back up again. Because all those people were playin', man, they were famous when I was a little boy, some before I was born."[88]

Part of their magic was their ability to meld the best of the old with something vibrant and new. Jimmy went on record as saying he and Little Walter dragged Muddy kicking and screaming into the modern '50s while Muddy kept both of them firmly rooted in the deep blues.[89] It deserves mentioning that the attitude toward the next generation taking over the blues was not necessarily something that the old guard was against. To the contrary, the musical impact of the blues youth had the opposite effect on most of the veterans, as Jimmy attested: "They'd come around to hear us play to see what we were doin' and every one of them gave us a good compliment. 'You're doin' somethin' for the blues. I'm glad somebody's bringin' 'em back alive.' And we livened the blues back up again, and more people decided they wanted to try to play the blues."[90]

Notes

Epigraph. John Brisbin, "Jimmy Rogers: I'm Havin' Fun Right Today," *Living Blues* 135 (September/October 1997): 19.

1. Ibid., 24.

2. Ibid.

3. Ibid., 20.

4. Jim O'Neal, Steve Wisner, and David Nelson, "Snooky Pryor: I Started the Big Noise around Chicago," *Living Blues* 123 (September/October 1995): 14.

5. John Brisbin, "Pryor Arrangements," *Blues Access* (Winter 1999): 52.

6. Brisbin, "Jimmy Rogers: Havin' Fun," 20.

7. Jim O'Neal and Bill Greensmith, "Living Blues Interview: Jimmy Rogers," *Living Blues* 14 (Autumn 1973): 14.

8. Jim O'Neal, phone interview with Jimmy Rogers, February 26, 1982.

9. Ibid.

10. O'Neal and Greensmith, "Living Blues Interview," 13.

11. Chris Smith, "Words, Words, Words," *Blues & Rhythm* 228 (April 2008): 22.

12. O'Neal, phone interview with Rogers, February 26, 1982.

13. *Down Home Blues Classics Chicago, 1946—1954* [Disc 1], Boulevard Vintage (BVB DC1014S-UK), 2005.

14. George Paulus, "Rare Jams: George Paulus Discovers Jimmy Rogers' First Record," *Blues & Rhythm* 18 (1993): 167.

15. Les Fancourt and Bob McGrath, *The Blues Discography, 1943—1970* ([West Vancouver] Canada: Eyeball Productions, 2006), 468.

16. George Paulus, Robert Campbell, Robert Pruter, Robert Stallworth, Dave Sax, and Jim O'Neal, "Ebony, Chicago, Southern, and Harlem: The Mayo Williams Indies," June 13, 2011, revised April 2, 2014, http://myweb.clemson.edu/~campber/ebony.html.

17. Norman Darwen, "The Chess Boys Got to It and It Exploded," *Blues and Rhythm* 82 (1993): 6.

18. Tony Glover, Scott Dirks, and Ward Gaines, *Blues with a Feeling: The Little Walter Story* (New York: Routledge, 2002), 40.

19. Justin O'Brien, "The Dark Road of Floyd Jones," *Living Blues* 58 (Winter 1983): 5.

20. Ibid., 11.

21. Fancourt and McGrath, *Blues Discography*, 468.

22. O'Neal and Greensmith, "Living Blues Interview," 14.

23. Mike Rowe, *Chicago Blues: The City and the Music* (New York: Da Capo Press, 1973), 52.

24. Brisbin, "Jimmy Rogers: Havin' Fun," 22.

25. O'Neal and Greensmith, "Living Blues Interview," 14.

26. Wayne Goins, phone interview with Jim O'Neal, January 9, 2008.

27. O'Neal and Greensmith, "Living Blues Interview," 14.

28. Glover, Dirks and Gaines, *Blues with a Feeling*, 40.

29. O'Neal and Greensmith, "Living Blues Interview," 14.

30. O'Neal, phone interview with Rogers.

31. Robert Palmer, *Deep Blues* (New York: Penguin Books, 1982), 82.

32. O'Neal, phone interview with Rogers.

33. O'Neal and Greensmith, "Living Blues Interview," 20.

34. Ibid.

35. Brisbin, "Pryor Arrangements," 54.

36. O'Neal, Wisner, and Nelson, "Snooky Pryor," 15.

37. Tim Schuller, "Jimmy Rogers: Not Giving Up on the Blues," *Blues Access* 5 (Spring 1991): 12.

38. Ibid., 6.

39. Robert Palmer, "Muddy Waters: The Delta Son Never Sets," *Rolling Stone* 275 (October 5, 1978): 54.

40. Brisbin, "Jimmy Rogers: Havin' Fun," 23.

41. Robert Gordon, *Can't Be Satisfied: The Life and Times of Muddy Waters* (Boston: Little, Brown, 2002), 91.

42. Brisbin, "Jimmy Rogers: Havin' Fun," 23.

43. Gordon, *Can't Be Satisfied,* 93.

44. Ibid., 96.

45. Nadine Cohodas, *Spinning Blues into Gold: The Chess Brothers and the Legendary Chess Records* (New York: St. Martin's, 2000), 49.

46. Tom Townsley, "Jimmy Rogers: His Legacy Still Lives On," *Blues Revue* 14 (Fall 1994): 24.

47. Ibid.

48. Ibid., 25.

49. Ibid.; emphasis added.

50. Brisbin, "Jimmy Rogers: Havin' Fun," 23.

51. Mary Katherine Aldin, liner notes to "Muddy Waters: The Chess Box" (MCA Records 1989), 4.

52. Ibid.

53. Cohodas, *Spinning Blues into Gold,* 43.

54. Malcolm Chisholm, quoted in Palmer, *Deep Blues,* 162.

55. Glover, Dirks and Gaines, *Blues with a Feeling,* 57.

56. Palmer, *Deep Blues,* 162.

57. Palmer, "Muddy Waters: Delta Son," 55.

58. Brisbin, "Jimmy Rogers: Havin' Fun," 26.

59. Ibid., 24.

60. Townsley, "Jimmy Rogers: Legacy," 25.

61. Glover, Dirks, and Gaines, *Blues with a Feeling,* 60.

62. Palmer, *Deep Blues,* 208.

63. Robert Pruter and Robert Campbell, "Tempo-Tone," June 16, 2009, revised October 25, 2013, http://myweb.clemson.edu/~campber/tempotone.html.

64. Ibid.

65. Glover, Dirks, and Gaines, *Blues with a Feeling,* 47.

66. Brisbin, "Jimmy Rogers: Havin' Fun," 22.

67. Ibid.

68. O'Neal and Greensmith, "Living Blues Interview," 13.

69. Gordon, *Can't Be Satisfied,* 87.

70. O'Neal and Greensmith, "Living Blues Interview," 13.

71. Brisbin, "Jimmy Rogers: Havin' Fun," 22.

72. Robert Campbell et al., "JOB," Red Saunders Research Foundation, October 8, 2011, revised September 10, 2013, http://myweb.clemson.edu/~campber/rsrf.html.

73. John Brisbin, liner notes to *Sunnyland Slim: House Rent Party*, Apollo Series (Delmark DD-655), 1992.

74. Mary Katherine Aldin, liner notes to *The Aristocrat of the Blues: The Best of Aristocrat Records*. MCA/Chess (CHD2–9387), 1997, 22.

75. Michel Ruppli, *The Chess Labels: A Discography*, Vol. 1 (Westport, CT: Greenwood Press, 1983), 9.

76. Mary Katherine Aldin, liner notes to *Muddy Waters—Rollin' Stone: The Golden Anniversary Collection*, Chess Records (MCA/Chess 088112301–2), 2000.

77. Bob Eagle, "Big Town Playboy: Johnnie Jones," *Living Blues* 12 (Spring 1973): 28.

78. Author e-mail interview with Dick Shurman, December 23, 2011.

79. O'Neal and Greensmith, "Living Blues Interview," 12.

80. Glover, Dirks, and Gaines, *Blues with a Feeling*, 58.

81. O'Neal and Greensmith, "Living Blues Interview," 12.

82. Dan Forte, "Jimmy Rogers and the Pioneers of Chicago Blues," *Guitar Player* 21 (August 1987): 67.

83. Brisbin, "Jimmy Rogers: Havin' Fun," 26.

84. Ibid.

85. Ibid.

86. Peter Guralnick, *Feel Like Going Home: Portraits in Blues and Rock 'n' Roll* (New York: Bay Back Books, 1999), 72.

87. Gordon, *Can't Be Satisfied*, 95.

88. Glover, Dirks, and Gaines, *Blues with a Feeling*, 56.

89. Bob Margolin, "What Was Muddy Like?" July 2003, http://bobmargolin.com/327–2.

90. Glover, Dirks, and Gaines, *Blues with a Feeling*, 56.

2

Nobody's Sweethearts

Gender, Race, Jazz, and the Darlings of Rhythm

SHERRIE TUCKER

From *American Music* 16, no. 3 (Autumn 1998): 255–288

The latest threat to male supremacy in the musical world is a bevy of beautiful swingsters known as the Darlings of Rhythm.
—*Pittsburgh Courier,* March 18, 1944

The Darlings of Rhythm was a very fine all-girl Black band and they never got the recognition that the Sweethearts did.
—Sarah McLawler

The Darlings . . . were just a bunch of raggedy women out there playing, you know. Playing hard for the money.
—Frannces "Frann" Gaddison

Despite their easily confusable band names, rosters that included many of the same musicians, and similar road schedules during the 1940s, the Darlings of Rhythm and the International Sweethearts of Rhythm were separate entities with significantly different histories. Both were African American all-female big bands that played swing hits of the day, both were extremely popular with black audiences in the 1940s, both spent much of their time traveling rugged routes of strictly Jim Crow one-nighters with bands that sometimes straddled the color line. But the origins of the two bands were markedly different, as were some of the distinct types of survival strategies they employed on Southern road trips.

The Sweethearts began as a fundraising band for Piney Woods Country Life School for poor and orphaned black children in Mississippi, and maintained the image of schoolgirls long after they went "pro" in 1941. The "International" in their title referred to the presence of members who were at least part Chinese,

Puerto Rican, Mexican, Native American, and white, and served as both protection for this band that blurred the black/white color line in the Jim Crow South, and an appealing advertising gimmick for black audiences appreciative of representations of global blackness that burst beyond subordinated and segregated minority status in the United States.

The Darlings, on the other hand, were professional from the get-go, organized in New York, and did not pattern themselves after schoolgirls or international ambassadors. Numerous differences in the ways the two bands were characterized are evident in advertisements, reviews, publicity photos, and in the accounts narrated to me fifty years later by musicians and fans. Those who remembered the Darlings of Rhythm often portrayed them in distinct contrast to the Sweethearts, pointing to areas of divergence that ranged from musical styles, costumes, and stage presence to the strikingly different representations of black women musicians delivered by their performances.

"The Darlings were just a little opposite of the Sweethearts," insisted Frann Gaddison, who played in the saxophone sections of both bands, as well as with Eddie Durham's All-Star Girls, at various times during the 1940s. When I spoke with her in 1994, she was still a busy professional musician, playing piano in Dallas. In fact, our phone interview took place well after midnight because she was working every evening in the foreseeable future. Energized, rather than exhausted, after a lengthy late-night recording session in 1994, Gaddison elaborated what she saw as a great contrast between the two bands. "The Sweethearts played," she reflected, "but they were pretty girls." Curiously, the "prettiness" of the band, in Gaddison's appraisal, seemed to indicate for her a lack of musical substance. The Darlings, on the other hand, were "raggedy," but they swung. "They'd come in there like they just got through washing dishes or something. Or washing clothes. And people liked them; they were swinging. But the Sweethearts were very lavish, you know, beautiful. They had hairdos and make-up. . . . But they didn't swing."[1]

Whether or not one agrees with the decree that the Sweethearts didn't swing (I, for one, think they swung!), the image of the "raggedy-but-swinging" Darlings of Rhythm suggests a striking range of representations in "all-girl" bands. Such descriptions evoke a jazz sphere where women didn't necessarily present a glamorous image; where women's nonglamorous or "raggedy" appearance might in fact be positively equated with a "swinging" sound; where women commanded audiences to listen to their music rather than ogle their bodies; and where women produced a kind of "powerhouse" aesthetic that was variously described as "rougher," "more masculine," and "better" than what audiences expected from an "all-girl" band.

Gaddison's use of the term "raggedy" seemed to refer to both the Darlings' musical and physical dimensions. On the physical side, "raggedy" evoked images of women who presented a bedraggled antithesis to glamorous stage norms. "They didn't keep themselves up. They were rough-looking women." Gaddison compared the Darlings' "look" with that of women tired from "washing dishes" or "washing clothes." There is a class connotation in this physical description that must be noted as well. Even though World War II brought expanded opportunities for many African American women to earn a living doing something besides washing other people's dishes or clothes, domestic labor was still the largest employer of black women in the 1940s. Historically, evoking an image of black women tired from scrubbing would refer to "washerwomen," women who washed for a living, rather than to middle-class housewives. Angela Davis notes that blues singer Bessie Smith's tribute to poor and working-class black women (recorded during the same session that she recorded "Poor Man's Blues") was called "Washwoman's Blues," and spoke to the "countless numbers of black women for whom domestic service was the only available option."[2] Gaddison laughed when she described the "look" of the Darlings, apparently enjoying her memory of musicians who looked more like tired everyday women rather than glamorous stars. Even Hollywood actresses were most often restricted to roles as domestic workers, if they were black, but the movies depicted them not as hard-working, tired, and poor, but as lazy, doting, and/or comical, inevitably beloved and well treated by white employers. The image Gaddison describes of tired women "working hard for the money" might have proven a truthful antidote to Hollywood cinema versions of most poor and working-class black women's relationships to their labor. The familiar image of tired, hardworking women, combined with the fact that these particular hardworking women did not wash for others, but spent their labor energies on performing music, traveling, and earning rave reviews in national black newspapers may well have been a welcome combination for working-class black audiences. But why did Gaddison, who herself was a member of the Darlings, delight in the memory of appearing on the stage as a member of the band she describes as "raggedy"? She described the appearance of the band with great enjoyment, even a note of pride. What other social meanings did "raggedy women" "playing hard for the money" hold for fans and musicians? Another key lies, perhaps, in Gaddison's equations of physical descriptions of the Sweethearts and the Darlings with their sounds. If "pretty" doesn't swing, "raggedy" jumps.

In narratives of African American jazz musicians, to call a band "raggedy" is not necessarily a criticism. The late nineteenth-century jazz precursor, "ragtime," got its name, according to some sources, from its syncopated rhythm or "ragged" approach to musical time. In the context of jazz and swing bands, "raggedy" has often been used to distinguish a relaxed, more individuated, more variably textured approach to ensemble playing from other kinds of methods that value such things as meticulously coordinated sections, strict unison playing, and highly polished executions of elaborate arrangements. As trombonist Dicky Wells put it, sometimes certain bands sounded

> almost too perfect. That's the funny thing about jazz. You may rehearse until you're hitting everything on the head, and here come a band like the Savoy Sultans, raggedy, fuzzy sounding, and they upset everything. "What am I doing here?" you wonder. But that's the way it is. That's jazz. If you get too clean, too precise, you don't swing sometimes, and the fun goes out of the music.[3]

This distinction between bands that are so "perfect" they don't swing and "fuzzy sounding" bands that "upset everything" is precisely the contrast evoked by some musicians and listeners when explaining the musical differences between the Sweethearts and the Darlings. In analyzing why she preferred the Darlings of Rhythm, jazz organist Sarah McLawler said that they sounded "more spontaneous." Though McLawler didn't play with either band, she attended performances by both, and wound up hiring three former Darlings—Lula Roberts, Vi Wilson, and Hettie Smith—to round out her successful "all-girl" combo, the Syncoettes, in the late 1940s. Unlike the Sweethearts, stressed McLawler, the Darlings played music that was "more jazz than it was show. By show," she elaborated, "I mean everything was sort of mechanical. With the Darlings of Rhythm, it was more improvisation, it was more spontaneous. That's what jazz is about. You know, it's like playing off the top of your head, not something that's really set. So that's where the Darlings, to me, were the better group."[4] Spontaneity and power are two qualities that came up again and again in interviews with musicians and fans who described the Darlings' sound. In fact, the references to the group as "rough-looking women" may serve as a link between the visual and musical elements in how the Darlings' performances were understood. Another musical context for "rough-looking women" is the term's application to certain blueswomen of the 1920s and 1930s, often with favorable connotations. Trumpet player Doc Cheatham described blues singer Clara Smith as "rough and mean-looking" and "louder than all of them" and attributed these qualities to her popularity over Bessie Smith and Ma Rainey among Southern working-class black audiences.[5] A "rough-looking" image may have resonated with this blues tradition, which provided a strong cultural precedent for the popularity of black women musicians who delivered performances brimming with "spontaneity" and "power."

Not everyone I spoke with agreed that the Darlings was the better band—some, in fact, disagreed. Jazz trumpeter Clora Bryant, who sat in with the Darlings at the Plantation Club in Watts, observed that the Darlings personnel changed often and the sound changed with it. "It was an up and down thing. The turnover was so fast. Sometimes they were good and sometimes they weren't so good. They were being exploited, more than anything. I think the Sweethearts was the best of all [of the "all-girl" bands] and then I would say the Prairie View

Co-Eds are next."[6] It is possible that the moments memorialized in spirited descriptions by Gaddison, McLawler, and others represent high points in the Darlings' turbulent career.

Unfortunately, those of us who don't have memories of hearing or playing with these bands are unable to experience for ourselves the variety of musical and visual representations that might be revealed from a comparison of performances by the Darlings (and other unrecorded African American "all-girl" big bands) with what little archival film and audio footage exists of the Sweethearts.[7] There appears to be no recorded evidence of the music played by the Darlings of Rhythm, let alone "Soundies" that would allow us to see them perform. One wonders how much the contrasting musical and visual "raggedy/spontaneous" performance style described in positive terms by Gaddison and McLawler might have contributed to the lack of recording and film opportunities for the Darlings. Were they seen and heard as less "lady-like"? Did it matter that they lacked a upward mobility myth to match what *Jet* magazine called the Sweethearts' "cotton-fields-to-Cadillac success" story?[8] Did it matter that they were not perceived as Piney Woods orphans or schoolgirls or even as youthful? That they were not celebrated as "international"? Were the Darlings considered "too black"? Several women, including Frann Gaddison and bass player Vi Wilson, who played in the Sweethearts briefly before joining the Darlings, mentioned that the Darlings tended to hire darker-skinned women than the Sweethearts. Trumpet player Thelma Lewis remembered that when she played for the Sweethearts, band manager Rae Lee Jones made her change her appearance through the use of light makeup and a wig. "I had to buy hair," she recalled. "And color, they doctored me up. You had to be a certain color for her. If I was any darker, she wouldn't have hired me." When Lewis played with the Darlings, however, she noticed no such color bias. As she put it, "The Darlings were all different colored flowers."[9] Was colorism a factor in the unequal documentation of the two bands?

Whatever factor or combination of factors accounts for the Sweethearts having made five "Soundies," several Armed Forces Radio broadcasts, and a record produced by Leonard Feather—and the Darlings having enjoyed none of these opportunities—also in part accounts for disproportionate documentation in recent years. The 1980s, which brought us two documentaries, a book, several chapters in books, and numerous reissued recordings of the Sweethearts, only rendered sketchy references to the Darlings.[10] It may be reasonable to speculate that the "lightness" of the Sweethearts contributed to the sense of inclusiveness celebrated by nonblack Second Wave feminists (a problematic "inclusiveness," since it appears that some white women could more readily pass as the light-skinned black women desired by the Sweethearts' management than could some dark-skinned black women).[11] It is also possible that the Darlings' eschewing of color bias and glamorous norms would have found an appreciative audience among Second Wave feminists. Ultimately, it is impossible to know for sure how the Darlings' story would have been consumed under the rubric of "womyn's music" if films and records had been available. Indeed, it would be difficult to produce a documentary or entire book about the Darlings considering the lack of archival materials. For these reasons, it is tempting to assume simply that the Darlings were a poor replica of the Sweethearts, an inferior spinoff. But there is also the possibility that we know less about the Darlings because they were somehow less acceptable to the white male-dominated recording and film industries. With this hunch come technical difficulties, however, since the lack of recorded information daunts their prospective historians. While the Darlings of Rhythm were distinct from the International Sweethearts of Rhythm and other African American "all-girl" bands, they also shared historical contexts. Regrettably, there are woefully few interview opportunities (most of the members were older than the Sweethearts members, so more of them are deceased), no recordings, no films, scattered sentences and paragraphs in articles and books about women in jazz or about the Darlings' leader Clarence Love, a smattering of publicity photos, and yet a surprisingly vast amount of news coverage. Taken together, the sources suggest that the Darlings of Rhythm were, at one time, also darlings of the black press, even if (excuse the pun) they are nobody's Sweethearts now.

I am by no means suggesting that the Sweethearts have been overdocumented. On the contrary, the International Sweethearts of Rhythm is one band we know enough about to recognize that they were underrecorded, underdocumented, and underacknowledged in jazz history. What I am suggesting is that histories of bands such as the Darlings that were even less recorded may add to our knowledge of sexism and racism (and colorism) in the "all-girl" band business in significant ways. As I attempted to research how the Darlings were organized and managed, how they played, who they were, and how they traveled the rough roads of the segregated South, a variety of what I think are revealing stories about gender, race, class, and jazz emerged in rough-edged, often noninterlocking remnants. I will lay out some pieces but I won't try to fit them together. It seems important to leave space for the ones that remain missing.

Some Origin Stories

The International Sweethearts of Rhythm were organized at Piney Woods Country Life School in Mississippi by the African American male founder of a black school in 1937, and traced their origins to the tradition of black schools sending out musical messengers to raise money and publicize black educational institutions.[12] The Darlings of Rhythm, on the other hand, were apparently organized in Harlem in late 1943 by an African American female saxophonist who hoped to improve what she saw as the deplorable working conditions of black women musicians in the Sweethearts and other bands. This part of the story is somewhat disputed, depending upon whom you talk to.

Saxophonist Lorraine Brown (later Guilford) told her story of organizing the Darlings in a questionnaire that she filled out for D. Antoinette Handy's path-breaking 1980 study of the Sweethearts. Portions of this questionnaire appeared in Handy's indispensable volume, and I am grateful to Handy for sending me the entire questionnaire when I was unable to locate Brown myself for further comment. In it Brown wrote, "Having been a member of 'the Sweethearts' I observed primarily that the musicians were always BROKE also their health did not seem to be a major concern of management."[13] She went on to describe how, in her efforts to combat these problems, she invested $5,000 in organizing a band of her own in Harlem in 1943. She claimed to have recruited experienced women musicians from all over the United States, then fed them, housed them, supplied costumes, and secured auditions with such well-known talent agents as William Morris and Moe Gale. The agents were interested, she noted, but wanted the musicians to remain in rehearsal a bit longer before signing them on—an option Brown could not afford.

At this time, the Ferguson Brothers agency in Indianapolis was actively seeking female groups. Though Ferguson was a smaller company than those headed by William Morris and Moe Gale, it was one of the largest black-owned talent agencies in the country, handling such popular black bands as the Carolina Cotton Pickers and the King Kolax Orchestra. Most talent agencies were white-owned, even those that specialized in black talent, including Moe Gale and Joe Glaser. Denver Ferguson, president of the Ferguson Brothers agency, was himself African American, as were the agents who worked for him, and the performers the agency represented. The agency maintained a high profile in the black press, often running large advertisements in the entertainment pages—ads that sometimes appeared, by accident or design, directly adjacent to the press reviews of various Ferguson Brothers' acts. In addition to the talent agency, Ferguson Brothers also owned a ballroom in Indianapolis, where the bands they handled were frequently booked. Brown decided to give Ferguson a try.

> I went out west and we negotiated all day and night until I got what I wanted for the band. One of the *main* features of [the] contract was "a minimum pay check" whenever *we were not* performing. I don't recall the amount but it was adequate; another was *band outfits* to be responsibility of the *agency* at no cost to the musicians, etc., etc. After fighting all day and night, I returned to New York with a *good* contract [emphases in original].[14]

Just when it appears that Brown's tale will end in feminist victory, the story grows hazy. Brown's written account claims that at the same time that Clarence

Love, an agent from Ferguson Brothers, came to New York to assist her with getting the band together, misunderstandings of some kind occurred between herself and the musicians. Brown's intentions and management decisions appear to have come under some doubt by individual band members. Undone with exhaustion, she took a weekend off to rest. According to Brown, Love took advantage of the rift by choosing that moment to hit the road with the band, leaving Brown and her "good contract" in the dust.

> In the meantime, I was *invited* to join the band as a musician only *not* as owner, organizer. I *refused*. Through the years, I ran into a few of the members of the band who confided to me that they now, too late, realized what I had attempted to do for *girl* musicians. Of course they *again* were done in by having *no* contract to their advantage.[15]

Curiously, none of the Darlings alumnae I talked to were familiar with this story. (One musician expressed disbelief that Brown would have known enough about music to organize a band on her own.) I was unable to speak with any of the original Darlings, though I did speak with members who joined within the first year.

Clarence Love's participation in the Darlings of Rhythm story adds a number of puzzles. For one thing, Love was a well-known, though unrecorded, African American bandleader and arranger in the 1920s and 1930s, whose style was described as "sweet" and "romantic," never as "raggedy." In contrast to the Blue Devils and other African American bands that played jazz in Kansas City during those jumping years when Tom Pendergast's corrupt behind-the-scenes grip on city management protected gambling and disregarded Prohibition (thus providing venues that employed jazz musicians), Love's bands spent the 1930s producing "sweet" music for white audiences in Kansas City ballrooms. "My hero was Guy Lombardo," Love told an interviewer on the occasion of his induction into the Oklahoma Jazz Hall of Fame in 1990. "Romance with Love" was the slogan of the all-male band he was leading prior to his "discovery" and subsequent leadership of the Darlings of Rhythm.[16] How did this leader of "sweet" male bands segue into a leadership role in a female band that would be remembered by many as "raggedy," "rough," and "spontaneous"? Contrary to the black press, which frequently referred to Love as "musical director and arranger" of the Darlings, two former band members with whom I spoke could not remember performing any arrangements by Love, recalling instead that the band usually played stock arrangements, augmented by riffs invented by their section-mates.

The chronology available in the black press indicates that Love lost his male band in 1941 (interestingly enough, it was allegedly stolen from him by another talent agent).[17] The last gig of the Clarence Love Orchestra was at the Sunset

Terrace in Indianapolis, a ballroom that just so happened to be owned by the Ferguson Brothers. Out of a band, Love accepted a position with the talent agency in whose lap he had landed, working as a booking agent, newswriter, and developer of talent. Love's interest in "all-girl" bands may have been sparked by the success of a vocalist with whom he had once worked, who had taken a job directing the International Sweethearts of Rhythm at Piney Woods School, and then engineered their great escape. Love later claimed that he had planned to manage and book the Sweethearts through Ferguson Brothers when they ran away and went "pro," except that his former coworker, Rae Lee Jones, had gotten "obstinate" and decided to manage the band herself.[18] Certainly, visions of lost revenue must have crossed his mind in subsequent years as he read about the Sweethearts' success.

According to a press clipping sent to me by Love, he traveled East when "a young girl in New York contacted [him] in Indianapolis, looking for a booking for her all girl band. . . . The band had talent, so Clarence Love and the Darlings of Rhythm set out to conquer America."[19] We might well assume that the "young girl" was Lorraine Brown, though this version little resembles her own telling of the story, in which she figures as owner/organizer of the band; nor does it describe anything like the negotiation process she proudly remembered or explain how or why she was not among the "talented" musical *conquistadoras* who tackled America with Love in the spring of 1944.

A mention by entertainment columnist Billy Rowe places Love's trip to New York in late January 1944: "Clarence Love, former orchestra leader, now a member of Ferguson Bros. staff" was in New York "making Eastern connections."[20] Less than six weeks later, black newspapers heralded the arrival of the "Darlings of Rhythm, Ferguson Brothers' latest musical finds, who are giving other aggregations a good run for their money."[21] From the onset of Love's tenure as leader of the Darlings, news stories portrayed the new band as a serious event. The musicians were conceived as contenders, bursting full-blown onto a jazz scene full of formidable female players. "Like thunder out of a blue sky," raved the *Chicago Defender*, "the Darlings of Rhythm, America's all-girl band is on the horizon of fame with Gene Ray Lee, hot trumpeter and Clarence Love, musical director. This all girl orchestra compares with any in the business."[22] The *Pittsburgh Courier* praised Ferguson Brothers for "unearth[ing]" the Darlings, and proceeded to describe them as "one of the nation's fastest bands." Though speed was not always a sign of expertise in dance bands, and "fast" as applied to an "all-girl" band could have been taken as a pun for "loose" women, the reporter apparently intended a compliment, for the copy continued with an accolade, clearly emphasizing musical skills. "They do not depend upon their beauty alone to sway their audiences, they really play, all thirteen of them."[23] The story went on to list most of the players by name. The Darlings, in fact, were frequently listed individually by name. Perhaps this evocation of women's names served as a way of hyping the femininity of the group. And, perhaps, the players were named because they were likely to be remembered by audiences who had heard them in other bands. The *Chicago Defender* went so far as to describe the Darlings' musical lineup as "celebrity studded."[24]

Trumpet player Jean Ray Lee (sometimes spelled "Gene" in the press) had been a member of the Harlem Playgirls, a popular African American "all-girl" band, off and on from 1935 to 1940.[25] Other Darlings often promoted by name in the black press included trombonist Jessie Turner, alto saxophonist Josephine Boyd, and drummer Henrietta Fontaine. Fontaine was a veteran of another 1930s band, having held down the trapset of the Dixie Rhythm Girls in 1937 and 1938. Trumpeter Thelma Lewis, who moved back and forth between Eddie Durham's All-Star Girls and the Darlings of Rhythm, told me that the Darlings were formed from a nucleus of Eddie Durham's musicians. Indeed, Eddie Durham's All-Stars was the last band in which Lorraine Brown played before organizing the Darlings; lo and behold, among the first lineup of the Darlings, Jean Ray Lee, Josephine Boyd, and Jessie Turner had all been playing with Durham's band just prior to joining the Darlings for their ascent on the "horizon of fame." Other Durham All-Stars would also cross over to the new band, including tenor star Margaret Backstrom, also known as "Padjo," whose continuous presence in the Harlem Playgirls between 1935 and 1940 contributed to the excitement reflected in the black press when she joined the Darlings' reed section. *Music Dial*, a jazz magazine produced largely by black musicians in New York, was just one of many publications to proclaim the Darlings' acquisition of Backstrom as news, describing the tenor player as a "nationally famous saxophonist."[26]

The unequivocal "stardom" accorded to certain African American women musicians in the black press was accompanied by debates over which band was the "number one" "all-girl" band in the nation. The practice of comparing and contrasting the Darlings and the Sweethearts did not originate in my interviews with women musicians in the 1990s, but seems to have been a continuation of an ongoing speculation by musicians, audiences, and reviewers. An item in the *Pittsburgh Courier* in 1945 invited readers to weigh the skills of star tenor players from the Sweethearts and the Darlings.

DETROIT—Jessie Harper of the Motor City writes that Margaret Backstrom, of the Darlings of Rhythm, is the lick on tenor sax, stating that she is as great or greater than Vi Burnside of the Sweethearts of Rhythm.

". . . Anyone who can hold an audience under her spell for twenty minutes, execute with excellency any request and demonstrate the complexities of jazz must have something on the ball."

Does anyone challenge the Harper statement?[27]

It is too bad that the debate initiated by *Courier* reader Jessie Harper didn't unfold in subsequent issues, as it would have perhaps been useful in teasing out the aesthetic differences that audiences attributed to the two representatives of the two bands. But the artifact of the debate is significant in that it implies that while the more "feminized" and "arrangement-oriented" performances of the Sweethearts were preferable to producers of "Soundies," they were not necessarily always more popular with black audiences than the visual and musical performances of the Darlings.[28] Bassist Vi Wilson recalled in our 1994 interview that it wasn't unusual for fans to engage in lively speculation over which band possessed the superior soloists. Recalling the rare occasions when the two bands would cross each other's paths on the road, Wilson described the ways the women would entertain fans and enjoy each other's company at jam session showdowns.

> Fellas in those days had a competition between the Sweethearts and the Darlings. But the Darlings could play. Boy, we would get in jam sessions with them like, whatever town we were in. The fellas, it was a novelty to them to come see these girls play. They said, "Those girls play like men." We'd have a big jam session. Boy, Vi Burnside would really play. And Padjo she would really play. And, see, the best players, tenor players were Padjo and Vi Burnside. And Vi Burnside would call Padjo, I think one was Lester Young and the other one called Ben Webster. And they'd come shake hands and get on the bandstand, "Let's blow these fellas down!" Oh, we'd have some good times.[29]

This evocation of the good-spirited "battles" waged between Sweethearts and Darlings in jam sessions is another interesting indication of a special relationship between the two bands. Many of the members knew each other from earlier bands. Vi Burnside and Margaret Backstrom may have represented opposing teams and divergent styles to fans in the 1940s, but they had spent two years in the same saxophone section when Burnside joined the Harlem Playgirls from 1938 to 1940. One year previously, Burnside had played in the Dixie Rhythm Girls, which was owned by the same man who managed the Harlem Playgirls, so it is likely that the consumer "sound test" levied on the two tenor players had begun in 1937. The differences between the two tenor saxophonists' playing styles continued to provide useful points of reference when musicians in the 1990s attempted to elucidate the lost music of the Darlings. "Vi Burnside was show, but Padjo actually played," explained Thelma Lewis. "Padjo could play fifty choruses, all different." Burnside played "riffs," or patterns, according to Lewis, but Backstrom "played the changes," meaning the latter saxophonist conceived her musical lines as negotiating the chord changes of the tune. The performance styles of the two tenors contrasted in Lewis's memory as well. She recalled that Burnside was a crowd-pleaser who moved a lot and got the audience to clap.

Backstrom, on the other hand, didn't move, but "stood straight up and played a lot of saxophone." In addition, the Darlings' star tenor "could read a fly-speck too" and doubled on clarinet.[30]

Another musician that former Darlings remembered as one of the band's brightest stars is alto saxophonist Josephine Boyd, who also had played in Eddie Durham's All-Stars. "She was a genius," murmured Sarah McLawler, who heard Boyd play in the Darlings at the Sunset Terrace Ballroom in Indianapolis. "I've seen her blow men off the stage," said Lillian Carter (later Wilson), who played with Boyd in Baltimore with the International Sweethearts of Rhythm. Carter insisted that Boyd helped Dizzy Gillespie with the invention of bebop. "Diz was there, backstage. And Josephine was there. And there was something about what they were doing, that they dug it. They dug each other." The fact that Gillespie didn't remember Boyd when I communicated with him through his road manager Charlie "the Whale" Lake didn't deter Carter's belief that Boyd had helped "set the egg" for bebop. "Sometimes Josephine would just get to herself. Just her and her horn. And run these dumb sounding changes, you know, like what bebop sounds like. And we'd be saying to ourselves, what in the world is she doing, you know?" Carter's character sketch of Boyd is consistent with other descriptions of the Darlings as a whole. "She played sax, and I mean she *played* it. She didn't just get up there and stand there and look halfway cute. She wasn't a cute person. She was Josephine."[31]

The network provided by the several African American "all-girl" bands in the 1940s made it possible for musicians such as Lewis, Gaddison, and Wilson, all three of whom played in a number of bands, to exercise some agency in their careers by moving back and forth among bands. Decisions to move were based not only on aesthetic preferences, but also on the location of one's friends, on working conditions, travel conditions, management, and money. Gaddison joined the Darlings after clashing with the stringent band rules of the Sweethearts. "The woman that was over the band, Mrs. Jones, she was very strict," explained Gaddison. "She was like having a matron." Gaddison's dismissal, ironically, was due to her desire to see Mary Lou Williams play piano with Andy Kirk's otherwise all-male band. The Sweethearts had a gig in New Jersey that evening, and Andy Kirk's band was playing in New York. Though there was a rule against wearing band uniforms in public when not on a job, Gaddison knew she would not have time to change if she tried to go hear Mary Lou Williams play. So she put a coat on over her band uniform and went out to hear Kirk's band. She missed the band bus to New Jersey, but hitched a ride through the tunnel and arrived at the Armory where the Sweethearts were playing a dance before the music started. Although Gaddison considered herself punctual and her behavior reasonable, "I got fired from the time I walked in the door."[32] The Darlings did not have such strict rules about what musicians did with their free time.

Thelma Lewis remembered leaving Eddie Durham's All-Stars on several occasions when "the money got funny" and then returning when the band reorganized.[33] She learned to stay alert to opportunities with other bands, such as the Darlings, during down periods, and she also learned how to be "stingy," as she put it, in order to make what little money she earned last as long as possible. "I could hold a dollar until it cried," she said. Her laughter had a sad ring to it, conveying a sense of the accumulated experiences that taught her to be so protective of her earnings. To this day, she said, she still remembers who owes her money. The network of bands meant that musicians weren't depending on the fortunes and fair-play of only the band to which they belonged at any given moment, but had several bands that could possibly pick them up if they wanted a change or found themselves stranded. The constant personnel shifts meant that there was a reliable communication system among the major African American "all-girl" bands.

Vi Wilson transferred from the Sweethearts to the Darlings in order to be with her cousin, reeds player T.Sgt. Gurthalee Clark, a veteran of the only African American band in the Women's Army Corps. Wilson recalled that Clark and some other members of the WAC, including trumpet player Constance Hurley, joined the Darlings after returning to civilian life in late 1945. They preferred the Darlings, according to Wilson, because they felt that the "Darlings had the best players. And the Sweethearts were growing more feminine, and had all the beautiful uniforms. They had some money behind them. The poor Darlings didn't have too much behind them. We only had two changes, two uniforms." The difference in investments afforded by the Sweethearts' management and the expenses incurred by Ferguson Brothers on behalf of the Darlings is perceptible in publicity photos (see fig. 2.1). Unlike the Sweethearts, whose photos present them artistically posed, and dressed in trademark flowing peasant dresses or smart traveling suits, the Darlings are lined up in rows, many of the musicians unsmiling and seemingly uncomfortable within the frames of their photos, and dressed in one of the sensible and unromantic uniforms described by Wilson. "We had a red coat with a black skirt and a white blouse. Then we had another one with a checkered jacket with a white blouse. That's all we had. But the Sweethearts had all these beautiful gowns, all kind of gowns, short dresses and all, and they were fabulous with make-up and all, but we just had what we had. But we could play." Without money for the kinds of elaborate arrangements written especially for the Sweethearts by such arrangers as Eddie Durham, Jesse Stone, Maurice King, and even Mary Lou Williams, the Darlings relied on musicians' abilities to improvise and to play head arrangements, riffs thought up by the musicians themselves ahead of time and then memorized. "Our music was a little bit more down to earth," said Wilson. "We had more jazz musicians, more rock and roll, and we could ad lib more."[34]

BRASS SECTION
DARLINGS OF RHYTHM ORCHESTRA

Personal Management
FERGUSON BROS. AGENCY, Inc.
328 No. Senate Ave., Indianapolis, Ind.
Indianapolis - New York - Hollywood

FIGURE 2.1 Brass Section, Darlings of Rhythm Orchestra *(Left to right:)* (Unidentified), Toby Butler, Marie Johnson, trumpets; Autora Bell, trombone. Courtesy Vi Wilson.

Wilson's reference to the "femininity" of the Sweethearts, as opposed to the skill level of the Darlings who "could play," is typical of a kind of division of labor evoked by Darlings alumnae explaining the differences between the two bands. The Darlings' music was frequently described as "masculine" by the women I interviewed, especially those who appreciated the band's style. And perhaps, considering the masculine "norm" in the jazz scene, it is understandable that even women musicians would consider "feminine" a pejorative descriptor, and would term music they enjoyed as "more masculine." "She plays like a man" was a compliment, freely doled out by the press, male musicians, and audience members, which women sometimes complained about during our interviews. But playing "like men" also represented a set of usually positive terms that women musicians sometimes used to describe themselves and other women who played in ways that were undifferentiated from the ways that men played. In Wilson's jam-session story, both Backstrom and Burnside took nicknames of famous male tenor soloists before leaping into a coed cutting session. To perform jazz without audible gender difference meant playing instruments and styles that were associated with men. It meant women's refusal to restrict themselves to "soft" or "sweet" timbres. It meant improvisation. Women whose jazz didn't produce "feminine difference" challenged audiences' definition of "woman" and they also challenged male ownership of the most highly valued instruments and styles. Surely, this is another clue as to why the Darlings alumnae with whom I spoke tended to refer proudly to the band's emphasis on musical skills and deemphasis on feminine accoutrements such as makeup and gowns. The Darlings were not the only "all-girl" band to adopt this particular mode of presenting and interpreting their music, but the interviews concerning this band raised these issues as inextricable from the band's history. Through their emphasis on an aggressive approach to the music, on thunderous volumes, on authoritative horn and saxophone soloists, the Darlings represent one strategy for women's claims to identities as jazz musicians. But this is not the formula by which all women jazz musicians conceive their art and their gendered musical identities.[35] Billie Holiday, for instance, arguably the most influential female musician in jazz history, was less than thrilled with the Darlings' approach when the band accompanied her at the Grand Terrace Ballroom in Chicago in June 1944.

Un-"Lady"-like Sounds

The Darlings hadn't been on the road a month when newspaper reports began to point excitedly toward their forthcoming appearance at Chicago's Grand Terrace. The famous ballroom ("world-renowned," according to the *Chicago Defender*) had been closed for three years, but retained its eminence as the site where Earl "Fatha" Hines "rode to music's peak" during his long reign as the ballroom's resident bandleader from 1928 to 1938. Other bands that had held forth on the celebrated bandstand included those led by Fletcher Henderson and Count Basie. To play for the grand reopening of the Grand Terrace was a coup for any band. There would be a nationwide radio hookup. The Darlings were fortunate to have such a high-profile booking so soon in the band's history.[36] Immediately upon Love's securing of this prestigious booking, press releases and news copy having anything to do with the Darlings managed to work in some mention of the Grand Terrace.

"Prior to their opening at the Grand Terrace, the Darlings of Rhythm are scheduled to do a string of one-nighters in Florida as well as dates at the Roller Rink, Louisville, KY and the Colosseum, Evansville, Ind.," announced the *Pittsburgh Courier* in early March 1944.[37] "The Darlings of Rhythm, America's dream band are headed eastward playing Norfolk and Newport News and several engagements later this month," reported the *Chicago Defender* in April. "These famous girls have broken attendance records in more than a dozen cities and are receiving requests for return engagements galore. After closing Tidewater area, they trek southwestward, playing engagements in Georgia and Louisiana enroute to Chicago where they open the Grand Terrace sometime early in June."[38] All that spring, items reporting where the Darlings were playing now—Tennessee, Ohio, Michigan, Georgia, Virginia, Texas, Oklahoma, Kansas—also reminded readers of the band's June destination.

As the anticipated booking approached, the *Chicago Defender* announced that the Darlings' vocalist Helen Taborn had begun sharing the "honors as canary with Joan Lunceford."[39] According to jazz historian Frank Driggs, Joan Lunceford was one and the same as Baby Briscoe, who had led the Harlem Playgirls in the late 1930s. D. Antoinette Handy notes that Briscoe led a male band known as the Dukes of Rhythm in New Orleans in the early 1940s.[40] In addition to Briscoe/Lunceford handling some of the vocal numbers and eventually wielding the baton, the band now consisted of Lula Roberts, Grace Wilson, and Josephine Boyd in the sax section; Marie Johnson on first trumpet and Jean Ray Lee on second and "hot" (jazz) trumpet; trombonists Jessie Turner and Autora Bell; Ozzie "Bumps" Huff (who would later marry Clarence Love) on piano (some reports say her specialty was boogie-woogie); bassist Lillian Jones; drummer Henrietta Fontaine; and vocalist Helen Taborn.

Curiously, although the grand reopening was repeatedly hyped in both the *Pittsburgh Courier* and the *Chicago Defender,* neither of these national weekly African American newspapers indicated that Billie Holiday would appear on the same bill, nor that her singing would be accompanied by the Darlings of Rhythm. Oddly enough, the famous jazz singer would not be mentioned in either paper until the reviews were filed. Holiday herself had vowed never to sing at the Grand Terrace again after being fired in 1936 by ballroom proprietor Ed Fox for singing "too slow."[41] Less than two weeks before the anticipated booking, *Variety* announced that the Grand Terrace grand-reopening bill would consist of the "Darlings of Rhythm 14 piece girl orchestra, a line of 14 girls, Two Bits of Rhythm, Mayberry and Johnson, Joe Stack, Jessie Davis and others, still to be booked."[42] Apparently, Holiday's starring role had yet to be confirmed.

By the time the Darlings arrived in Chicago for the rehearsal at the Grand Terrace, the news had reached them that they would be appearing with Billie Holiday. The instrumentalists, at least, were thrilled. It is difficult to imagine how the two vocalists would have felt about performing in the same show as the great jazz singer. Several members of the International Sweethearts of Rhythm told D. Antoinette Handy that when Holiday appeared with the Sweethearts in August 1941—three years before her date with the Darlings—she had resented sharing the bill with the band's vocalist, Evelyn McGee.[43] McGee (later Stone) fondly remembered the incident. "Billie Holiday was the featured attraction that week and I sang first and broke up the house. And she went to Mrs. Jones and told her, 'Put that little McGee girl on after the band plays the opening number.' I intimidated her, but she was paying me a great compliment."[44] In the spring of 1944 reviewers in the black press were in the habit of comparing Darlings' vocalist Helen Taborn with Billie Holiday, an opinion that might not have boded well for smooth relations between the band and the famous singer. Despite such comparisons, Holiday's popularity among jazz fans and critics, if not the general public, was unsurpassed in 1944. In January of that year, she was easily elected "best jazz vocalist" by jazz critics in the first-ever *Esquire* poll. As part of that honor, Holiday had recently appeared at New York's Metropolitan Opera House in an all-star band with the other poll winners—becoming the first African American to sing at the Met.[45] It was also the first time Holiday had ever been invited to sing in a concert hall.

By June 1944 the Darlings had also enjoyed their share of honors, which were considerable for a band so recently formed. Beginning in April, the *Chicago Defender* occasionally let slip its usual allegiance to the International Sweethearts of Rhythm, dubbing the Darlings "America's No. 1 all-girl orchestra" (along with ravings about Darlings' vocalist Helen Taborn being "in the same class with Billie Holiday and Ella Fitzgerald").[46] All reviews since the band's formation, in fact, had been wildly favorable, and the Darlings were riding high on the attention. So while the Darlings had heard about Holiday's occasional foul temper through the musicians' grapevine, and may have even anticipated possible resentment of Taborn's vocal numbers, they did not foresee the magnitude of her unfavorable reaction to the instrumentalists' handling of her charts.

"She screamed at us!" exclaimed Frann Gaddison, who vividly remembered the scene. "She called us a bunch of names. . . . She just cussed us out in rehearsal. Called us a bunch of bitches, you know. She had a bad mouth, anyway." The "cussing out" didn't surprise the musicians so much as the content of Holiday's critique. "She was saying, 'Haven't you heard of Paul Whiteman?'" Whiteman, a famous white band leader of the 1920s, whose all-male band specialized in "sweet" numbers and elaborate arrangements, often stated that his mission was to "make a lady out of jazz," a goal that was, oddly enough, antithetical to that of the Darlings of Rhythm. The Darlings didn't want to "make a lady out of jazz"—for them, that would have meant crafting some kind of "feminine" imitation of jazz, and they considered themselves "real" jazz musicians. The Darlings emphasized the very qualities—power, spontaneity, drive—that Whiteman hoped to eradicate by making jazz "symphonic"—the musical equivalent to the pedestal. Whiteman's project was to elevate jazz, to make it respectable, to bring it into the concert hall. By the 1940s Whiteman's band was considered "square," "corny," and "watered down" by many white and black jazz listeners alike. As the Darlings played Holiday's charts with characteristic punch, the musicians felt themselves in fine form. That is, until Holiday rebuked the very attributes that were prized by the band members. The Paul Whiteman comment was intended to dampen their volume, as well as their spirits. "She wanted us to soften down," mused Gaddison. "And we were busting those notes! We had a drummer that was, you know, *bad* as any guy out there."[47]

Clearly, Gaddison meant "bad" in the African American vernacular sense of "extremely good," but her description of the drummer's skills as "bad as any guy out there" gives a clue as to the grounds for Holiday's objection. Holiday's own approach to crafting an identity as a female jazz artist did not consist of "busting notes," nor did it entail straining to be heard over instrumentalists who "busted notes" behind her. Holiday's intervention into the usual gender division of jazz labor included her insistence that instrumentalists, who were usually male, listen to her as she listened to them, and to interact with her with the same spirit of collaboration and respect they would accord any other soloist in the band. In this way, she not only transformed the role of the jazz singer, but the role of the jazz instrumentalist. Her preference for tenor saxophonist Lester Young's softer-toned, behind-the-beat style to Herschel Evans's bigger, harder-swinging, Coleman Hawkins–inspired sound explains, in part, why she might try to "soften down" the Darlings.[48]

The musical collaborations of Billie Holiday and Lester Young and other members of Count Basie's band in the mid- and late 1930s heralded not only a new approach to modern jazz, but also a new approach to the traditional gender organization of the music. "He played music I like," Holiday said about Lester Young in a conversation with jazz writer Max Jones, elaborating that Young "didn't try to drown the singer."[49] In place of a convention where the "girl singer" stood in front as a kind of audiovisual decoration, Holiday and Young charted new territory where a female vocalist and male horn player might find places to meet as equals, inspire each other, create new approaches to both voice and saxophone, and expand the possibilities of jazz itself. Young once told an interviewer that when he played the records he and Holiday made in the 1930s, it sounded to him like "two of the same voices . . . or the same mind."[50] References to this musical relationship abound in jazz literature, often accompanied by quizzical speculations regarding the nature of their personal relationship, frequently described not only as platonic, but as "amazingly" (John Chilton's qualifier) platonic.[51] Interestingly, Young's voice-like approach to his horn, a radical departure from Coleman Hawkins's aggressive tenor style, also frequently inspired ridicule and curiosity that he might be homosexual—the very reactions that met women instrumentalists who "played like men."[52] Holiday's critique of the Darlings strangely echoes a well-documented incident in Young's career. During the unhappy months he spent in Fletcher Henderson's band as a replacement for Hawkins who had left, Henderson's wife, trumpet player Leora Meoux, spun Coleman Hawkins's records for Young, coaxing, "Lester, can't you play like this?"[53]

Interestingly, when Billie Holiday "cussed out" the Darlings, she did not say, "Can't you play like Lester Young?" or "Haven't you ever heard Count Basie's band, the way the musicians supported the vocalist . . .?" Instead, she invoked the name of a white bandleader who came to prominence in the 1920s by "sweetening" jazz and making it appeal to a mass white audience; who described his contribution as that of a musical missionary who set out to tame jazz of its "demonaic energy, and fantastic riot of accents."[54] *Metronome* editor Doron K. Antrim went so far as to congratulate Whiteman for "rescu[ing] jazz from the jungles" and "civiliz[ing] it."[55] These ways of understanding Whiteman's music were current during the times in which he was dubbed by white historians "the King of Jazz." His claim to have made "a lady out of jazz" most certainly meant "white lady," since African American women were not accorded the status of respectable "cult of true womanhood" "lady-ness" in the United States at that time. Yet Billie Holiday called herself "Lady." As Susan Cook has pointed out, Holiday's adherence to the nickname "Lady" (personalized to "Lady Day" by Lester Young) represents a significant challenge to the racial and gender stratification of the United States of the era.[56] Even as Holiday redefined the role of the jazz singer to equal status (rather than inferior opposite) to the jazz instrumentalist, she staked claim to the socially respectable feminine difference represented by the word "lady." Holiday made the title "Lady" cross the color line and transformed it to include a range of backgrounds and behaviors traditionally excluded from the pedestal. Women from poor families, who "cussed" people out, who were jazz singers—all were traditionally disqualified from the definition "lady," regardless of race. Her reworking of the term "lady" is similar to what Angela Davis has described as Holiday's ability to "relocate" "the sentimental love songs" of the white popular song idiom into "a specifically African American cultural tradition and simultaneously challenge the boundaries of that tradition."[57] Yet it appears that Holiday's transformation of the boundaries of "lady" and "jazz" did not encompass black women players of horns, reeds, and rhythm, who owned only two costumes changes and were proud of their loud, powerful big-band sound.

Was Holiday trying to "make ladies" out of the Darlings? If so, why was it necessary to evoke Whiteman's white men's "symphonic jazz" band? More troubling is the possibility that Holiday objected to the Darlings' music as "too black," that somehow an element of musical whiteness, or crossover at least, was necessary to make black women musicians into "ladies." Was the evocation of Whiteman's white band meant to discourage qualities in the Darlings' playing style associated with African American working-class culture—"jump" tunes, boogie-woogie, blues, head arrangements, and riffs? Or perhaps the Darlings delivered their aesthetic with such determination that Holiday felt an extremist tack was necessary just to cut the decibels enough to get her songs across. Perhaps the Darlings' own embattled sense of themselves as big-band jazz players who happened to be women could not afford the reworking of the roles of vocalist and instrumentalist that Holiday demanded; perhaps their ability to "drown the vocalist" was an important element of their proof to audiences that they were "real" jazz musicians, not feminine imitations.

If Holiday had launched her critique during a rehearsal of "Trav'lin' Light," the one tune (and a hit) she recorded with Whiteman's orchestra in 1942, the reproach would make a more literal kind of sense—she may have wanted the Darlings to play it more as it sounded on the record. (This would have been a good trick, however, since Whiteman used strings under Holiday's vocal and, other than the bass in the rhythm section, the Darlings had no strings.)[58] But Gaddison did not remember the repertoire from this otherwise unforgettable rehearsal. Her explanation, that Holiday wanted the band to "soften down," makes musical sense in terms of Holiday's well-documented preferences for a sensitive collaboration among instrumentalists and vocalists. Still, there was something else going on in her mention of Whiteman, an insult perhaps, a rejection, a pulling of rank, though we may never know what exactly was intended. The Darlings were proud of their mighty brass and driving rhythm. Surely the great jazz singer recognized (from the way they "busted those notes") that they had no intention of sounding like Whiteman. The sting of Holiday's remark was detectable in Gaddison's telling of the story; she returned several times to the comment. "She kept saying, 'You all ever heard of Paul Whiteman?' Because she recorded with Paul Whiteman. It was strange, you know, and la de da."

The story of Billie Holiday and the Darlings of Rhythm represents for me not the superiority of one method for black women to craft identities as jazz artists over another, but rather a fascinating instance of a clash between two entirely different strategies in a single historical moment, both of which were sometimes successful in carving out spaces for black female musicians to do their art and to get some degree of respect and remuneration. Though it is Holiday who is known today as the quintessential woman jazz artist, and the Darlings who are virtually unknown, some reporters in the black press actually seemed more enthused with the Darlings' performance at the Grand Terrace. A reviewer from the *Chicago Defender* devoted accolades to the "musical gyrations" of the "14 collaborators of Swing" and to Joan Lunceford as "petite and vivacious songstress and Lady of the Baton," before praising Holiday's "magnificent chirping" and "fashionable gowns."[59] Columnist Al Monroe got personal (might he have heard about the Darlings' rehearsal?) when he pronounced that Holiday's behavior at the Grand Terrace "didn't help her popularity here. . . . She responded to none of the few encores received and coworkers say she 'sat' on everyone who sought her friendship."[60] It appears that the Grand Terrace represented an unhappy booking for Holiday's sense of herself as both an artist and a "lady"; she didn't like to sing in variety acts, she didn't like singing with loud bands, and she could have seen her booking with an "all-girl" band as an insult. For the Darlings, however, the Grand Terrace represented a milestone. Its perks were rare for black women who were not singers or dancers. Three shows nightly (11:00 P.M., 1:00 A.M., and 3:00 A.M.), playing behind the acts of forty artists ranging from comedians to chorus lines may sound grueling but, for musicians accustomed to one-nighters, it meant four weeks of steady work in one place. It also meant rare access to one of swing's primary technologies for success—live radio broadcasts, the opportunity to work with the greatest jazz singer in the world, and a source of fame that would linger in press mentions of the band throughout its lifetime.

Darlings on the Road

On July 22, the *Chicago Defender* announced that "Clarence Love, leader and director of America's Class A all-girl orchestra will close his Grand Terrace engagement to take to the highways latter part of July" on a tour of "Indiana, Illinois, Ohio and Pennsylvania."[61] The band was so popular between the summer of 1944 and the early months of 1946 that it is actually possible to track their road schedule from newspaper stories and band listings in the black press, as well as in the "Top-Flight Bands" column in the American Federation of Musicians' magazine, *The International Musician*. They never were included in *Down Beat's* "Where the Bands Are" column, though the International Sweethearts of Rhythm were frequently listed.

News items during July and August indicated that the Darlings had acquired two additional experienced trumpet players, Ann Cooper and Estelle Handy, and that after barnstorming the dance halls of the Midwest, they had worked their way east, hitting Delaware, Virginia, New Jersey, Maryland, Pennsylvania, New York, Connecticut, and Massachusetts. The *Courier* greeted their upcoming arrival in New York City, Newark, Albany, Boston, and New Haven with the exclamation, "This will be their first Eastern appearance after a long stay at the Grand Terrace Cafe in Chicago."[62] September and October found them traveling and playing their way through Arizona, California, Oregon, and Washington, delighting entertainment-starved black soldiers at Fort Huachuca, Arizona, and making other notable appearances at the Silver Slipper in San Diego and Seattle's Turf Room. While on the West Coast, Love brokered more talent, signing on tenor star Margaret Backstrom and vocalist Pat LaMar. Of his selection of LaMar ("delineator of sweet numbers"), the *Courier* praised Love for his "keen eye for talent and eye for the beautiful," and Love was paraphrased as saying something to the effect that "Pat adds just the touch needed to make the Darlings the perfect picturesque and musically superior orchestra."[63] November found the Darlings headlining in such venues as the Village Barn in Tulsa, Oklahoma; the Cotton

Club in Longview, Texas; the East Texas Cotton Club in Lufkin, Texas; and the Harvest Club, in Beaumont, Texas.

The new year, 1945, brought more onslaughts of one-nighters, moments of glory, and personnel changes, all glowingly reported in the press. The year started off with a bang as the Darlings were selected out of twenty-five nominated bands to play the annual private dance known as the Twelve Mo Ball, held annually at the Walker Casino in Indianapolis. *Music Dial* reported Clarence Love as declaring with a publicist's flair for overstatement that "this affair will be the crowning point of his life."[64] A Southern tour followed, with standing-room-only appearances in Mississippi and Tennessee. At one point in the spring or summer of 1945, drummer Hettie Smith replaced Henrietta Fontaine. In April, the *Chicago Defender* noted that "Little Toby of the SWEETHEARTS OF RHYTHM band is out of the organization."[65] By June, Toby Butler was showing up in photographs and stories as a member of the Darlings of Rhythm. The acquisition of a white member was not publicized—the integrated status of the band would be covert until Butler's arrest in 1946.

In June 1945 the Darlings finally outdid their Grand Terrace publicity by traveling to Los Angeles in what the *Pittsburgh Courier* referred to as "real style. The Army has provided them transportation in a B-29 bomber from Amarillo Texas where they entertained GIs."[66] After their spectacular airborne entrance into Los Angeles, the band opened at the Plantation Club in Watts on June 21. Newspaper reports hinted at exciting golden opportunities that awaited the band on the West Coast. "A recording session and a probable movie is in the making if the deal jells. After the Coast bash a series of Eastern dates is being lined up."[67] A publicity photo showed the Darlings lined up in front of their eighteen-passenger sleeper coach at the Metro-Goldwyn-Mayer studios, smiling, perhaps at their good fortune in the City of Angels (see fig. 2.2). Yet, despite the hoopla, rumors of MGM contracts, recordings, and overseas tours, it appears that what greeted the Darlings after their four weeks in Los Angeles was yet another string of stateside one-nighters, this time hitting such swinging towns as Yakima, Everett, and Walla Walla, Washington; and adding to their list of venues such places as the Pelican Theater in Klamath, Oregon; the Civic Auditorium in Oakland, and the Brown Bomber ballroom in San Francisco.[68] A month later, they were still doing one-nighters, only now in the Midwest, where in a single week in September they played dates in Norfolk, Nebraska; Worthington, Minnesota; Des Moines, Iowa; Waterloo, Iowa; Omaha, Nebraska; Sioux Falls, South Dakota; and Battle Lake, Minnesota, in that order. By Christmas, they were still on one-nighters, this time in Florida.

What is missing from these breezy newsprint itineraries, is, of course, the working and traveling conditions of the musicians, who were, after all, African American women and one white woman, racing from gig to gig in a bus across terrain that was often inhospitable, even dangerous, and where integration was

DARLINGS OF RHYTHM Coming To the Casablanca Lounge Personal Management
In Hollywood Monday Nite August 5th FERGUSON BROS. AGENCY, Inc.
328 No. Senate Ave., Indianapolis, Ind.
Indianapolis · New York · Hollywood

FIGURE 2.2 Darlings of Rhythm Orchestra. In front of Metro-Goldwyn-Studios in Hollywood, 1945. Courtesy Vi Wilson.

against the law. These missing "road hazards" were remembered and described vividly by bassist Vi Wilson. By matching events from Wilson's memory with stories from the press, it appears that she joined the Darlings in either late 1945 or early 1946. A Los Angeles native, she had never been to the Jim Crow South before her tenure with the Darlings, and noted that the band had less money behind them, fewer resources, and a more poorly equipped bus than the Sweethearts, but the same problems. Among her memories of traveling with the Darlings were many stories of the particular challenges faced by the band and their strategies for meeting them. One strategy of the Ferguson Brothers agency, she recalled, was the hiring of a white bus driver.

"Bob was our bus driver," said Wilson. "He would tell the white sharecroppers down there, 'These are my girls and they work for me.' And that's how we could get by." Interestingly, the famous African American radio choir, Wings Over Jordan, also used a white bus driver when they toured the South, apparently as a strategy for mitigating against disaster. It seems that the hiring of white men to drive the buses and communicate with white men in charge of various things like gas stations and dance halls was, ironically, one kind of integration that actually eased Jim Crow travel for some black entertainers.[69] According to Wilson, Bob had other qualities useful for the task of safely conveying African American travelers in the South—he was a former race-car driver from Indianapolis.

> We had a word that we'd say: "West." That was our password. When any trouble would happen, he would just shoot down one street and up another and we'd holler, "West, west," that was the danger word, and we would run. Wherever we were we would drop everything and run. . . . Bob would gun his motor three times . . . and we knew something was wrong. And the person would hold at the door and as he'd drive past, we'd run for the bus and he'd reach down and grab hands and swing 'em in. And he'd turn the corner until the last one was in, and when the last one was in, we'd say "West" and we'd pull the cord three times and we'd slam the door and make it out of town.

Not long after Wilson joined the Darlings, Clarence Love rushed home to Tulsa to care for his dying father. He would not return, but would remain in Tulsa, eventually opening a nightclub. In his place, Ferguson Brothers installed a one-armed trumpet player named Leroy McCoy. Wilson vaguely recalled that the band accidentally left McCoy on the road somewhere during a bathroom break in the middle of the night. A typical latrine stop, Wilson recalled, involved the women going around on one side of the bus, and the men (Bob and McCoy) on the other. "Now, the last person in is supposed to check to see that everybody's in the bus," she explained.

> Somehow or another down there, we were in Louisiana or Mississippi or somewhere, [McCoy] went out to the rest room. He went out over here and we were on this side. . . . So Bob hit the cord and he says, "All clear?" and somebody said, "Aw, go ahead. We're okay." Hit the cord three times and they closed the door. They left McCoy out there on the road with nothing but his stocking cap on his head, his robe, his pants, and his undershirt. And drove off! We had this gig, we had to be there the next night. Pretty soon, somebody said, "Where's McCoy?" And we had gone about fifteen or twenty miles down the road. And we had to be at that gig, because, you know, whenever you missed a gig, they could dock you if you didn't have the number of [musicians] to fulfill the contract. We said, "Oh my God. He's not in the bus!" We must have left him on the road.

The band went ahead to the gig and trombonist Jessie Turner, who had studied music at Wayne State University, led the band, while McCoy trudged the miles of Southern highway by foot in his night clothes. Wilson confided that she often wondered if the band had left McCoy on the road on purpose, acknowledging that most of the musicians preferred Jessie Turner as a leader. "But they said they really didn't know he wasn't on the bus." McCoy arrived safely at the dance hall by the break and, as Wilson recalled, he took over the baton without recriminations. In June McCoy was still listed in the press as leader of the Darlings. By July, however, Jessie Turner would appear in newspaper reports as the band's leader, the William G. Powell Agency would be advertised as the booking agent, and the band would be referred to as the "newly reorganized" Darlings of Rhythm.

Women from Mars

As with the International Sweethearts of Rhythm, many of the "road hazards" incurred by the Darlings revolved around police suspicions that the band was breaking Jim Crow laws. It wasn't safe for the band to advertise itself as integrated, nor did its membership lend itself to a construction as "international." Yet the band did include some light-skinned members, and one white member, trumpet player Toby Butler, who had been raised by a black family and who had spent her career up to that point playing in black women's bands. The interracial aspect of the Darlings was covert. Still, the highest profile the Darlings would ever achieve occurred due to an incident with the police in Milledgeville, Georgia, over their breaking of Jim Crow laws. "I have a clipping that I'll have to show you one time where they caught us in the Darlings," informed Wilson by way of introducing her telling of the incident. "They had arrested Toby."

The story of Butler's arrest would move the Darlings of Rhythm out of the entertainment pages of the *Pittsburgh Courier* and on to the front page, complete with a photo of the white trumpet player, captioned "Georgia Law Got Her." The headlines read, "Out of Tune! White Girl in Mixed Orchestra Arrested by Georgia Police." Other black newspapers ran the story, and the incident even rated the Darlings a page-one story in *Down Beat*, which had, up to that moment, not been much interested in the band.[70] The *Courier* news copy stated the facts: "Charging that Toby Butler, trumpet player with the 'Darlings of Rhythm' all-girl orchestra, is white, and therefore breaks a law when she travels with Negro members of the unit in Georgia, police officers here halted the band's itinerary last week by arresting her."

According to Wilson, the police threw Butler in their squad car and were preparing to drive her down to the station.

> Toby had to sit in the back seat and she whispered to us, "I will never let them take me to jail, because you know what they do to white girls that are with [black bands. They misuse them] just like they misuse colored girls." She said, "They'll never do that to me." She had a little 32 pistol in her purse. And she said, "When he puts his foot on that starter, I'm going to blow him away." And we would just cringe; we said, "We're not going to let them take you."

Now, this is Wilson's memory of the event, her version of what she believed was happening. Butler's own account made no mention of a pistol in her purse, a sensible omission from any number of perspectives. Butler simply informed me that she was indeed detained in Georgia, and that the newspaper clippings were accurate. If, however, a Southern white woman in 1946 believed that rape was a possible consequence of being jailed for breaking Jim Crow laws, it would hardly have been an irrational fear. Nor would it have been irrational for such a woman to carry a weapon to protect herself. Not only would a white woman have been seen as a criminal for associating with black people, she would be perceived as a "fallen woman," a race traitor, disqualified from Southern chivalry, and deserving of social, as well as legal, punishment.

As she told the story, Wilson reached into an envelope of memorabilia and retrieved a photograph of a young white woman with long, brown hair.

> Now this is Toby, the one I told you about, who was going to blow the cops away? . . . But you know what happened? Jessie went and leaned up on that car with her cigarettes and started talking. . . ."Now wouldn't you feel real stupid going to your supervisor, telling them that you've got a white girl in the car, and this girl is my cousin? Now look at me." Jessie was very fair, same color as Toby. . . . Well, in our band we had light girls and darker girls mixed up. . . . So she said, "Now this girl is my first cousin, now you can take her if you want to, but you're going to probably get fired." Oh, she just kept talking and they kept looking, country hicks, they kept looking at one another. And, you know she talked Toby out that car?

Before the police officers could change their minds, the musicians calmly but swiftly escorted Toby to the bus, all boarded it, and they were out of town in a matter of minutes. The police watched them disappear, perhaps kicking themselves for letting that white-looking, light-skinned black woman plant the doubt in their mind that that white-looking white woman wasn't really white. In Wilson's telling, the story ended with this twist: "They don't know that today they should be thanking Jessie for saving their lives."

Another tactic of Jessie Turner's survives in something she told the press, a statement that appealed to so many reporters in both the black press and the white-owned mainstream trades that the trombonist was quoted in nearly every report of the incident. Identified as the leader of the Darlings by this point, Turner explained the integration of the band in matter-of-fact, merit-based, color-blind terms: "Since the reorganization of the Darlings of Rhythm, my sole interest is in building the best musical unit possible and as long as my girls conduct themselves properly and display ability, I do not see that it would matter even if there were a few women from Mars mixed in."[71]

The "color-blind" rhetoric of Turner's defense is fascinating in this Jim Crow context. By invoking the mainstream integrationism brandished by postwar white liberals, Turner made it seem as though "race" was something that only police believed important, and that black women musicians gave "race" little thought, even as they risked their lives by traveling in the South with a white member. The irony, of course, is that African American residents and travelers in the South were forced by circumstances to think a great deal about "race," and to know the rules in order to survive. Turner's awareness of the life-and-death stakes, and her expertise in manipulating the loopholes of Jim Crow laws, is evident in her successful rescue of Butler from the police car, in getting the entire band safely out of Milledgeville, and in shaping a statement to the press that would circulate widely. Even in the North and West, entrance into previously segregated spheres was not achieved by "color-blind" gate-keeping practices or "merit-based" hiring policies, but by active protest mostly engaged in by people who had been historically excluded and who fought to have these exclusions acknowledged and corrected.

Turner's press statement built on the logic of this formula: Toby Butler "displayed ability" and "conducted herself properly," therefore, she could be in the band. In this way, Turner reversed the kind of integration usually imagined in discussions of "merit-based" hiring. Because the black woman leader of the Darlings was "color-blind," she could see that the white woman employee was "able" and "properly" behaved enough to remain in her organization. Is there an implicit social critique in Turner's statement? She was, after all, modeling values of integration that were still preached more often than practiced in bands covered by *Down Beat*. Even though magazines such as *Down Beat* frequently praised certain bands as paragons of "color-blind" virtue, other news items and editorials betrayed mixed feelings about mixed bands. One 1937 *Down Beat* editorial actually held up music's "color-blind" quality as an argument against integration in bands. Praising music for having "no racial lines," the editorialist captured the ambivalence of many mainstream swing liberals by arguing that "mixed groups" are unfair to musicians because such a band "arouses racial prejudice and focuses the public's attention on its social aspects—NOT ITS MUSICAL VALUES!"[72] In other words, *because* music was color-blind, bands shouldn't "arouse" race consciousness. Certainly, leaders and bookers of white "all-girl" bands were not yet prepared to say, "I don't care if you're black or white or green and from Mars, if you can play, you can be in my band." Nor was mainstream U.S. gender and race ideology accustomed to black womanhood being held up as the able and proper category to which a gifted white woman might aspire.

In casting the one white member as the "woman from Mars," Turner turned the tables on who is normal and who is the "Other." While *Down Beat* may have been entranced with Turner's "color-blind" language, which appeared to fit so neatly with the magazine's own claims to rise above race, African American readers of the story in both the trades and in the black press surely caught the ironies of Turner's reframing of the situation. For once, the black female members of the Darlings of Rhythm were depicted as normal, and the singular white member was an "Other" so exotic that she was not only of another color, but from another planet. She wanted to play with the Darlings and they accepted her. The Sweethearts may have been international, but the Darlings were intergalactic.

Yet, as we have seen, the Darlings of Rhythm were so alien to the paradigm of even that forgotten category of "all-girl" bands that no recordings or films document their performances and their history is all but lost. Turner's "common-sense" remark about musical ability mattering more than race, color, or gender was not the way the industry worked, a fact certainly known by the Darlings of Rhythm.

Indeed, all of the "all-girl" bands were vulnerable to perceptions of being "women from Mars" in varying degrees, and not all employers were as tolerant of inter- and intraplanetary differences as Jessie Turner. Women who broke too many rules tended to wind up on the cutting-room floor of earthly history: excluded as "women from Mars," regardless of merit. As the Darlings' case suggests, some exclusions were more complete than others.

Notes

1. Frannces "Frann" Gaddison, telephone interview, July 7 and 8, 1994 (hereafter Gaddison interview).

2. Angela Y. Davis, *Blues Legacies and Black Feminism* (New York: Pantheon Books, 1998), 102.

3. Dicky Wells, as told to Stanley Dance, *The Night People: The Jazz Life of Dicky Wells* (Washington, D.C.: Smithsonian Institution Press, 1991), 68. Many jazz musicians have spoken of this distinction. See bassist John Brown's discussion of the liability of tight arrangements on a band's ability to swing: "Basie's was a looser type of thing, and Lunceford's swing wasn't as relaxed because the arrangements were more complicated." Quoted in Stanley Dance, *The World of Swing* (New York: Da Capo Press, 1979), 23. Even Duke Ellington, whose writing was a primary factor in his orchestra's sound, instructed his soloists to "keep some dirt in there, somewhere." Robert O'Meally, "Improvisation," in *Seeing Jazz: Artists and Writers on Jazz*, ed. Elizabeth Goldson (San Francisco: Chronicle Books, 1997), 43.

4. Sarah McLawler, telephone interview, July 12, 1994.

5. Doc Cheatham, quoted in Dance, *World of Swing*, 307–9.

6. Clora Bryant, telephone interview, October 7, 1990.

7. For film clips of the International Sweethearts of Rhythm, see Rosetta Reitz, *Jazz Women* (video), Rosetta Records RRV-1320; and Greta Schiller and Andrea Weiss, *International Sweethearts of Rhythm* (film/video), Jezebel Productions, 1986. Audio recordings are available on *International Sweethearts of Rhythm* (LP), Rosetta Records RR-1312, 1984; *Forty Years of Women in Jazz* (CD), Stash, Jass CD-9/10, 1989; and *Women in Jazz: All-Woman Groups* (LP), Stash Records, ST-111, 1978.

8. The Sweethearts' humble background and ultimate fame was often framed in the black press as a rags-to-riches Horatio Alger narrative. See *Jet*, February 1954. This framework is somewhat misleading, for despite the band's musical triumphs and popularity, the original Sweethearts were grossly exploited and never paid according to the stipulations of the union except when they traveled on USO.

9. Thelma Lewis, telephone conversation, March 26, 1998 (hereafter Lewis conversation).

10. In addition to the archival film and audio sources mentioned earlier, see documentaries by Greta Schiller and Andrea Weiss: *International Sweethearts of Rhythm* (film/video), Jezebel Productions (1986), and *Tiny and Ruby: Hell-Divin' Women,* Jezebel Productions (film/video, 1988). For written histories about the Sweethearts, see D. Antoinette Handy, *Black Women in American Bands and Orchestras* (Metuchen, N.J.: Scarecrow Press, 1981) and her *The International Sweethearts of Rhythm* (Metuchen, N.J.: Scarecrow Press, 1983); Marian McPartland, "The Untold Story of the International Sweethearts of Rhythm," in her *All in Good Time* (New York: Oxford University Press, 1987); Sally Placksin, *American Women in Jazz: 1900 to the Present* (New York: Wideview Books, 1982), and Linda Dahl, *Stormy Weather: The Music and Lives of a Century of Jazzwomen* (New York: Limelight Editions, 1989).

11. I would like to thank Kyra Gaunt for encouraging me to think about the effects of colorism on Second Wave consumption of the Sweethearts.

12. The tradition of traveling entertainment emissaries as fundraisers and advertisements for black educational institutions dates nearly as far back as the establishment of the institutions themselves. Perhaps the best remembered today are the Fisk Jubilee Singers. The choir embarked on their first concert tour in 1871 to raise money to enlarge Fisk University (founded in 1867), and continued this touring tradition, traveling both in the United States and Europe, for sixty years. Other choral groups based out of black educational institutions included the Hampton Institute Choir, the Tuskegee Institute Choir, the Morehouse College Quartet (which performed for both Franklin D. Roosevelt and Herbert Hoover), the Wilberforce College Octette, and the Howard University Glee Club. Maud Cuney Hare, *Negro Musicians and Their Music* (1936; New York: Simon and Schuster, 1996), 55–57, 248–52.

13. Some of the content of this questionnaire appears in Handy's *The International Sweethearts of Rhythm,* 191. I am grateful to Handy for sharing with me the entire questionnaire that Lorraine Brown (Guilford) filled out for her project in 1980.

14. Ibid.

15. Ibid.

16. Advertisement, "Merry Xmas and Happy New Year. Clarence Love and His Orchestra." *Down Beat,* December 15, 1941.

17. Albert McCarthy, *Big Band Jazz* (New York: Exeter Books, 1974), 41–47.

18. Clarence Love, interviewed by Nathan Pearson and Howard Litwak, Kansas City, Mo., April 13, 1977. Transcript, Western Historical Manuscript Collection, Kansas City, Mo.

19. Clipping sent to me by Clarence Love, January 22, 1998. Source unknown.

20. Billy Rowe, "Billy Rowe's Note Book," *Pittsburgh Courier,* January 29, 1944, 15.

21. "Darlings of Rhythm Newest 'Find': The Darlings of Rhythm Are the Current Darlings of Orchestra Whirl," *Pittsburgh Courier,* March 18, 1944, 13.

22. "Swing's Newest Rave Sensations Capture Nation," *Chicago Defender,* March 18, 1944, 8.

23. "All-Girl Crew Set to Reopen Grand Terrace," *Pittsburgh Courier,* March 18, 1944, 13.

24. "Darlings Build Business," *Chicago Defender,* June 10, 1944, 8.

25. I am grateful to Mark Miller and Ron Sweetman for alerting me to Howard Rye's article, "What The Papers Said: The Harlem Play-Girls and Dixie Rhythm Girls (and Dixie Sweethearts)," *Storyville,* Chigwell, Essex, England (1996–97). Most of the information on 1930s personnel in this chapter is drawn from Rye's study of "Traveling Musicians" listings in American Federation of Musicians local reports in *International Musician.* I have studied the listings from the 1940s issues of *International Musician* in my attempts to track the movement of personnel among the Darlings of Rhythm, Eddie Durham's All-Star Girls, and the International Sweethearts of Rhythm.

26. "Margaret Backstrom Joins Darlings' Reed Section," *Music Dial,* November 1944, 15.

27. "Who's Best Sax—Backstrom or Vi?" *Pittsburgh Courier,* June 16, 1945, 13.

28. It is important to note that all "all-girl" bands were marginalized in relation to men's bands, and no version of feminized image or sound was a guarantee for commercial success. In fact, coming off as "commercial" was dangerous for "all-girl" bands who were already suspected as being novelty bands, inferior, "Mickey Mouse." The performance burden for "all-girl" bands was twofold: they had to prove that they were "real musicians" and that they were "real women," and since "real musicians" were already presumed to be men, and women who played instruments associated with men were often sexually suspect, this was no simple task. The Sweethearts' performances also incorporated improvised solos, blues, and jump tunes in their more arranged style; and the Darlings' sometimes included "sweet" vocal features. These balancing acts were different for different women, also, depending upon what gender ideologies they had access to and whether those images would accommodate professional musicianship. Some white bands, such as Phil Spitalny's Hour of Charm orchestra that went for a hyperfeminized look and sound may have been commercially successful, but they were also ridiculed. And the "Angel of the Hearth" image promoted by Spitalny's group was right out of the Victorian "cult of true womanhood," an ideology of white femininity that excluded African American women. Issues of "feminine" representations were especially fraught for African American women's bands, as it was for African American women in entertainment in general, plagued as they were by exclusion from dominant versions of "femininity" and by racist representations in dominant culture and often by issues of colorism. When the Sweethearts made Soundies and a few records near the end of the band's ten-year existence, they crossed into a realm of white-male-producer approval and historical documentation that was never accorded the Darlings. However, it would appear that the Darlings' strategy was also viable in the circuits they moved in for a variety of reasons, even though it also contributed to their slipping farthest outside the paradigms of jazz history.

29. Vi Wilson, interview, Los Angeles, June 12, 1994 (hereafter Wilson interview).

30. Lewis conversation.

31. Lillian Carter (Wilson), telephone interview, August 24, 1991.

32. Gaddison interview.

33. Thelma Lewis, telephone interview, June 12, 1994.

34. Wilson interview.

35. I discuss a wide range of both black and white women instrumentalists' strategies for claiming and maintaining identities and careers as jazz and swing musicians in my book and dissertation in progress (of which this work is a part): Changing the Players/Playing the Changes: "All-Girl" Jazz and Swing Bands During World War II (to be published by Duke University Press). Until recently, very little work in jazz studies has incorporated gender as a salient category of analysis. The few jazz studies scholars who have begun to include gender have focused primarily on masculinity. I am most heartened by the work in this area that is meticulous in its specificity of both constructions of "what is masculinity" and "what is jazz" at particular historical moments, and in its attention to intersections of gender and race. Among these welcome analyses of jazz and gender are: Ingrid Monson's interrogation of "white hipness" as patterned after "a style of black masculinity" that "held, and continues to hold, great appeal for white audiences and musicians"; Steven Elworth's analysis of a transformation of masculinity in the swing context represented by the popularity of "boy singer" Frank Sinatra; and David Ake's recent analysis of the figure of Ornette Coleman as representing one of the "alternative masculinities" that Krin Gabbard has observed has been frequently offered by jazz performances and musicians. Ingrid Monson, "The Problem with White Hipness: Race, Gender, and Cultural Conceptions in Jazz Historical Discourse," Journal of the American Musicological Society 48, no. 3 (Fall 1995): 402; Steven B. Elworth,

"Jazz in Crisis, 1948–1958," in *Jazz Among the Discourses,* ed. Gabbard (Durham, N.C.: Duke University Press, 1995), 61–62; David Ake, "Re-Masculating Jazz: Ornette Coleman, 'Lonely Woman,' and the New York Jazz Scene in the Late 1950s," *American Music* 16, no. 1 (Spring 1998): 25–44; Krin Gabbard, *Jammin' at the Margins: Jazz and the American Cinema* (Chicago: University of Chicago Press, 1996), 7. My concern is that gender analyses that focus on masculinity threaten to replicate the omissions of women musicians from jazz history that has been one of the glaring continuities between jazz studies and earlier jazz historiography. While I agree with Gabbard that jazz has historically offered an intriguing "number of alternatives" to "conventional notions of masculinity and male sexuality," I would also add that a complex variety of notions about race-specific femininities and female sexualities have also flourished in jazz contexts; that ideas about femininity have also been historically embedded in discourses of jazz authenticity, boundaries, performance elements, and genre; and that analyses of both women's and men's jazz practices will benefit from explorations of historical struggles over competing and related ideas about masculinity and femininity. Implicit in this article is a scholarly wish-list for more studies that encompass jazz, race, gender, and women.

36. "Swing's Newest Rave Sensations Capture Nation," 8.

37. "All-Girl Crew Set to Reopen Grand Terrace," 13.

38. "Darlings of Rhythm Score," *Chicago Defender,* April 22, 1944, 8.

39. "Helen Tabor Scores," *Chicago Defender,* June 3, 1944, 8.

40. Rye, "What the Papers Said," 176. Handy places Lunceford as leading her Dukes of Rhythm in New Orleans in 1941, in *Black Women in American Bands and Orchestras,* 45.

41. Ed Fox's firing of Billie Holiday is described in most Holiday biographies. Billie Holiday, with William Dufty, *Lady Sings the Blues* (New York: Avon, 1956), 63; John Chilton, *Billie's Blues: The Billie Holiday Story: 1933–1939* (New York: Da Capo, 1975), 35–37; Stuart Nicholson, *Billie Holiday* (Boston: Northeastern University Press, 1995), 76. Interestingly, though the newspapers reviewed her Grand Terrace return and appearance with the Darlings in 1944, I have yet to find a Billie Holiday biography that mentions the "all-girl" band. Two posters advertising the event are reprinted, however, in Ken Vail, *Lady Day's Diary: The Life of Billie Holiday, 1937–1959* (Surrey: Castle Communications, 1996), 71, 72.

42. "Grand Terrace, Chicago, Preps Colored Show," *Variety,* June 24, 1944, 45.

43. Handy, *International Sweethearts of Rhythm,* 163.

44. Evelyn McGee (Stone), telephone interview, November 30, 1996.

45. Nicholson, *Billie Holiday,* 134–35. Holiday's Met appearance predates Marian Anderson's by over a decade. Anderson, who is most often credited with being the first black person to sing the Met, was indeed the first African American to sing a role with the Metropolitan Opera Company in 1955. Jon Michael Spencer, *The New Negroes and Their Music: The Success of the Harlem Renaissance* (Knoxville: University of Tennessee Press, 1997), 105.

46. "Darlings Score for Camp Hill," *Chicago Defender,* May 8, 1944, 8.

47. Gaddison interview.

48. I am grateful to Angela Davis for sharing insights about Billie Holiday's transformative contributions that inform how I am reading this clash with the Darlings.

49. Max Jones, *Talking Jazz* (New York: Norton, 1987), 249.

50. From Chris Albertson's 1958 interview with Lester Young, reprinted in *A Lester Young Reader,* ed. Lewis Porter (Washington, D.C.: Smithsonian Institution Press, 1991), 167.

51. Chilton, *Billie's Blues,* 42. Sexual overtones abound in labored textual explanations of what Stuart Nicholson called Holiday and Young's "deep, platonic love affair." The tendency in the jazz literature to either present Young as a feminine man or to present the Holiday/Young

collaboration/friendship as sexually overdetermined warrants further scholarly jazz/race/gender analysis. James Lincoln Collier refers to their musical collaboration as a "marriage," and includes Young in a list of Holiday's lovers: "She had had her affairs in the past, one with Basie's guitarist, Freddie Greene; another with sometime accompanist Bobby Henderson. And she had had some sort of platonic friendship with Lester Young." Nicholson, *Billie Holiday,* 51; James Lincoln Collier, *The Making of Jazz: A Comprehensive History* (New York: Dell, 1978), 309.

52. Clora Bryant told interviewer Steve Isoardi that her "main purpose" of dressing in irrefutably feminine clothes was to avoid the stigma of lesbianism; the assumption being that if a woman played trumpet, she "had to be a man." Bryant et al., *Central Avenue Sounds: Jazz in Los Angeles* (Berkeley: University of California Press, 1998), 356.

53. This story appears in most biographical material on Lester Young. Young told the story himself in a 1959 interview with François Postif, reprinted in *Lester Young Reader,* ed. Porter, 191.

54. Paul Whiteman and Mary Margaret McBride, *Jazz* (New York: J. H. Sears, 1926), 210.

55. Doron K. Antrim, ed., *Secrets of Dance Band Success* (New York: Famous Stars Publishing, 1936), 61.

56. Susan Cook spoke eloquently on Holiday's claiming of the name "Lady" during an era when black women were denied this title. Cook, "Billie Holiday and the Performance of Race and Gender," Feminist Theory and Music II, Eastman School of Music, Rochester, N.Y., June 17–20, 1993. (As an anonymous referee reminds me, Lester Young's use of the term "Lady" presents even more of a challenge, since he incorporated the title in nicknames for black men as well!)

57. Davis, *Blues Legacies and Black Feminism,* 165.

58. *Trav'lin' Light,* Paul Whiteman and His Orchestra, with Billie Holiday, was recorded for Capital Records on June 12, 1942 (CAP-30-A).

59. "'Darlings of Rhythm' Hit Peak at Terrace," *Chicago Defender,* July 8, 1944, 8.

60. Al Monroe, "Swinging the News," *Chicago Defender,* July 22, 1944, 6.

61. "Darlings of Rhythm Take to Road," *Chicago Defender,* July 22, 1944, 6.

62. "Lady with a Horn," *Pittsburgh Courier,* August 26, 1944, 13.

63. "Darlings' Feature Pat Lamarr, Helen Taborn," *Pittsburgh Courier,* November 25, 1944, 13.

64. "Darlings of Rhythm Set for Twelve Mo Ball," *Music Dial* (March–April 1945): 10.

65. Al Monroe, "Swinging the News," *Chicago Defender,* April 14, 1945, 17.

66. "B-29 Drops 'Darlings' in Los Angeles," *Pittsburgh Courier,* June 23, 1945, 13.

67. "'Darlings of Rhythm' to Play Coast's Plantation," *Chicago Defender,* June 23, 1945, 10.

68. "All Girls' Band Scores," *Chicago Defender,* August 11, 1945, 14.

69. Madalin O. Price, "Fifty Years of Memories: The Radio Program *Wings Over Jordan,*" conference paper, Oral History Association, New Orleans, Sept. 25, 1997.

70. "Out of Tune! White Girl in Mixed Orchestra Arrested by Georgia Police," Pitts*burgh Courier,* July 13, 1946, 1; "Jail Girl Musician: 'Too Light' for All Negro Orchestra," *Chicago Defender,* July 13, 1946, 16; "Jim Crow Stuff Still Spreading! Girl Trumpeter Tastes Southern Chivalry and Color Ousts Mab's Men," *Down Beat,* July 29, 1946, 1.

71. Ibid.

72. "Negro and White Band Folds," *Down Beat,* December 1937, 12.

3

The Genesis of *Black, Brown and Beige*

MARK TUCKER

From *Black Music Research Journal* 13, no. 2 (Autumn 1993): 67–86

Ellington's descriptions of the creative process often emphasized speed and efficiency. Like a reporter trained to work under deadline, he knew how to compose under pressure—usually for his orchestra's next recording date or concert appearance—and took pride in this ability. Ellington filled his memoirs, *Music Is My Mistress,* with anecdotes showing him swiftly, even effortlessly, turning out new pieces, often at the last minute. He claimed to have dashed off the extended work *Creole Rhapsody* (1931) overnight, writing "so much music . . . that we had to cut it up and do two versions" (Ellington [1973] 1976, 82). Similarly, his labors on the 1925 musical revue *Chocolate Kiddies* reportedly lasted a single night: "I sat down that evening and wrote a show. How was I to know that composers had to go up in the mountains, or to the seashore, to commune with the muses for six months in order to write a show?" (Ellington [1973] 1976, 71). Shorter compositions, like the popular "Mood Indigo" (1930) and "Solitude" (1934), apparently required less than thirty minutes to complete (Ellington [1973] 1976, 78–79, 87). While these accounts may contain elements of exaggeration,[1] Ellington's generally swift rate of composition has been confirmed by other witnesses. His son Mercer was impressed when Duke wrote three numbers for *Jump for Joy* (1941) on a train between Salt Lake City and Los Angeles (Dance [1970] 1981, 40). And Jimmy Jones, the pianist and arranger who occasionally worked with the Ellington orchestra in the sixties and early seventies, once observed, "The amazing thing about Ellington is that he can think so fast on the spot and create so quickly. I watched Duke write once and it was astonishing. When he knows what he wants and has got it in his mind, he can write awfully fast" (Dance [1970] 1981, 217).

In recounting how he came to write *Black, Brown and Beige,* the massive, three-movement "Tone Parallel to the History of the Negro in America," Ellington once again stressed the seemingly casual and spontaneous nature of his work habits. According to *Music Is My Mistress,* an impromptu suggestion by Ellington's manager caused him to undertake one of the largest and most ambitious pieces of his career: "One day William Morris, Jr., said, 'I want you to write a long work, and let's do it in Carnegie Hall.' So out came *Black, Brown and Beige*" (Ellington [1973] 1976, 180–181). The actual writing, Ellington recalled, began in December 1942—the month before the piece premiered in Carnegie Hall on January 23, 1943. Ellington started composing during a theater appearance by his orchestra in Hartford, Connecticut, on a bill that included the singer Frank Sinatra and a film titled *The Cat Woman.* While the film was being shown, Ellington would go to the piano onstage behind the screen and compose: "It sometimes got pretty scary back there in the dark" (Ellington [1973] 1976, 181). Ellington revealed little else about the process of writing *Black, Brown and Beige,* only noting blandly that the piece "came off well" and its premiere was an "overwhelming success" (Ellington [1973] 1976, 181).

In this "official" version of the circumstances surrounding *Black, Brown and Beige,* Ellington reduced the work's long and tangled early history to a simple, easily digestible account. While Ellington may have composed *Black, Brown and Beige* quickly—and evidence suggests he did just that—he had been conceiving a large-scale work based on themes from African-American history for more than a decade. Contrary to the story given in his memoirs, neither William Morris Jr. nor an impending Carnegie Hall debut played a role in the origins of *Black, Brown and Beige.* They simply provided a deadline—the one crucial part of the creative process that Ellington himself, over a period of years, had been unable to secure. During these years, however, Ellington had worked on other projects that paved the way for *Black, Brown and Beige:* the Paramount film short *Symphony in Black* (shot in 1934, released in 1935), the socially conscious, race-proud musical *Jump for Joy* (1941), and, most important, the opera *Boola,* a work often cited in the Ellington literature but long shrouded in mystery. These sources, together with a series of tantalizing hints in the press about a major Ellington project, suggest a genesis much more arduous and protracted than the one revealed by the composer in his memoirs. Rather than polishing off *Black, Brown and Beige* with dispatch, Ellington had to "commune with the muses" long and hard before realizing his artistic ambition.

The first signs of Ellington's interest in writing the piece that eventually became *Black, Brown and Beige* appeared late in 1930.[2] At the time Ellington and his band were nearing the end of their roughly three-year stint at Harlem's Cotton Club (December 1927–February 1931). In an interview, published December 13, 1930, in the *Christian Science Monitor,* Ellington spoke of his desire to explore the African roots of black music and to compile some kind of musical history of the black American experience. "The tragedy," he told journalist Janet

Mabie, "is that so few records have been kept of the Negro music of the past. It has to be pieced together so slowly. But it pleases me to have a chance to work at it" (Mabie 1930). A few weeks later these vague plans had crystallized into something more definite, as an article in the *New York Evening Graphic* revealed: "At present [Ellington] is at work on a tremendous task, the writing, in music, of 'The History of the Negro,' taking the Negro from Egypt, going with him to savage Africa, and from there to the sorrow and slavery of Dixie, and finally 'home to Harlem'" (Zunser 1930).

Such a serious, large-scale project may seem to have been a surprising choice for a bandleader carving out a career in the field of popular entertainment. But several factors in Ellington's background and professional experience probably inspired the idea.

To begin, Ellington had grown up in Washington, D.C., surrounded by people proud of their heritage and dedicated to preserving it. In *Music Is My Mistress* Ellington wrote that in grade school "Negro history was crammed into the curriculum, so that we would know our people all the way back" (Ellington [1973] 1976, 17). Outside the classroom, historical pageants turned textbook descriptions into living drama. During Ellington's youth the most elaborate such presentation was *The Star of Ethiopia,* a show brought to Washington in 1915 by W.E.B. Du Bois and produced in the American League Ball Park, where, as a teenager, Ellington worked selling refreshments. According to the program, the pageant covered "10,000 years of the history of the Negro race" and featured "music by colored composers, lights and symbolic dancing" (Tucker 1991, 7–8). Similar historical productions were staged in local concerts and theaters, such as *The Evolution of the Negro in Picture, Song, and Story,* seen at the Howard Theater in 1911.[3]

Even if the young Ellington did not attend such events in his hometown, he would encounter other representations of black history—designed more to entertain than educate—through working with his band in New York's black nightclub revues during the twenties. Historical scenarios, for example, figured repeatedly in black stage shows produced by prominent white impresario Lew Leslie. The first scene of Leslie's revue *Dixie to Broadway* (1924), starring Florence Mills, was titled "Evolution of the Colored Race," while his famous *Blackbirds of 1928*—which, according to James Weldon Johnson ([1930] 1944, 212), "set a pace for all revues, white as well as black"—began "Way Down South," took a detour for a "Scene in Jungleland," and later moved to modern-day Harlem. Leslie's *Rhapsody in Black* of 1931, similarly, featured "a musical transition of the Negro from Africa to Harlem" (Sampson 1980, 288).[4]

These revues drew on various musical genres to evoke aspects of the African-American heritage—a practice Ellington would follow later in *Black, Brown and Beige.* Just as the gradual rise in the Negro's status was depicted dramatically— from plantation days through Emancipation to modern life in Harlem—so musical "progress" might accompany the narrative, from "savage" dance numbers and stylized "jungle" ditties (in the vein of Cole and Johnson's 1902 "Under the Bamboo Tree") to plantation and minstrel songs, to refined concert spirituals and red-hot jazz. Hence Lew Leslie's *Blackbirds of 1929* began, as did the 1928 edition, with scenes "Way Down South" and in "Jungleland" (featuring the mock-primitive number "Diga Diga Doo") but ended in a New York music studio with cast members depicting such characters as "Inspiration" and "The Composer" in an "Operative" rendition of the Jimmy McHugh and Dorothy Fields song, "I Can't Give You Anything but Love" (Sampson 1980, 155). The 1930 edition of Sissle and Blake's *Shuffle Along* opened with laborers on a showboat singing "Work, Work, Work," while later a group performed spirituals and a number called "Go Harlem." And *Chocolate Kiddies*—the European traveling production to which Ellington and Jo Trent contributed a handful of songs in 1925—featured a similar progression in its third act; spirituals and Stephen Foster songs, followed by "Jungle Nights in Dixie" and "Jim Dandy" (a comic "minstrel" song by Ellington and Trent), opened the act, which later shifted to present-day Harlem with two more Ellington–Trent songs, "With You" and "Jig Walk" (Tucker 1991, 121–131).

At the Cotton Club, where the idea for *Black, Brown and Beige* was born, Ellington encountered similar theatrical conventions in shows portraying African Americans and their heritage. As is well known, the Harlem nightspot created an illusion of exotic primitivism for its white clientele with sensuous dancers, skimpy costumes, and naturalistic decor. In this setting, Ellington and his orchestra furnished stage acts with evocative "jungle" music, featuring colorful sound effects provided by the pounding tom-toms and spooky temple blocks of drummer Sonny Greer, the growling plunger-mute solos of brass players Cootie Williams and Joe "Tricky Sam" Nanton, and the eerie dips and swirls of clarinetist Barney Bigard. A September 1929 Cotton Club show called *Blackberries* offered a number entitled "Congo Jamboree" (an "exhibition of unrestrained Nubian abandon," according to the program), while the next year's *Blackberries of 1930* featured "Jungle Gestures on Lenox Avenue" (Stratemann 1992, 689, 691). Recordings made by the Ellington orchestra during this period—sometimes under the pseudonym "The Jungle Band"—included "Diga Diga Doo," "Jungle Nights in Harlem," "Jungle Blues," and "Jungle Jamboree" (from the 1929 revue *Hot Chocolates*). Beyond the African motifs, the South-to-North geographical movement of earlier black shows could also appear—as in a segment titled "Dixie to Harlem" in the Cotton Club's 1930–1931 *Brown Sugar* revue (Stratemann 1992, 692).

Ellington's notion in late 1930, then, to write a musical "history of the Negro" reflected both his exposure to black history in Washington (via the classroom and possibly pageants and stage productions) and, in more stylized form, in New York (via theaters and nightclubs). Yet the question arises: As Ellington worked in show business at the Cotton Club—observing snappy comic routines and sensual dance numbers, accompanying satirical skits set in Africa and the Old South—what prompted him to attempt a serious and extended musical treatment of these historical themes? One strong possibility is that he absorbed ideas about promoting race consciousness from figures associated with the Harlem Renaissance. While it is not known how closely Ellington followed events in black literary and artistic circles during the twenties—the publicity, say, surrounding such emerging talents as Langston Hughes and Claude McKay or the New Negro ideals set forth by Alain Locke—later, in the British danceband magazine *Rhythm*, Ellington did compare his artistic aims to those of black poet Countee Cullen and unnamed "others in literature" (Ellington 1931, 22).

Another source of inspiration for Ellington may have been black composers who were producing extended works forged directly from the African-American historical experience. His friend and earlier piano mentor James P. Johnson, for example, had written *Yamekraw* in 1927, described in the score as "a genuine Negro treatise on spiritual, syncopated and 'blue' melodies" (Brown 1986, 185).[5] And William Grant Still, the orchestrator of *Yamekraw*, had produced such race-conscious works as *Darker America* (1924), *Levee Land* (1925), and *Africa* (1928), while his *Afro-American Symphony* would receive its premiere in 1931. The theme of a people's progress, as has recently been noted, is common to both *Darker America* and the *Afro-American Symphony* (Oja 1992, 159–160). Moreover, the symphony's journey (in movement titles) from "Longing" and "Sorrow" to "Humor" and "Aspiration" would be retraced by Ellington from *Black's* "Work Song" and "Come Sunday" sections to *Brown's* "The Lighter Attitude" and *Beige's* sophisticated waltz, "Sugar Hill Penthouse."

After Ellington announced his intent in late 1930 to write a large-scale work based on the history of the Negro, references to this project recurred periodically over the next decade. They showed that while Ellington had settled on the chronological scheme outlined in the *New York Evening Graphic*—moving from Africa to the South to Harlem—he was undecided about the ultimate shape of the piece. In the 1931 *Rhythm* article, for example, Ellington claimed to be working on "a rhapsody unhampered by any musical form in which I intend to portray the experiences of the coloured races in America in the syncopated idiom. . . . I am putting all I have learned into it in the hope that I shall have achieved something really worth while in the literature of music, and that an authentic record of my race *written by a member of it* shall be placed on record" (Ellington 1931, 22). By 1933 the "rhapsody" had become a suite in five sections: "Africa," "The Slave Ship," "The Plantation," "Harlem," and a finale that recapitulated earlier themes (Hobson 1933, 94). And the following year *Variety* announced that Ellington had written "a full length Negro opera [tracing] Negro life from the jungle to Harlem" ("Ellington's Opera" 1934, 1).[6]

Despite these references to a work in progress—whether a rhapsody, suite, or opera—no extant evidence suggests that Ellington had gotten beyond the planning stage with his project. In 1934, however, he did have an opportunity to explore some of the work's main themes in the film *Symphony in Black*.[7] In this nine-minute Paramount short, Ellington, playing himself, is shown in the process of writing a "new symphony of Negro moods" (the world premiere, typically, is only two weeks away). Glimpses of Ellington composing in his studio and his orchestra performing the finished piece alternate with scenes depicted in the score: groups of men at work ("The Laborers"), a lover spurned ("A Triangle" in three parts: "Dance," "Jealousy," and "Blues"—the last of these featuring a young Billie Holiday), a child's funeral ("A Hymn of Sorrow"), and an exuberant nightclub dance ("Harlem Rhythm"). Various writers have noted parallels between *Symphony in Black* and *Black, Brown and Beige* (see, e.g., Schuller 1989, 72–73; Knauer 1990, 21–22; Priestley and Cohen 1993, 186–187). Both works feature—as do their antecedents in nightclub revues and stage productions—a "Dixie to Harlem" progression, beginning in the rural South and ending in the urban North. "The Laborers" sequence in *Symphony in Black* could be seen as a sketch for the much more extensive "Work Song" of *Black*. A slow and heart-wrenching blues stands at the center of both the film and the tone parallel. The consoling power of religion is treated in the *Symphony's* "Hymn of Sorrow" as well as in *Black's* "Come Sunday" section—and a musical thread even connects the two, as Brian Priestley and Alan Cohen have pointed out: a descending gesture from the main theme of "Hymn of Sorrow" returns in an interlude in "Come Sunday" (Priestley and Cohen 1993, 187n). Formally, however, as Gunther Schuller (1989, 72) has noted, the two works are quite distinct: *Symphony in Black* resembles a suite fashioned from discrete units,[8] while *Black, Brown and Beige* represents an effort at integrated, large-scale composition.

Although a successful fusion of evocative music and expressive images, *Symphony in Black* did not satisfy Ellington's urge to write a large-scale historical piece. In 1938, according to biographer Barry Ulanov, Ellington emerged from a brief stint in New York's Wickersham Hospital to declare that his next project would be a five-part *African Suite*. He had "formulated the program" for the work and "done a lot of solid thinking about it at the hospital"; soon he would complete it (Ulanov [1946] 1975, 205–206). That same year, *Down Beat* announced that, after "six years of spare time composing," Ellington had finished an opera dealing with "the history of the American Negro, starting with the Negro back in the jungles of Africa, and following through to the modern Harlemite" ("Ellington Completes Negro Opera" 1938, 2). The *Down Beat* article also mentioned that Ellington had written the score for a "Broadway show" on a subject sounding by now rather familiar: "episodes in Negro life in America, both in the South and in the North . . . mainly concerned with Negro folklore." Such notices may have been placed by Irving Mills, Ellington's manager, in hopes of attracting potential sponsors who might arrange for performing venues—thereby providing Ellington with incentive to finish (or actually write) the piece in question.

As before, though, none of these works materialized. The next large project Ellington completed was *Jump for Joy*, a musical revue produced at the Mayan Theater in Los Angeles in the summer of 1941. Although not based on historical themes, *Jump for Joy* had a didactic, consciousness-raising function—as would *Black, Brown and Beige* two years later. The show attempted, as Ellington wrote in his memoirs, "to correct the race situation in the U.S.A. through a form of theatrical propaganda" (Ellington [1973] 1976, 175). Unlike *Black, Brown and Beige*, the tone of *Jump for Joy* was bitingly satirical, especially in such numbers as "I've Got a Passport from Georgia" and "Uncle Tom's Cabin Is a Drive-in Now." And with its dynamic roster of singers, dancers, and comedians, it sought unabashedly to entertain. Even so, *Jump for Joy* apparently served as a kind a creative catalyst for Ellington, reminding him to return to the themes and ideals of *Black, Brown and Beige*. He acknowledged this in *Music Is My Mistress* when introducing the subject of *Black, Brown and Beige*: "The feeling of responsibility that *Jump for Joy* had aroused sustained itself, and one day William Morris, Jr., said, 'I want you to write a large work'" (Ellington [1973] 1976, 180).

It was around the time of *Jump for Joy* that references to Ellington's long-delayed opera began to resurface. One West Coast newspaper article described it as telling "the story of the Negro people, [tracing] the history of this great nation from its beginning here through chattel slavery, reconstruction, to the present." It also alluded to difficulties Ellington was having: "Ellington is still working on this opera. He is looking for ideas. He admits having trouble in representing the Negro American as he is today, what he wants, what he's got, what he's tried to get and didn't, how he is going to get it" (Pittman [c. 1941] 1993, 150).

A fuller account of the opera appeared in a column by *San Francisco Chronicle* music critic Alfred Frankenstein, who identified the work as *Boola* and reported that Ellington had been laboring on it for the past nine years (Frankenstein 1941). Parts of the opera remained unfinished, Frankenstein noted, but "you gather that he could finish it if he wanted to in less time than it takes to run through a couple of choruses." Among the most striking features in Frankenstein's account were Ellington's explanation of the opera's title and overview of its structure:

"Boola," says Ellington, is the name Negro historians use to symbolize their race. "If they want to tell you that Negroes took part in this or that event," said Ellington, "they will say 'Boola was there.' My opera traces Boola's whole history in four scenes. The first scene is laid in Africa. The music there is mostly imaginary, because no one today knows what African Negro music was like in the days of the early slave traders. The second scene is Negro life in slave times, the third, Negro life in the period after the Civil war, and the fourth, Negro life today. There isn't any continuous plot, but there is one symbolic figure—Boola himself—who appears throughout" (Frankenstein 1941).[9]

Ellington claimed to have supplied both libretto and music for *Boola* and expressed his aim to supervise the production. He also gave Frankenstein his reason for composing the work: "'I wrote it because I want to rescue Negro music from its well-meaning friends. . . . All arrangements of historic American Negro music have been made by conservatory-trained musicians who inevitably handle it with a European technique. It's time a big piece of music was written from the inside by a Negro'" (Frankenstein 1941).

Despite the hopeful tone, Ellington never did finish *Boola*. Instead, as a reading of the Frankenstein article now makes clear, he developed it into *Black, Brown and Beige*, dropping the first "African" scene and reworking the other three as individual movements of his tone parallel. This process of adaptation, it should be said, was noted in passing by some contemporary commentators—Howard Taubman, for one, who wrote in a *New York Times Magazine* preview of Ellington's Carnegie Hall debut: "Ellington's most elaborate composition is an opera, still unproduced, called 'Boola.' . . . He has taken some of the music from this opera and turned it into a half-hour tone poem for his band . . . called 'Black, Brown and Beige'" (Taubman 1943, 30). And a few years later, Ellington biographer Barry Ulanov would state that *Boola* had "yielded much of the material for [*Black, Brown and Beige*]" (Ulanov [1946] 1975, 253).

Yet despite such acknowledgments of *Boola*'s importance to *Black, Brown and Beige*, the opera has long remained a shadowy work, and its precise links to the orchestral tone parallel have gone unexamined. Recently, though, two documents have surfaced—both texts without music—that conclusively show *Boola*'s relationship to the structure and content of *Black, Brown and Beige*. The first is an untitled, twenty-nine-page manuscript—part poem, part prose—written in Ellington's hand on unlined three-quarter size tablet paper and now located in the Smithsonian's Duke Ellington Collection. The second is an edited and expanded version of this draft, a thirty-three-page typescript titled "*Black, Brown and Beige* by Duke Ellington," which had been in the possession of Ruth Ellington Boatwright, the composer's sister.[10] Both the autograph draft (hereafter "*Boola* sketch") and the typescript suggest that *Boola* and *Black, Brown and Beige* shared the same scenario and sprang from a single creative impulse.

While dating these two sources is difficult, the *Boola* sketch clearly preceded the typescript. Its text, for example, makes only one direct reference to the piece *Black, Brown and Beige*—on page 21, where Ellington writes "Brown 2nd mvt" (this appears to be a later addition to the manuscript, in fact)—and breaks off at the point where *Beige* should begin with the words "Harlem/Black Metropolis." The typescript, by contrast, is divided into three sections and is labeled according to the movements of the composition, with *Beige* taking seven pages. Given the various press references to an opera between 1934 and 1941, Ellington may have drafted the *Boola* sketch some time during this period. The typescript was probably produced closer to the January 1943 premiere of *Black, Brown and Beige*—completed before the event (for use in publicity or the printed program) or even afterward.[11]

In both sources the narrative revolves around the character Boola, an African brought to the New World aboard a slave ship. After opening with a lurid description of the horror of the journey, Ellington follows Boola's trials and triumphs in North America, as he takes up a life of hard physical labor, meets a female companion named Voola, discovers Christianity, and eventually participates in the unfolding pageant of African-American history. Boola—as Ellington had explained to Alfred Frankenstein in 1941—is more symbol than fully realized character, someone whose individual experience embraces, in a fundamental way, that of all African Americans. It would be difficult to represent him on the operatic stage, especially in those later sections where the time sequence speeds up considerably and Boola is swept along by the tide of historical events—the Civil War, Emancipation, the Spanish-American War, World War I, and the flowering of African-American culture in Harlem during the twenties. Rendering the story through a tone parallel, then, as Ellington eventually chose to do, avoided some of the obvious dramaturgical problems of Ellington's conception.

Although no music accompanies the two treatments of the *Boola* story, Ellington does note possible musical settings for the scenes he depicts. The opening, describing Boola's experience in the hold of the slave ship, contains references to a "symphony of torture," a "crescendo to a new climax," and a "cacophonous rhapsody" mingling sounds of lashing whips, memories of pounding jungle drums, and Boola's throbbing pain. As noted above, Ellington omitted this section in *Black, Brown and Beige* and started instead with "Work Song." Nevertheless, "Work Song" opens with the echo of jungle drums, as Sonny Greer's timpani strokes recall Ellington's text at the beginning of the *Boola* sketch (Ellington n.d., 1):

> A message is sent through the jungle by drums
> Boom Boom Boom Boom
> Like a Tom Tom in Steady Precision

The pounding rhythmic motive that pervades the "Work Song" section of *Black* serves as the central rhythmic idea uniting the three sections of the typescript poem, and it takes on the character of different activities—for example, the laborers singing while working ("Sing! Sing! Sing! Sing!") and the bells summoning Boola to church ("Ding! Dong! Ding! Dong!").

This percussive leitmotif, in fact, forms the strongest musical point of contact between the two texts and *Black, Brown and Beige*. A *Variety* article from early December 1942—appearing just before the engagement in Hartford where Ellington began composing *Black, Brown and Beige*—reinforces the connection, reporting that at the upcoming Carnegie Hall concert Ellington would perform a

> jazz symphony, composed of the themes taken from his original and as yet unproduced opera, "Boola."
> The first movement will show the origin of Negro music, with an African tomtom beat as a background; the second will show the development of early American jazz; the third present day swing, and then a futuristic finale, all four parts tied together with the beat of the original tomtom ("Ellington on Negro Music" 1942, 37).[12]

A tom-tom motif also occurs in the celebrated Ellington composition "Ko-Ko" (1940), which was identified by Ulanov ([1946] 1975, 253) as an excerpt from *Boola*. The introductory rhythmic figure in "Ko-Ko," shared by Greer's tom-tom and Harry Carney's baritone sax (♫♫ | ♩) may reflect a unifying device Ellington had considered for the *Boola* score.

Other key musical references in the two *Boola* sources emerge in the program of *Black, Brown and Beige*. In discussing the early experience of Africans in the New World, Ellington writes, "The first thing [they] did was WORK . . . and there the Work Song was born/not a song of great Joy—not a triumphant song—but a song of Burden—a song punctuated by the grunt of Heaving a pick or axe" (Ellington n.d., 6–7). Ellington renders these words musically explicit in a call-and-response passage of the "Work Song" in which a solo line by trombonist Joe "Tricky Sam" Nanton is answered by the orchestra's collective heaving shout (see Ex. 3.1). Later Ellington describes Boola standing outside a church, not yet permitted to enter: "And now Come Sunday—that nice quiet little house with the steeple—Everyone who went into it was dressed up—courteous—smiled—it was all so nice—So he watched and waited. He listened—the music was so sweet and tender even from that distance" (Ellington n.d., 9). Ellington's introduction to "Come Sunday" captures the same mood and effect of distance—so much so that it is difficult to hear on the 1943 Carnegie location recording.

EXAMPLE 3.1 "Work Song," autograph score, mm. 186–193.

The two *Boola* texts include a host of other musical references to portions of *Black, Brown and Beige*. Among them are the "broken walk" or "todalo" of the workers (Ellington's own "East St. Louis Toodle-O," quoted in the middle of "Come Sunday"); the patriotic and Revolutionary War tunes heard in "West Indian Influence" and the transition to "Emancipation Celebration"; the blues resulting from love triangles formed during the Spanish-American war ("The Blues" or "Mauve"); and (in the later typescript source only) the "jungle" music of Harlem in the twenties heard in the opening of *Beige*, as well as the concluding patriotic anthem ("The black, brown, and beige for the red, white, and blue"), which was ultimately cut before the premiere.

While the *Boola* sketch and the typescript provide expansive textual commentary on the program for *Black, Brown and Beige*, they also range beyond it, touching on issues that would appear in Ellington's later works. These included the dramatic and didactic depiction of the African-American experience, as found both musically in *A Drum Is a Woman* (1956) and historically in the show *My People* (1963); the social commentary of the *Deep South Suite* (1946), especially the second and third sections ("Hearsay" and "There Was Nobody Looking"); the spirituality of the Sacred Concerts; the hopeful vision of *New World A-Comin'* (1943); and the celebration of Harlem, both in the tone parallel *Harlem* (1950) and in many shorter works. Together with *Black, Brown and Beige*, these works, in a sense, grow out of *Boola*—just as the roots of *Boola*, as well as those of *Symphony in Black*, extend back to the Cotton Club period and to Ellington's youth in Washington, D.C.

After *Black, Brown and Beige's* unusually long period of gestation—extending at least twelve years, from 1930 to 1942—the work fell into place quickly once Ellington started writing it for his Carnegie Hall debut. Several sources provide evidence of the rapid rate of composition.[13]

In his memoirs, as mentioned above, Ellington claimed to have started writing *Black, Brown and Beige* at an engagement in Hartford in December 1942. The Ellington orchestra appeared at Hartford's State Theatre December 11–13 on a bill featuring Frank Sinatra—who had recently left Tommy Dorsey's orchestra—and the dancers Baby Laurence and "Jig Saw" Jackson ("Duke Ellington and His Famous Band" 1942). The "scary" film remembered by Ellington as part of the show was not *The Cat Woman* but another with fright potential: *Secrets of the Underworld*, or, as a review listed it, *Secrets of the Underground* ("Duke Ellington Has Lively Show" 1942).

Extant portions of Ellington's autograph short score for *Black, Brown and Beige* confirm late 1942 as the time when Ellington began writing.[14] Marginalia in *Black*, for example, link the work to the Ellington orchestra's engagements in Connecticut. At the top of the first page Ellington jotted down the name and address of his co-headliner at the State Theatre: "Frank Sinatra, 143 Bergen

Avenue, Jersey City, New Jersey." Later in the movement (on the page containing measures 85–116) Ellington wrote an address and phone number for "Allen and Mrs. McMillan" of Wilson, Connecticut (he probably meant *Wilton*, a town close to Danbury). The McMillans may have met Ellington during the run in Hartford or (closer to Wilton) at the Lyric Theatre in Bridgeport, the site of the band's next engagement (December 14–16; see Stratemann 1992, 238).

Other evidence in the autograph score points to a compressed period of writing the entire piece. In one four-page gathering from *Black*, for example (beginning at m. 187), Ellington sketched out portions of Joe Nanton's solo from "Work Song" and notated some of the popular songs to be quoted in *Brown* (Dan Emmett's "Dixie," Stephen Foster's "Old Folks at Home," and "Yankee Doodle"). At the bottom of the third page of this gathering, Ellington made notes about both form and instrumentation for the piece, writing "Pastel" (perhaps a working title for one of the sections), "Brown" (referring either to the movement or to trombonist Lawrence Brown), "5 sax clar" (i.e., saxophones, clarinets), "7 brass cups" (i.e., with cup mutes), "4 sax," and "Ben" (for tenor saxophonist Ben Webster). On the next page he seems to be drafting a press release for the upcoming Carnegie concert: "to read D. E. [Duke Ellington] playing the original things he loves that won him acclaim with his serious audiences at home and abroad," then "Program of interpretive music by D. E. and played by the musicians who inspired this great work." Finally, looking ahead either to the printed program or to his own spoken remarks, he writes "Synopsis of Symphony—Meaning a Tone Parallel." These notations suggest that the actual working out of the composition occurred in tandem with preparations for his Carnegie Hall debut.

Yet another detail in the score linking *Black, Brown and Beige* to late 1942 is the trumpet part marked for Harold "Shorty" Baker, who had joined the orchestra in September. Baker had played with Ellington for a few days in 1938, but the orchestra then had only four saxophones, while the autograph score of *Black, Brown and Beige* shows five.

In addition to these clues in the original score, other sources reinforce the evidence suggesting that Ellington wrote much of *Black, Brown and Beige* in the six weeks prior to the premiere. A journalist visiting Ellington shortly before the event reported that the composer had been up all night at work on a "fairly long new piece" with band members at his side copying parts as quickly as he wrote them: "Several times, when Duke's muse seemed to be slowing up, his copyists jogged him, 'C'mon Duke,' they said, 'you're holding us up.' And Ellington worked a little faster" (Taubman 1943, 10). More recently, Gunther Schuller (1989, 147) has speculated that Ellington's quick writing habits helped sabotage the third movement, *Beige*: "Its formal uncertainty reveals signs of hasty patching together of materials." Indeed, one section of *Beige*—Lawrence Brown's trombone solo in the "Sugar Hill Penthouse" section, with the band accompanying—is in the hand of Billy Strayhorn, suggesting that Ellington, pressed for time, turned to his writing partner for assistance as the premiere's deadline approached.

Ellington does quote or interpolate a handful of earlier pieces in *Black, Brown and Beige*, but they add up to only a few minutes of music (out of roughly forty-five minutes overall) that can be dated before December 1942 (see Table 3.1). The two most substantial borrowings are Ben Webster's saxophone interlude in "The Blues" section of *Brown*, and Ellington's piano solo in *Beige*. As Andrew Homzy (1991) has discovered, Webster's sixteen-bar solo and the accompanying reed and trombone backgrounds in "The Blues" come directly from *Jump for Joy's* "Concerto for Klinkers"—a piece never recorded by Ellington but unearthed by Homzy in the Smithsonian collection. And toward the beginning of *Beige*, where Ellington evokes Harlem nightlife of the twenties, he interpolated a piano piece, "Bitches' Ball," which he later identified as dating from his early years in Washington. Following the practice of "ragging" a piece, Ellington first plays the theme in a moderate, rocking tempo then doubles it in a sudden burst of virtuosity (see Tucker 1991, 39–41). In the overall context of *Black, Brown and Beige*, however, these borrowings make up a minuscule part of the entire work—reinforcing the impression that much of the music was devised specifically with the 1943 Carnegie Hall premiere in mind.

The evidence, then, strongly suggests that Ellington composed most of *Black, Brown and Beige* between December 11–13, 1942, and the January 23, 1943, premiere. Quite likely most, if not all, of the work was completed by January 16 or so, when the orchestra began a week of rehearsals for the concert at New York's Nola Studios, on Broadway between Fifty-first and Fifty-second streets. On

TABLE 3.1 Earlier Works by Ellington Quoted or Incorporated in *Black, Brown and Beige*

Black
  "Come Sunday"
    "East St. Louis Toodle-O" (1926), accompaniment quoted behind Ray Nance violin solo (Priestley and Cohen 1974a, 37)
    Melodic cell from "A Hymn of Sorrow" (from *Symphony in Black*, 1934/1935) occurs throughout this section, also used in "Light" (Priestley and Cohen 1993, 187n)
  "Light"
    Passage in opening chorus related to "Riding on a Blue Note" (1938) (Priestley and Cohen 1974b, 29)

Brown
  "Blues"
    Ensemble quotation from "Way Low" (1939) between the first vocal chorus and Ben Webster's saxophone solo (Priestley and Cohen 1974b, 32)
    Ben Webster tenor saxophone solo and accompaniment taken from "Concerto for Klinkers," from the show *Jump for Joy* (1941) (Homzy 1991)

Beige
    Piano solo from "Bitches' Ball" (ca. 1914–1915), a piece from Ellington's early days in Washington, D.C. (told by Ellington to Brooks Kerr; see Tucker 1991, 39–41)

Friday, January 22, the Ellington orchestra tried out the piece at Rye High School in Rye, New York; on this occasion, according to Ulanov, the "flag-waving" finale featuring vocalist Jimmy Britton was cut from the score (Ulanov [1946] 1975, 250). The following night Ellington at last unveiled his long-awaited opus at Carnegie Hall. After two repeat performances of the Carnegie program that same year—in Boston (January 28) and Cleveland (February 20)—Ellington would never again perform *Black, Brown and Beige* in its entirety.[15]

My account has focused chiefly on how Ellington came to conceptualize and compose *Black, Brown and Beige*. Further exploration of the work's origins, however, might involve pursuing several leads that can only be mentioned here by way of conclusion.

One fruitful area of inquiry would be to examine Ellington's composition against the backdrop of earlier large-scale jazz works designed for the concert hall. During the period of *Black, Brown and Beige's* conception, bandleader Paul Whiteman was the key figure in this field. Beginning with his commission of Gershwin's *Rhapsody in Blue* in 1924 and continuing through his series of "Experiment in Modern Music" concerts held between 1926 and 1938 (all but one at Carnegie Hall), Whiteman served as a vigorous advocate of symphonic-length jazz compositions, helping to create a climate favorable for the emergence of a piece like *Black, Brown and Beige*. Like Ellington's tone parallel of 1943, the works performed by Whiteman and his orchestra at these concerts featured little or no improvisation, evoking jazz through various melodic, harmonic, and timbral effects instead. And, like *Black, Brown and Beige*, they tended to be programmatic—as in Ferde Grofé's *Mississippi (A Tone Journey)* (1926) and better-known *Grand Canyon Suite* (1931) or John Green's *Nightclub* (1933), which gave impressions of a fancy cabaret (DeLong 1983, 175). For his eighth Experiment concert in 1938, Whiteman commissioned a half-dozen composers to write short pieces on the subject of bells; one was Ellington, who contributed "Blue Belles of Harlem" (which he also performed at his first Carnegie concert). Later Ellington would pay tribute to Whiteman in *Music Is My Mistress*, praising the bandleader for his "dignity" and "class" (Ellington [1973] 1976, 103). And in 1943, just before the premiere of *Black, Brown and Beige*, Ellington told an interviewer: "Don't let them kid you about Whiteman. He has been a big man in our music. He's done a lot for it, especially with his concerts where he gave composers a chance to write new, extended works" (Taubman 1943, 10).

Another retracing of *Black, Brown and Beige's* roots might connect its themes with those treated earlier by figures during the Harlem Renaissance and the New Negro movement of the twenties. *Black, Brown and Beige's* race pride, historical focus, and celebration of African-American identity had antecedents in the poetry of Langston Hughes and Countee Cullen, the fiction of Claude McKay, the art of

Aaron Douglas, and the writings of Alain Locke and James Weldon Johnson. In a way, by fashioning an extended work from black vernacular idioms, Ellington fulfilled one of the New Negro criteria for artistic excellence—as foreshadowed by James Weldon Johnson's protagonist in *Autobiography of an Ex-Colored Man* (1912), who dreamed of one day writing classical music based on ragtime and authentic Negro themes.[16] Yet a later parallel to Ellington's work in *Black, Brown and Beige* was provided by the African-American painter Jacob Lawrence, whose extensive series of panels under the title "The Migration of the Negro" (1940–1941) graphically portrayed scenes and themes Ellington explored musically.

A third approach to *Black, Brown and Beige* might be to read it as an autobiographical document—a personal historical invention blurring fact and fiction, like Zora Neale Hurston's *Dust Tracks on a Road*, Sidney Bechet's *Treat It Gentle*, or Alex Haley's *Roots*. For Ellington's composition, after all, not only presented a panoramic view of the black experience but retold his own story. The audience at the Carnegie Hall premiere saw standing before them an American whose African ancestors had struggled under slavery. His grandparents had lived in the rural South—Virginia on his mother's side, North Carolina on his father's. Both parents had worked in service positions. Early in life, like Boola, Ellington had discovered the Bible and the solace of religion. Later he participated in the historic journey north, traveling to New York and the dynamic black metropolis of Harlem.

As the Ellington orchestra gave a tone parallel to the history of African Americans, its leader offered a human parallel. Elegant, urbane, talented, and successful, Duke Ellington was a living symbol of his people's progress. By using his Carnegie Hall debut to celebrate African-American achievement with a work of heroic proportions and bold ambition, Ellington wrote himself into the script—assuming the lead role of Boola in the grand historical pageant he called *Black, Brown and Beige*.

Notes

My thanks to Steven Lasker and Art Pilkington for answering questions that arose in the course of writing this article.

1. *Chocolate Kiddies*, for example, included only five songs by Ellington and Jo Trent, and one of them, "Deacon Jazz," had been composed the previous year. So the "show" written by Ellington overnight may in fact have been a total of four songs.

2. Previous accounts of the genesis of *Black, Brown and Beige* have tended to cite 1933 as the starting point (see, e.g., Jewell 1977, 52–53; Knauer 1990, 21). More recently, Klaus Stratemann has alluded to a *Chicago Defender* article from early 1931 that mentions Ellington's idea for "a musical stage play about the progress of the black race in America" (Stratemann 1992, 115).

3. These productions were not limited to Washington. In 1921 the black newspaper the *New York Age* gave considerable coverage to a Carnegie Hall performance of *The Open Door*, a "pageant with music" originally produced at Atlanta University (with undergraduate Fletcher

Henderson playing piano in the orchestra). A preview of *The Open Door* described it as "built up around the 'spirituals' and folk songs of the race, and showing symbolically its development from jungle dance and barbaric ritual through slavery and oppression, to the present day when the door is open to education and larger opportunity" ("The 'Open Door' Pageant" 1921). Music for the pageant was provided by the well-known black composer and violinist Clarence Cameron White, who conducted the Clef Club Orchestra at the Carnegie Hall performance.

4. Such historically structured scenarios dated back to nineteenth-century minstrelsy, especially post–Civil War productions mounted by black companies. A reviewer's description of *Darkest America* in 1896, for example—starring the noted black minstrel men Billy McClain and Sam Lucas—could almost serve as a summary of the program for Ellington's *Black, Brown and Beige*: "[The performers'] delineation of Negro life, carrying the race through all their historical phases from the plantation, into the reconstruction days and finally painting our people as they are today, cultured and accomplished in social graces, holds the mirror faithfully up to nature" (Sampson 1980, 5).

5. A film short based on *Yamekraw* was released by Vitaphone in 1930. Klaus Stratemann compares its integrated plot and music to Ellington's *Symphony in Black* of 1934/1935 (Stratemann 1992, 123).

6. This announcement appeared around the same time as two highly publicized operas about African Americans (both, however, written by white composers): Louis Gruenberg's *Emperor Jones,* produced in blackface at the Metropolitan Opera in 1933, and Gershwin's *Porgy and Bess,* which the composer began in early 1934 and which premiered in Boston in 1935.

7. The title, of course, plays off Gershwin's *Rhapsody in Blue* of 1924. The film's subtitle was "A Rhapsody of Negro Life," and an early working title was "Black Rhapsody." A Paramount cue sheet for the film located by Ellington researcher Steven Lasker identifies the musical score as "A Composition of Negro Moods." For detailed discussion of *Symphony in Black,* see Stratemann (1992, 118–128).

8. Three sections of the film, in fact, had been recorded by Ellington earlier as independent pieces: "Dance" and "Harlem Rhythm" as "Ducky Wucky" and "Merry-Go-Round," respectively (both 1933), and "Blues" as "Saddest Tale" (1934).

9. The "Boola was there" quote also appeared in Irving Kolodin's annotation for *Black, Brown and Beige* in the January 23, 1943, Carnegie Hall program: "'Boola' is the term Negroes use to symbolize the perpetual spirit of the race through time. Thus when a discussion of some important phase of American history is under way—Valley Forge, for example—one of the group is sure to say: 'Yes, 'Boola' was there all right'—referring to some heroic Negro little known to the white man who made a valiant contribution to the Revolutionary cause" (Kolodin 1943).

10. The first published reference to this typescript, to my knowledge, appears in conductor Maurice Peress's liner notes to *Four Symphonic Works by Duke Ellington* (1989). Peress generously shared a copy of this typescript with me in early 1992. For more on this source and its relationship to *Black, Brown and Beige,* see Peress (in this issue).

11. Later in 1943, for example, *Variety* reported that Ellington was preparing a book that would explain the story behind *Black, Brown and Beige* and would contain both the score and the accompanying descriptive text (Stratemann 1992, 243).

12. Interesting that here, less than a month before the *Black, Brown and Beige* premiere, Ellington's work was announced as tracing the development not of African-American history but of African-American *music.* In a way, this description looks ahead more to *A Drum Is a Woman* (1956) than *Black, Brown and Beige.* It also relates to the project (never finished) on which Ellington worked with Orson Welles around this time—a film called *It's All True,* which was to have traced the history of jazz (see Ellington [1973] 1976, 240–241).

13. Wolfram Knauer takes issue with what he calls the "legend" of *Black, Brown and Beige's* speedy, last-minute composition (see Knauer 1990, 21–22, 37n3). But he provides no evidence to show that any significant portions of the work were completed before December 1942. It is certainly intriguing that the composer and pianist John Lewis told Knauer he had heard portions of *Black, Brown and Beige* performed by the Ellington orchestra as early as 1939 or 1940. Without corroborative testimony, however, this isolated recollection cannot support Knauer's claim that the actual composition of *Black, Brown and Beige* unfolded over a period of years. Instead, as I argue below, signs point to most of the composing taking place in the six weeks before the Carnegie premiere. For a piece lasting three-quarters of an hour, this is quick work by anyone's standards.

14. Autograph scores for the following sections have been located at the Smithsonian: from *Black,* all of "Work Song" and virtually all of "Light" (except for the introductory trumpet cadenza); from *Beige,* the introduction and "Sugar Hill Penthouse" to the clarinet solo. For more on sources for *Black, Brown and Beige*—including scores, transcriptions, and recordings—see Homzy (in this issue) and Peress (in this issue).

15. In 1959 Robert D. Crowley recalled hearing the Carnegie program—including, it seems, all of *Black, Brown and Beige*—repeated in Chicago some time in the winter of 1943 (Crowley 1943, 99). At this writing I cannot verify that he heard the uncut, premiere version. For a more detailed account of the piece's revisions and performance history, see Homzy (in this issue).

16. This aim, in turn, might be traced to Antonin Dvorák, who in the 1890s had called upon American composers to use indigenous materials—especially the Negro spiritual and plantation songs and music of the Indian. The link between Ellington and Dvorák is Will Marion Cook, who studied with the Czech composer at the National Conservatory in New York and served as a mentor to Ellington in the twenties (see Peress 1990).

References

Brown, Scott E. 1986. *James P. Johnson: A case of mistaken identity.* Metuchen, N.J.: Scarecrow Press and the Institute of Jazz Studies.

Crowley, Robert D. 1959. *Black, Brown and Beige* after 16 years: An album review. *Jazz* 2 (Spring):98–104. (Reprinted in *The Duke Ellington reader,* edited by Mark Tucker, 179–185. New York: Oxford University Press, 1993.)

Dance, Stanley. [1970] 1981. *The world of Duke Ellington.* New York: Da Capo Press.

DeLong, Thomas A. 1983. *Pops: Paul Whiteman, king of jazz.* Piscataway, N.J.: New Century.

Duke Ellington and his famous band. 1942. Advertisement in the *Hartford Daily Courant* December 10.

Duke Ellington has lively show on State stage. 1942. *Hartford Daily Courant* December 12.

Ellington, Duke. n.d. *Boola* sketch. Manuscript. Held in the Duke Ellington Collection, Smithsonian Institution, Washington, D.C.

———. 1931. The Duke steps out. *Rhythm* March:20–22. (Reprinted in *The Duke Ellington reader,* edited by Mark Tucker, 46–50. New York: Oxford University Press, 1993.)

———. ca. 1943. *Black, Brown and Beige* by Duke Ellington. Typescript. Held in the Duke Ellington Collection, Smithsonian Institution, Washington, D.C.

———. [1973] 1976. *Music is my mistress.* New York: Da Capo Press.

Ellington completes Negro opera at bedside. 1938. *Down Beat* October:2.

Ellington on Negro music. 1942. *Variety* December 9:37.

Ellington's opera. 1934. *Variety* July 10:1.

Frankenstein, Alfred. 1941. "Hot is something about a tree," says the Duke. *San Francisco Chronicle* November 9.

[Hobson, Wilder.] 1933. Introducing Duke Ellington. *Fortune* August: 47–48, 90, 92, 94, 95. (Reprinted in *The Duke Ellington reader*, edited by Mark Tucker, 93–98. New York: Oxford University Press, 1993.)

Homzy, Andrew. 1991. Presentation given at the Tenth Annual International Ellington Conference, Los Angeles, California, June 14.

Jewell, Derek. 1977. *Duke: A portrait of Duke Ellington.* New York: W. W. Norton.

Johnson, James Weldon. 1912. *Autobiography of an ex-colored man.* Boston: French.

———. [1930] 1977. *Black Manhattan.* New York: Atheneum.

Knauer, Wolfram. 1990. "Simulated improvisation" in Duke Ellington's *Black, Brown and Beige. The Black Perspective in Music* 18:20–38.

Kolodin, Irving. 1943. Program notes, "Duke Ellington and his orchestra: Twentieth anniversary concert," Carnegie Hall, January 23. (Reprinted in *The Duke Ellington reader*, edited by Mark Tucker, 160–165. New York: Oxford University Press, 1993.)

Mabie, Janet. 1930. Ellington's "Mood in indigo." *Christian Science Monitor* December 13. (Reprinted in *The Duke Ellington reader*, edited by Mark Tucker, 42–43. New York: Oxford University Press, 1993.)

New York packs Carnegie Hall to see "The Open Door." 1921. *New York Age* November 26.

Oja, Carol J. 1992. "New Music" and the "New Negro": The background of William Grant Still's *Afro-American Symphony. Black Music Research Journal* 12, no. 2:145–169.

The "Open Door" pageant for Atlanta Univ. at Carnegie Hall. 1921. *New York Age* November 19.

Peress, Maurice. 1989. Liner notes, *Four symphonic works by Duke Ellington.* Music Masters 7012-2-C.

———. 1990. Dvorak and African-American musicians, 1892–1895. *Black Music Research Bulletin* 12, no. 2:26–29.

Pittman, John. n.d. [probably August or September 1941]. The Duke will stay on top! Unidentified clipping. (Reprinted in *The Duke Ellington reader*, edited by Mark Tucker, 148–151. New York: Oxford University Press, 1993.)

Priestley, Brian, and Alan Cohen. 1974a. Black, Brown & Beige—1. *Composer* 51:33–37.

———. 1974b. Black, Brown & Beige—2. *Composer* 52:29–32.

———. 1974–1975. Black, Brown & Beige—3. *Composer* 53:29–32.

———. 1993. Black, Brown & Beige. Rev. ed. of 1974–1975 article. In *The Duke Ellington reader*, edited by Mark Tucker, 185–204. New York: Oxford University Press.

Sampson, Henry T. 1980. *Blacks in blackface: A source book on early black musical shows.* Metuchen, N.J.: Scarecrow Press.

Schuller, Gunther. 1989. *The swing era: The development of jazz, 1930–1945.* New York: Oxford University Press.

Stratemann, Klaus. 1992. *Duke Ellington: Day by day and film by film.* Copenhagen: JazzMedia ApS.

Taubman, Howard. 1943. The "Duke" invades Carnegie Hall. *New York Times Magazine* January 17:10, 30. (Reprinted in *The Duke Ellington reader*, edited by Mark Tucker, 158–160. New York: Oxford University Press, 1993.)

Tucker, Mark. 1991. *Ellington: The early years.* Urbana: University of Illinois Press.

Ulanov, Barry. [1946] 1975. *Duke Ellington.* New York: Da Capo Press.

Zunser, Florence. 1930. "Opera must die," says Galli-Curci! Long live the blues! *New York Evening Graphic Magazine* December 27. (Reprinted in *The Duke Ellington reader*, edited by Mark Tucker, 44–45. New York: Oxford University Press, 1993.)

4

Black Women Working Together

Jazz, Gender, and the Politics of Validation

TAMMY L. KERNODLE

From *Black Music Research Journal* 34, no. 1 (Spring): 27–55

In the essay "Black Women and Music: A Historical Legacy of Struggle" (2001), Angela Davis chronicles the cultural and historic trajectory black women musicians have advanced through music in their transition from free people to enslaved persons to free but oppressed people in relation to the context of their lives in Africa and America. While Davis situates her discussion in how black women have used spirituals and the blues as a means of developing social and political consciousness, her theoretical scope could easily be enlarged to include other forms of black music, most notably jazz. One of the arguments Davis raises concerns the common reading of black women's relationships with each other in the larger scope of popular culture. These relationships are often framed as competitive and antagonistic. Rarely has the complex and layered engagement between black women been acknowledged. In recent years, popular culture has perpetuated the trope of competitiveness, hostility, and violence between black women through social networks (e.g., Facebook, Twitter) and reality television (e.g., "Basketball Wives," "Real Housewives of Atlanta"). These depictions have been used to stereotype black women, discredit their viability in certain social environments, and reject them as intellectual beings. But close examination of the social and familial relationships between women exposes a complex culture of engagement and socialization. These relationships are at times defined by layered and multifarious praxes through which collectives of black women have engaged in self-definition; created systems of knowledge that provided the skills to navigate political, social, and economic spheres; and formed "safe spaces" that have supported their process of brokering power.

Why has this competitive narrative permeated popular culture and our readings of how black women engage with one another? One reason is that this narrative has been defined by emotional responses generated from the engagement between black men and women in public and private spheres. The supposed lack of "good" black men who can sustain "good" relationships with "good" black women serves as the undercurrent for competitive and sometimes toxic relationships between black women. This is furthered with the proliferation of the mythology of the "strong black woman" and her engagement with "weak black men" and the supposed subversion of social and power structures that define masculinity. These ideological beliefs raise a number of questions when considered in relation to the interactions between black women and men in larger contexts of popular culture. How has the competitive narrative framed how black women musicians are read and defined within popular culture history and criticism? To understand this we must interrogate how the narrative of competition and the engagement of black women musicians have been documented in the historiography of jazz.

The narrative of the competitive personality or the inability to "get along" among black women musicians has become paramount to the mythologies that have shaped the public understandings of the culture of jazz.[1] It is often used as one of the rationales for why women are "disruptive" to the work being done in spaces where jazz is created. The prevailing thought is that the competitiveness that women exhibit in these spaces is one that is destructive rather than productive to the working environment. The male competitive spirit in jazz, however, is the essence of the creative energy generated. It is "the" necessary constant, for it produces cultural hallmarks, real-time moments of genius and frames the infinite nature of possibility that occurs when men *work together* even when poised or posed in competitive stances. When this type of analysis is extended to women musicians, it is often subverted from its role as the tool of empowerment that helps one develop her individual musical voice to one where she is forced into battle to be the "one" female creative voice that survives and earns a place in the historical narrative. The result, as evidenced in the written, recorded, and cinematic histories of jazz, is what several scholars have described as the phenomenon of the "exceptional woman" (Tucker 2001/2002, Rustin 2005). The exceptional woman becomes the rationale for the exclusion of other women and lends support to a narrative of invisibility that occurs in jazz histories as it relates to women musicians. Sherrie Tucker describes this as follows:

> Women are invisible because they weren't good enough. Playing good enough meant playing like men. Women who play like men are "exceptional women," and exceptional women can enter the discourse without changing it. We can acknowledge the importance of an exceptional woman in jazz history while retaining the belief that women cannot play powerfully enough or women can't improvise. We can use her inclusion to argue that our historical vision of jazz is not sexist, but merit-based. (2001/2002, 384)

Most important to this discussion is how this narrative of the exceptional woman has defined common understandings of how these women *worked* and created art. Much of jazz scholarship and criticism has equally contributed to the widespread notion that exceptional women work in a space of "gendered isolation," and collaboration occurs only with male peers or husbands. Examples of this would include the working relationships of Lil and Louis Armstrong, Lovie Austin and her Jazz Hounds, Mary Lou Williams and the Andy Kirk band, John and Alice Coltrane, and Bertha and Elmo Hope. One is left to believe that exceptional women work primarily in isolation from each other because while the stage can accommodate as many exceptional men as possible, there is space for only one exceptional woman. These notions became increasingly important in the years following World War II due the expanding subtext of masculinity and race that permeated jazz culture. Only in the reclamation histories of the 1980s and 1990s have such beliefs been refuted. This work seeks to expand the analytical lens of jazz histories to consider what happens when two or more exceptional women *work together*.[2]

The potential of this type of analytical and methodological approach raises a number of questions. How does the narrative accommodate professional and personal relationships between exceptional women who have similar life and career trajectories? What does the collaborative praxis engaged in by these musicians reveal about the systems of knowledge building that black women engaged in apart from their male peers? How did these women create support systems and networks that enabled them to subvert social power structures and create "spaces" for themselves within male-defined environments? This essay seeks to answer these questions through an analysis of the professional collaborations and personal relationships trombonist/arranger Melba Liston developed with peer black women musicians, most notably Mary Lou Williams. Liston and Williams first collaborated during the 1957 Newport Jazz Festival in a performance that marked Williams's return from a self-imposed three-year hiatus from public performing, and offers one of the first documented instances in which these two "exceptional women" performed on stage together. In preparation for the performance, Liston, a trombonist and arranger for Dizzy Gillespie's orchestra, arranged segments of Williams's 1945 symphonic composition *The Zodiac Suite* into the first big band setting of the work. This would come to signify the essence of Liston and Williams's musical collaborations—Liston's reworking of material drawn from the pianist/arranger's vast oeuvre that created new "readings" of Williams's musical contributions to jazz.

Over the next six years (1957–64), Liston and Williams worked on a number of projects that revealed a progressive vision of jazz, as evidenced in their compositional efforts and their marketing of jazz through the inaugural Pittsburgh Jazz Festival in 1964. Although these collaborations are documented through recordings and newspaper and personal accounts, there are several interpretative challenges that emerge when trying to chronicle or historicize the collaborative process used by the two. Neither left any written documentation that specifically outlines the praxis they engaged in while writing certain arrangements.[3] Nor did either speak specifically in personal interviews of who initiated what. So it is not always clear who did what and when. This lack of written documentation may be indicative of a focus on verbal dialogue versus written correspondence. Considering the expansive holdings associated with the Mary Lou Williams Collection at the Institute of Jazz Studies at Rutgers University in Newark and the Melba Liston Collection at the Center for Black Music Research at Columbia College Chicago and the obvious absence of written correspondence contained within, one can surmise that their physical proximity to each other (they both resided in Harlem during this time) framed their collaborative process.[4]

Emblematic of this is Liston's selection and reworking of specific musical material that Williams used for particular events (e.g., recording dates and live performances) and the pianist's acknowledgement of Liston's importance and assistance. Although the focus of this essay is the collaborative and personal relationships that developed between Liston and her female peers, in order to understand these relationships, one must also consider her relationships with male peers such Dizzy Gillespie. Historicizing the relationship between Liston and Williams requires an interrogation of the triangular relationship that developed between the two women and Gillespie and how it refutes the commonly held notion that black women are incapable of forming emotional/professional relationships due to their chronically competitive personalities, especially when black men are also engaged in these scenarios (Davis 2001, 230). This work also seeks to explore how Liston and other black women collaborators sought to redefine the knowledge base associated with jazz, reposition the importance of the solo as the badge of legitimacy, and subvert the power structure of the bandstand through the intricate and innovative nature of their arrangements.

I Am Who I Say I Am: Self-Definition and Survival

First you are a jazz musician, then you are black, then you are female. I mean it goes down the line like that. We're like the bottom of the heap.[5]
—Melba Liston (Stokes 1983)

In the landmark book *Black Feminist Thought: Knowledge, Consciousness and the Politics of Empowerment*, feminist theorist Patricia Hill Collins explores the methods through which black women, as a subordinate group, engage in the acquisition of the knowledge deemed necessary to integrate into the power structures and social spaces that exclude them. She also discusses how black women engage in redefining themselves in contexts that extend beyond common readings of black femininity. The investigation of such processes is necessary in understanding the homosocial networks that black women musicians created to counter the growing resistance to their presence on the bandstand during the mid-twentieth century. The culture of jazz is one that is defined in the development of homosocial networks that enable the individual musician to gain knowledge, develop a certain skill set, and refine his/her individual musical voice. In the early 1940s, these practices extended beyond the bandstand to the after-hour jam sessions. While these sessions provided musicians with opportunities to interact socially, they often became spaces that benefitted male musicians only. Dizzy Gillespie describes the environment of the jam session as follows:

> Amongst musicians when I came up, we had a very close feeling of camaraderie. We were all trumpet players together—Charlie Shavers, Benny Harris, Bobby Moore, and I—and we were unified socially; not just trumpet players, other musicians too.
>
> We traded off ideas not only on the bandstand, but also in the jam sessions. We had to be as sensitive to each other as brothers in order to express ourselves completely, maintain our individuality, yet play as one. Jam sessions, such as those wonderfully exciting ones held at Minton's Playhouse were seedbeds for our new, modern style of music. (Gillespie and Shipton 1979, 134)

Gillespie's account of the jam session's critical role in the development of bebop and other modern jazz styles is centered on its importance to the development of the male musician. Although he does not suggest that women were not welcome, it is clear that the jam session was a masculine space that men inhabited for character building, self-actualization, and knowledge acquisition. Trumpeter Clora Bryant, who participated in many of the jam sessions associated with Central Avenue in Los Angeles, substantiates the notion of the jam session as a masculine space. "A woman would rarely venture into a club unaccompanied . . . Women instrumentalists, no matter how well known, steered clear of the jam sessions. Women who did venture into the performing arena found the range of opportunities limited" (Dje Dje and Meadows 1998, 285).

With the jam session becoming the center of knowledge acquisition and character building during the postwar years, it became increasingly important for black women musicians to find alternative methods of knowledge building. Most continued in a practice black women have engaged in for centuries—the development of grassroots networks that enable the transference of knowledge. The act of "knowing" for female jazz musicians became increasingly essential for the development of personal consciousness and the necessary skill set to traverse male spaces like the jam session and bandstand.[6] While the act of "knowing" (especially in relation to prevailing performance aesthetic) accomplished this goal, it did not ensure their emotional survival. For this, one had to develop wisdom. Wisdom occurs when knowledge intersects with experience. Experience, not abstract concepts, became the important factor in black women developing the wisdom that is key to their survival. Collins explains: "As members of a subordinate group, black women cannot afford to be fools of any type, for our objectification as the Other denies us the protection that white skin, maleness and wealth confer. This distinction between knowledge and wisdom and the use of experience as the cutting edge dividing them, has been key to black women's survival" (2000, 257). When this theoretical lens is applied to the activities of black women musicians that were active in the years following World War II, it reveals how these women promoted among themselves a type of social knowledge that provided solutions to the issues that developed out of the engagement of the black female body and male-defined spaces. The professional trajectory of Liston uncovers how the homosocial networks created by black women musicians stimulated knowledge acquisition and the development of wisdom. These networks centered largely on the trinity of church, home, and community.

The black church, since its beginnings in slavery, has historically provided a space for public music making among black women. It also served as a means through which black women brokered for power within male-centered social/power structures. Outside of women's ministries, such as missionary societies and kitchen ministries, the role of church musician, choir director, or song leader provided black women with limited possibilities of leadership in the black community. Music also allowed women to subvert prevalent power structures of the church (men held decision-making positions despite being the minority) and frame the theological perspective and common practice within specific denominations. Evidence of this can be found in the roles Lucie Campbell and Mattie Moss Clark played in elevating and defining gospel performance practice in the Baptist and Church of God in Christ (COGIC) denominations during the twentieth century (Boyer 1992; George 1992; Walker 1992; Kernodle 2006). Liston spoke often of the importance the black church had in framing her earliest contexts of music making and in the development of the consciousness of her female relatives. She weekly attended church with her family, regularly engaging in congregational singing. While Liston never sang in any of the choirs of the church or played her trombone during the services, her reflections indicate that she viewed these experiences as being key to her understanding of how important music was in defining the black experience.[7]

The home also served as an important site for knowledge development for Liston. The piano, radio, and records served as conduits of knowledge building as they exposed the young musician to performances that featured some of jazz's most influential musicians of the time (Liston 1996, Dahl 1984). Liston acquired a historical and performative knowledge of jazz through these media, which translated into her developing a method through which she learned to replicate the music she heard on her instrument (Dahl 1984, 253). One of Liston's earliest memories of performing in the home was playing "Deep River" and "Rocking the Cradle of the Deep" while sitting on the back porch with her grandfather (Liston 1996, 4). The development of Liston's musical voice was furthered by her family's migration to Los Angeles in 1937 and the larger black community's acknowledgment of her extraordinary talent. She participated in a highly developed and active music scene that consisted not only of the nightlife associated with Central Avenue but also a strong public school music program.

In addition to playing in school bands, Liston also participated in Alma Hightower's WPA children's band. Although she was a drummer, Hightower's legacy in jazz history has been defined more so through her role as teacher and mentor. Alma Hightower and her Melodic Dots proved to be an important training ground for both female and male musicians. The band during Liston's tenure included pianist Alice Young and saxophonists Vi Redd and Dexter Gordon. According to Liston, the young musicians received a full range of training that included tap and hula dancing, singing lessons, theory, and basic musicianship (Liston 1996, 7). Youth, a lack of knowledge regarding the racial and gender politics of the cultural industry, and the mentorship by Hightower shielded Liston from many of the issues that derailed many female musicians. By the time she joined professional union bands at age sixteen, Liston had begun the process of developing a strong performance personality.

Liston's knowledge base grew even more when she joined the all-male bands of Gerald Wilson and Count Basie. Through her stints with these bands, Liston gained more advanced musical skill but also an awareness of how the female body can disrupt and challenge the social structures and spaces that defined the culture of jazz—tour buses, jam sessions, and bandstands. Like many of her peers, Liston learned that life on the road as the only woman encouraged the development of various types of "knowing" that was based in how you engaged with men in those spaces. These forms of knowledge reveal 1) the vulnerability of the black female body; 2) the devaluation of the black female body within certain cultural/social spheres; 3) how the presence of the female body in male-centered spaces could be read as promoting a type of sexual currency that disrupted the power/social relationships among men. Liston's experiences with physical and sexual violence at the hands of band members will be discussed more thoroughly in the Tucker/O'Connell essay contained in this issue. As a female body and trombonist, Liston's presence on the bandstand was often read as "taking" or robbing black men of professional opportunities. Such readings reflect how black males were valued more in the cultural industry that promoted jazz during the postwar years and how jazz narratives sexualized the presence of women's bodies in certain spaces.

Liston's most quoted account of being viewed as the "other" or outside the camaraderie of men pertained to the time she was asked to join Dizzy Gillespie's band in 1956. Commonly referred to as Gillespie's State Department band, this group was one of the first jazz aggregations to tour Europe, the Middle East, and South America as part of the Eisenhower administration's strategy to use global mass mediation of American music to combat the spread of communism. Gillespie was already engaged in Norman Granz's famous Jazz at the Philharmonic tour when the official announcement was made, so he left the assembly of the band to Quincy Jones. Jones had two distinct mandates from Gillespie. The first was to ensure that the group was to include both men and women and be racially diverse. The second was to strategize a plan that reconciled the issues of racial inequality with the strong propaganda element of the tour without seeming complacent to the failure of the government. To address the first, Jones added white musicians Phil Woods (alto sax), Rodd Levitt (trombone), singer Dotty Saulter, and Liston. But, in relation to the second issue, Gillespie decided to create a program that surveyed the history of jazz through accompanying lectures by Marshall Stearns. While there seemed to be little resistance to the addition of white musicians or Saulter, the decision to hire Liston versus a male trombonist was met with profane negativism. She recounts her invitation to join the band as follows:

> Dizzy was in Europe. Quincy Jones was the musical director and was organizing the band for Dizzy. Dizzy said, "Get the band together, but include Melba, and Melba is to write some of the music." So those were orders no questioning that. But when I got to New York I heard some comments, about, "Why the hell did he send all the way to California for a bitch trombone player?" They didn't know me at all, but as Dizzy instructed, I arranged some things and brought them with me, "Stella by Starlight" and "Anitra's Dance." . . . When we got into the initial rehearsals and they started playing my arrangements, well, that erased all the little bullshit, you see. They say, "Mama's all right." Then I was "Mama," I wasn't bitch no more. (Gillespie and Shipton 1979, 416)

In later years Liston would explain this reaction as being fueled by the fact that members of the band had friends who wanted the job (Liston 1996, 16). But, further reading might reveal other reasons. In the previous section of this essay I discussed how the jam session and the bandstand had increasingly become male-centered spaces in the years following World War II. Musicians, critics, and fans created a spectrum of readings that defined the woman's role in this culture. The use of the term "woman" was a reference to females who inhabited this space as wives, girlfriends, patrons, or groupies. All of these roles positioned women as being diametrically "outside" of the culture, on the periphery, but comprising central networks that supported the creative activities of men. Most importantly, these "women" did not disrupt the *work* or camaraderie of the men, but enabled it. They were essentially participating in a manner that maintained their status as "women" or as female bodies who acknowledged and exercised in appropriately gendered spaces. The counter to the "woman" was the "bitch." In this case "bitch" became the reading of the female body that disrupted male-defined spaces. The bitch did not support the creative efforts of the male artist; she took away from his art by taking his place on the bandstand and devaluing what he does. The bitch also creates conflicts between him and other men by challenging the power structure of jazz in an attempt to manage the business affairs or correct perceived injustices against her lover or husband. The lack of any real historicizing of jazz wives has allowed for the proliferation of negative readings of their engagement with public jazz culture. Readings of Bud Powell's wife, Buttercup, is a good example of this.[8]

The juxtaposition between the "woman" and the "bitch" and the male jazz musician is further complicated when race is considered. Although there are a number of white women instrumentalists who were associated with the postwar scene (e.g., Marian McPartland), the white woman's place in modern jazz history has largely been defined as groupie, lover, patron, and wife. In the book *To Be or Not to Bop*, Gillespie explains the juxtaposition between white and black women and jazz musicians:

> There's not too much difference between black and white women, but you'll find that to gain a point, a white woman will do almost anything to help if it's something that she likes. There's almost nothing, if a white woman sees it's to her advantage that she won't do because she's been taught that the world is hers to do with, as she wants. This shocks the average black musician who realizes that black women wouldn't generally accept giving so much without receiving something definite in return. A black woman might say; "I'll love him . . . but not my money." But a white woman will give anything, even her money, to show her own strength. She'll be there on the job, every night, sitting there supporting her own goodies. She'll do it for kicks, whatever is her kick. . . . As a patron of arts in this society, the white woman's role, since white males have been so preoccupied with making money, brought her into close contact with modern jazz musicians and created relationships that were often very helpful to the growth of our art. (Gillespie and Shipton 1979, 282)

Gillespie's assertions not only substantiate a prevailing reading of the role of women in jazz spaces, but they also reveal that race complicated these issues. Liston (and many of her peers) had not only to challenge social constructs that marginalized them as women but also to negotiate the racial issues that defined them. Revisiting the earlier quotation regarding the reaction to Gillespie's decision to hire Liston for his State Department band exposes how she, like many of her peers, had to move beyond the point of "knowing" what their presence represented to these spaces to developing and enacting the wisdom to survive these potentially hostile situations. Rather than suppress her femininity, apologize for her presence, or try to prove her musical prowess as a soloist, Liston allowed her skills as an arranger to argue her position. From extant accounts, Liston never responded to questions about why Gillespie sent to California for a "bitch"; she follows the instructions of the bandleader, which are to distribute the arrangements he asked her to prepare. Thus Gillespie and Liston make the jazz arrangement, not the solo, the equalizer. In so doing, they allowed Liston to reflect a knowledge base that exceeded the skill set of the musicians and qualified her presence. Moreover, as the conduit for the artistic expression of her male peers, Liston's arrangements provided a means for developing, rather than stifling, the creative symmetry of the band.

The jazz arrangement provided the means through which Liston also transitioned from "bitch" to "mama," indicating another level to the spectrum of reading female bodies in jazz. While the term "mama" is often used to acknowledge the strength, power, and nurturance of black women, in this case the use of "mama" is duplicitous. It is an acknowledgement of Liston's strength as musician, yet it is also reflective of her willingness to take on certain domestic needs of the band. In an interview with Linda Dahl in 1982, Liston explained that her willingness to sew buttons, cut hair, and attend to the domestic, nonsexual needs of the band members meant that she was being a "woman" or operating in a gendered role that precipitated camaraderie with her male peers (Dahl 1984, 256). But her refusal to engage in sexual relationships with band mates also led to the marginalization of her sexuality. Thus the use of the term "Mama" takes on a new meaning, which extends out of the readings of black women's sexuality that formed the binary of the asexual Mammy and the oversexed Jezebel. "Mama" becomes the modern representation of the nurturing, asexual black woman, whose presence in certain social spaces is framed by her service to the men around her. Although Liston accepted being identified as "mama" because of the gender politics of the time, in later years she was insistent that female musicians define themselves and not be marginalized through such characterizations:

> The male-female thing is really something else. And that has not changed too much. You don't see it quite so clearly, and you don't hear it quite so clearly, but nothin' changed. Like, well, they're doin' it to Janice Robinson. I worry about Janice, who is a most talented girl. And she is not accepted just for that by the musicians. And they don't even know it. It's not what they intend to do—the brothers would not hurt for nothin'. But this attitude is just a deeply imbedded thing. It's just a *habit* . . . They used to call her "Little Melba." I told them that's wrong . . . all the cats was standin' there, and they said, "Hey little mama!" I said, "She ain't no little mama." I said, "That's *Janice Robinson*. Hopefully, she's not goin' to follow in *my* footsteps and let you do the same thing to her that you did to me. And you just quit it." (Dahl 1984, 258)

Liston's assertions reflected her growing knowledge of the importance of self-definition for black women musicians in light of the ever-shifting cultural contexts that defined the jazz scene of the late-twentieth century. For Liston as well as many of her peers, it became increasingly important for black women not to allow their identities to be completely defined by their work environments or engagement with various power structures. Instead they should engage in defining themselves through their own social and/or professional networks. These circles facilitated the development of a social knowledge base that would frame how they engaged not only with one another but also in the male-centered spaces they inhabited. Liston's acquisition of such knowledge and engagement with this social/professional network began first during her early years with Hightower and extended to her experiences touring with Billie Holiday in the summer of 1950.

The interactions between Holiday and Liston, during a short-lived tour of the South in 1950, reveal how the relationships between black women sometimes developed into a type of mother-daughter dynamic. The relationship of mother to daughter frames one of the most immediate and intimate ways in which knowledge is transferred among black women. This type of bond developed between Holiday and Liston largely out of a need to ensure that the singer remained sober and drug-free during this tour. Shortly after Holiday's manager John Levy hired Gerald Wilson's band to accompany the singer, he asked Liston to "keep an eye on [Holiday]" (Blackburn 2005, 245). Holiday's struggles with her addiction were significant during this period, and Levy thought that the tour would be a good way to keep her clean. At twenty-three years of age, Liston had acquired a great deal of professional experience but had had little experience with what she called "night-life people" (Blackburn 2005, 245). Part of her assignment was to share a room with Holiday, and it was during those moments that the singer began to impart strategies about surviving the demands that society placed on black women. "She talked about her childhood and the chaotic life she had lived in Baltimore, maybe with certain memories reawakened by the recent visit there," recalled Liston. Although she claims to not have understood half of what Holiday said, Liston developed a close relationship with the singer. "I thought she was really great. I loved her. Lady was an easy person to like because she was a very warm person, you couldn't help it. If she liked you, she liked contact. I'd see her and she'd always hug me" (Blackburn 2005, 245). Billie took to calling Liston her "little girl," inferring a type of mother-daughter relationship. Through this relationship Holiday warned Liston about "getting messed up in life." Liston would assert in later years that looking back on this time she realized how she became the daughter Holiday never had, but longed for (Blackburn 2005, 245). But, most importantly, Holiday, like many black mothers, understood that if Liston accepted the sexual politics and role of "mammy" that would be offered to her by the social constructs of the cultural industry, she would become a willing participant in her subordination. Acting in the role of mother to Liston meant Holiday provided the necessary knowledge that would ensure her physical and mental survival in hostile spaces (Collins 2000, 183). Despite a disastrous end to the tour, Liston and Holiday remained close throughout the years, and the mother-daughter dynamic never ceased.[9] Liston, while touring with her all-female quintet in 1958, saw Holiday for the last time in an airport. Although the singer was struggling with health issues, Liston recalls that she "was looking beautiful and she was dressed real nice . . . Billie gazed at this little group of female musicians and then addressed the agent in a voice filled with maternal authority. 'Now you take care of my children!'" (Blackburn 2005, 248). Holiday died a year later, but the knowledge she imparted to Liston framed how the trombonist engaged with other women musicians during the remainder of her career.

Melba, Mary Lou, and Dizzy

The bebop era, socially speaking, was a major concrete effort of progressive thinking black males and females to tear down and abolish the ignorance and racial barriers that were stifling to the growth of any true culture in modern America.
—Dizzy Gillespie (Gillespie and Shipton 1979, 282)

In order to understand the circuitous factors that brought Melba Liston and Mary Lou Williams together in the summer of 1957, one would have to look at the relationship that developed between each of these musicians and Dizzy Gillespie. The triangular relationship that developed between these three reveals how varied and layered the relationship between black male and female musicians were. Where most triangular relationships are generally based on competition that is rooted in sexual attraction, this one was based on 1) support systems that ensured the personal survival of jazz musicians; 2) a progressive view of jazz and the desire to expand the music beyond the commercialized trends orchestrated by the culture industry; and 3) a collective desire to redefine the persona of the black jazz musician from the common reading of the "other" to that of artist.

Williams met Gillespie in the early 1940s following her departure from the Kirk band and her subsequent move to New York with a small band she led that included drummer Art Blakey. Liston first encountered Gillespie while working with Gerald Wilson's band during the late 1940s. Both Williams and Liston credit Gillespie with being key to their survival during the 1940s and 1950s. "During that period, I was living at the Dewey Square Hotel, and that was the beginning of what they later called 'bop,'" Williams recalled in Gillespie's memoir *To Be or*

Not to Bop. "I used to go around the corner to Minton's and I met Dizzy there. He knew that I was in New York and wasn't working, and he began to give me some of his gigs. And most of them were non-union gigs" (Gillespie and Shipton 1979, 148). Williams's successful performance during some of these gigs led to her being able to join the union before the traditional three- to six-month window and transition fully into the New York scene. "He always looked out for me, and I never realized how wonderful he was until years later. Anytime he thought I wasn't working or something wasn't happening right, he'd always come to my rescue" (Gillespie and Shipton 1979, 149). Liston's experience with Gillespie was similar and led to her playing in his band:

> I had come back East with Gerald Wilson's band, and the band disbanded. Somehow or another, I wound up in New York. Dizzy had the big band at what I think was Bop City, and he heard that I was in town, and there was one trombone player that he wanted to get rid of, so he immediately fired him. And I went by to visit. He says, "Where ya goddamned horn? Don't you see this empty chair up there? You're suppose to be working tonight." (Gillespie and Shipton 1979, 356)

Liston ended up working with the band, which included John Coltrane, Jimmy Heath, and John Lewis, for four to five months before the group disbanded.

In both scenarios, Gillespie, who was quickly growing as one of the leading voices in modern jazz, gave access to the bandstand to two extraordinary black women. By the time both encountered Gillespie, they each had earned a reputation for not only being strong soloists but also innovative arrangers. Both had escaped the narrative of invisibility, not through their instrumental performances, but through their arranging skills, which allowed them to legitimize the eclectic and diverse knowledge systems from which they had drawn as black women. It was also through the jazz arrangement that Gillespie provided each woman the means to subvert the power structure of the bandstand. In 1949 Williams wrote the bop fairytale "In the Land of Oo Bla Dee" for Gillespie's band, and the tune became a staple in his repertory throughout the 1940s and 1950s. But the most striking example of Gillespie's acknowledgement of and challenge to the subordination of female musicians is seen in his selection of Liston for the State Department band. Let's revisit the earlier quoted anecdote:

> Dizzy was in Europe. Quincy Jones was the musical director and was organizing the band for Dizzy. Dizzy said, "*Get the band together, but include Melba, and Melba is to write some of the music.*" So those were orders no questioning that [emphasis added]. But when I got to New York I heard some comments, about, "Why the hell did he send all the way to California for a bitch trombone player?" They didn't know me at all, but as Dizzy instructed, I arranged some things and brought them with me, "Stella by Starlight" and "Anitra's

Dance." . . . When we got into the initial rehearsals and they started playing my arrangements, well, that erased all the little bullshit, you see. They say, "Mama's all right." Then I was "Mama," I wasn't bitch no more. (Gillespie and Shipton 1979, 416)

Note how Gillespie prepared Liston for the reaction to her presence. He did not instruct Jones to have her prepare her best tune in order to prove her prowess as a soloist, instead he has her *write some tunes*. Gillespie was fully aware that Liston was a capable instrumentalist and soloist and that that would not be enough to quell the simmering tensions. He understood that her innovative musical voice as an arranger would be the factor that would legitimize her presence. The arrangements she chooses are significant—the jazz standard "Stella by Starlight" (this would have been known by most of the musicians in the band) and a reworking of Edvard Greig's composition "Anitra's Dance," from *Peer Gynt Suite no. 1*, which she renamed "Annie's Dance." The latter was an important statement about the breadth of Liston's musical knowledge and her ability to reconceive any musical idea or motive as a jazz theme. The reaction was exactly what Gillespie had surmised. According to Liston, when he heard the negative comments, Gillespie said, "Go on and take one of those arrangements out and see if they can play it. Two or three bars later, he said 'Now who's the [bitch]?'" (Dahl 1984; Liston 1996).[10] The advanced musicianship that Liston's arrangements required challenged the musicians and their initial dismissal of her as the "bitch" who took an opportunity from another man.

Liston's arrangements became an important part of the identity of Gillespie's 1956 State Department band as "Annie's Dance" and a reworking of Debussy's "Reverie" became signature pieces of the band. The latter—another work that pointed to the trombonist's love for the lush harmonies and emotional nuances of nineteenth-century Romantic composers like Debussy and Ravel—served as a showcase for Liston, who played an extensive solo during live and recorded performances. "Annie's Dance" was used to "break the ice" with audiences. Their knowledge of the theme, which Liston used as the main motivic material, made the music played by the band more accessible with international audiences (Liston 1996, 36).

Gillespie's benevolent attitude toward other musicians eventually led to Liston and Williams meeting in 1957. In the years preceding this meeting, Williams had positioned herself as one of the purveyors of modern jazz through her arrangements and recorded performances and had been one of the few jazz pioneers to champion bebop. She had also experimented with new forms of jazz composition, which had resulted in the performance of her set of symphonic poems called the *Zodiac Suite* at Town Hall in 1946. In 1952 she went to Europe for what was supposed to be just a series of performances in England and ended up traversing the continent for two years before settling in France and suffering from physical and mental exhaustion. When she returned to the States in 1954, she renounced public performance, converted to Catholicism, and began working with drug-addicted jazz musicians. Gillespie and his wife, Lorraine, were the pianist's primary link to the jazz world, and each urged Williams to return to her music. When she refused, Gillespie began sending Liston to check on the mental and physical health of the pianist. There is no indication that Liston and Williams had met each other before 1957, but it is quite likely that they knew of each other because of their individual relationships with Gillespie and close proximity of living in Harlem. It is also not clear if Liston, who took on many different musical and nonmusical roles in the Gillespie band, protested or tried to avoid these visits. Williams's accounts of these visits indicate that the two connected in a personal way, and, in time, Liston inspired her to begin playing piano again and composing new works. Williams would describe these first interactions as follows:

> Dizzy would send Melba. "Go up there and see what Lou's doing. See how she's playing." Melba, I understand, would go back and say, "Man, Lou played some chords and you ought to hear them. They're really great." He said, "well, get her out." Melba would come here and when he took me out to the Newport Jazz Festival, Melba arranged some things. He said, "Those arrangements were really good." She said, "I didn't do them. That was Lou's arrangement and I just sat down and took the music down." He said, "What! Get her out here!" (Williams 1973, 149)

Williams's account indicates that one approach to the collaborative process between her and Liston during these early interactions consists of the trombonist writing down the musical ideas played by Williams. This points to a similar mode of working that developed between Liston and Randy Weston. Although Lisa Barg's essay will contextualize the working relationship between Liston and Weston, it bears noting that in that collaborative scenario, Liston generally wrote down initial ideas and then began working them into intricate arrangements. This might have also defined how Williams and Liston worked together, but beyond the citation above, there is no evidence to substantiate this further. Although there is a lack of definitive evidence regarding the collaborative process used, what results in the subsequent years reveals how Liston and Williams worked to expand the scope of jazz performance, created new spaces for the elevation of the music, and mentored a generation of musicians.

Getting the *Work* Done

Few could have deduced that Gillespie sending Melba Liston to check on the wellbeing of friend and fellow musician Mary Williams would spark a musical partnership between the two. In preparation for Williams's performance with the Gillespie band at the 1957 Newport Jazz Festival, Liston not only wrote arrangements based on several of the pianist's well-known tunes but also led the rehearsals that prepared the band for this segment of the performance. Williams's performance with the group consisted primarily of three movements drawn from the *Zodiac Suite*. In addition to these reworkings of the *Zodiac Suite*, Liston also produced a short musical interlude that accompanied Williams as she entered the stage. The medley was based on two well-known melodies—the blues "Roll 'Em" and the bop tune "In the Land of Oo Blah Dee." "Roll 'Em" resulted from a request by Benny Goodman for Williams to write a blues for his band. In 1937 she presented him with the tune arranged in the boogie-woogie piano style she had been exposed to in Kansas City. It was just one of a few of Williams's compositions that would translate the rhythmic and motivic structure of the boogie-woogie genre into the big band idiom. "Roll 'Em" became a hit for Goodman, who continued to work with Williams throughout the 1940s and 1950s. "Oo-Bla-Dee" was a highly rhythmic tune that drew on bebop's short melodic phrases and the jive dialect that framed the genre's culture. It was written for and recorded by Gillespie in 1949 and featured vocals by Joe Carroll. The medley, though less than a minute long, displayed Liston's ability to master Williams's sound and create a snapshot of her musical contributions to big band and modern jazz. Liston would later expand this medley to include "What's Your Story Morning Glory" and "A Fungus Amungus," and this would serve as Williams's entrance music for the 1964 Pittsburgh Jazz Festival.

Liston's synthesis of Williams's style is most evident in her arrangement based on selected movements of *The Zodiac Suite*. Written in 1945, the *Zodiac Suite* was based on jazz musicians born under the astrological signs and had initially been written for combo (piano, bass, and drum). It was later scored for small chamber orchestra by Williams and Milt Orent but had never been arranged for big band. Liston's arrangements of "Virgo," "Libra," and "Aries" transformed these movements from works reflecting the chamber-jazz aesthetic into swinging big band arrangements. The medley started with "Virgo," a bop-influenced blues that Liston reconceived through motivic interplay between various sections of the band and Williams's piano. Williams's original melody is not altered, but Liston does score the full, lush chords that the pianist played on the original recording from 1945 (Asch 620 and Asch 621) into material played at different points by first the sax section, then the brass instruments, and later the entire band. Although the performance swings, its recording, *Dizzy Gillespie at Newport*, reveals the difficulty that the band had at various points trying to navigate the intricate nature of Liston's arrangement.[11]

Williams calls out with a few notes, which are answered by the saxes, to initiate the transition into "Libra." Liston did not alter the original tempo of "Libra," deciding instead to remain true to the slow and rhapsodic nature of the work. No doubt this was done to create an emotional contrast to the previous movement. "Libra" is impressionistic in nature and features the band playing lush, colorful, and expansive chords. But the interplay between band and piano is suspended early in this movement, and Williams moves into a solo that becomes more and more disjointed rhythmically as she continues. Eventually the drummer and bassist drop out, leaving Williams to improvise in a manner that completely obscures the rhythmic pulse initiated at the beginning of the work. There is a return to tempo with the entrance of a muted trumpet solo under which Williams plays lush arpeggios. The band once again drops out as Williams begins another solo. The band re-enters with saxes playing the main motive before Williams once again plays the next phrases of the melody that segue into full-band ascending chords before the final loud dissonant chord. Williams goes right into the melody for "Aries" before the band enters with dissonant punctuations. Overall, "Aries" received less treatment by Liston, and the majority of the movement featured Williams offering up segments of the main theme.

The performance not only documented that the pianist had not lost her musical prowess as a soloist but also indicated that Liston had developed the ear to synthesize Williams's music in new ways without compromising the uniqueness of Williams's sound. Another highlight of the 1957 Newport performance was Liston's solo on the swinging blues tune "Cool Breeze." While the tune had been recorded a year earlier featuring a solo by trombonist Frank Rehak, at the Newport it became illustrative of Liston's role as an instrumentalist in Gillespie's band. Liston's solo, the first, reveals an aggressive, advanced technique and a progressive approach to improvisation. Most important, it is one of the few recordings documenting Liston in a live performance setting with the Gillespie band.[12]

In the months following the performance, Liston and Williams collaborated in a recording session for Roulette Records. The three-hour session, consisting of Liston's arrangements of some of Williams's most well-known works, was never released, and all that remains as evidence of the session are the tapes that Williams kept and a photo essay created by famed photographer Chuck Stewart.[13] Despite Liston's work with other musicians during this period, Williams continued to procure her assistance with various projects. In the early 1960s, this would include two hallmarks of Williams's career: the album *Mary Lou Williams Presents The Black Christ of the Andes*, and the 1964 Pittsburgh Jazz Festival.

"Black Christ of the Andes"

In the early 1960s, Williams, more committed than ever to her faith, began experimenting with writing sacred jazz compositions. These works fused biblical scripture and portions of the Catholic liturgy with modern jazz harmonies and nuances to create a new form of jazz and sacred music. The emergence of these compositions coincided with Vatican II, and, in time, Williams's music became central in advancing the inclusion of diverse music in the celebration of the mass as well as the Church's evolving position on civil rights. It would also become an important aspect of Williams's evangelistic efforts, which positioned jazz as music that could minister to mental and emotional needs of people. She would not refer to her music as sacred jazz, but as "music for the soul." The first composition in this vein was the vocal work entitled "A Hymn in Honor of St. Martin De Porres," an anthem written for eight-part choir (SSAATTBB) and based on a text commemorating the life of De Porres, the first Negro saint canonized by the Catholic Church. The work was first performed in November of 1963 at St. Francis Xavier Church (Kernodle 2004, 201). At some point during this period, Liston scored "St. Martin" for a small chamber orchestra (instrumentation included flute, clarinet, two alto saxes, two tenor saxes, baritone sax, four trumpets, three French horns, four trombones, piano, bass, and drums).

While the score for this arrangement exists, there is no evidence that Williams ever performed this setting. I believe, based on the activities the two were engaged in during the period, that Liston's arrangement was prepared for a 1963 performance of jazz at Philharmonic Hall that featured Gillespie and Williams. The concert, a benefit for the Symphony of Musical Arts, marked the first time black performers were allowed to perform at the venue. Integrating Lincoln Center had seemingly been one of the initiatives discussed by Liston, Williams, and several other musicians. According to Williams, "The whole thing was prejudiced . . . Melba Liston and a lot of the musicians [were] having meetings up in Harlem and [they were] talking about Philharmonic" (1973, 166). It is not clear from the extant sources what the group had planned, but close friends of Williams asked that she dissuade the group from protesting. Instead, Father Anthony Woods, the religious confidant of Williams, raised enough money to book the Philharmonic and sponsored the concert that featured Gillespie's band and Williams. This raises the question as to what motivated Williams and Liston to produce this new setting of "St. Martin De Porres." Were they hoping to replicate the 1946 collaboration with the Carnegie Pops Orchestra in the performance of her *Zodiac Suite*? Had she planned to include the work as one of the final excerpts of the "History of Jazz" retrospective that she ultimately performed during the concert? Unfortunately a definitive answer to these questions cannot be given at this time. However, what is clear is that Liston worked with Williams in not only creating this new genre of sacred jazz but also promoting it to sacred and secular audiences.

Liston's role in advancing Williams's sacred music extended into the 1964 recording sessions that would produce the LP *Mary Lou Williams Presents The*

Black Christ of the Andes. The album, the first of three released on the Williams's own label Mary Records, featured a mixture of sacred and secular pieces recorded in late 1963. In addition to standards like Billy Taylor's "A Grand Night for Swinging" and Gershwin's "It Ain't Necessarily So," the session produced performances of Williams's originals—"A Fungus Amungus," "Dirge Blues," and "Miss D. D." The focal point for some scholars of Williams's music, however, has been the religious works debuted on this album (Kernodle 1997; Kernodle 2004; Murchison 2002). In addition to "St. Martin De Porres," the album featured three other vocal works, a cantata in a style similar to "St. Martin" called "The Devil," and two swinging hymns—"Anima Christi" and "Praise the Lord"—that were written by Liston. These two hymns reveal that Liston's conceptions of sacred jazz were different from those heard in "St. Martin De Porres." Her arrangements reflected more of the gospel and congregational traditions she had been exposed to during her early years. "St. Martin De Porres" and "The Devil" reflected a connection with the music of the post–Council of Trent Catholic church, with its emphasis on an intricate, unaccompanied, homophonic choral style. But "Anima Christi" and "Praise the Lord" displayed a stronger musical and cultural connection between gospel, blues, and modern jazz.

"Anima Christi" was written in standard hymn or strophic form, and the 6/8 meter evoked the feeling of the swinging gospel ballad style popularized by gospel composer Lucie Campbell and the gospel group the Angelic Gospel Singers. The instrumentation was expanded beyond the traditional combination of piano, bass, and drums and included electric guitar and B-flat bass clarinet. It was also scored for male soloist (tenor) and small mixed group, which pointed back to the gospel group sound that had become a signature of black gospel practices. Notations in the extant scores indicate that Liston had a clear sense of the style and feeling that the hymn's prayer should invoke. The soloist was instructed to sing in a "funky gospel style," which was periodically accompanied by the background voices interjecting with harmonized responses. The text is a prayer to God for protection against the evils of the world and for a merciful response toward sins. The mood of the composition is established by the clarinet, which plays a rhythmic figure that serves as the underlying ostinato heard throughout the entire performance. Unlike the techniques employed in "The Devil" and "St. Martin De Porres," "Anima Christi" displayed more flexibility in the singer's rendition of the text and melody. There is no doubt in hearing this work that Liston was drawing on the congregational singing practices she heard during her early years.

"Praise the Lord" further established the connection between gospel, jazz, and blues with a rhythmic vamp established by bass, drums, guitar, and piano, and a tenor solo, played by Budd Johnson, that was reminiscent of the shouts and moans of the black church. Johnson's solo segued into vocalist Jimmy Mitchell rhythmically reciting (or "rapping") the lyrics that combine scriptural references from Psalms 148 and 150 with excerpts of a Medieval prayer. This act of "rapping" is suspended on the chorus, as Mitchell transitions to singing the text "everybody clap your hands." The next chorus featured Mitchell's verbal exclamations being answered by a chorus of singers. The track ended with the song mirroring the frenetic and improvisatory nature of the Baptist and Pentecostal church before fading out. In addition to writing these works, Liston also conducted the band and singers during the recording session. "Amina Christi" and "Praise the Lord" were significant contributions to Williams's repertory of sacred works, and they greatly influenced her compositional approaches, as in subsequent years she would include many of these stylistic elements in her jazz masses.

Pittsburgh Jazz Festival

In addition to promoting the *Black Christ of the Andes* LP, in 1964 Williams began traveling back and forth to Pittsburgh to visit her ailing mother. Father Woods initiated a meeting between the pianist and the Bishop of Pittsburgh, John J. Wright, in hopes that he could assist Williams while she was in the city. Woods wrote to Wright, explaining Williams's importance and her deep abiding faith, and, upon her arrival, she met with the Bishop. After a short conversation about her family and faith, Mary explained to him the benefits of adding jazz education to the curriculum of the city's Catholic schools. He was hesitant, stating that he had always associated jazz with drugs and drug addicts. She corrected him, stating that drugs were more prevalent in commercial rock than in jazz and that the latter provided a more positive means for expression. Bishop Wright, who had been quite invested in revitalizing black neighborhoods and providing educational and recreational activities for underprivileged children, was receptive to Mary's ideas but felt that the schools were not ready to integrate jazz into the curriculum just yet. Instead, he proposed that the Church sponsor a citywide jazz festival.

By 1964, the jazz festival, first introduced in 1948, had grown to be a very important venue in terms of advancing and promoting jazz. The first American festival, the Newport Jazz Festival, was established in 1954 by the collective efforts of George Wein and Elaine and Louis Lorillard. The festival's structure, which included live musical performances and academic panels, became a blueprint for subsequent festivals. In time, the Newport not only became a vehicle for the performance of more experimental works but also was instrumental in resurrecting the careers of a number of musicians including Duke Ellington and Miles Davis. The Festival was documented in the 1958 film *Jazz on a Summer's Day*, and, over the years, numerous recordings of performances were released. In the decade since its debut, the Newport Festival had grown in popularity and importance, and Williams hoped to achieve similar results with the Pittsburgh Jazz Festival.

The primary objective of the festival was to raise money to fund the Catholic Youth Organization (CYO), which provided educational and recreational facilities in underprivileged areas. But, Williams also viewed it as an opportunity to highlight Pittsburgh's importance in jazz history, which had contributed some notable musicians including Earl Hines, Errol Garner, and Billy Strayhorn (H. Garland 1964, 13). The festival's dates were set for June 19–20, and the excitement surrounding the endeavor escalated as the date approached. The governor of the state served as honorary chairman, and the Mayor of Pittsburgh, Joseph Barr, proclaimed June as "Jazz Month" (H. Garland 1964, May, 23).

Although Pittsburgh had cultivated a strong musical scene in the early twentieth century, in the decades that had passed since the end of World War II its musical activity had dissipated. Wiley Avenue, which had become the training ground for many early jazz musicians in the city, including Williams, had become an urban wasteland inhabited by vacant buildings and drug addicts. Only two clubs offering live jazz performances remained in the city—the Crawford Grill and the Hurricane. The possibilities of a major jazz festival coming to Pittsburgh would not only bring revenue to the city but could also resurrect the jazz scene. Wright assigned Father Michael Williams, Director of the Pittsburgh CYO, to work directly with the pianist and allotted $30,000 as seed money.

Williams focused on the planning of the festival, which provided her with a temporary escape from the ailing health of her mother and the consuming debt she faced back in New York. She enlisted the help of George Wein, who assisted in the planning, promotion, and solicitation of some of the performers. Williams also called upon Liston, who aided in the coordination of the festival's activities and was named musical director. In this capacity the responsibility of outlining the musical focus of the festival resided with Liston. Although each of the headliners planned their own set list, Liston was responsible for determining what the festival big band would play during their own set and as incidental music. Liston selected the band's personnel, which consisted of a number of musicians she had worked with over the years and some local jazz musicians. The band would be called the Pittsburgh Jazz Orchestra and would take on many different manifestations over the course of the next forty years.

Liston began work on several arrangements that coincided with the various sets she outlined in her notes on the Festival. These works included arrangements of Ellington's "Cottontail" and the "Blues" from *Black, Brown, and Beige* for Ben Webster's performance as well as a number of tunes for Pittsburgh native and singer Dakota Staton. But much of time was devoted to the music that would form Mary Lou Williams's set, which was being heralded as her "homecoming" (P. Garland 1964, 9).

The two began working immediately on a new arrangement of "St. Martin De Porres," which, in its new form, was written for big band instrumentation and a solo vocalist. Williams thought the spiritual message of text could best be conveyed through an interpretation in dance, so she contacted Alvin Ailey in hopes he would choreograph a series of dances to the composition. Ailey was unavailable, so she contacted Bernice Johnson, the wife of saxophonist Budd Johnson and the founder of the Bernice Johnson Dancers. The two conceptualized dances for not only "St. Martin De Porres" but also for the composition "Praise the Lord." Williams also wanted to include her early arrangements into the program Liston was developing for the all-star big band's performance that featured Thad Jones, Snooky Young, Ben Webster, Budd Johnson, and Wendell Marshall. Liston came up with an arrangement that expanded the short medley she had composed years earlier for Williams's Newport performance into a more developed overture that included thematic material drawn from "Roll 'Em," "What's Your Story Morning Glory," "In the Land of Oo Bla Dee," and "A Fungus Amungus." The work served as the opening for both days of the festival.

The preparatory work conducted by Liston and Williams coalesced into a two-day festival that drew a crowd of over thirteen thousand to the Civic Arena in June 1964. The festival featured performances from Thelonious Monk, Dave Brubeck, Art Blakey, Jimmy Smith, and local musicians such as Walt Harper, Dakota Staton, and Harold Betters. The evening, however, belonged to Pittsburgh's first lady of jazz—Mary Lou Williams—whose performance was highly acclaimed. Liston was also singled out as one of the festival's stars because of her intricate arrangements and strong leadership of the festival big band. The critic for the *Pittsburgh Courier* asserted the following in relation to the Saturday night performance:

> The big band sounded better, now that the musicians had had a day to become acquainted with the arrangements. Now Melba Liston paused to speak of her long romance with the trombone—such an unlikely instrument for a lady. "I've been playing it since I was a little girl . . . I didn't even know what it was, at first, but I just liked the way it looked. Everyone kept trying to get me to play something else, but every time they took it away from me, I'd cry. I just like the way it looks. . . . It's such an elegant instrument. I even try to look like one myself." I noted the long lines of her white gown and black lace bolero. Yes, Melba did look like a trombone, in some surrealist way. When a fan commented on the complexity of her arrangements, Melba laughed, "Don't mind that I do the tough ones because those are the sort of jobs I usually get. Deep down inside, I have a big streak of rock 'n' roll in me." (P. Garland 1964, 1)

In addition to her role as conductor, Liston also played trombone on the set featuring Ben Webster, which included the arrangements referenced above as well as Liston's composition "Len Sirrah" and the Al Grey original "Tacos and

Grits." Reviewers for *Down Beat* and *Stereo Review* made specific references to Liston's solos during this set (Kohler 1964; Dance 1964). Both nights ended with Williams and the dancers returning for performances of "Anima Christi" and "Praise the Lord."

At the end of the second day, Father Williams announced that the Festival was a "go" for the following year. Despite the enthusiasm the Festival sparked, no profit was made. The fragile financial health of the Festival would greatly undermine its viability over the next few years.

While Mary Lou Williams and George Wein returned as coproducers of the 1965 Festival, Liston did not return as musical director. It is not clear, from the extant documents, why she did not reprise her role as musical director. The program for the 1965 Festival indicates that there was no festival big band and that the concerts consisted primarily of guest artists such as the Miles Davis Quintet, Thelonious Monk, The Modern Jazz Quartet, and the orchestras of Count Basie and Duke Ellington. Even Williams, who had been the headliner for the 1964 Festival, was noticeably absent except for the piano workshop held on Sunday afternoon and a short set of solo piano. There seems to have been a power shift in the production staff of the Festival in subsequent years. While Williams and Wein returned in 1965, the following year the Festival listed only Wein's name as producer. Williams is only credited with helping behind the scenes in program notes (Pittsburgh Jazz Festival Program). There is no evidence that Williams or Liston returned as performers in subsequent years, and the festival's inability to generate a substantial profit eventually led to it ending. But for those two days in 1964, Williams and Liston earned a place in jazz history as the first African American women to produce a major American jazz festival. Their roles as producer and musical director would also foreshadow the emergence of the women-directed and women-focused music festivals of the 1970s and 1980s.[14]

Conclusion

> I had to prove myself, just like Jackie Robinson. Now I belong to all the guys, and they will take care of me. I don't have to worry. I'm free all over the world. Musicians will take care of Melba. Not to worry. But another young woman musician comes along, they're not going to get that.
> —Liston (Dahl 1982, 258)

Melba Liston and Mary Lou Williams would professionally go in different directions in the 1970s, but they maintained a close and personal relationship that is documented in the cards and letters housed in the Mary Lou Williams Collection at the Institute of Jazz Studies at Rutgers University. Their professional experiences during the 1970s situated both of them as agents of knowledge as they transitioned into teaching positions. In the early 1970s, Liston went to

Jamaica, where she served as director of the Afro-American Department of the Institute of Music in Jamaica, and, in 1977, Williams joined the faculty of Duke University as its first Artist in Residence. Through these positions, both women created inclusive and innovative pedagogies that integrated the teaching of jazz history with the performance of corresponding repertory. They would also be championed and celebrated for their contributions to jazz throughout the 1970s. And while each would eschew the terminology "feminist" or any connections with many of the social movements of the time, their mentorship of younger musicians would position them in a larger ideological struggle surrounding race in the feminist movement.

During the 1970s the personal and professional networks that women musicians had created among themselves coalesced into organizations and programming initiatives that were initially outgrowths of the feminist movement. While these festivals, conferences, and organizations sought to promote women musicians, a problematic trend emerged—the noticeable exclusion of young, emerging black women musicians. Where jazz histories had previously constructed and promoted the trope of the exceptional woman as a means of rationalizing the exclusion of women musicians, the feminist movement expanded this trope through its perspective on race. The movement came to promote what I call the *exceptional black woman*. This concept defines the impact and influence of black women only in relation to the contributions of pioneering black women musicians like Liston, Williams, Bessie Smith, and Ma Rainey. While these efforts to reclaim and situate the pioneering contributions of these women musicians in larger contexts of jazz and blues history were laudable, they served as a means through which the exclusion or subordination of contemporary black women musicians could be rationalized. Black women were generally excluded from leadership roles within these organizations and festivals, while their white female peers were heavily promoted. Although Melba Liston and Mary Lou Williams emerged out of the scene as celebrated women, their younger black counterparts were largely ignored (Gossett and Johnson 1979, 4).

As a result, black women musicians, much like their counterparts in other social movement organizations, began to create their own collectives and support groups (Springer 2001; Dahl 1984). The Universal Jazz Coalition (UJC), started in the late 1970s by Corbi Narita, provided much-needed support to emerging women musicians regardless of race and ethnicity. The organization not only hosted concerts (Annual Women in Jazz Festival) and panel discussions, it also sponsored workshops and served as a repository of information that educated young musicians in how to manage their careers. Liston became associated with the UJC in 1980 when she formed the coed band Melba Liston and Company, which featured various women, most notably bassist Carline

Ray, drummer Dottie Dodgion, pianist Francesca "Chessie" Tanksley, and tenor saxophonist Erica Lindsay—all of whom were members of the UJC. This band facilitated the transference of knowledge between Liston and a generation of black women musicians that was similar to that found in the relationships she formed with Alma Hightower and Billie Holiday. The group toured Asia and the U.S. throughout 1980 and was highly acclaimed for its musicianship. Over the next few years, Liston would perform with varying personnel—both male and female—until a stroke left her partially paralyzed (Watrous 1999)

This essay began with a discussion of scholar/activist Angela Davis's work, in which she posits that for too long the emotional relationships shared by black women have not been acknowledged for their importance in enabling these women to achieve a certain level of autonomy and independence. The professional and personal experiences recounted in this work seek to refute the notion that the competitive personalities of black female jazz musicians prevented them from forming significant and lasting relationships. These experiences not only speak to the type of relationships that developed between these women but also reveal how these women created opportunities that validated their presence in certain spaces and developed systems that promoted the transference of knowledge to one another, insuring their mental and physical survival in the environments and scenarios they functioned in. Finally, these exchanges also indicate how black women musicians: 1) established lived experience as a criteria for establishing meaning and relevance; 2) prioritized verbal communication as a primary means of transferring knowledge; and 3) developed an ethic of accountability that defined how they engaged with each other and their social/ professional circles.[15]

Notes

Special thanks goes to Cecilia Smith for her willingness to help me gather important information used in the writing of this essay and her work in establishing the legacy of Mary Lou Williams through her work. I would also like to thank the library staff at the Center for Black Music Research at Columbia College, Institute of Jazz Studies at Rutgers University (Newark) and Special Collections at Rubenstein Library at Duke University for their assistance. Thanks to the blind readers and members of the Melba Liston Collective for their valuable feedback.

1. There are several examples of jazz critics "pitting" female jazz musicians against each other. An example of this is the criticism written around Mary Lou Williams and Hazel Scott, who were often compared to each other, with the latter dismissed as not being a "real" jazz musician. In reality Scott and Williams were close personal friends and never viewed each other as professional competitors. For more information, see Kernodle (2004).

2. Much of the scholarship of Sherrie Tucker, especially in relationship to all-girl bands and female jazz musicians on the West Coast, has documented these issues. See Tucker (2000); and Tucker (1996).

3. The extant correspondence between the two is from the 1970s and consists mainly of holiday cards.

4. Randy Weston discusses in *African Rhythms: The autobiography of Randy Weston* (2010) how Williams's home had become the hangout for musicians and that Liston lived close to her.

5. Liston as quoted in Stokes (1983, 100).

6. In relation to jazz, Sherrie Tucker discusses this in "West Coast Women—A Jazz Genealogy" (1996).

7. Liston and Mary Lou Williams discuss the influence of the church in the development of their respective musical voices in a number of places, but most notable are both of their oral history interviews with the Smithsonian Jazz Masters. However, Williams talks more about the impact of music on the life of black migrants. See Kernodle (2004).

8. Robin D. G. Kelley has addressed such misreadings of jazz wives. See his obituary of Nellie Monk (2002).

9. There were a number of missteps that placed the tour in a financial bind. Holiday refused to continue, and the musicians were left stranded in South Carolina. Wilson and Liston eventually made their way back to Los Angeles, but the experience proved to be too much for Liston. Soon afterwards she took a hiatus from playing and found a clerical job with the Board of Education.

10. Liston discusses further how Wilson and Gillespie championed her skills to other musicians and how this shaped how other musicians viewed her in the NEA oral history interview (1996, 16).

11. This analysis is based on the recording "Dizzy Gillespie at Newport" Polygram Records, 1992.

12. "Cool Breeze" is also contained on the recording "Dizzy Gillespie at Newport."

13. It is not clear from extant documents why Roulette did not release the recording. The tapes and photos from the session are now contained in the Mary Lou Williams Collection at the Institute of Jazz Studies at Rutgers University in Newark, NJ.

14. The festival was resurrected during the 1980s, and the Pittsburgh Jazz Orchestra, resurrected by Nathan Davis, became a fixture at the event.

15. Chapter 6 of Collins's *Black Feminist Thought* (2000) outlines these as emblematic of how black women create their own system of validation.

References

Blackburn, Julia. 2005. *With Billie*. New York: Pantheon Books.

Boyer, Horace Clarence. 1992. Lucie E. Campbell: Composer of the National Baptist Convention. In *We will understand it better by and by: Pioneering African American gospel composers*, edited by Bernice Johnson Reagon, 81–108. Washington, D.C.: Smithsonian Institution Press.

Bryant, Clora, Buddy Collette, William Green, Steve Isoardi, and Marl Young, eds. 1998. *Central Avenue sounds: Jazz in Los Angeles*. Berkley: University of California Press.

Collins, Patricia Hill. 2000. *Black feminist thought: Knowledge, consciousness and the power of empowerment*. New York: Routledge Books.

Dance, Stanley. 1964. Jazz in Pittsburgh. *Saturday Review* July 11: 43.

Dahl, Linda. 1984. *Stormy weather: The music and lives of a century of jazzwomen*. New York: Limelight Edition.

Davis, Angela Y. 2001. Black women and music: A historical legacy of struggle. In *Black feminist cultural criticism*, edited by Jacqueline Bobo. Maiden, Mass: Blackwell, 217–232.

Dje Dje, Jacqueline, and Eddie S. Meadows, eds. *California soul: Music of African Americans in the West*. 1998. Berkley: University of California Press.

Garland, Hazel. 1964. Mary Lou Williams spearheads drive to bring jazz festival to Pittsburgh. *Pittsburgh Courier* April 18: 13.

———. 1964. Interest mounts in first Pittsburgh Jazz Festival. *Pittsburgh Courier* May 20: 23.

Garland, Phyl. 1964. Mary Lou Williams conceived idea: Pittsburgh Jazz Festival began as a dream. *Pittsburgh Courier* July 4: sect. II, 1.

George, Luvenia. 1992. Lucie E. Campbell: Her nurturing and expansion of gospel music in the National Baptist Convention. In *We will understand it better by and by: Pioneering African American gospel composers,* edited by Bernice Johnson Reagon. Washington, D.C.: 109–120.

Gillespie, Dizzy and Al Fraser. 1979. *To be or not—to bop: Memoirs.* Garden City, NJ: Doubleday.

Gossett, Hattie, and Carolyn Johnson. 1979. Jazzwomen: They're mostly singers and piano players only a horn player or two hardly any drummers. *Jazz Spotlite News* 1, no. 2 (August).

Kelley, Robin D.G. 2002. Jazz wife: Muse and manager. *New York Times* July 21: sect. A, 24.

Kernodle, Tammy. 1997. "Anything you are shows up in your music: Mary Lou Williams and the sanctification of jazz." PhD diss., Ohio State University.

———. 2004. *Soul on soul: The life and music of Mary Lou Williams.* Boston: Northeastern University Press.

———. 2006. Work the works: The role of African American women in the development of contemporary gospel. *Black Music Research Journal* 26, no. 1: 89–109.

Kohler, Roy. 1964. Caught in the act: First Annual Pittsburgh Jazz Festival. *Down Beat* July 30: 13.

Liston, Melba. 1996. Interview by Clora Bryant. Smithsonian Oral History Program NEA jazz master interview. December 4–5. Liston's home, Los Angeles. http://www.smithsonianjazz .org/oral_histories/pdf/Liston.pdf.

McRae, Barry. 1988. *Dizzy Gillespie: His Life and Times.* New York: Universe Books.

Murchison, Gayle. 2002. Mary Lou Williams's hymn "Black Christ of the Andes" (St. Martin de Porres): Vatican II, civil rights, and jazz as sacred music." *Musical Quarterly* Winter 86, no. 4: 591–629.

Pittsburgh Jazz Festival program. 1964. Linda Dahl Collection. Duke University Special Collections.

Pittsburgh Jazz Fesitval program. 1965. Linda Dahl Collection. Duke University Special Collections.

Rustin, Nicole. 2005. "Mary Lou Williams plays like a man!": Gender, genius, and difference in black music discourse. *South Atlantic Quarterly 104, no. 3*: 445–462.

Shipton, Alyn. 1999. *Groovin' high: The life of Dizzy Gillespie.* New York: Oxford University Press.

Springer, Kimberly. 2001. The interstitial politics of black feminist organizations. *Meridians: feminism, race, transnationalism* 1, no. 2: 155–191.

Stokes, W. Royal. (1983). The big band sound of Melba Liston. *Ms. Magazine*: January, 1983; 99–101.

Tucker, Sherrie. 1996. West Coast women: A jazz genealogy. *Pacific Review of Ethnomusicology* 8, no. 1: 3–22.

———. 2000. *Swing shift: All-girl bands of the 1940s.* Durham: Duke University Press.

————. 2001/2002. Big ears: Listening for gender in jazz studies. *Current Musicology* (Spring): 375–408.

Walker, Charles. 1992. Lucie E. Campbell Williams: A cultural biography. In *We will understand it better by and by: Pioneering African American gospel composers,* edited by Bernice Johnson Reagon. Washington, D.C.: Smithsonian Institution Press, 121–139.

Watrous, Peter. 1999. Melba Liston, 73, trombonist and prominent jazz arranger. *New York Times* April 30.

Weston, Randy, and Willard Jenkins. 2010. *African rhythms: The autobiography of Randy Weston.* Durham, N.C.: Duke University Press.

Williams, Mary Lou. 1973. Smithsonian Oral History Program NEA jazz master interview. Washington, D.C.

Discography

Gillespie, Dizzy. *Dizzy Gillespie at Newport.* Verve (1992).

Williams, Mary Lou. *Zodiac suite.* Smithsonian Folkways. SFW CD 40810 (1995).

————. *Mary Lou Williams presents "The black Christ of the Andes."* Smithsonian Folkways. SFW 40816 (2004).

5

New Monastery

Monk and the Jazz Avant-Garde

ROBIN D. G. KELLEY

From *Black Music Research Journal* 19, no. 2
(Autumn 1999): 135–168

The musician who once terrified us all no longer seems to disturb a soul. He has been tamed, classified, and given his niche in that eclectic Museum of Great Jazzmen which admits such a variety of species, from Fats Domino to Stan Kenton.
—André Hodeir on Thelonious Monk, circa 1959

A 1972 press release announcing the reissue of Thelonious Monk's Prestige recordings included the following observation:

[I]n the early Sixties, with the emergence of "avant-garde" jazz and the appearance of Ornette Coleman, John Coltrane and Cecil Taylor, Monk's music no longer seemed quite so strange. He was finally able to whittle away at the "Mad Monk" tags that had been laid upon him by smug critics and listeners who had neither the equipment nor the desire to comprehend. There was even the introduction to polite society in the form of a *Time* magazine cover story in 1964, and Monk finally and without compromise began to receive the widespread attention and adequate financial remuneration that was his due. ("Thelonious Monk" 1972)

Although hyperbole is unavoidable in any press release, there is a kind of truth here. At the very moment that Coltrane, Ornette Coleman, Albert Ayler, Cecil Taylor, and others were bringing about a revolution in "modern jazz," Monk's career finally began to soar. After enduring almost two decades of confused and often vicious criticisms from writers and musicians alike, by the early 1960s, Juilliard students were studying his compositions, Martin Williams (1963; 1964) had insisted that he was a "major composer," and French critic André Hodeir (1986, 164) had hailed him as the first jazz artist to have "a feeling for specifically modern esthetic values" (see also Kotlowitz 1961; Lapham 1964). By 1961, Monk had established a more-or-less permanent quartet consisting of Charlie Rouse on tenor saxophone, John Ore (later Larry Gales) on bass, and Frankie Dunlop (later Ben Riley) on drums. He performed with his own big band at Town Hall, Lincoln Center, and the Monterey Jazz Festival, and the quartet toured Europe in 1961 and Japan in 1964. He left the Riverside label for a more financially lucrative contract with Columbia Records in 1962, and by the mid-1960s, his quartet reportedly earned nearly $2,000 a week for a gig (see de Wilde 1997, 171–178; Gourse 1997, 153–211; Ponzio and Postif 1995, 201–267; Williams 1963; Williams 1964).

The mainstreaming of Monk and the emergence of the jazz avant-garde—or what has been called "free jazz" or the "New Thing"—was not merely coincidental. In several respects, both musically and politically, these developments were interdependent if not mutually constitutive. The emergence of the jazz avant-garde during the early 1960s did indeed change the field of reception for Monk as well as for other musician/composers (e.g., Charles Mingus) who only a decade before were considered too "far out" and experimental. However, the shifting critical response to Monk's music vis-à-vis the avant-garde partly reflected the changing political landscape—one in which black nationalism, Third World solidarity, and even the more localized struggles against racism and exploitation in the music industry challenged Cold War liberalism. In this war of words, conservative and some liberal critics embraced Monk as a foil against the free jazz rebellion, while defenders of the avant-garde often sought to claim Monk as one of their own. Given Monk's complicated, often iconoclastic relationship to the history of modern jazz, it should not be surprising that all of these constituencies could legitimately lay claim to him. Whereas Monk, like most musicians of his generation, expressed disinterest if not outright hostility to free jazz, artists identified with the avant-garde found his music to be a major source of ideas and inspiration. Indeed, as I demonstrate below, no matter how much Monk tried to distance himself from these new developments, he helped give birth to the jazz avant-garde. And yet, as has been the case with all cultural progeny, these young musicians not only built on but challenged Monk's musical conceptions altogether.

Criss Cross: Monk Meets the Avant-Garde

The term *avant-garde* obscures as much as it reveals. There have been many self-proclaimed avant-garde movements in music and in the arts more generally, and depending on how one defines avant-garde or the specific historical context in which these movements emerged, one might argue that jazz's unique position as neither "folk" culture nor a product of mainstream Western arts institutions, combined with its ever-changing improvisational character, renders the entire genre avant-garde. Or one could point to the apparent, although largely unacknowledged, role that black improvisational music has had on American and European avant-garde composers such as John Cage (Lewis 1996). If we simply limited our scope to avant-garde developments in jazz itself, one could easily include the work of Duke Ellington, Charlie Parker, or Thelonious Monk at particular historical junctures. But for the purposes here, I will limit the definition to a particular generation of musicians (e.g., John Coltrane, Ornette Coleman, Don Cherry, Cecil Taylor, Archie Shepp, Bill Dixon, Albert Ayler, Eric Dolphy, and Sun Ra and his Arkestra, to name a few) who emerged in the late 1950s and developed a self-conscious movement in the 1960s (see, for example, Carles and Comolli 1971; Jost 1994; Litweiler 1984; Radano 1985; Radano 1993; Such 1993; Szwed 1997; Wilmer 1980). Of course, it is impossible to lump all of these artists together; terms such as *avant-garde* or *free jazz*—like the word *jazz* itself—simply cannot contain the diverse range of music that they have produced. Nevertheless, most of these artists not only identified themselves as part of a new movement, but their work taken collectively reveals some common elements. By moving away from traditional sixteen- and thirty-two-bar song structures, standard chord progressions, and the general rules of tonal harmonic practice, they opened up new possibilities for improvisation by drawing on non-Western music; experimenting with tonality, flexible parameters, and variable rhythms; and developing forms of collective improvisation based on linear rather than harmonic qualities. The music may or may not have a tonal center; it may have a fixed pulse or some recurring rhythmic pattern, or the music may be suspended "out of time"; and there may be composed themes or prearranged rules for improvisation. In other words, free jazz is hardly chaos, and it certainly is not uniform. By some accounts, free jazz was to music what abstract expressionism was to painting, because it embraced the abstract features of postwar modernism (see Block 1990; Block 1993; Jost 1994; Litweiler 1984; Pekar 1963; Reeve 1969; Such 1993).

Yet at the birth of the free jazz movement—indeed, before there really was a movement to speak of—a few critics and musicians recognized some of these elements in Monk's music. Monk had been on the scene since the late 1930s, developing a reputation among musicians as an innovative—if not strange or difficult—pianist and composer. Like many artists ahead of the mainstream, Monk's distinctive sound (discussed below) generated both a small but enthusiastic following and a somewhat marginal existence in the commercialized world of jazz during the 1940s and early 1950s. Although he did not record as a leader until 1947 (when he was 30 years old), he had already by that time penned some of the most distinctive compositions in the history of modern jazz, including "'Round Midnight," "Epistrophy," "Well, You Needn't," and "Ruby, My

Dear." His career suffered a major setback in 1951, when he was falsely arrested for possession of drugs. Deprived of his cabaret card—a police-issued "license" without which jazz musicians could not gig in New York clubs—Monk barely worked in his hometown for the next six years. Aside from a few jobs in the neighborhood clubs in Brooklyn and the Bronx and sporadic appearances in a couple of Manhattan venues, he was forced to take out-of-town jobs to survive (see Fitterling 1997, 30–70; Goldberg 1965, 30–37; Gourse 1997, 32–102; Ponzio and Postif 1995, 41–153).

It is significant that as soon as Monk's cabaret card was reinstated in 1957, he secured a long-term engagement at the Five Spot with a quartet consisting mainly of saxophonist John Coltrane, bassist Wilbur Ware, and drummer Shadow Wilson.[1] That Monk made his triumphant return to the New York scene at the Five Spot, leading one of the most celebrated quartets in the history of modern jazz, put him squarely at the center of the avant-garde revolution. First, the venue had become a haven for the postwar avant-garde both on and off the bandstand. Originally a tiny, nondescript bowery bar at 5 Cooper Square inherited by the brothers Joe and Iggy Termini, the Five Spot became a neighborhood hangout for abstract expressionist painters, sculptors, Beat poets, and genre-crossing artists such as painter/saxophonist Larry Rivers. The performers who appeared just prior to Monk's engagement represented a fairly diverse group, stretching from the subtle experimental works by composer and French horn player David Amram and the "hard bop" and Afrodiasporic music of pianist Randy Weston to the kinetic, extremely abstract sounds of pianist Cecil Taylor and bassist Buell Neidlinger. While Monk's Five Spot appearance attracted fans from all over the city, he also inherited an audience attracted to experimental music (see Gourse 1997, 132–137; Ponzio and Postif 1995, 174–175; Porter 1998, 109–110; Weston 1999; Wilmer 1980, 47).

Monk's return also coincided with larger national and international cultural developments that helped create the kind of audiences that would patronize places like the Five Spot. Bohemia and elements of a self-proclaimed postwar avant-garde produced some of Monk's most dedicated followers. They represented an audience that could find the boundary-crossing and genre-breaking work of abstract expressionist painters, conceptual artists, and atonal composers both intellectually engaging and politically relevant. Included in this group were young black writers such as LeRoi Jones (later Amiri Baraka), Frank London Brown, Ted Joans, Jayne Cortez, and others who discovered in Monk a startling modernism as well as a direct link to the rich traditions of black music making. All of these artists contributed profoundly to the modernist, multimedia qualities that have come to characterize the new music and that resonate powerfully with Monk's own performance practices. For some of his followers, for instance, the way Monk danced around the piano while his sidemen continued to play rendered Monk more than a jazz musician—he became a performance artist (Kelley 1997; Joans 1995).

The avant-garde writers and artists of the postwar generation, particularly the Beats, held a special reverence for Monk and black jazz musicians. In some respects, their attraction to Monk was partly linked to a larger crisis in masculinity during the 1950s. As Norman Mailer argues in his controversial essay "The White Negro" (published in *Dissent* the same year that Monk opened at the Five Spot), black men—particularly the hipsters and the jazz musicians—offered an alternative model of masculinity in the age of the gray flannel suit, suburbia, and other emasculating forces. Beat artists often characterized jazz musicians as emotionally driven, uninhibited, strong black men capable of reaching into their souls to create a pure Negro sound (Panish 1997, 56–66; see also Ehrenreich 1983, 56; Mailer 1957, 332–358; Monson 1995, 396–422; Ross 1989, 65–101). To their ears and eyes, Monk had the perfect combination of abstract qualities and unbridled, authentic Negro sound (and also an extremely stylish wardrobe). He was a towering figure at six feet, three inches, with a large upper body and dark brown skin. He was black masculinity in its most attractive and threatening form, and his tendency to dance around the bandstand to his own music put his body on display in a unique way. Moreover, even musicians and critics at the time interpreted his dissonant harmonies, startling rhythmic displacements, and swinging tempos as distinctively "masculine." This is precisely how Steve Lacy described Monk's music in the pages of *The Jazz Review*. He not only stated that Monk's music possessed, among other traits, a "balanced virility," but in the context of a discussion about Sonny Rollins he observed that "[Rollins'] masculinity and authority can only be matched in jazz by that of Thelonious Monk" (quoted in Lacy 1964, 269, 271). In the liner notes to his first all-Monk album, *Reflections,* Lacy also characterized Monk's music as "masculine" (quoted in Gitler 1958). Gitler concurred, calling Lacy's remark "an interesting and pointed observation in the light of the numerous effeminate jazz offerings we have heard in the past five years. The inner strength of songs like *Ask Me Now* and *Reflections* demonstrates that it is not slow tempos and low decibels which necessarily indicate an effeminate performance."

By "effeminate offerings," was Gitler referring to the so-called cool jazz movement coming primarily from white West Coast musicians, the chamber music/jazz fusions of the Modern Jazz Quartet, or the romantic lyricism of Bill Evans? My guess is that Gitler equated effeminate performance with consonance, steady, often slow tempos, major keys, a light touch, and a romanticism that one associates with the balladeer. Although most of Monk's compositions—as well as the old standards he favored—were written in major keys, he virtually unhinged the major tonalities on which the tunes were built by adding minor seconds to melodic lines and emphasizing tritone, dominant, and minor ninth intervals in his improvisations and melodies. Critics used words like "assault," "pulverize," "savage," or "playing havoc" to describe what Monk did to pop tunes; they tended to see his interpretations as delightfully iconoclastic or as deliberately terroristic acts of disfiguring the romanticism of standards such as "Just a Gigolo" and "Darn That Dream" (Hodeir 1986, 166–167; Mehegan 1963, 4).

Ironically, in Western classical music parlance, consonance, major tonalities, and romanticism would be gendered masculine and Monk's music "feminine," because of its dissonance, its tendency to float away from tonal centers, and its employment of cadences in which the functionally dissonant chord (i.e., the dominant) resolves into a "weak" bar or beat. The discourses of Western music theory, however, are not neatly applicable here precisely because black vernacular musics are understood through different historical filters and systems of meaning. Gendered constructions of music, as with anything else, are always racialized. For example, as Susan McClary (1991, 7–19) argues, dissonance in Western classical music is gendered female precisely because it is imagined as disruptive—at best a voice of resistance, at worst a voice of hysteria. On the other hand, in the 1950s and 1960s, part of the attraction to black music was its disruptive capacity, its resistance to order and the dominant culture, and its rebelliousness. Rebellion in this age was inextricably tied to masculinity, and black men were regarded by this growing generation of "white Negroes" as the role models of manhood.[2]

Monk's masculinity, evident in his music and his body, was only one aspect of his attractiveness. The cultural avant-garde was also drawn to Monk's image as a visionary, seer, mad artist, and nonconformist—in part, a construction of the popular press dating back to the 1950s. By the early 1960s, when the Beat poet and hipster were fused together in popular media and parodied—and a new counterculture sought spiritual, cultural, and intellectual alternatives to suburbia—in walked Monk. Writer Barry Farrell (1964, 84) linked Monk with Jack Kerouac and the Beats: "[Monk's] name and his mystic utterances . . . made him seem the ideal Dharma Bum to an audience of hipsters." Many musicans looked upon Monk as a guru. Coltrane, Sonny Rollins, and pianists Randy Weston and Dollar Brand (Abdullah Ibrahim), to name a few, echoed Steve Lacy's assessment of Monk as "a teacher, a prophet, a visionary" (Lacy 1995).

But Monk turned out to be a most unwilling guru. Although he had always helped young musicians, inviting them over to his tiny apartment on West 63rd Street and providing valuable advice in his quiet way, Monk was not very receptive to the music of the avant-garde. He usually kept his opinions to himself, but on those rare occasions when he did have something to say about the new music, it was not very flattering. When asked by an interviewer in 1961 about Ornette Coleman, he claimed not to have listened to the saxophonist's work but added, "I don't think it's going to revolutionize jazz" (quoted in Gourse 1997,

175). Nat Hentoff (1995, 74) relates a similar story. One night, Hentoff and the Baroness Pannonica (Nica) de Koenigswarter—long-time patron of jazz musicians and a close friend of Monk's—were listening to Coleman's records when Monk entered: "Suddenly he interrupted a record. 'That's nothing new. I did it years ago.' Monk got up and started to go through the piles of Nica's records, without envelopes, stacked on the floor. He found what he wanted, played his old performance, which made his point, and said, 'I think he has a gang of potential though. But he's not all they say he is right now. After all, what has he contributed?'" In other, more public contexts, he was much less charitable: "I think he's nuts" (quoted in Coleman 1993). He seemed especially frustrated with the avant-garde's interpretation of his music, although he certainly did not hear all or most of what these artists were trying to do with it. As bassist Buell Neidlinger recalled:

> When I was with [clarinetist] Jimmy Giuffre, . . . we opened for Ornette Coleman at the Jazz Gallery and we played a lot of Monk tunes. But Thelonious hated the way we played his music. He was working at the Five Spot and the Baroness would drive him over. She'd sit in the car while he came into the kitchen to get a hamburger or a whiskey and storm around. There was a big, metal fire door that he used to slam during our numbers. Of course, when Giuffre played Monk's music, the chords were all wrong. (Quoted in Silsbee 1987, 8)

Besides slamming doors, Monk occasionally voiced dismay over the direction of the music, as in a conversation he had with singer Delores Wilson arranged by the *Toronto Telegram*. When Wilson criticized modern composers for "going so far out" and losing the basic "soul expression" of opera, Monk concurred: "I agree with you wholeheartedly because in jazz they're doing the same things, what they call avant-garde, they do anything, make any kind of noise. A lot of young musicians are doing that." Even more interesting was Wilson's own characterization of Monk's music, which she believed embodied the romanticism of earlier Western musics: "I just want to go and be moved by the beauty of it, I want to feel it. Mr. Monk does that beautifully with his music. There is soul, there is expression, but some of our modern composers are now just trying for just plain sound" (Bassell 1966). For someone whose playing had been compared to the sound of a jackhammer, this is a surprising assessment.

For young musicians drawn to free jazz, Monk's criticisms must have hurt, or at the very least, surprised them. Monk, after all, was their man. The avant-garde not only claimed him as one of their main progenitors and leaders but actively sought to canonize him. They regarded him as perhaps the most important forefather of what some called the "New Thing" in jazz (Goodman 1976, 72). Indeed, the first wave of the avant-garde performed more tunes by Monk than by any other composer outside their immediate circle. These artists also wrote what amounted to tributes to Monk—Coleman, "Monk and the Nun"; Eric Dolphy, "Hat and Beard"; Andrew Hill, "New Monastery"; Charles Mingus (a reluctant but very important figure in the free jazz movement), "Jump Monk" and "Monk, Bunk, and Vice Versa"; and Grachan Moncur III, "Monk in Wonderland."[3] For saxophonist Steve Lacy and trombonist Roswell Rudd, Monk was such an important composer and improviser that they eventually formed a band in the early 1960s devoted to studying and playing only Monk's music. Graduates of the Manhattan School of Music and Yale University, respectively, both understood that they were engaged in the canonization of Monk by forming what Lacy (1995) described as a repertory band: "What Roswell and I wanted to achieve at that time was a repertory band. But they thought we were crazy. And we started as a repertory band, and we played Ellington, Strayhorn, Kurt Weill, and Monk. And then we started really getting more interested in the Monk thing, and it turned into a band that only played Monk. But the idea from the get go was repertory. And at that time it was unheard of."

Who Knows? (E)Race-ing Monk in an Era of Black Liberation

The divide between Monk and the jazz avant-garde reflected not simply different musical tastes or a misunderstanding. It was also a matter of politics. Conservative and Cold War–liberal critics drove a wedge between Monk and the avant-garde by promoting Monk as a foil against the radicalization of black musicians. Ironically, some of Monk's most enthusiastic supporters during his meteoric rise to fame commented on his disinterest in race or politics as a particularly attractive feature of his life and work.

The context for such a response is very important. The emergence of the avant-garde in the early 1960s coincided with the sense of betrayal that white liberals felt from an increasingly militant, uncompromising Civil Rights movement, a rise in black nationalist sentiment reflected in groups such as the Nation of Islam and the Revolutionary Action Movement, and growing protests over U.S. foreign policy in the Third World. The same crisis occurred in the world of jazz—a world that many white critics believed ought to be color-blind. Critics who were uncomfortable with the increasing militancy of musicians identified with the "New Thing," particularly black musicians, declared war on the new music and its proponents. And they attempted to enlist anyone, willing or not, who would stand up for "real" jazz—swinging and free of politics. Critic Ira Gitler (1962) published a highly defensive critique of black protest politics in jazz in the guise of a review of Abbey Lincoln's album *Straight Ahead*. Gitler attacked Lincoln's militant politics, criticized the fact that there were no white musicians on the date, and called her "misguided and naïve" for her support of

African nationalism. For Gitler, this album and the current trends in jazz were precursors to a powerful black separatist movement. He warned, "[W]e don't need the Elijah Muhammed [sic] type thinking in jazz" (24).[4] The major record labels also attempted to silence musicians who were openly critical of American racism or supportive of black liberation. In 1959, Columbia Records—which was soon to be Monk's label—refused to issue Charles Mingus's original version of "Fables of Faubus," which included a biting call-and-response between Mingus and drummer Dannie Richmond criticizing Governor Orval Faubus, President Eisenhower, and the entire white South for the school integration crisis in Little Rock, Arkansas. Columbia's executives believed that they would lose a good portion of their southern market if they released the song with the lyrics (Priestley 1984, 119). Furthermore, the fact that the interracial avant-garde was dubbed the "New Black Music" by critic/poet LeRoi Jones (1967, 15–16, 172–176, 180–211) made the white critical establishment and some musicians, including some who were sympathetic to free jazz, uncomfortable.

Although the avant-garde was by no means united on political issues or even uniformly interested in politics, some of the most vocal proponents identified with the Black Freedom movement and/or were organizing to fight racism, exploitation, and inequity in the music industry itself. For many black musicians of the 1950s and early 1960s, both inside and out of the avant-garde, the emancipation of form coincided with the movement for African freedom. The convergence of these political and aesthetic forces, combined with a search for spiritual alternatives to Western materialism, led to the formation of collectives such as Abdullah, The Melodic Art-tet, the Aboriginal Music Society, and the Revolutionary Ensemble. The new wave of musicians also formed collectives for economic security, developing structures for cooperative work that anticipated the Black Arts movement's efforts of the late 1960s (see Baker 1986; de Jong 1997; Hunt 1974; Jost 1994, 107–121; Kelley 1997, 18–19; Litweiler 1984, 183–187; Neal 1965; Porter 1997, 176–206; Thomas 1995; Weathers 1973; Wilmer 1980, 213–227). One of the most visible institutions was the Jazz Composers Guild, an interracial collective intended to protect musicians' interests and heighten the public's awareness of exploitation and racism in the jazz industry. It was formed from the infamous "October Revolution in Jazz," a series of avant-garde jazz concerts at the Cellar Café on New York's Upper West Side, which were organized by trumpeter Bill Dixon in 1964. The participants included Dixon; a quartet led by John Tchicai and Roswell Rudd; the Free Form Ensemble; bassist Ali Jackson and his trio; and many others. Some of the more prominent musicians—Cecil Taylor, Archie Shepp, Steve Lacy, Sun Ra, and pianist Andrew Hill—took part in a midnight panel discussion on music and politics. Overall, it was a huge success, although the infusion of politics disturbed even the more sympathetic critics (Levin 1965; Morgenstern and Williams 1964; Wilmer 1980, 213–215).

For many of these musicians, collectives were necessary in order to ensure their survival. They paid a dear price not only for their artistic integrity but also for their activism. A good number of the avant-garde musicians lived in dire poverty and could hardly get a gig. Cecil Taylor worked on and off as a dishwasher; just months after Monk's feature in *Time* appeared, he was actually living on welfare. Drummer Sunny Murray was so poor that he could not afford a drum set for a time. The Steve Lacy–Roswell Rudd group devoted solely to playing Monk's music could only secure gigs in coffee shops and restaurants for almost no money (Lacy 1995; Russell 1964, 6; Spellman 1966, 12–25). Nevertheless, collectives were not merely unions under a different name; the idea was to develop collaborative artistic relationships without leaders, to mirror the experiments in group improvisation that had become a central characteristic of the new music, and to challenge the star system perpetuated by the music industry. Archie Shepp said it best when he remarked on the various critics' pools that jazz musicians had to endure: "I mean, did you ever see [Artur] Rubinstein awarded stars for performance? Bach wasn't no threat to Beethoven and they're both great—right? Nobody says who gets five stars. It's a way of treating Black culture which is discriminatory and divisive because it always creates competitiveness on the very jivest, lowest level" (quoted in Wilmer 1980, 222).

But in 1964, the year of the great "October Revolution," Monk was a star: *Down Beat* voted his quartet the best small group in jazz. To the critics, many of whom ignored or disparaged him a decade earlier, Monk now epitomized what they believed that jazz should be about: a music that transcends color and politics. A year after his Five Spot debut, Monk told black novelist/critic and activist Frank London Brown: "My music is not a social comment on discrimination or poverty or the like. I would have written the same way even if I had not been a Negro" (quoted in Brown 1958, 45). Seven years later, in an interview with English jazz critic Valerie Wilmer, he was even more emphatic about his disinterest in politics:

> I hardly know anything about [race issues]. . . . I never was interested in those Muslims. If you want to know, you should ask Art Blakey. I didn't have to change my name—it's always been weird enough! I haven't done one of these "freedom" suites, and I don't intend to. I mean, I don't see the point. I'm not thinking that race thing now; it's not on my mind. Everybody's trying to get me to think it, though, but it doesn't bother me. It only bugs the people who are trying to get me to think it. (Quoted in Wilmer 1977, 50)

The right-wing *National Review* jazz critic Ralph de Toledano (1965, 940–941) took notice of Monk's attitude and praised him for not confusing music with politics: "Like most of the best jazzmen . . . he doesn't believe that he must make his art a sledge hammer to pound away at political themes."

While conservative and liberal critics tried to promote Monk as a foil against an increasingly radical, antiracist musicians' movement, neither the jazz avant-garde nor the black activist community in general ever viewed Monk as a "sell out." On the contrary, he was elevated to the status of cultural icon in some radical nationalist circles. In an article published in the Harlem-based *Liberator*, actor/critic Clebert Ford (1964, 15) included Monk on his list of black revolutionary artists who drew on the "Negro experience" for their art. The list included a broad range of artists, from Miles Davis, Charles Mingus, Rollins, Coltrane, and Parker to "the avant-garde nationalism of an Ornette Coleman and [a] Cecil Taylor." A few months later, the *Liberator* carried another article, this one critiquing *Time* for its portrait of Monk. Written by Theodore Pontiflet (1964), the article is really about the exploitation of Monk—by his record label, by managers and clubs, and especially by his white patron, the Baroness Pannonica de Koenigswarter. "She serves as a bitter insinuation," writes Pontiflet, "to both black and white Americans alike that a rich white woman is the black jazzman's salvation." Pontiflet goes on to suggest that *Time*'s focus on Monk's relationship with the baroness not only implied wrongly that "black women are in the background reduced to domestic chores" but "warns white America that in these days of talking integration and on the fatal eve of passing a watered-down civil rights bill, they should remember that it could mean more of their daughters will be bringing home an occasional black genius." The author implies, however, that Monk was unaware of the exploitation that he had to endure as a black artist in the United States, thus unintentionally reinforcing the dominant image of him as naïve and childlike. Throughout the struggles of his career, Pontiflet writes, "Thelonious Monk and his wife Nellie remain as pure as honey. The patron baroness? She was part of the deal—the bitter part of the sweet."

All of these portraits of Monk, from the *Liberator* to the *National Review*, treat him as though he were oblivious to politics. Of course, the reality is much more complicated. As Ingrid Monson (1999) points out, Monk not only played a benefit for Paul Robeson in 1954 and performed at various fund-raisers for the Student Nonviolent Coordinating Committee (SNCC), but at times he made relatively militant statements denouncing discrimination in the music industry and condemning police brutality. He told Valerie Wilmer: "In the United States the police bother you more than they do anywhere else. The police heckle you more. You don't have that much trouble anywhere else in the world except the United States. The police just mess with you for nothing. They just bully people and all that kind of shit. They carry guns, too, and they shoot people for nothing" (quoted in Wilmer 1977, 50). It is also interesting to note that, when he was interviewed by Stanley Dance in 1963 and asked to name one of the "greatest Americans of the century," he chose George Washington Carver. The person whom he admired most in *sports* was Paul Robeson (quoted in Gourse 1997,

197–198). But this side of Monk—the "race" man, patron of the black freedom movement, critic of police brutality—was not the dominant image projected by the mainstream media. Instead, Monk came across as the kindly eccentric with the funny hats who, unlike the "angry" young lions, knew how to swing.

Played Twice: Musical Encounters

All of these factors help us understand the great chasm between Monk and the avant-garde as well as the timing and meaning of Monk's sudden success. Nevertheless, I think that the most important and, in some ways, most elusive explanation for the unique, interdependent, often strained relationship between Monk and the avant-garde lay in the music itself. Interestingly, LeRoi Jones (1964) took a mildly critical stance toward the development of Monk's music in the early 1960s, but not because of politics. Like many others, Jones praised Monk for his contribution to bebop and to the New Music and still saw him as a revolutionary of sorts but wondered why, suddenly in 1963, the artist was being feted after two decades of hard times. In raising this question, Jones hinted that something in the music, in his playing, might be faltering that could be related to his canonization, his migration to the Columbia label, and his overnight fame. He then issued a warning of sorts: "[O]nce [an artist] had made it safely to the 'top,' [he] either stopped putting out or began to imitate himself so dreadfully that early records began to have more value than new records or in-person appearances. . . . So Monk, someone might think taking a quick glance, has really been set up for something bad to happen to his playing" (21). To some degree, Jones thought that this was already happening and placed much of the blame on Monk's sidemen. "[S]ometimes," Jones conceded, "one wishes Monk's group wasn't so polished and impeccable, and that he had some musicians with him who would be willing to extend themselves a little further, dig a little deeper into the music and get out there somewhere near where Monk is, and where his compositions always point to" (22).

The question, of course, is, to where did Monk's compositions point? Did his music point forward, as in Jones' view, to the experiments of the free jazz movement? Did it point back to the old stride pianists with whom Monk so strongly identified? This question is critical if we are going to understand how Monk's music could be so attractive to the avant-garde as an opening for their own experimentation. In the final section of this article, I show how Monk's compositions and piano style actually promoted greater freedom while simultaneously placing certain restrictions on instrumentalists and how specific avant-garde artists built on elements of Monk's music to extend his conception of rhythm, timbre, group improvisation, and the eventual emancipation from functional harmony.

Although few of our leading canonizers place Monk within the realm of "free jazz," many writers and musicians recognize his contributions to the New Music. Musicologist James Kurzdorfer (1996, 181) has suggested that Monk "in some ways foreshadows the often atonal 'free' jazz of some of the musicians of the next generation." Likewise, pianist Ran Blake (1982, 29) identified Monk as one of the major figures "responsible for loosening the grip of tonality and thus paving the way for the later free jazz experiments of Ornette Coleman and others." Randy Weston, an extraordinary pianist/composer, insisted that what Monk had been doing all along was not so different from what free jazz was attempting to do, both musically and politically. Disturbed by all the hype surrounding the avant-garde, Weston told Arthur Taylor: "I don't see how this music is more free than another. I've heard Monk take one note and create unbelievable freedom. One note can be a whole composition. . . . There have been musicians throughout the years who have protested musically and also protested in other ways than in their music. In other words, this freedom thing is not new" (quoted in Taylor 1993, 27).

Unlike his fellow boppers, Monk was less inclined to take chord changes from other tunes.[5] Instead, he created a new architecture for his music—not just new progressions and new chord structures but also a different relationship between his harmonic and rhythmic foundation and the melody. Monk asked his sidemen to do more with the melody when improvising, and what he played underneath was often a restatement of the melody or even a countermelody (Williams 1992, 437). One might also point to his use of ostinato in "Thelonious," "Think of One," and "Shuffle Boil," pieces built on one or two notes played repeatedly over a harmonic movement that dominates—even defines—the theme (Blake 1982, 26; Floyd 1995, 182). He also placed greater emphasis on dissonant harmonies than his contemporaries in bebop. Although it was not uncommon for pianists of this era to play clusters (clumps of notes—usually chromatic—played at the same time) in order to achieve tone colors, Monk's closed-position voicings sometimes sounded as if he were playing clusters when he was not. He might voice a major-seventh chord by playing the seventh in the bass, the root next, and then the third—the bottom interval would be a minor second. Sometimes he would voice a chord with the root in the bass and the major third and fourth played together, which would generate harmonic ambiguity because the suspension (created by the fourth) and resolution (the third) occur in the same harmony. It was also common for Monk to play the minor seventh and major seventh, or the minor ninth and the major ninth, at the same time-either in the same chord or a melody note relative to the chord. By thus pushing functional harmony to the edge but never abandoning it, he invented unique ways to voice his chords, exploiting major- and minor-second intervals and emphasizing the highly dissonant and unstable tritone (interval of three whole steps), which gave his music a whole-tone feel and created harmonic ambiguity (Blake 1982, 28; DeVeaux 1997, 223–225; Koch 1983, 67–68; Kurzdorfer 1996, 181–201). One hears these elements in virtually all of his music, although they are particularly pronounced in tunes such as "Epistrophy," "Misterioso," "Introspection," "Off Minor," "Crepuscule with Nellie," "Ask Me Now," "Hornin' In," and "Raise Four."

Whereas most pianists of the bebop era adopted Bud Powell's style—simplifying their instrument by playing sparse chords in the left hand and placing more emphasis on right hand melodic lines built on eighth notes—Monk combined an active right hand with an equally active left hand, combining stride, distinctive arpeggios, bass counterpoint, and whole-tone runs that spanned the entire keyboard. He influenced an entire generation of avant-garde pianists to reassert the left hand and use the lower registers.[6] As mentioned previously, Monk was also a master of rhythmic displacement—the extension or contraction of a musical phrase that falls outside the established bar lines. Of course, this is not new—one can find numerous examples of rhythmic displacement in standard bebop licks. But for Monk, rhythmic displacement was more than an improvisational strategy; in some respects, it was an essential element of his compositional technique. He wrote and played phrases that might extend four-and-a-half or five bars, or he would frequently play the same phrase at a different place in the rhythm. One can hear these elements in most of his compositions; obvious examples include "Straight, No Chaser," bars 9–11 of "Ba-lue Bolivar Ba-lues-are," and bars 5–6 of "Hackensack" (Haywood 1994–95, 25–45; Koch 1983; Kteily-O'Sullivan 1990; Somers 1988, 44–47).

Often celebrated for his use of space, Monk would "lay out" fairly regularly, enabling his horn players as well as bassists and drummers to explore the possibilities of new tonalities. Freed from the piano as harmonic cage, it is no accident that so much of the avant-garde discarded the piano altogether or used it in new ways. In fact, this is partly what Coltrane meant when he said, "Monk gave me complete freedom. He'd leave the stand for a drink or to do his dance, and I could just improvise by myself for fifteen or twenty minutes before he returned" (quoted in Thomas 1976, 88). Coltrane was not alone. Monk's absence from the piano allowed for musical experimentation within the ensemble itself, opening the door for various kinds of collective improvisation (Williams 1992, 439). Especially memorable were Coltrane's interactions with bassist Wilbur Ware during the Five Spot engagement. Ware's inventive playing, use of substitute chords, and strategic avoidance of the tonic challenged Coltrane in other ways, particularly without Monk's piano leading the way. "[Ware] plays things that are foreign," Coltrane remarked. "[I]f you didn't know the song, you wouldn't be able to find it. Because he's superimposing things. He's playing around, and under, and over—building tensions, so when he comes back to it you feel everything sets in. But usually I know the tunes—I know the changes anyway. So we manage to come out at the end together anyway" (quoted in Porter 1998, 112).

Yet, although Monk freed the music and musicians in some ways, the structure of his compositions and his unique playing style also had a constricting effect. Ironically, because everything fit together so well and was so tightly structured, Monk's sidemen could not go anywhere they wished with the music. His melodies were not only difficult to learn but improvising on them was always a challenge. Many great musicians lost their bearings playing with Monk, which sometimes led to new discoveries or, more often than not, utter confusion. As Coltrane succinctly put it, "I lost my place and it was like falling into an open elevator shaft" (quoted in Blake 1982, 27). Fellow tenor saxophonist Johnny Griffin, who later replaced Coltrane during Monk's extended stay at the Five Spot, found playing with Monk "difficult" and felt that the pianist left his sidemen little "elbow space": "I enjoyed playing with him, . . . but when I'm playing my solos, for instance, the way his comping is so strong, playing his own music, that it's almost like you're in a padded cell. I mean, trying to express yourself, because his music, with him comping, is so overwhelming, like it's almost like you're trying to break out of a room made of marshmallows. . . . Any deviation, one note off, and you sound like you're playing another tune, and you're not paying attention to what's going on" (quoted in Sidran 1995, 201–202).

Monk also placed certain limitations on his sidemen—at least by the early 1960s when he was fronting his own permanent quartet. For example, although he always gave his bassists plenty of space and let them solo frequently, he also insisted that they not use the bow and wanted them to "swing" all the time. This frustrated Butch Warren, who eventually left Monk's band (Gourse 1997, 206). By the time that drummer Ben Riley joined the group, Monk seemed to want even less clutter and more space; he wanted a drummer who would simply swing. When Riley first joined Monk, he was trying to play like Max Roach and Roy Haynes, constantly filling the space, exploring the polyrhythms, and experimenting. Monk was not too keen on this approach and thought Riley was too busy. "Now you don't have to do that, you know," Monk told him. "Just learn how to swing and make everybody move to certain places and then the rest of it will take care of itself" (quoted in Riley and Troupe 1998, 105). As Frankie Dunlop, the drummer whom Riley replaced, discovered, Monk wanted a drummer who stayed in the background and kept a steady, swinging beat. "Monk demanded rather this solid, dead on-the-beat backing of Dunlop," wrote critic Jef Langford (1971a, 7). "Truly, he was a melodic drummer at his best, but I gather that he played what was requested."

We cannot underestimate the political meanings of "swing" in the era of free jazz. The lack of swing in the new music upset many critics because "swing," in their view, was constitutive of jazz itself. Ironically, critics not only regarded swing as the element that made the music authentic, and thus linked to black folk traditions, but they considered it representative of the good old prepolitical days when the music was color-blind, melodic, and pleasurable. In an otherwise sympathetic 1964 review of the "October Revolution," Dan Morgenstern lamented the loss of "swing," which to him was a defining characteristic of jazz. The New Thing, he noted, "is a form of 20th century 'art music' rather than that unique blend of popular and 'true' art that has been (and is, and will be) jazz as we know it" (Morgenstern and Williams 1964, 33). For some critics, swing not only rendered the music more authentic but also more emotional. Those who were most opposed to raising issues of race and racism in jazz accepted a racialized construction of the music as more physical and emotional than cerebral—the latter a label usually associated with European classical music. Thus it is fitting that Ralph de Toledano (1965, 942) chided Monk for being *too cerebral* and not swinging enough. While praising Monk, he accused him of too much intellectualism, for not reaching down to his "soul" in order to make great music, and for removing any sense of "dance" from his music! In other words, while Monk was not too black politically, and thus a safe symbol in the age of ghetto uprisings, Black Power, and the rantings of the avant-garde, musically, de Toledano considered him not black enough.

Interestingly, the leading pianist/composer of the first-wave avant-garde, and the most direct descendant of Monk, was also accused of not "swinging." A product of a middle-class family on Long Island, Cecil Taylor began playing piano at age five and later explored percussion. In 1951, at age eighteen, he studied piano, theory, and composition at the New England Conservatory, where he became familiar with the works of Schoenberg, Webern, and Berg and was deeply influenced by Bartók and Stravinsky (Coss 1961, 19–21; Goldberg 1965, 213–227; Spellman 1966, 3–76; Wilmer 1980, 45–59). His training in European classical music impressed Gunther Schuller, who, in a review of Taylor's early albums (*Jazz Advance* and *At Newport*), emphasized that his trajectory paralleled European music's move toward atonality. Schuller then suggested that Taylor, unlike other "jazz" musicians, played from his mind rather than his soul and hence did not really play the "blues." The comment, although made in the context of a glowing review, deeply upset Taylor, who saw himself in the blues tradition: "I play an extension of period music—Ellington and Monk" (quoted in Spellman 1966, 29). On the question of his atonality, Taylor responded to Schuller in the liner notes to his album *Looking Ahead,* again invoking Monk as a precursor of his experiments, not European music:

> Some people say I'm atonal. It depends, for one thing, on your definition of the term. . . . Basically it's not important whether a certain chord happens to fit some student's definition of atonality. A man like [Thelonious] Monk is concerned with growing and enriching his musical conception, and what he does comes as a living idea out of his life's experience, not from a theory. It may or may not turn out to be atonal. (Quoted in Spellman 1966, 27–28)

Taylor's classical training—which was variously treated by critics either as a benefit, a liability, or both—not only shaped his reception but also *Monk's* reception vis-à-vis the avant-garde. Schuller, for example, used Taylor as a foil to define Monk's relationship to the new music almost as much as Taylor invoked Monk to stake out his own position. In an essay in *The Jazz Review,* Schuller (1964, 232) suggested that it would never occur to "a man of Monk's temperament" to practice and perhaps change his technique in order to improve his music. The implication was that Monk, the allegedly self-taught pianist, came out of an improvisational tradition in which study and transformation were not essential. Moreover, Monk's playing was so integral to his compositional style that it had never occurred to him to change it. Schuller was not alone in his assessment. Despite Monk's often-cited 1948 quote that he and his fellow boppers "liked Ravel, Stravinsky, Debussy, Prokofiev, Schoenberg and maybe we were a little influenced by them" (quoted in Panish 1997, 10), jazz critics consistently characterized Monk as an untrained primitive whose musical knowledge was largely intuitive. French critic André Hodeir (1986, 162), whose praise for Monk could hardly be contained, nonetheless insisted that this "true jazzman" had no interest in "serious music." He assured his readers that "no twelve-tone sirens have lured Monk away from jazz. He probably doesn't even know such music exists. I can safely say that the gradual development of his language has been the result of intuition and intuition alone." Pianist and teacher John Mehegan (1963, 2–3) said much the same thing:

> The idea of Monk enrolling in music school to seek some course of systematic instruction as many of his peers have done . . . is alien to every breath of his life in jazz. This is a central facet of Monk's image—the unsullied subcultural artist who has steadfastly retained the sum total of his oppression, unspoiled by the slick artifices of the glossy white world. . . . The entire body of resources of Western man relating to the playing of the piano, which dates back to the 16th century, remains unknown to Thelonious Sphere Monk for the simple reason that Monk is not Western man. He is a Black man.

Indeed, at the height of Monk's popularity, even the "genius" label was qualified by adjectives such as "naïve," "primitive," or "intuitive." Lewis Lapham's (1964, 72) sympathetic portrait of Monk for the *Saturday Evening Post* described him thus: an "emotional and intuitive man, possessing a child's vision of the world, Monk talks, sleeps, eats, laughs, walks and dances as the spirit moves him."

Cecil Taylor once again responded to Schuller, using the occasion of a forum sponsored by the United Nations Jazz Society (organized by Bill Dixon and attended by Martin Williams, John Lewis, Jimmy Giuffre, and George Russell, among others) to defend Monk as well as the artistic integrity of African-American culture and the limitations of viewing black music in relation to

European developments: "I asked them, 'Would it ever occur to Horowitz to practice to change *his* technique?' I said, 'Monk can do things that Horowitz can't, and that's where the validity of Monk's music is, in his technique.' I told them that the Schullers wanted to change jazz to fit their own needs; that, essentially, they couldn't recognize the tradition that came from a black subculture as being valid in the face of European culture" (quoted in Spellman 1966, 31–32).[7]

On the surface, Taylor's identification with Monk appears more philosophical than musical because their approaches to improvisation and composition seemed so dramatically different. Taylor played with a kinetic energy that could not be contained within a steady beat, producing waves of sound that continue to build. His early recordings can sound rather strained, with drummers and bassists playing in tempo and horn players falling back on standard licks. And unlike Monk, Taylor abandoned functional harmony altogether and embraced a more dissonant and chromatic tonal vocabulary. However, close listening to Taylor's early recordings reveals similarities in how both he and Monk used the piano in an ensemble setting. Like Monk, Taylor never accompanies a soloist by simply feeding chords; rather he sounds like he's soloing himself, filling every space with two-handed tremolos and jagged runs up and down the piano over several octaves. Taylor himself described the role of the pianist in this fashion in his essay/poem "Sound Structure of Substance Becoming Major Breath/Naked Fire Gesture" (1966) published as liner notes to *Unit Structures*: "internal dialogue mirror turns: player to nerve ends, motivation 'how to' resultant Unit flow. The piano as catalyst feeding material to soloists in all registers. . . . At the controlled body center, motors become knowledge at once felt, memory which has identified sensory images resulting social response." Taylor's "comping," if one can call it that, must be understood as essential to his conception of piano playing, which in many ways is "orchestral" (see Bartlett 1995, 279; Jost 1994, 75; Levin 1991).

Taylor also drew on Monk in developing a kinetic philosophy of performance. Playing was a physical activity that required the whole body; it was dance. Dance was inseparable from music, Taylor (1966) insisted, and he understood dance as "a visible physical conversation between all body's limbs: Rhythm is the space of time danced thru." He maintained a long-standing interest in dance and even studied dance and wrote for ballet (see Bartlett 1995; Jackson 1965; Miller 1988). He regarded Monk's dance as part of a long tradition of musicians dancing around their instruments going back before Delta blues musician Charley Patton to the present, with avant-garde drummer Milford Graves doing the same thing (Wilmer 1980, 50). Bassist Buell Neidlinger recognized the critical importance of dance in black musics and the impact that Monk's dancing had on his generation of artists. Echoing his former collaborator and mentor, Neidlinger remarked, "Dance is the core of all great musics, whether it's Monk, Ellington, or Stravinsky" (quoted in Silsbee 1987, 9).

Finally, during his formative years as a composer/player, Taylor turned to Monk's music as a tool for the development of his own system of composition and improvisation—what he called "constructivist principles." The basic idea was to compose, learn, and perform music by ear, to produce structured music that was not written down. A musical score, Taylor argued, "is subjugated to the feeling of jazz—they swung, 'swing' meaning the traditional coloring of the energy that moves the music. It is the physicality of the musician, and the physicality of the musician is determined by a particular tradition that he comes out of—by the blues." Here again, Taylor stakes out his connection to Monk, who wrote out lead sheets but insisted that his players learn by ear. At the time that Taylor developed his constructivist principles, he noted, "We used a lot of Monk's tunes. We used to take the Monk tunes out of themselves into the area in which I was going" (quoted in Spellman 1966, 71). In the process, he introduced Monk to his sidemen through the terms of experimental music and helped usher in a new generation of "students" who regarded Monk's music as a road to greater freedom.

Of Taylor's sidemen, the most committed student of Monk's music was the phenomenal soprano saxophonist Steve Lacy. Born Steven Lackritz in New York City, Lacy studied with Cecil Scott and played with several Dixieland revival bands before meeting Taylor. Together, Taylor's and Monk's music had a revolutionary impact on Lacy. He went on to record with Taylor on *Jazz Advance* (1956), *At Newport* (1957), and *New York City R&B* (1961) and then made several albums on his own. He was so taken with Monk's music that his second album as a leader, *Reflections* (1958), consisted entirely of Monk compositions. Indeed, it was the first all-Monk album ever recorded by an artist other than Monk. Joined by Mal Waldron on piano, Buell Neidlinger on bass, and Elvin Jones on drums, Lacy chose to record more difficult, less well-known compositions such as "Four in One," "Skippy," and "Hornin' In," as well as the lovely ballads "Ask Me Now" and "Reflections." With the exception of "Bye-Ya," none of the pieces Lacy selected had been recorded before by anyone except Monk. To prepare for the album, Lacy learned approximately thirty Monk tunes and "listened to Monk's records hundreds of times" (Gitler 1958). Monk's music became something of an obsession, although one that would prove to be a hallmark in Lacy's musical education and his path to greater freedom.

If Monk heard Lacy's album, he certainly did not give any indication of it. Nevertheless, Lacy sought Monk out in order to extend his musical education, and Monk befriended the young soprano saxophonist. He even hired Lacy for a sixteen-week gig at the Jazz Gallery (another club owned by the Termini brothers).[8] But when Monk hired Lacy for his big band recordings at Lincoln Center in 1963, he would not allow the saxophonist to solo (see Gervais and Bouliane 1977; Gitler 1961; Gourse 1997, 168–173; Lacy 1964). "I think Monk was trying to teach me a lesson," he recalled. "I was too anxious" (Lacy 1995). Anxious or not, Lacy had already proven himself to be a brilliant and conscientious interpreter of Monk's music. That Monk reined Lacy in and, in fact, never hired him again (with the exception of the big band concert) suggests that something else was going on besides a lesson in patience.

Lacy's engagement with Monk's music pushed him in new directions—partly toward the experiments of Ornette Coleman and Don Cherry. Evidence of this comes from Lacy's third album, *The Straight Horn of Steve Lacy*, recorded in November 1960 while he was working with Monk. On this date, he led a piano-less quartet consisting of bassist John Ore, drummer Roy Haynes (both members of Monk's rhythm section at the time), and Charles Davis, a bop-influenced baritone saxophonist who had recorded earlier with Sun Ra. Lacy included three Monk compositions: "Criss Cross," "Played Twice," and "Introspection." Both in choices of songs and interpretation, these recordings reveal Lacy moving away from a tonal center. "Introspection," for example, is built on whole tones and a kind of wandering chordal movement that only occasionally lands on the tonic. Davis and Lacy constructed solos that stretched the limit of functional harmony and sounded somewhat akin to Coleman, although they remained loyal to Monk's conception by constantly finding ways to restate the theme. Equally surprising is the work of John Ore, who is more adventurous rhythmically (and harmonically) on these recordings than he was with Monk. One can almost hear the influence of Charles Mingus, Wilbur Ware, and possibly Charlie Haden as he breaks up the beat and turns the bass into more of a melody instrument.

One year later, Lacy returned to the studio to lead another piano-less quartet. This time he was joined by Don Cherry on trumpet, Carl Brown on bass, and Billy Higgins on drums—all associates of Ornette Coleman. The timing of this collaboration is important: Higgins had recently recorded and gigged with Monk on the West Coast, and Don Cherry had been playing Monk's music more frequently without Coleman. Indeed, Cherry had been exploring songs such as "Monk's Mood" and "Crepuscule with Nellie" in the New York Contemporary Five, and he had recently recorded a version of "Bemsha Swing" with John Coltrane. On this date, Lacy recorded four Monk compositions: "Evidence," "Let's Cool One," "San Francisco Holiday," and "Who Knows." The result is a brilliant fusion of Monk's ideas with Coleman's "harmolodic theory" (his idea that harmony, melody, and rhythm should be given equal weight in order to break out of the constrictions created by improvising on chord changes). Coleman's intention was to eliminate chord progressions and move to free improvisation generally built on tonal centers, although, as his own ideas evolved, even the need for tonal centers became less important (see Litweiler 1992). Don Cherry believed that Monk's music was especially open to harmolodic explorations "because his melodies are where you can hear the harmonies in the melody, and you can improvise Monk's tunes from the melody or from the chords" (quoted in Sidran 1995, 409). Lacy's collaboration with Cherry, Brown, and Higgins moves even closer to free improvisation built on tonal centers than his previous album, and yet both Lacy and Cherry seem even more committed to building their solos on the melody. As Lacy explained at the time of this recording, playing with Monk had taught him "to try to get more with the melody, to have what I play relate to the melody, and to get inside the song" (quoted in Hentoff 1961). Indeed, the theme is so important that on "Evidence," Lacy plays the role of Monk's piano by restating the theme under Cherry's solo.

In trombonist Roswell Rudd, who was also a renegade from the Dixieland revival scene and a rising figure in the avant-garde, Lacy met a Monk soul mate—not to mention an astounding improviser and brilliant arranger (Danson 1982; Heckman 1964; McRae 1975). In about 1961, the two formed a band that was to function as a kind of school for them to study Monk's music. Joined by drummer Dennis Charles, with whom Lacy had played in Cecil Taylor's band, and a succession of different bass players, the group spent the next three years playing on and off together and getting gigs where possible—restaurants, coffee houses, and so on. Unfortunately, the group never went into the studio; only one amateur recording exists from a 1963 gig at the Phase Two Coffee House in New York ("Liner Notes" 1994). By the time the recording was made, however, the group was regularly playing all of Monk's recorded compositions—fifty-three in all (see "Liner Notes" 1994; "Steve Lacy" 1963; Lacy 1995). (Monk's own group rarely had more than twenty songs in its book at one time.) As Lacy recalls, getting to this point required hard work and patience: "We played the tunes very strictly, especially at first, when we didn't dare deviate at all. We improvised right on the structure whether there were five bars or seven bars or funny keys or whatever. . . . The thing is, though, it was a nightly experience—we wanted to play on those tunes every night. So, after a while, if you do things every night you start to take liberties, and the liberty was what interested us—a liberty through this discipline" (quoted in "Liner Notes" 1994).

Liberty is precisely what they achieved. They continued in the Monkish tradition of using elements of the theme as the essential building blocks but found new ways to tear apart the melody and rebuild it—exemplified in their interpretation of Monk's ballad "Pannonica." Lacy and Rudd offer two different interpretations of the theme simultaneously, reduced to short staccato phrases and played over a steady march tempo. By the fourth bar, "Pannonica" is hardly recognizable—they strip it to its bare essence just as Monk had distilled "Just You, Just Me" to create "Evidence." They stretch Monk's music beyond anything he had ever done, using more variable rhythms, abandoning functional harmony, and extending Coleman's concept of harmolodics to achieve a level of group improvisation in which no one seems to be in the background.

A wonderful example of this transformation process can be heard in their version of "Brilliant Corners." The first chorus is played as a slow dirge and then in double time on the second chorus. The melodic and harmonic movement is shaped like a circle, except for the bridge, which is more of a descending movement. In the Lacy–Rudd recorded version, the bass of Henry Grimes becomes the harmonic foundation as he essentially keeps restating the melody, playing around with it, turning it inside out, tearing it apart, and reconstructing it. Lacy and Rudd respond by playing circles around his circular statement of the theme, following the bass notes as a roving tonal center—sometimes hovering over it, sometimes landing directly on it. On the choruses that are doubled in tempo, Charles and Grimes play a *clave* rhythm that gives the song a funkier, Caribbean feel while Rudd's trombone explores a range of harmonic and rhythmic patterns, from Dixieland-style phrases to short staccato lines that seem to puncture the "circle." Moreover, all four musicians continually vary dynamics; they shift easily from forte to pianissimo, shouting and whispering when the mood of the song requires it.

The addition of bassist Henry Grimes to the group contributed enormously to the success of these recordings. A rising giant in the avant-garde, Grimes had played with a range of people, from Arnett Cobb and Anita O'Day to Cecil Taylor, Archie Shepp, and Albert Ayler. His style fit perfectly with Lacy and Rudd's vision because they could not use a bass player who just swung steadily in $\frac{4}{4}$ time—the kind of bass player Monk wanted by the early 1960s. With no piano and a conception rooted in group improvisation, they required a bass player who could change up rhythms and tempos easily, play melodically, and provide a strong harmonic foundation when needed. At the time, there were few bassists with those capabilities who were sympathetic to the new music; the most notable examples were Mingus, Charlie Haden, Reggie Workman, Buell Neidlinger, David Izenzon, and Ronnie Boykins. Indeed, their biggest problem was finding imaginative bass players who could do all of these things and stick to the project of learning Monk's music. They eventually went through seventeen bass players and several rewritings of the bass book ("Steve Lacy" 1963, 14).

Although the Lacy–Rudd quartet has not been adequately documented, the group succeeded in finding unexplored areas to which Monk's music pointed where few—Monk included—had gone. "What we wanted to do," Lacy explained, "was to eliminate the compromises Monk had had to make recording [his compositions], due to the lack of sufficient preparation of his sidemen. It seemed there wasn't a strong enough relationship between the improvisations and the piece itself. This was true not only in Monk records but in most of the jazz we'd heard" (15). In other words, Lacy believed that Monk's sidemen did not explore all the improvisational possibilities embedded in his music because they tended to be stuck in the bop mode of soloing on the chord changes. Lacy and Rudd recognized the possibilities of freedom in Monk's music. "Now we're at a point," Lacy added, "where our flexibility is at least equal to that of any of the so-called free players. However, our freedom has been won through a long—and some people would say, arbitrary—discipline. It's also been an extremely enjoyable one" (15).

Not all of the avant-garde artists developed Monk's ideas by working through his repertoire. Eric Dolphy is rarely associated with Monk; they never played together, and Dolphy recorded only four different Monk compositions—and only one of those as a leader.[9] Yet, in some ways, Dolphy worked more to advance Monk's harmonic ideas than his saxophonist contemporaries who attributed much of their music development to Monk—namely, Rollins and Coltrane. Flutist/composer James Newton was one of the few observers to make the Dolphy–Monk connection. In the liner notes to Dolphy's *Other Aspects* (previously unreleased recordings discovered posthumously), Newton (1987) observed: "One point that is not dealt with too often is the influence of Thelonius [*sic*] Monk on Dolphy. Monk's incredibly advanced timbral knowledge would lead him to use the full range of the piano. As with Ellington, it is not uncommon for a Monk phrase to cover three or four octaves. Each register's color has a strong tie to what is trying to be accomplished rhythmically and emotionally. The same qualities that are often inadequately called 'angular' can be found in Eric's playing." Careful listening to Dolphy's improvisations on bass clarinet and alto saxophone bears this out. Like Monk, Dolphy often employed whole-tone scales, and his tendency to explore the upper structures of chords (ninths, elevenths, thirteenths) created minor- and major-second intervals that became Monk's trademark. Dolphy's composition "Hat and Beard" from his *Out to Lunch* album suggests that he listened to Monk's music and developed a clear conception of what lay at its core. Recorded in February 1964 with Dolphy (bass clarinet), Freddie Hubbard (trumpet), Bobby Hutcherson (vibes), Richard Davis (bass), and Tony Williams (drums), "Hat and Beard" was not the sort of piece that Monk would have embraced, despite the many compositional and harmonic affinities with his music. Although composed in the "free jazz" idiom with obvious shifts in time signature (it begins in $\frac{5}{4}$, moves to $\frac{9}{4}$, and eventually evolves into a more free-form rhythm), the theme of "Hat and Beard" works somewhat like Monk's "Friday the Thirteenth" in that the bass counterpoint is played so forcefully against the melody that it emerges as the principal motive. And while the tonal center fades in and out during improvisations (supported by Davis's strong bass playing), the theme outlines a G7($\sharp$5)–E$\flat$7($\flat$5) giving the song's opening statement a whole-tone feel.

"Hat and Beard" reveals Dolphy's conception of the essential elements in Monk's music, and at the same time, it tells us how he—together with Hubbard, Hutcherson, Davis, and Williams—could use these elements to find openings for freer improvisations. Another example to consider in this light is Dolphy's version of "Epistrophy," recorded in the Netherlands in 1964 with pianist Misha Mengelberg (released on Dolphy's *Last Date*). What makes this recording so fascinating is that the Ukranian-born Mengelberg, one of Holland's leading avant-garde musicians/composers, plays so much like Monk that one could almost imagine what a Dolphy/Monk collaboration might sound like. Dolphy develops an extremely chromatic solo on bass clarinet, which works well with the piece's chromatic melody. Meanwhile, Mengelberg's comping is somewhat Monkian—sparse clusters, dissonant block chords, tremolos, insistent restatements of the melody. Dolphy moves further outside when he returns to trade eighths with the drummer and then turns the melody "inside out" by coming in on the first beat of the measure rather than the second. (After a couple of choruses, it all works itself out, although it is not clear if Dolphy's early entry was intentional or not.) Mengelberg sounds even more Monkish on his original composition titled "Hypochristmutreefuzz." Although the piece was not intended as a Monk tribute, he and Dolphy play it as if it were. Built on a descending chromatic chord progression similar to Monk's "Thelonious," Mengelberg's solo and comping are full of whole-tone phrases, tritone and minor-ninth intervals, and a storehouse of quotes lifted directly from Monk.

Monk's musical spirit appears in another of Dolphy's collaborations, this one with pianist Andrew Hill. Hill grew up in Chicago and found his way to the avant-garde via various R&B and bebop bands in the 1950s. By the early 1960s, he was drawn to experimental music; moving away from chord progressions, he began composing works based on a single tonal center around which musicians could remain or leave. Hill drew much of his inspiration, especially as a composer, from Monk. He told writer A. B. Spellman (1963), "Monk's like Ravel and Debussy to me, in that he's put a lot of personality into his playing, and no matter what the technical contributions of Monk's music are, it is the personality of the music which makes it, finally." Monk's personality is quite apparent in Hill's "McNeil Island," recorded on *Black Fire*, his first album as a leader. Accompanied by Joe Henderson (tenor saxophone), Richard Davis (bass), and Roy Haynes (drums), Hill constructs a ballad akin to "Monk's Mood" and "Crepuscule with Nellie." Henderson and Hill play the melody in unison in a slow, halting rubato tempo, over Davis's area bass. Hill fills in the space with bass counterpoint, arpeggios, and truncated runs, occasionally landing on an isolated seventh or ninth in the bass—"orchestral" strategies characteristic of Monk. And like Monk, all of Hill's "fills" seem to have been carefully composed.

Dolphy's collaboration with Hill took place about six months after "McNeil Island" was recorded and one month after Dolphy recorded "Hat and Beard" (and, incidentally, one month after Monk's *Time* profile). Hill led the date but used the rhythm section with which Dolphy had worked the previous month—namely, Richard Davis on bass and Tony Williams on drums. Besides Dolphy, he hired Joe Henderson again on tenor saxophone and Kenny Dorham, who replaced Hubbard on trumpet. Thus, only weeks after making "Hat and Beard," some of the same band members found themselves exploring one of Hill's most Monk-influenced pieces, "New Monastery," which apparently got its name after Frank Wolff of Blue Note remarked that the tune reminded him of "something Thelonious Monk wrote long ago" (quoted in Hentoff 1964b). "New Monastery" does contain hints of Monk's "Locomotive" and "Played Twice." The horns simultaneously play slightly different countermelodies over Hill's simple motive, which shifts back and forth between intervals of a perfect fourth and augmented fourth (tritone). Hill's two-note phrase is constantly displaced, rhythmically and harmonically, for it floats up and down the keyboard along with the tonal center. The work's structure is unusual: twenty-two bars consisting of two A sections of eleven bars each. Like Monk, Hill keeps returning to the theme when he's comping and soloing. And although the song lacks a fixed tonal center, the augmented fourth emphasizes whole-tone harmony (particularly on Dolphy's solos) while the perfect fourth creates a sense of suspension. Although "New Monastery" contains many elements of Monk's sound and compositional techniques, there is no mistaking Hill's tune for the music to which he is playing tribute. Unlike "McNeil Island," Hill does not try to reproduce Monk's sound here. It does swing in places, but the goal of this tune and all of Hill's composi- tions on *Point of Departure* is freedom. Indeed, because Davis and Williams are not concerned with sustaining the pulse or keeping steady tempos, rhythmically they bring the same energy and freedom they had brought to Dolphy's *Out to Lunch* session that produced "Hat and Beard." Hill recalled, "I was certainly freer rhythmically. And the way I set up the tunes, it was more possible for the musicians to get away from chord patterns and to work around tonal centers. So harmonically too, the set is freer" (quoted in Hentoff 1964a). Thus, like so many artists of the 1960s avant-garde, Hill and Dolphy were quite willing to jettison traditional notions of swing and functional harmony in the name of freedom.

Coda

During one of his infamous "blindfold tests," Leonard Feather played for Monk "Flight 19" from Andrew Hill's *Point of Departure* (Feather 1966). The recording apparently bored Monk; he looked out the window, complimented Feather on his stereo system, and made no comment whatsoever about Hill's playing or the song. Monk's reaction to Hill, which took place in 1966, is telling. As much as I would like to imagine Monk recording with Ornette Coleman and Don Cherry, Eric Dolphy, Archie Shepp, Henry Grimes, Buell Neidlinger,

Steve Lacy, and Roswell Rudd in a small combo, Monk had no such interest in collaborating with the avant-garde. His opposition to the new music was primarily aesthetic. As I have attempted to demonstrate, neither professional jealousy, fame, nor what has wrongly been identified as Monk's conservatism or apolitical attitudes adequately explains why those collaborations never happened (although the latter certainly shaped the ways in which critics and fans responded to him in the early 1960s). Certainly, Columbia's interest in making Monk as salable as possible served as a much greater fetter for such collaborations.

To find our answers, we have to understand and acknowledge Monk's deep investment in his musical conception. In some ways, Monk can be seen as an architect who built a unique structure to house his music. The jazz avant-garde was interested in demolishing all houses, letting the music sprawl out into the expanse. Yet it was through his Old Monastery, if you will—equipped with so many windows and doors in unusual places—that this new generation of artists could *see* the expanse, could imagine the emancipation of the music from functional harmonies, standard song forms and time signatures, and Western notions of musicality. The irony is not that they found avenues to freedom in such highly structured music or that Monk could not see all the possibilities his music had to offer. Rather, it is that the avant-garde helped create Monk's audience, contributing indirectly to his canonization and rise to fame, yet they could hardly make a living playing his music—let alone their own.

Notes

This essay would never have been published had it not been for the insights and suggestions of T. J. Anderson, Dwight Andrews, Anthony Davis, Ann Douglas, Maxine Gordon, Farah Jasmine Griffin, James Hall, George Lipsitz, Eric Porter, Ron Radano, Guthrie Ramsey, Paula Giddings, Robert G. O'Meally, Franklin Rosemont, Mark Tucker, Michael Washington, Randy Weston, Arthur Woods, the entire Columbia Jazz Study Group, and the participants in the University of North Carolina symposium on Monk.

1. Monk actually opened at the Five Spot on July 4, 1957, with a trio consisting of himself, Frankie Dunlop, and Wilbur Ware; Coltrane did not join the group until July 18. Wilbur Ware stayed on until the second week of August, when he was fired for failing to appear. Ahmed Abdul-Malik subsequently replaced Ware, and Shadow Wilson replaced Frankie Dunlop, who at the time was having problems with the musicians' union. There were also other replacements and various artists sitting in, including drummers Max Roach, Art Blakey, Willie Jones, Philly Joe Jones, and Kenny Dennis; French horn player Julius Watkins; and alto saxophonist Sahib Shihab (Porter 1998, 109–110).

Larry Rivers takes credit for persuading the Termini brothers to hire Monk, although his account is questionable. For example, he claims that Monk was the first black musician to perform there and that Rivers suggested Monk because "jazz is black." He makes no mention of Cecil Taylor or Randy Weston, who performed there in 1956 (Rivers 1992, 341–342).

2. My arguments here draw mainly from McClary (1991). McClary's analysis is far more nuanced than what is presented here and, in fact, can account for black/white opposition

because she maintains that the Other need not always be interpreted as female. Rather, the dissonant Other can stand for anything that is an obstacle and must be brought into submission. On the other hand, these readings of masculinity in jazz position the black voice as heroic and ultimately masculine. Charles Ford's study of Mozart's operas offers an alternative approach to gendering music that might better explain dissonance as masculinity. For him the dominant modulation—the leap to the augmented fourth (tritone interval)—is a masculine move because it connotes struggle and striving. He also suggests that metric dynamism is masculine, whereas "decorative stasis" connotes femininity (Ford 1991). Both of these elements are characteristic of Monk's music—composed and improvised (see also Green 1997, 117–121). Whether any of these readings are "right" has no bearing on my point, however, which is to introduce ways in which critics and/or musicians make gendered meanings out of harmonic and rhythmic elements. One excellent example of a gender analysis of music that consistently accounts for race and class is Davis (1998).

3. Examples of avant-garde recordings of Monk's music or tributes to him include Cecil Taylor's 1956 recording of "Bemsha Swing" on *Jazz Advance;* New York Contemporary Five's 1963 recording of "Monk's Mood" and "Crepuscule with Nellie" on *Archie Shepp: The New York Contemporary Five;* Don Cherry and John Coltrane's 1960 recording of "Bemsha Swing" on *The Avant-Garde;* Andrew Hill's 1964 recording of "New Monastery" on *Point of Departure;* and Charles Mingus's "Jump Monk" (1956) on *Mingus at the Bohemia* and "Monk, Bunk, and Vice Versa" (which Mingus sometimes called "Monk, Funk, and Vice Versa") on *Epitaph.* Lead sheets for Mingus's tunes can be found in Sue Mingus (1991).

4. The controversy led to a panel discussion on "Racial Prejudice in Jazz" that included Gitler, Lincoln, Nat Hentoff, Max Roach, and *Down Beat* editor Don DeMichael. The exchange turned quite nasty, with Gitler defending his review (and defending the fact that he never interviewed Lincoln but based his critique on Hentoff's liner notes) and DeMichael raising the issue of "Crow Jim"—the idea that white musicians were being discriminated against. Of course, white critics nervous about the presence of black nationalist sentiment in jazz directed most of their criticism at artists identified with the avant-garde (see for example, Gitler 1965, 8; Hentoff 1966, 36–39; Jones 1963, 143–152). In other words, the white critical insistence that jazz ought to be "color blind" is hardly new (see Gennari 1991; Gennari 1993; Kofsky 1998,83–122; Panish 1997).

5. This is not to say that he did not borrow progressions from pop tunes: "In Walked Bud" is based on "Blue Skies," "Let's Call This" on "Sweet Sue," "Hackensack" on "Lady Be Good," "Rhythm-n-ing" on "I Got Rhythm," "Evidence" on "Just You, Just Me," and "Bright Mississippi" on "Sweet Georgia Brown." Nevertheless, even the borrowed changes were altered so significantly through unique voicings and substitutions that they often bore only a passing resemblance to the original.

6. Critic Michel-Claude Jalard (1960) linked Monk, Cecil Taylor, and Duke Ellington together precisely because of their strong use of the left hand, although he argues that they do not use it to the same effect.

7. To be fair, Schuller's essay enthusiastically praised Monk and defended his technique at every point. Indeed, the statement to which Taylor refers was made in a footnote. Nevertheless, although Taylor's reading of Schuller's piece may not do justice to Schuller's arguments and intentions, he does hit upon the very real and pervasive problem of racism in jazz criticism.

8. Unfortunately, there are no extant recordings of this group, which included Charlie Rouse on tenor saxophone and the inimitable Roy Haynes on drums.

9. Altogether, Dolphy recorded a version of "'Round Midnight" with John Lewis's Orchestra (September 1960) and another version with George Russell (May 1961); "Blue Monk" with

Abbey Lincoln (February 1961); and "Epistrophy" as a leader with Misha Mengelberg, Jacques Schols, and Han Bennink (June 1964). He was also a featured soloist on Gunther Schuller's "Variants on a Theme of Thelonious Monk (Criss Cross)" (Simosko and Tepperman 1996, 108, 110–111, 112, 126).

Discography

Cherry, Don, and John Coltrane. *The avant-garde.* Atlantic SD 1451 (1960).

Coleman, Ornette. *Beauty is a rare thing: The complete Atlantic recordings of Ornette Coleman.* Rhino Records R2 71410 (1993).

Coltrane, John. *Coltrane time.* Blue Note CDP 7 84461 2 (1958).

Dolphy, Eric. *Last date.* Fontana 822 226 2 (1964).

———. *Other aspects.* Blue Note CDP 7 480412 (1987).

———. *Out to lunch.* Blue Note CDP 7 46524 2 (1964).

Hill, Andrew. *Black fire.* Blue Note CDP 7 841512 (1963).

———. *Point of departure.* Blue Note CDP 7 84167 2 (1964).

Lacy, Steve. *Evidence.* Prestige NJ-8271 (1961).

———. *Reflections: Steve Lacy plays Thelonious Monk.* Prestige 8206 (1958).

———. *The straight horn of Steve Lacy.* Barnaby/Candid Jazz BR-5013 (1960).

Lacy, Steve, and Roswell Rudd Quartet. *School days.* Hat Hut Records CD 6140 ([1963]1995).

Mingus, Charles. *Epitaph.* Columbia C2K-45428 (1991).

———. *Mingus at the Bohemia.* Debut 123 (1956).

Monk, Thelonious. *The complete Blue Note recordings.* Blue Note CDP 830363.

———. *Thelonious Monk: Always know.* Columbia 469185 2 (1979).

———. *Monk.* Prestige 7053 (1954).

———. *Thelonious Monk / Sonny Rollins.* Prestige 7075 (1954).

New York Contemporary Five. *Archie Shepp: The New York Contemporary Five.* Storyville STCD 8209 ([1963]1991).

Taylor, Cecil. *Jazz advance.* Blue Note CDP 7 84462 2 (1956).

———. *At Newport.* Verve MGV8238 (1958).

———. *Looking ahead!* Contemporary 7562 (1959).

———. *New York City R&B.* Candid CCD-79017 (1961).

———. *Unit structures.* Blue Note CDP 7 85237 2 (1966).

References

Baker, Malcolm Lynn. 1986. "Black nationalism and free jazz collectives: The black musician's approach to economic self-determination." *Jazz Research Papers* [6]: 24–29.

Bartlett, Andrew W. 1995. "Cecil Taylor, identity energy, and the avant-garde African American body." *Perspectives of New Music* 33 (Winter/Summer): 274–293.

Bassell, John. 1966. "Encounter: an interview with Thelonious Monk and Delores Wilson." *Toronto Telegram* (November 12): 9.

Blake, Ran. 1982. "The Monk piano style." *Keyboard* 8 (July): 26–30.

Block, Steven. 1990. "Pitch-class transformation in free jazz." *Music Theory Spectrum* 12, no. 2: 181–202.

———. 1993. "Organized sound: Pitch-class relations in the music of Ornette Coleman." *Annual Review of Jazz Studies* 6: 229–252.

Brown, Frank London. 1958. "More man than myth, Monk has emerged from the shadows." *Down Beat* (October 30): 13–16,45–46.

Buin, Yves. 1988. *Thelonious Monk*. Paris: P.O.L.

Carles, Philippe, and Jean-Louis Comolli. 1971. *Free jazz / Black power*. Paris: Editions Champ Libre.

Coleman, Ornette. 1993. Liner notes, *Beauty is a rare thing: The complete Atlantic records of Ornette Coleman*. Rhino Records R271410.

Coss, Bill. 1961. "Cecil Taylor's struggle for existence: Portrait of the artist as a coiled spring." *Down Beat* (October 26): 19–21.

Danson, Peter. 1982. Roswell Rudd. *Coda* [183] (April): 4–9.

Davis, Angela Y. 1998. *Blues legacies and black feminism: Gertrude "Ma" Rainey, Bessie Smith, and Billie Holiday*. New York: Pantheon.

de Jong, Nanette. 1997. "Chosen identities and musical symbols: The Curacaoan jazz community and the Association for the Advancement of Creative Musicians." Ph.D. diss., University of Michigan.

de Toledano, Ralph. 1965. "Thelonious Monk and some others." *National Review* (October 19): 940–941.

de Wilde, Laurent. 1997. *Monk*. New York: Marlowe.

DeVeaux, Scott. 1997. *The birth of bebop: A social and musical history*. Berkeley: University of California Press.

Ehrenreich, Barbara. 1983. *The hearts of men: American dreams and the flight from commitment*. London: Routledge.

Farrell, Barry. 1964. "The loneliest Monk." *Time* 83 (February 28): 84–88.

Feather, Leonard. 1966. "Blindfold test, T. Monk." *Down Beat* (April 21): 39.

Fitterling, Thomas. 1997. *Thelonious Monk: His life and music*. Berkeley, Calif.: Berkeley Hills Books.

Floyd, Samuel A., Jr. 1995. *The power of black music: Interpreting its history from Africa to the United States*. New York: Oxford University Press.

Ford, Charles. 1991. *Cosi? Sexual politics in Mozart's operas*. Manchester [England]: Manchester University Press.

Ford, Clebert. 1964. "Black nationalism and the arts." *Liberator* 4, no. 2 (February): 14–16.

Gennari, John. 1991. "Jazz criticism: Its development and ideologies." *Black American Literature Forum* 25, no. 3 (Fall): 449–523.

———. 1993. "The politics of culture and identity in American jazz criticism." Ph.D. diss., University of Pennsylvania.

Gervais, Raymond, and Yves Bouliane. 1977. Interview with Steve Lacy. Translated by Effie Mihopolous. *Brilliant Corners: A Magazine of the Arts* 5 (Spring): 77–112.

Gitler, Ira. 1958. Liner notes, *Reflections: Steve Lacy plays Thelonious Monk*. Prestige 8206.

———. 1961. "Focus on Steve Lacy." *Down Beat* (March 2): 15, 46.

———. 1962. "Racial prejudice in jazz." *Down Beat* (May 24): 24.

———. 1965. "Chords and discords: To Hentoff from Gitler." *Down Beat* (September 9): 8.

Goldberg, Joe. 1965. *Jazz masters of the 50's*. New York: Macmillan.

Goodman, Alan. 1976. "Thelonious gestalt: Monk disrobed." *Crawdaddy* [66] (November): 72.

Gourse, Leslie. 1997. *Straight, no chaser: The life and genius of Thelonious Monk*. New York: Schirmer.

Green, Lucy. 1997. *Music, gender, education*. Cambridge, England: Cambridge University Press.

Haywood, Mark S. 1994–95. "Rhythmic readings in Thelonious Monk." *Annual Review of Jazz Studies* 7: 25–45.

Heckman, Don. 1964. "Roswell Rudd." *Down Beat* (January 30): 14–15.

Hentoff, Nat. 1961. Liner notes, Steve Lacy, *Evidence*. Prestige NJ-8271.

———. 1964a. Liner notes, Eric Dolphy, *Out to lunch*. Blue Note CDP 7 46524 2.

———. 1964b. Liner notes, Andrew Hill, *Point of departure* CDP 7 84167 2.

———. 1966. "New jazz: Black, angry, and hard to understand." *New York Times Magazine* December 25:36–39.

———. 1995. *Listen to the stories*. New York: HarperCollins.

Hodeir, André. 1986. *Toward jazz*. Translated by Noel Burch. 1962. Reprint, New York: Da Capo Press.

Hunt, David C. 1974. "Black voice lost in white superstructure." *Coda* 11, no. 6 (February): 12–14.

Jackson, Harriet. 1965. "Daniel Nagrin, at YM-YWHA, New York, April 24." *Dance News* 46, no. 6 (June): 13.

Jalard, Michel-Claude. 1960. "Trois apôtres du discontu." *Jazz Magazine* 6, no. 65 (December): 42–46, 63.

Joans, Ted. 1995. Interview with the author. New York, December 15.

Jones, LeRoi [Amiri Baraka]. 1963. "White critics, black musicians, new music." *African Revolution* 1, no. 6 (October): 143–152.

———. 1964. "The acceptance of Monk." *Down Beat* 31, no. 6 (February 27): 20–22. (Reprinted in LeRoi Jones, *Black music* [New York: Quill, 1967], 26–34.)

———. 1967. *Black music*. New York: Quill.

Jost, Ekkehard. 1994. *Free jazz*. 1975. Reprint, New York: Da Capo Press.

Kelley, Robin D. G. 1997. "Dig they freedom: Meditations on history and the black avant-garde." *Lenox Avenue* 3 (Winter): 13–27.

Koch, Lawrence. 1983. "Thelonious Monk: Compositional techniques." *Annual Review of Jazz Studies* 2: 67–80.

Kofsky, Frank. 1998. *Black music, white business: Illuminating the history and the political economy of jazz*. New York: Pathfinder Press.

Kotlowitz, Robert. 1961. "Monk talk." *Harper's Magazine* 223 (November 15): 21–23.

Kteily-O'Sullivan, Laila Rose. 1990. "Klangfarben, rhythmic displacement, and economy of means: A theoretical study of the works of Thelonious Monk." M.M. thesis, University of North Texas.

Kurzdorfer, James. 1996. "Outrageous clusters: Dissonant semitonal cells in the music of Thelonious Monk." *Annual Review of Jazz Studies* 8: 181–201.

Lacy, Bobbie. 1964. "Introducing Steve Lacy." In *Jazz panorama: From the pages of* The Jazz Review, edited by Martin Williams, 268–272. New York: Collier.

Lacy, Steve. 1963. "The land of Monk." *Down Beat* (October 10): 14–15.

———. 1995. Interview with the author, Paris, May 12.

Langford, Jef. 1971a. "Monk's horns, part II." *Jazz Journal* 24 (January): 7–8.

———. 1971b. "Monk's horns, part III." *Jazz Journal* 24 (February): 3–4.

Lapham, Lewis H. 1964. "Monk: High priest of jazz." *Saturday Evening Post* 237 (April 11): 70.

Levin, Robert. 1965. "The Jazz Composer's Guild: An assertion of dignity." *Down Beat* (May 6): 18.

———. 1991. Liner notes, *Coltrane Time*. Blue Note B2-84461.

Lewis, George. 1996. "Improvised music after 1950: Afrological and Eurological perspectives." *Black Music Research Journal* 16, no. 1: 91–122.

Liner notes. 1994. Steve Lacy and the Roswell Rudd Quartet, *School Days*. Hat Hut 6140.

Litweiler, John. 1984. *The freedom principle: Jazz after 1958*. New York: Quill.

———. 1992. *Ornette Coleman: A harmolodic life*. New York: William Morrow.

Mailer, Norman. 1957. "The white Negro." *Dissent* 5 (November). (Reprinted in Norman Mailer, *Advertisements for myself* [New York: Putnam, 1959], 337–358.)

McClary, Susan. 1991. *Feminine endings: Music, gender, and sexuality*. Minneapolis: University of Minnesota Press.

McRae, Barry. 1975. "Roswell Rudd: All the way from Dixie." *Jazz Journal* 28 (May): 20–22.

Mehegan, John. 1963. "Crepuscule with Monk." Held in the Monk vertical files, Institute for Jazz Studies, Rutgers University.

Miller, Mark. 1988. "Cecil Taylor: Musician poet dancer." *Coda* [220] (June/July): 4–6.

Mingus, Sue, ed. 1991. *Mingus: More than a fake book*. New York: Jazz Workshop.

Monson, Ingrid. 1995. "The problem with white hipness: Race, gender, and cultural conceptions in jazz historical discourse." *Journal of American Musicological Society* 48, no. 3 (Fall): 396–422.

———. 1999. "Monk meets SNCC." *Black Music Research Journal* 19, no. 1: 61–74.

Morgenstern, Dan, and Martin Williams. 1964. "The October revolution: Two views of the avant-garde in action." *Down Beat* (November 19): 15, 33.

Neal, Lawrence P. 1965. "Black revolution in music: A talk with drummer Milford Graves." *Liberator* 5, no. 9 (September): 14–15.

Newton, James. 1987. Liner notes, Eric Dolphy, *Other Aspects*. Blue Note B2–48041.

Panish, Jon. 1997. *The color of jazz: Race and representation in postwar American culture*. Jackson: University Press of Mississippi.

Pekar, Harvey. 1963. "Experimental collective improvisation." *Jazz Journal* 16 (November): 8–9.

Pontiflet, Theodore H. 1964. "The American way." *Liberator* 4, no. 6 (June): 8–9.

Ponzio, Jacques, and François Postif. 1995. *Blue Monk: Un portrait de Thelonious*. Paris: Actes Sud.

Porter, Eric. 1997. "'Out of the blue': Black creative musicians and the challenge of jazz, 1940–1995." Ph.D. diss., University of Michigan.

Porter, Lewis. 1998. *John Coltrane: His life and music*. Ann Arbor: University of Michigan Press.

Priestley, Brian. 1984. *Mingus: A critical biography*. 1982. Reprint, New York: Da Capo Press.

Radano, Ronald. 1985. "The jazz avant-garde and the jazz community: Action and reaction." *Annual Review of Jazz Studies* 3: 71–79.

———. 1993. *New musical figurations: Anthony Braxton's cultural critique*. Chicago: University of Chicago Press.

Reeve, Stephen. 1969. "The new piano in the new jazz." *Jazz Journal* 22 (September): 25.

Riley, Ben, and Quincy Troupe. 1998. "When the music was happening then he'd get up and do his little dance." In *The jazz cadence of American culture*, edited by Robert G. O'Meally, 102–110. New York: Columbia University Press.

Rivers, Larry, with Arnold Weinstein. 1992. *What did I do? The unauthorized autobiography of Larry Rivers*. New York: HarperCollins.

Ross, Andrew. 1989. *No respect: Intellectuals and popular culture*. London: Routledge.

Russell, Charlie L. 1964. "Has jazz lost its roots?" *Liberator* 4, no. 8 (August): 4–7.

Schuller, Gunther. 1964. "Thelonious Monk." In *Jazz panorama*, edited by Martin Williams, 216–238. New York: Collier.

Sidran, Ben. 1995. *Talking jazz: An oral history*. Expanded ed. New York: Da Capo Press.

Silsbee, Kirk. 1987. "Thelonius [sic]: Exploring the Monk canon." *L.A. Reader* (February 20): 8–9.

Simosko, Vladimir, and Barry Tepperman. 1996. *Eric Dolphy: A musical biography and discography*. Rev. ed. New York: Da Capo Press.

Somers, Steven. 1988. "The rhythm of Thelonious Monk." *Caliban* [4]: 44–49.

Spellman, A. B. 1963. Liner notes, Andrew Hill, *Black Fire*. Blue Note CDP 7 84151 2.

———. 1966. *Four lives in the bebop business.* New York: Pantheon.

Such, David G. 1993. *Avant-garde jazz musicians performing "out there."* Iowa City: University of Iowa Press.

Szwed, John. 1997. *Space is the place: The lives and times of Sun Ra.* New York: Pantheon.

Taylor, Arthur. 1993. *Notes and tones: Musician-to-musician interviews.* 1977. Reprint, New York: Da Capo Press.

Taylor, Cecil. 1966. "Sound structure of subculture becoming major breath/naked fire gesture." Liner notes, *Unit structures.* Blue Note CDP 7 84237 2.

Thelonious Monk Prestige 24006. 1972. Prestige Records press release (January). Held in the clippings file, Institute of Jazz Studies, Rutgers University.

Thomas, J. C. 1976. *Chasin' the Trane: The music and mystique of John Coltrane.* 1975. Reprint, New York: Da Capo Press.

Thomas, Lorenzo. 1995. "Ascension: Music and the Black Arts movement." In *Jazz among the discourses,* edited by Krin Gabbard, 256–274. Durham, N.C.: Duke University Press.

Weathers, Diane. 1973. "The collective black artists." *Black World* 22, no. 1 (November): 74–77.

Weston, Randy. 1999. Interview with the author, New York City, February 5.

Williams, Martin. 1963. "Thelonious Monk: Arrival without departure." *Saturday Review* [46] (April 13): 32–33.

———. 1964. "Thelonious Monk: Prelude to success." *Jazz* [3] (October): 8–10.

———. 1992. "What kind of composer was Thelonious Monk?" *Musical Quarterly* 76 (Fall): 433–441.

Wilmer, Valerie. 1977. *Jazz People.* New York: Da Capo Press.

———. 1980. *As serious as your life: The story of the new jazz.* Westport, Conn.: Lawrence Hill.

6

Production Line

(Excerpt)

NELSON GEORGE

From *Where Did Our Love Go? The Rise and Fall of the Motown Sound,* by Nelson George (2007)

From 1957 to 1963—the period of Berry Gordy's rise to prominence within the American record industry—black popular music was the industry's bastard child and mother lode, an esthetic and economic contradiction that was institutionalized by white record executives. The major labels—Decca, Columbia, RCA in New York, Mercury in Chicago, and Capitol in Los Angeles—all recorded a few black singers. Capitol had Nat "King" Cole, Columbia had Johnny Mathis, RCA had Sam Cooke, each of whom were known for crooning styles that owed much to the mellow Big Band vocal style epitomized by Frank Sinatra. Not that there was no art in this approach; Cole, Mathis, and Cooke all made many spellbinding, beautiful records. Still, anyone who had heard, for example, Cooke's gospel recordings with the Soul Stirrers, knew that there was a whole world of emotional power he had access to that his RCA recordings rarely tapped. Underneath the glistening strings, Broadway show tunes, and relaxed vocal styles was a music of intense feeling. In the spirit of the Eisenhower era, the major labels dismissed real black music as a curiosity, recording this gutsier style first as "race music," then as "blues," and by 1960 as "rhythm and blues," all on subsidiary lines, such as Columbia's Okeh Records, which were not pushed in the white marketplace. (Harry Belafonte's calypso ditties had in fact received more mainstream exposure and been extremely popular.) Blacks simply weren't considered good enough to sit in the front of the record industry bus with the Sinatras, Comos, and other white angels that men such as Columbia A&R director and television personality Mitch Miller so steadfastly supported. Like a bastard child, this music was shunted to a corner and left to fend for itself.

Yet, for all the prejudice aimed at blocking its growth, this rambunctious sound was quietly "poisoning" the minds of young white Americans. Its vehicles were small independent record companies, called "indies," usually owned by white entrepreneurs who knew that an expanding market existed for blues, gospel, and rhythm and blues. New York's Atlantic Records, founded by Ahmet and Nesuhi Ertegun, the sons of a Turkish diplomat, built an impressive enterprise, with Ray Charles, Ruth Brown, the Drifters, and the Coasters. Chicago's Chess Records had been catering successfully to black tastes with Muddy Waters and Howlin' Wolf, and to white teens with Chuck Berry and Bo Diddley, since the early 1950s. Fats Domino, a portly New Orleans pianist with a quavering tenor, a bluesy delivery, and access to the Crescent City's unceasing stream of rhythms, had found white and black fans by way of the Los Angeles–based Imperial label. The big labels knew that this music, labeled "rock and roll" by deejay Alan Freed, but really rhythm and blues in disguise, was making deep inroads into the youth market. Sam Phillips, with his Sun Records in Memphis, had taken the logical step of recording white singers, most prominently Elvis Presley and Jerry Lee Lewis, in this rock and roll style, sending a tremor through America's popular culture and tapping black music in ways that the big boys couldn't ignore. Presley's signing with RCA in 1955 could have been the moment that the majors went all the way, acknowledging the appeal of Presley *and* the musicians who had inspired him. Instead, after Presley, more white rock and rollers—and only a few blacks—made the leap. Lloyd Price, once a New Orleans R&B shouter, was suddenly cutting cutesy pop (like "Personality" for ABC-Paramount); most other blacks were left safely in their place on the indies.

During the seven years from 1957 to 1963, black music, performed by whites and blacks, was being either co-opted by the majors through whites in black face (or, in Presley's case, black shakes) or being picked up by adventurous young whites through airplay on rhythm and blues stations located on the AM dial's far right end.

In this environment, success for a black performer was characterized by sales of 45-rpm records in the 100,000 to 300,000 range, a lack of substantial album sales, headline status in a national network of ex-vaudeville houses in black neighborhoods (labeled "the chitlin circuit") and a rapid rise and fall. The indies found it more economical to emphasize hit records over hit singers, and so black music was rife with one-hit wonders and performers who bounced from label to label in search of hits. For all its wondrous musical energy, the world of black music was marked by chaos. When Berry sold one record to Chess, one to United Artists, and one to End, or when he used Smokey Robinson first as part of the Miracles and then as part of a duo (Ron & Bill), he wasn't innovating—he was just surviving in a business that demanded improvisation and flexibility.

Starting in 1963, Motown would change black music's position in the record industry and in American culture. The Motor Town Revue, shortened by now to the Motown Revue, was just a start. Over the next four years that gamble would be overshadowed by artistic and economic triumphs, triumphs made all the more amazing by the fact that Motown was owned and largely operated by blacks.

Until Motown, the history of black-owned record labels had been marked by frustration, cynicism, and unfulfilled potential. Black Swan, the first important black record company, had been founded in 1921 by Henry Pace and W. C. Handy, the latter a Northern bandleader who made his fortune committing blues songs he'd heard in the South to paper. The money he made from blues standards like "The St. Louis Blues" financed Black Swan's operations, including the hiring of famed big-band arranger-writer Fletcher Henderson as music director. While Pace and Handy recorded some "down-home" blues artists such as Trixie Smith, they had a definite crossover philosophy, as their recordings of the Broadway-flavored voice of Ethel Waters and the following ad attest:

> Only bonafide Racial Company making talking machine records. All stockholders are Colored, all artists are Colored, all employees are Colored. Only company using Racial Artists in recording high class song records. This company makes the only Grand Opera Records ever made by Negroes. All others confine this end of their work to blues, rags, comedy numbers, etc.

But, despite its potential (and Handy's dollars), Black Swan didn't last three years in competition with the two major labels, Columbia and Paramount, who had entered the "race" record market in the 1920s.

Don Robey's Duke–Peacock of Houston had no such upscale intentions. This tough former taxi-company owner specialized in the blues, recording Bobby "Blue" Bland, Junior Parker, O. V. Wright, and the late great Johnny Ace, as well as the young Little Richard. In his autobiography *Little Richard: The Quasar of Rock,* Little Richard says that Robey "would control the very breath that you breathed," and claims Robey punched Richard for talking back to him, giving the singer a hernia. Robey never made big money until he sold Duke–Peacock to ABC Records in 1972. Moreover, Bland, acknowledged master of the blues song, wasn't marketed to white audiences until after Robey had sold his company, thus becoming a victim of a profound lack of vision on Robey's part.

Chicago's Vee Jay Records, which in 1963 was bigger than Motown, took the chances that Duke–Peacock did not. Operated by James and Vivian Carter Bracken (and, later, with the aid of Harvey Fuqua's old friend Ewart Abner), Vee Jay seemed to have everything: solid R&B groups (the Dells, the Spaniels, the El Dorados), gutsy blues (John Lee Hooker did his most polished work for them), talented solo acts (Dee Clark, Gene "Duke of Earl" Chandler, Betty Everett, Jerry Butler), and some extremely popular white groups (the Four Seasons, and the Beatles' first American single, "Please Please Me"). But Vee Jay, in graphic contrast to Motown, was a poorly run family-owned company.

"Vee Jay could have been bigger than Motown," claims one black radio veteran, "but they wasted money." One case in point is the free junket to Las Vegas that Vee Jay sponsored for twelve influential R&B deejays in the early sixties. One participant remembers, "They asked us what we wanted. The guys didn't want free poker chips or liquor. They wanted women." So Vee Jay flew in twelve tall blondes from Oslo, Norway, via the North Pole to Los Angeles to Las Vegas, for a Friday, Saturday, and Sunday of fun. The deejays left for work happy on Monday morning. "They could have been bigger than Motown, but," the participant concluded, "they needed a bookkeeper." Eventually, the costs of maintaining Vee Jay's huge building on Chicago's Michigan Avenue as well as its large roster of talent, combined with the traditional hostility of the white distributors toward a black company, led Vee Jay into bankruptcy by 1965.

What was Motown's edge, the difference that made it work where so many others had failed? It was Berry Gordy, the talent he acquired, both on record and backstage, and the way in which he organized and motivated his personnel. In the fall of 1963 Berry was, at thirty-four, a veteran at songwriting, at production, and at dealing with checks that never came. His once directionless energy was now focused. The examples of achievement set by his father and mother, as well as the family lore about his grandfather, were inspirations to him.

Berry created an "all for one and one for all" atmosphere in this period at Motown that, for all its sentimentality, appealed greatly to young black men and women. It is easy to say that Berry was a "father figure" to his staff, and for some of the company's members—Smokey for one—there may be some truth to that description. But, more accurately, Berry was Motown's "corporate hero," a man who espoused certain beliefs, represented certain values, and made sure everyone around him knew and believed in them, too. He did so by emphasizing his accomplishments, exuding a confidence that bordered on arrogance, and brimming over with a strange charisma.

To most people who met Berry, that quality wasn't always immediately apparent. He spoke in a flat, slightly nasal manner, with a halting cadence that was rarely eloquent. Those who, because of his achievements, expected a bigger man, were often surprised by his shortness. Despite these handicaps, when Berry spoke about something that fascinated him—songwriting, performing, a sales report, or a sporting contest (be it boxing, baseball, or blackjack)—he could be mesmerizing.

Sitting at the head of a table or standing up, suddenly towering over his seated employees at the Monday morning staff meetings, Berry made himself a symbol of what could be attained and the desire it would take to make it. Berry also liked to illustrate his control of the company—by vetoing release of a record that his sixty or so staffers liked, by forcing a reluctant executive to sing the company song ("Hitsville, U.S.A."), or by surprising the loyal composer of that song, Smokey Robinson, into tears by unexpectedly naming him vice-president at a 1962 staff meeting. Berry constantly talked about songwriting, about what was good and bad, instructing and, perhaps not coincidentally, reinforcing the myth of his own rise. Hadn't he been young and hungry once, as they now were? Look at him today. Berry wore expensive if poorly cut suits, had a confident, commanding air, and a rapid, self-important strut. Writing hits for Jackie Wilson had given Berry a reputation, but he'd taken it further than anyone could have imagined. For the young producer-writers—hungry cats like Norman Whitfield and Eddie Holland—Berry was a constant reminder of how successful a song could be. To the artists, he was a magic man who held the power to turn dreams into cold hard cash. To the young blacks in the area, he was a black man employing local people in a town where Henry Ford supplied almost all the jobs.

Though he never spoke about the issue overtly, Berry's rise in the early 1960s linked him with the civil rights movement. (Dr. Martin Luther King, Jr., once visited Motown briefly, and Berry would release his "I Have A Dream" speech, along with a few other civil rights–related albums throughout the decade.) Naively, some saw Motown as the entertainment-business equivalent of the National Association for the Advancement of Colored People, or the Southern Christian Leadership Conference. To them Motown wasn't just a job; it was part of a movement.

It was in this spirit that several Motown staffers once volunteered to pick the dandelions from the front lawns of 2648 West Grand Boulevard; in this spirit they gathered on weekends to cement their sense of identity. "In the early days we were a family, man," says pianist Earl Van Dyke. "We had so many good times together. That is the gospel. We had picnics, Christmas parties or we just hung out. There was a closeness there, man." Rodney Gordy, son of Robert Gordy, currently a Jobete staffer, remembers that picnics at Detroit's Belle Isle "would be the whole staff and friends of the staff and musicians and whoever. I think they started off as Gordy picnics and then kind of blossomed into Motown picnics. . . . There would be sack races, playing football, getting drunk and getting drunk and getting drunk. It was good clean fun." The athletic competition could get fierce. Clarence Paul broke an arm and Marvin Gaye fractured a foot playing "touch" football. Motown staffers were no less combative on Fridays at marathon poker games convened weekly at the home of Berry's secretary Rebecca Jowles, where Berry himself was one of the regulars. "We would be there the whole weekend," says Van Dyke, "just drinking, eating barbecue, lying, dancing, playing cards, and just enjoying ourselves."

Looking back today, most black Motown veterans remember this period as a special golden time of laughing, of drinking—and of a warm feeling of blackness enveloping the company. Berry, however, had already learned a very valuable lesson about American business: his black enterprise needed whites inside it to prosper. Because of Berry's skin color, some may have romanticized his motives, but only if they misread his message. He was preaching success in 1963, not black success. Part of the Motown mystique has been that it was black-owned. It was, however, never entirely black-operated.

"First of all I make the money, it's my money," Berry once said to a black reporter who asked him why he hired whites. "I do what I want with it. But black people have shown a lack of understanding of what I'm doing as a general market businessman. They say, 'Why do you hire this white man, or why this or why that?' Because this white man can do what I've hired him for better than I can do it." Or, taking Berry's statement to its logical conclusion, better than any black he could have hired for the same job. Moreover, Berry's use of the phrase "general market businessman" in reference to his use of white employees shows that he felt whites were essential to helping Motown's sales and image outside the black community.

For all his hard work Berry played hard, too. His love of competition and risk, elements that had led him to pursue boxing as a career, manifest themselves in Berry's love of gambling. Ex-staff members say that once Motown was established it wasn't unusual for him to blow $50,000 to $100,000 a day in bets. They speculate that Berry's interest in Motown acts playing Las Vegas, at least partially, stemmed from his desire to be closer to the gaming tables. Representative of Berry's gambling obsession is a story told by Marvin Gaye, Beans Bowles, and others. In his biography, *Divided Soul,* Marvin related that "Berry's such a hardcore bettor that if you were in his office and it was raining, he'd pick out two raindrops that hit the window at the same time. He'd take one, you'd take the other, and he'd bet you ten bucks that his raindrop would slide down and hit the bottom of the window before yours."

Marvin also observed that for Berry power was an aphrodisiac. He thought "Berry was the horniest man in Detroit. . . . You'd think he was working, but he might be freaking with some chick up in his office." The singer, in addition, charged that Berry, like many black men in positions of power, was attracted to white women, as though possessing them was a symbol of their achievement. But Berry didn't flaunt his white liaisons, perhaps quite aware of his image in black America. "He married blacks," said Marvin, "and fooled around with whites."

Beginning with Barney Ales in distribution, whites became actively involved in the financial and administrative aspects of Motown. Ralph Seltzer, a lawyer and a friend of Ales, came aboard as a special assistant to the president, a vague title that gave him broad powers to dabble in all aspects of Motown's operations. Sidney Noveck was an accountant who eventually superseded George Edwards as chief supervisor of Motown and Jobete's books. His brother Harold Noveck, a lawyer, became an important Motown consultant. Ed Pollack, yet another lawyer, filled a number of administrative positions. In addition, Phil Jones and Irv Biegel, two promotion staffers, came in under Ales as part of Motown's expansion to some sixty employees by January 1963. Physically, Motown was expanding as well, adding buildings on both sides of West Grand Boulevard.

The effect this influx of whites had on Motown is captured in this story by Motown bandleader Choker Campbell: "We had been gone on tour ninety days. When we came back everything was in shipping and we brought all these bills and everything. The way my band was booked, each promoter sends a deposit of x amount of dollars before the tour went out. I would always say, 'Give me my band payroll and give me fifty dollars in pay and keep the rest of that money in escrow for me so when I come home I have a nice amount of money.'

"I come back. My car notes are behind two, three months. They're going to cut off my phone. They're going to cut off my lights. But I ain't worried about that 'cause I got to go on by there on a Sunday night and go down [to Motown] on Monday. When I go down there they say, 'Go to Barney.' I said, 'Where?' 'Oh, he's down the street two buildings.' 'Okay, where is International Talent Management?' 'Oh, it's the other building.'

"So I go to International Talent first and picked up a sixty-day tour. It opens up Tuesday at the Mosque Theater in Pittsburgh. That's fine. So next I go to finance to get my money and run downtown and pay my bills. I said to myself, 'Who is this?' When I walked in the door they say, 'Oh, Choker, you're the bandleader, right? I said, 'Right.' All the time saying to myself, 'Who the hell is these dudes?' So I said, 'I came to pick up my bread.' I opened my books. Seltzer came on over. My books tallied with his books.

"So he said, 'Fine, Choker, fine.' I said, 'Well, give me my check.' He says, 'Since you've been gone, Wednesday is finance day. No one gets any money except on Wednesday.' I said, 'Man, what are you talking about? I've been gone ninety days. I got to be in Pittsburgh Tuesday. And you tell me Wednesday is finance day. I want my money now.' And then we had a little problem there, but I got my money, you dig?"

Campbell was able to get Berry to intercede on his behalf, just as Berry would, over the next few years, often have to act as mediator in disputes between his black music makers and his growing white executive group. Over time, this tension would have a divisive effect on the company morale.

Undoubtedly, rumors linking Motown with organized crime coincided with this influx of whites into the company's management. According to legend, the Teamsters union loaned Motown money to pay some bills and never got out of the company. A now-defunct sixties magazine called *Rock* alleged that Berry had lost the company gambling in Puerto Rico and subsequently spent most of his time under house arrest. "Syndicate figures" reportedly tried to buy

Smokey's contract in the late sixties; Berry would say that "someone" offered to buy Smokey's contract for one million dollars cash. As a *Detroit Free Press* writer once put it, "Berry had almost as many hit rumors as hit records."

And the rumors have never stopped. It has, in fact, become a record industry truism that Motown is controlled by underworld figures; that they grabbed power at Motown by lending money to Berry when he was caught in a perilous cash flow bind similar to that of Harvey Fuqua's at Harvey Records; that Berry has been merely a figurehead at Motown, at least in financial terms, since about 1963.

Not an impossible scenario: organized crime has been involved with the entertainment industry since Prohibition. Las Vegas was reputedly the invention of racketeer Bugsy Siegel; New York's Copacabana, a symbol of success in mainstream entertainment to Motown in the sixties, was controlled by mobster Frank Costello (according to informer Joe Valachi). Many of the most chic discos of the seventies were created to launder money. In the entertainment industry it is unlikely that even the most honest citizen doesn't come into contact with some "underworld" figure. Owning a club or managing a superstar is a great way to hide money or camouflage any number of illegal activities.

However, despite twenty-five years of innuendos, there has never been any criminal investigation linking Motown to any segment of organized crime. Nor was Motown, a label that during the sixties would receive generous amounts of radio play, ever mentioned in any of the numerous payola scandals that have rocked pop music, particularly R&B, over the last quarter-century. Considering Motown's visibility since 1963, it is hard to imagine that the company has not been the subject of scrutiny from local, state, and federal law enforcement agencies (during this same period, black advancement proponents as diverse as Martin Luther King, Jr., and the Black Panthers were under covert investigation and attack by the FBI). It would have been a brilliant publicity coup for white prosecutors to catch Motown in bed with a criminal organization, and yet, in spite of the whispers, no mob connection has ever been proven.

Leaving aside the question of the validity of these rumors, it's interesting to note that, without any corroborating evidence, they have been so widely accepted. Perhaps it is hard for many to accept the idea that a black-owned company could be as successful as Motown. And in the early sixties, it was even harder to believe than it is today. Another aspect of Motown that has fueled outsiders' suspicions is the clannishness of Berry, his family, and the people who worked for him. Motown's lack of cooperation with the press is legendary. Artists, as we'll see, were trained *not* to give interviews of substance; for years, almost nothing about Motown—from the roles of its executives to the names of its musicians—was general knowledge. Berry's father, Pops, had encouraged self-reliance and togetherness. But Berry, Jr., instilled in his colleagues a suspicion of outsiders that bordered on paranoia. The rumors of underworld connections, though often denied, have never been aggressively attacked through a major public relations campaign, and this has given the company a subtly sinister mystique within the entertainment industry.

But whatever the rumors, the fact is that Berry Gordy wasn't a puppet manager; he was (and is) a powerful and demanding boss. If he gave you a job, you were expected to do it. If he gave you an assignment, you were expected to carry it out. He didn't usually care a great deal *how* it was accomplished. That was your problem. In fact, "That's your problem" is a phrase many former Motown employees associate with him. Or, as he explained his philosophy in 1969, "My point is to let them do their job and not get involved. When there is a situation that comes up and they want my view on it, then I would give them my view." He delegated authority easily, and the better the company did, the bigger the bonuses department heads received. Black people in business are traditionally perceived as doing a poor job of utilizing and motivating personnel. Usually self-made men, suspicious both of white authority and of black deceit or incompetence, black businesspeople tend to keep their hands on the backsides of everyone who works for them, stifling creativity in the process. In contrast, Berry's style allowed his lieutenants great autonomy—as long as they satisfied his demands.

"People had a lot more freedom then than I think the outside people realized," Lamont Dozier recalls. "[Berry] let you do what you wanted to do. You didn't have to get permission other than say, 'I want to go into the studio and I want to cut this.' Nobody looked at what you were doing. When you sent it to him finished, either he liked it or he didn't like it." Don Davis, a sometime session guitarist on early Motown recordings, remembers Berry lecturing him one day, "saying I wasn't cooperating enough with his producers. He said I was contributing a lot of ideas, 'But those guys down there are running the show.' He meant he had put them in charge and that I should go do what they say."

One of a series of mid-sixties weekly meetings between Berry, sales vice-president Barney Ales, A&R director Mickey Stevenson, and Billie Jean Brown—Whitfield's successor in quality control—to discuss the scheduling of new Motown releases provides a vivid picture of Gordy's management style and the power Ales and Stevenson wielded over their areas. One staffer remembers it as follows:

> The meeting opened with Barney Ales asking, "Where is the record?"
>
> "I gave it to your girl at quality control three days ago," says Stevenson. "You haven't heard it?"
>
> Berry turns to her. "Where is the record on the Miracles?"
>
> She reaches into the pile on her lap. "Oh, here it is."
>
> Berry takes it from her and puts it on his turntable behind his desk. Halfway through, he takes it off and says to Stevenson, "I thought you made a change."
>
> "She's got the changes on a tape dated two days later." Brown pulls it out. Ales interjects, "Come on. Give me the record. I got to get it on the street."

"You got your record, Barney."

"Thanks. Now where is the record on Marvin Gaye?" Ales asks.

"Well, where is it, Mickey?" says Berry.

"Nobody came up with anything worthwhile."

"You come up with it," Berry demands. "That's your problem."

"Okay," says Stevenson. "I'll have the record on Marvin by next Wednesday."

"Okay," says Ales. "I'll put the release down for two weeks from now." Then looking at his release schedule, he says, "But I don't want it then 'cause we already have the Supremes for then."

Berry moans. "Now Marvin's gonna go apeshit." He turns to Stevenson. "Okay, you have the problem 'cause you should have had the record. You go explain to him why it's not coming out."

Stevenson, trying not to reveal his dismay, says he'll handle it.

After the meeting, Stevenson asks Gaye to write and produce his next record himself, which, despite Gaye's immense musical gifts, Stevenson sometimes finds is like pulling teeth. Instead of asking Gaye directly, he takes him to dinner, and over drinks convinces Marvin to collaborate with him on a new song. A few days later, after the song's completion, Stevenson makes sure he lets Berry know he has completed his mission *ahead of schedule*. Berry may not have cared about the details, but his employees knew he rarely forgot an order.

"I got a surprise for you. I'm gonna have the Marvin Gaye record sooner than the next two weeks. If I go to Barney, you think he'll go on and put out the record?

"That's your problem," Gordy replies. Then he adds, "Let me hear the record first. Then if you can convince Barney, all right." Interestingly, Berry just wants to know if the record meets company standards; whether that particular record gets out or not is not his prime consideration. After Berry gives it his approval, Stevenson then stops by Barney Ales's house. Before playing it he builds it up, promoting its sales potential. At the end of their talk, Barney, all fired up about it, says, "That record belongs out. Let's put it on the market."

Further insight into Motown production comes from an unlikely source—Neil Young, founder of the pioneering folk-rock band Buffalo Springfield, and member of the late-sixties and early-seventies supergroup Crosby, Stills, Nash & Young. Young's first recording experience was at Motown, with the Mynah Birds, a Canadian band featuring future Springfield bassist Bruce Palmer and a long-haired, freaky-looking, rock-loving black dude named Ricky James. (The Mynah Birds were one of several white rock bands Motown would sign to no avail in the early to mid-sixties.)

We went in and recorded five or six nights, and if we needed something, or if they thought we weren't strong enough, a couple of Motown singers would just *walk* right in and they'd *Motown* us. A couple of 'em would be right there, and they'd sing the part. They'd just appear and we'd all do it together. If somebody wasn't confident or didn't have it, they didn't say, "Well, let's work on this." Some guy would just come in who had it. . . . And an amazing thing happened—we sounded hot.

Young recalls that they were the only group on Motown playing twelve-string guitars over the Motown beat. But if the music was different, the contract was standard Motown issue. "They had the hugest, *hugest,* most gargantuan contract you've ever seen in your life. Man, we were ushered into these offices, signing these huge publishing contracts. They still have my publishing: everything with the Mynah Birds," he recalled in 1984. However, the music never hit the street. At the time the single "It's My Time," was due out, Buffalo-born James was busted for draft evasion. Motown, fearful of bad publicity, cancelled its release. According to Young, none of the band members saw any income from the deal, since their manager took the money and "OD'd on our advance." Young and Palmer moved to L.A. and started Buffalo Springfield. James kept in contact with Motown, and, despite the bust, would re-sign with the label, not as a folk-rocker, but as a creation named Rick, not Ricky, James.

The A&R department was so active by 1964 that Stevenson downgraded his role as producer to concentrate on being a cheerleader-administrator. (And since the more hits Motown had, the more money he received in bonuses, this can be seen as enlightened self-interest.) But, on a deeper level, he saw Motown as very much *his* company; he recruited the session players and much of the talent, and he saw their triumphs as his triumphs.

Every Friday there would be a parade of writers and producers into Stevenson's office to give progress reports. If the Supremes needed a new song, he'd ask the Hollands and Lamont Dozier, "What's happening, man? We need some more tunes?" If producer Hank Cosby couldn't get studio time, Stevenson would rearrange the schedule to accommodate him. When Smokey complained that he couldn't find Benny Benjamin for a session, Stevenson would be on the phone to Van Dyke, telling him to chase Benny down. Significantly, while all these musical decisions were being made and these assignments handed out, there were, with the obvious exception of Smokey Robinson, never any artists present.

At night Stevenson would prowl Detroit, visiting Hitsville, nightclubs, and often the homes of Motown writers to check on how songs were developing— and they had better be developing, or the writers would catch hell. Even if a tune were coming along, Stevenson would put the pressure on, saying that it wasn't as good as H-D-H's or Smokey's latest effort, and if they didn't get it together he'd get laughed out of the next Monday morning meeting.

For the writer-producers, the feeling was one of constantly being scrutinized; if your music were consistently deemed inferior, ridicule and even dismissal were the consequences. In fact, encouraging this mentality was essential to the company's creative strength. Eddie Holland, for example, convinced his brother

Brian and Lamont Dozier to let him join their team by arguing that his presence as lyricist would accelerate their production process, making them more competitive with the other producer-writers—especially Smokey and Berry (who was then still spending a lot of time in the studio).

When an important act needed a hit, Motown would hold a contest to come up with that elusive hit song. The competition was keen. When the Temptations needed a breakthrough hit in 1964, Berry and Smokey battled to see who'd provide it. Driving back from a concert at the Apollo in New York, Bobby Rogers and Smokey composed a song while taking turns behind the wheel. When they arrived back in Detroit, they found Berry gloating. "Hey, look, I have got this great song on the Temptations, man," he said. "I have recorded it and know that it's gonna win the contest."

Smokey challenged him. "No, man," he said. "Give me two days, because I have got *the* song and I think it is going to wash your song away!" Smokey went down to the basement and cut it. A week later the contest was held with Mickey Stevenson, Clarence Paul, Harvey Fuqua, and about a dozen others sitting in judgment. Five records were played and only two got any votes; three people voted for Berry's now-forgotten ditty, and everyone else voted for Smokey and Bobby Rogers's "The Way You Do the Things You Do."

As a songwriter, Berry may have been somewhat chagrined to be so decisively defeated by his protege. But as Motown's president, he was delighted that "Things" established the Temptations as major hitmakers.

Even the annual Christmas shows at Detroit's Fox Theater were trials by fire. For five shows a day, over an entire week, Motown's top attractions attempted to outdo each other at Berry's instigation. He made it a point of honor that the better acts were placed later in the program. The only way they could be moved back "was if their act was so good that their applause drowned out the name of the following act," decreed Berry. All week long, between shows, while a movie was on, even while the artists were still onstage, Berry, his sisters, and anyone else in the Motown family could offer criticisms and suggest changes in each artist's show. Egos were hurt. Arguments were common. Everyone was forced to sharpen their presentation, which was just what Berry wanted in the first place.

This combative posture did have its dark side. Some writers suspected others of listening at keyholes to their compositions. There was talk of producers buying quality songs outright from low-level Jobete writers and putting their names on them, basking in the credit and collecting the royalties. Clarence Paul would later tell David Ritz that "tunes were stolen all the time, and often credit wasn't properly assigned." Later Beans Bowles would claim he deserved a writing credit on "Fingertips—Pt. 2." Marv Johnson told a Detroit newspaper that he, not Berry Gordy, wrote his hit "Come to Me." Yet in these two specific instances where rip-offs are charged, neither man has filed suit for back royalties.

Overall, this philosophy pushed the cream to the top and left the lazy far behind. Anything you got at Motown as a creative person you had to earn. The more Motown and Jobete grew, the more intense the competition was to get one's song used by hit artists. "The whole thing at the company was about competition," says Norman Whitfield, "and competition breeds giants."

This same spirited, aggressive attitude permeated the sales department. At one point Loucye Gordy Wakefield had to organize Motown's accounts receivable, and she is credited by Berry and Esther with keeping Motown solvent in the days when more records were being ordered and pressed than were being paid for by distributors. But by 1964, and certainly after Loucye's death in 1965, it was Barney Ales's persona and methods that dominated sales. Ales took no crap, demanding respect and Motown's money from the distributors (at Motown's height in the early sixties the label dealt with as many as thirty-three).

"I'd hear him on the telephone," says one Motown vet. "'Goddamn it, I want that record moved!' he'd say. That record would move, man. He would say, 'What do you mean? I don't want to hear that fucking shit!'" Ales manipulated distributors, threatening to delay or withhold hot recordings in their area, even saying that he'd change distributors in a particular area if payments were late or incomplete.

"You can always get your money when you're hot," says CBS vice-president LeBaron Taylor, looking back at indie labels in the 1960s. "People would say, 'One of these days Motown's gonna be cold and all those returns that they had all over the world will come back.' But it just so happens that they never did get cold." But Taylor acknowledges that even then "there had to be a certain amount of encouraging your distributors to pay. It wasn't uncommon in those days for guys to visit distributors and leave with their checks. And there were a lot of tough guys in the business a long time ago. They used to come in and break a guy's back. Yeah. It wasn't uncommon for you to know people. You might have difficulty collecting money in certain areas and call friends, and say, 'Well, hey, this guy's holding my money. Your friend would place a call and within a certain time you could get your money.'" In this hard-nosed environment, Barney Ales's abrasive style was perfect.

That's not to say that Motown didn't use milder methods to get what they wanted. As was standard among indie labels at the time (and as is still done widely in the record industry), Motown made extensive use of various "deals," or discount plans with distributors. The basic unit of a deal was 1,300 records; a "half-deal" was 650 records and a "quarter-deal" was 325. If a distributor ordered 1,000 records he got 300 free records or "free goods," 300 records that contractually Motown paid little or no royalties on. But, while 1,300 was the base, the orders for Motown, once the production line was in place, were usually a lot higher. This meant that an awful lot of ready cash was being made available.

This policy left plenty of room for abuse by sales staffers, but, as ex-Motown sales staffer Tom Noonan says, "Berry trusted him [Barney Ales] one hundred percent and Berry is that type of executive where he does delegate and Barney ran sales. It meant he ran it with a heavy hand and without interference."

So, in 1963, a year before the Beatles broke through in America and the British Invasion pushed most American pop out of the Top Forty, Motown was gearing up. There were still some pieces missing and some valuable teams to be formed. It was a transitional year in which the careers of the young veteran Smokey Robinson, the gifted rookie Stevie Wonder, and the patient Martha Reeves would all take center stage.

Since their marriage in November 7, 1959, Motown's favorite lovebirds, Smokey and Claudette Robinson, had battled the enemy of all show business couples, the road. Since Claudette was in the Miracles, she and Smokey were never separated for long periods of time, as were couples with only one performing member. Still, even when the two were touring together, Smokey's good looks and romantic voice had female fans pursuing him, with or without Claudette. ("Smokey wasn't henpecked," one musician remembers, "but she sure kept an eye on him.")

Their first major trial came only a few weeks after their marriage, following a New Year's Eve performance at Philadelphia's Uptown Theater. When they returned to their hotel, the Miracles found women wandering the halls looking for parties and musicians. Smokey, who had left his room to visit another of the Miracles, encountered two female fans in the hallway. Full of the holiday spirit and moved by Smokey's pretty eyes, the two pinned him against a wall and proceeded to place their lips upon his face. In a scene that could have been written for Doris Day, Claudette stepped into the hallway and became a surprise witness to the shocking scene.

Claudette slammed the door and started packing her clothes. Kelly Isley, the oldest of the Isley Brothers (with whom the Miracles were touring), ran down the facts of life on the road to Claudette. For the next two hours, he explained to her that the incident would actually strengthen the Robinsons' marriage, since it had shown them the extraordinary depth of trust they would need if their marriage was to withstand the physical and emotional demands of show business.

But that misunderstanding seemed inconsequential compared to the Robinsons' problems in 1963. In that year Smokey and Claudette suffered a series of personal tragedies that could have destroyed a weaker relationship. That fall, while performing at Washington, D.C.'s Howard Theater, Smokey contracted one of the first reported cases of Asian flu in the United States. Every day of the week-long engagement, a doctor visited the Robinsons' cramped quarters in a rooming house across from the Howard. And every night after the last show they'd stop at a local hospital. At one point Smokey's temperature rose as high as a life-threatening 106 degrees. At the end of the engagement Claudette rushed her ailing husband home to Detroit, and then she headed to South Carolina to join the rest of the Miracles, assuming Smokey's role as lead vocalist.

While convalescing, Smokey began getting news from the road that Claudette was losing weight. At first he chalked it up to fatigue. Besides, she never mentioned any problems when she called. But then bassist James Jamerson and Mary Wells, who was rooming with Claudette, called Smokey, imploring him to make Claudette come home. Unbeknownst to Smokey, his wife was pregnant and had been hemorrhaging for the past few weeks. Had Claudette suffered those symptoms at home, a responsible doctor would have ordered immediate bed rest. Instead, Claudette was touring the country, doing exhausting shows every day, all the while never letting on to Smokey that something was wrong. By the time Wells and Jameson called, Claudette had been losing blood for over a month. She hadn't told Smokey because she knew it would force the Miracles off the road, costing its members money and weakening the Motown Revue. Smokey called her and, after some debate, got her to agree to come home. "When she got off the plane, I didn't even know her. She was down to eighty-nine pounds," recalls Smokey. Doctors thought that the baby might be saved, but the strain proved too great, and Claudette miscarried. As soon as Claudette regained her health, she hit the road again. She became pregnant and miscarried again. And again. And again. Claudette suffered a total of six miscarriages before Smokey finally told her, "You gotta come off the road."

One can only imagine the anguish that filled their hearts. Before they had their first child (named Berry, of course) in 1968, Smokey and Claudette spent five years nagged by the fear that they'd never have children. Because of this ongoing personal trauma, Smokey's emotions were closer to the surface than most men ever allow. He says that only one song, the beautiful and uncharacteristically straightforward "More Love" (later a major hit for Kim Carnes), was written in direct response to Claudette's problems. "After she had a miscarriage she would always tell me she was sorry she had let me down. I would explain that she had not let me down because she was there, she was alive, I wanted the babies, but I didn't know them. I wrote 'More Love' to let her know how I felt about her. I wrote it as soon as I went home."

It is hard to imagine this painful experience not having a profound effect on Smokey's songwriting. That is not to say that Claudette's miscarriages were the sole inspiration behind his songwriting brilliance; his technique was too sophisticated to result purely from a raw emotional response, but we can't underestimate the deep well of emotions it tapped. The refinement of deep emotion is the springboard to great art, as these songs illustrate: "Ain't That Peculiar" and "I'll Be Doggone," recorded by Marvin Gaye; "Two Lovers," "My Guy," and "What's Easy for Two Is so Hard for One," recorded by Mary Wells; "The Hunter Gets Captured by the Game" and "Don't Mess With Bill" by the Marvelettes; "The Way You Do the Things You Do," "Don't Look Back," "It's Growing," "Since I Lost My Baby," and "My Girl," recorded by the Temptations; and "The Love I Saw in You Was Just a Mirage," "The Tracks of My Tears," "I'll Try Something New," and "Choosey Beggar," recorded by Smokey's own Miracles.

The great theme of Smokey's writing, one that echoed the conflict between the achievements of the Miracles and Motown with his personal turmoil, is the understanding and dissection of love's paradoxes. Sometimes, this is expressed by the words themselves. "My Girl," a song Smokey and Ronnie White composed backstage at the Apollo Theater, is built on paradoxical images: the singer has sunshine on a cloudy day, he is enjoying May weather in the dead of winter, all because of his lady's love. "I don't like you, but I love you," the opening of "You've Really Got a Hold on Me" is simple, too, but it hooks us right away with the singer's confusion and the overriding power of his love. In one sentence we know that the relationship between the speaker and the woman to whom he is speaking is passionate, loving yet quiet. Smokey wrote "Hold" after hearing Sam Cooke's classic "Bring It on Home to Me" in a New York hotel room. Note that while Cooke's original is a soulful, straightforward declaration of the desire for a lost lover, Smokey's special gift for lyrical invention results in something more realistic. A similar idea can be found in "Ain't That Peculiar," when Marvin Gaye muses, "I know that flowers grow from rain/But how can love grow from pain?" In the end, despite a catalogue of conflicting emotions, the listener is left to assume that love will go on anyway, with Gaye confessing that he still doesn't understand how love works, only that it does.

In the exquisite "Two Lovers," Smokey uses some of his most direct lyrics to put us in the midst of singer Mary Wells's seemingly adulterous relationship. In the first verse she sings the praises of a man "sweet, and kind, and mine all mine." In the second verse we find that Wells's other man "treats her bad" and "makes her sad." But by song's end we find she's loving a dude with a split personality; she loves them both, enduring his evil moods for just a little more of his good, true loving. Smokey based "Two Lovers" on his feelings toward Claudette, a Gemini. Smokey says that in the early years of their marriage she "had the power to really make me very happy or very sad with a word or with an action."

For Wells, who served as Smokey's most effective female mouthpiece, sex is a battleground in "You Beat Me to the Punch." Here common words take on several meanings. In the first verse, the word *punch* refers to the fact that Wells's prospective lover, guessing her attraction to him, makes the first move. By the second verse Wells has guessed that his aggressiveness means he is just a "playboy," so she beats him to the "punch" and tells him to take a hike.

Of course, Smokey's cleverness was sometimes used in the service of pure fun. "The Way You Do the Things You Do" is a celebration of style, and Smokey shows his by comparing his lady to a candle, a handle, a broom, and perfume, drawing smiles in the process and perfectly matching the syncopation of the melody. Better still are the series of unexpected comparisons between love and life that open the Temptations' "It's Growing." In the space of four lines, love is like a snowball rolling down a snow-covered hill, love is the size of a fish a man claims destroyed his reel, love is a growing rosebud, and love is an oft-told tale.

Of course, of his countless great songs, Smokey's masterpiece is "The Tracks of My Tears," a song so compelling, so beautiful, so resilient, that even Linda Ronstadt's wooden interpretation couldn't ruin it. As Smokey recalls, "I had that track for a while, but I really couldn't think of anything to fit it because it's such an odd musical progression. Finally, one day [in 1965] the chorus came to me. No one had ever said 'tracks of my tears.' The whole thought of tears was you wipe them away so no one could tell you've been crying. To say that I can't even wipe them away because they've left these tracks, you know, I thought it was a good idea."

The central image is of a smiling, joking guy at a neighborhood party with a pretty woman on his arm. But the singer soon reveals that his smile is like a clown's makeup, disguising the deep pain he feels at the loss of his true love. But the beauty of "Tracks" goes deeper than Smokey's lyrics. It possesses a wonderfully wistful melody (the "odd musical progression") and a brilliant production. For, while Smokey was so supple a lyricist that Bob Dylan once remarked, and not in jest, that he was "America's greatest living poet," it was Smokey's willingness to collaborate with the other Miracles and the Motown musicians that gave "Tracks" an extra dimension. Marv Tarplin's melancholy guitar introduction, a distant parody of circus music, was the song's basis, not Smokey's words. The melody was shaped with the help of another Miracle, Warren Moore, and then Smokey "fit" words to it.

In fact, most of the songs just cited were written by Smokey in tandem with others who provided melodic and rhythmic ideas: Moore also co-wrote "It's Growing"; Bobby Rogers co-wrote "The Way You Do the Things You Do"; Ronnie White contributed to "My Girl" and "You Beat Me to the Punch"; Motown staff writer Alfred Cleveland accidentally came up with the title of "I Second That Emotion" while he and Smokey were Christmas shopping in 1967; "Ain't That Peculiar," "The Love I Saw in You Was Just a Mirage," and Smokey's 1979 comeback hit "Cruisin'," like "Tracks," were all started by Marv Tarplin guitar figures.

Smokey's songs were sparked by stimuli of every kind. "Don't Mess With Bill" and "The Hunter Gets Captured by the Game," two of his wittiest love songs, were composed to accommodate what Smokey called Wanda Rogers's (of the Marvelettes) "little sexy" voice. The romantic "I'll Try Something New," in marked contrast, came to Smokey while watching the Detroit Tigers trounce the Cleveland Indians with his father at Detroit's Briggs Stadium. Smokey wrote the song's lyrics on the back of a crushed popcorn box.

Because of Smokey's ability to collaborate with others and find inspiration in a variety of ways, his songs never sounded formulated. There were certain recurring melodic and lyrical motifs—"My Girl" was obviously a companion piece to "My Guy"—but he avoided the kind of musical signatures and clichés that marked the work of many of his Motown contemporaries. Smokey's role as the Miracles' lead singer also influenced his writing. His voice, wrote David Morse, "recognizes no distinction between speech and song; it uncoils from a breathy, intimate whisper into a clear, bright, continuously intense verbal pressure" that was, perhaps, the most effective tool of seduction of the sixties. At house parties, bachelor pads, and, most profoundly, lovemaking sessions throughout America, Smokey's voice was cooing sweetly in the background. On the more rarefied level of musicianship, Smokey's sense of rhythm—an underappreciated aspect of singing—was remarkable. "While other singers land heavily on the beat," says Morse, "Smokey Robinson maintains a subtle, continuous contact with it, a kind of prehensile touching."

Ironically, it was Smokey's own creativity that would, after 1963, make him an inconsistent member of the Motown hitmaking machinery. One never knew what to expect from him, and so his songs and productions were never guaranteed hits. During his peak years as a writer, from 1963 to 1967, others at Motown would rack up more Top Ten hits and larger sales figures. Yet for durability and sheer beauty, no one at Motown would top him.

7

Hold My Mule

Shirley Caesar and the Gospel of the New South

CLAUDRENA N. HAROLD

From *When Sunday Comes: Gospel Music in the Soul and Hip-Hop Eras*, by Claudrena N. Harold (2020)

There is nowhere in the USA quite like America's South; there is no place more difficult to fully understand or fully capture. . . . The people who walk that land, both black and white, wear masks and more masks, then masks beneath those masks. They are tricksters and shape-shifters, magicians and carnival barkers, able to metamorphize right before your eyes into good old boys, respectable lawyers, polite society types, brilliant scholars, great musicians, history makers, and everything's-gonna-be-all-right Maya Angelou look-alikes—when in fact nothing's gonna be all right.
—James McBride, *Kill 'Em and Leave: Searching for James Brown and the American Soul*

If one thing doesn't work you shift and you do something else. If a fast song doesn't work, you use a slow one. . . . I change every time I get up to sing. . . . I take everything into consideration, what's going on around me, and I adjust my music for my audience. Yes indeed, I did it last night. Almost every time you hear me sing I do it. . . . Like for an example, the song my sister (Ann) sings "You can depend on Jesus." I'll say . . . in a sing-song fashion "Gonna be alright, gonna be, gonna be alright, everything's gonna be alright." Really what I'm waiting for, I'm waiting for the musicians to get into a pocket; by the time they get into that pocket, phone Aunt Jane. I'll give you a quarter if she ain't home.
—Shirley Caesar in Brooksie Eugene Harrington, "Shirley Caesar: A Woman of Words"

Thirty years into her recording career, the Grammy Award–winning artist Shirley Caesar showed no signs of slowing down. In 1988, Caesar returned to her traditional gospel roots with the release of her critically acclaimed record,

Live . . . in Chicago, which dominated the gospel charts for nearly eight months. It featured the hit single "Hold My Mule," a sermonette centered on the fictive character Shouting John, an eighty-six-year-old farmer who, in the words of Caesar, had joined "a dead church" controlled by ministers who frowned upon his expressive style of worship. To no avail, church leaders had repeatedly attempted to subdue John during his extended "praise breaks" by grabbing his limbs or forcing him to return to his seat. Their efforts always failed miserably. Frustrated by John's refusal to discipline his religious fervor, a small group of church officials traveled to the elder's home to chastise him for his behavior. Upon their arrival, they find John ("and a beat-up old mule") plowing in the field. The proud farmer approaches his guests and then listens to their complaints. Showing no compassion for the elder, the church leaders deliver an ultimatum to John: "If you don't stop shouting, if you don't stop dancing, we're going to put you out of our church."[1] John's demonstrative religiosity had crossed a dangerous line.

If church officials expected John to give in to their demands after their threat of disfellowship, they were in for a major disappointment. When granted the opportunity to speak, John details his many blessings: his ownership of land, his good health, and his trouble-free children. "Not one time have I been to the courthouse," he proudly informs his guests; "not one time have I been to the cemetery. But you don't want me to dance in your church?" The act of recounting his blessings leads John to make the following declaration to the delegation: "Well put me out, I can't hold my peace."[2] A spiritually ecstatic John then proceeds to shout and dance all over his property.

On this popular sermonette, which decades after its release still plays on gospel radio stations across the country, Shirley Caesar demonstrates both her unrivaled skills as a storyteller and her ability to capture the class tensions gripping black America during the post–civil rights era. She also gives voice to older black women and men still tied to the economies and cultural rhythms of the rural South. Caesar's attentiveness to the cultural richness and diversity of black America combined with her singularity as a performer and songwriter have enabled her to connect with multiple generations of gospel fans. One would be hard-pressed to find a gospel artist who has enjoyed her level of success for a longer period of time. First working with the famous Caravans from the late 1950s to the mid-1960s, then striking out on her own to become one of gospel music's most successful performers, Caesar boasts an incredibly impressive discography that captures her remarkable range as an artist. Her hits include sermonettes ("Don't Throw Your Mama Away," "Praying Slave Lady," and "Hold My Mule"), traditional hymns ("Don't Be Afraid" and "Jordan River"), soulful tunes ("Put Your Hand in the Hand"), and country ballads ("No Charge"). Her career is a marvel, and quite frankly trying to convey the brilliance of her artistry can be frustratingly difficult—not just because of her prodigious output but also because of the diversity of her work. Soul, funk, disco, and country—all of these genres have seeped into her music at one time or another. As a recording artist, Caesar has been at the cutting edge of both traditional and contemporary gospel music, refusing to allow anyone or anything to stifle her creativity.

Onstage, Caesar has also been in the vanguard of the art form, dazzling fans and critics alike with her legendary live performances. In her prime, her concerts featured spirited preaching, extended "praise breaks" during which she danced across the stage or down the aisles, and reworked versions of her most popular songs and sermonettes that captured her gift of improvisation. "I like to compare Shirley's performance to the well-known structure of a short story," writes Brooksie Eugene Harrington. "She gives you the introduction, the rising action, the climax, and the falling action. . . . Shirley knows what she is doing, and . . . she does it in such a meticulous manner that she carries her audience right along with the flow of the waters as she reaches the zenith of her concert."[3] Caesar's mastery as a performer was the by-product of her brilliant fusion of various traditions, modalities, and styles. One tradition was the black sermonic tradition. The "old-time Negro preacher," James Weldon Johnson writes in his classic 1927 text, *God's Trombones*,

> was a master of all the modes of eloquence. He often possessed a voice that was a marvelous instrument, a voice he could modulate from a sepulchral whisper to a crashing thunder clap. His discourse was generally kept at a high pitch of fervency, but occasionally he dropped into colloquialisms and, less often, into humor. He preached a personal and anthropomorphic God, a sure-enough heaven and a red-hot hell. His imagination was bold and unfettered. He had the power to sweep his hearers before him; and so himself was often swept away. At such times his language was not prose but poetry.[4]

Like the classic black preachers before her, Caesar transformed her sermonettes, particularly tunes like "Praying Slave Lady" and "Hold My Mule," into high art.

None of Caesar's success was by chance. Every move was a calculated one. Upon her departure from the Caravans in 1966, she signed with House of Beauty (HOB) Records. HOB and Caesar's partnership yielded some of her biggest hits and most critically acclaimed recordings. Then in 1977, the singer signed with Roadshow, a small secular label whose roster included the bands Enchantment and B. T. Express. Three years later, Caesar inked a deal with the Christian entertainment powerhouse Word Records, which for the first twenty-five years of its existence confined itself primarily to the white Christian market. As a testament to her commercial appeal, Caesar was high on the priority list of all three companies. Word, Roadshow, and HOB envisioned Caesar as a transcendent artist who could help them break into new markets and increase their profit margins considerably. Moreover, label executives regarded Caesar as a versatile performer whose expansive talent allowed her to thrive in a variety of musical settings. Such was the case in the early 1980s, when Word paired Caesar with country producer Tony Brown for her first three records on the label. Her Nashville sessions included some of the industry's most respected musicians and were carefully planned to generate the most commercially viable product. These sessions were radically different from those during her earlier days with the Caravans. "When I recorded with the Caravans," Caesar remembered, "the production budgets were always very meager. There weren't any allocations to hire musicians. Often we borrowed musicians from local churches. At best we had a drummer, a bass, a lead guitarist, and an organ player. We couldn't afford to pay for studio time for more than one day, so we would record ten to twelve songs in one session. If we made mistakes, the producer overlooked them. If the altos came in late or the sopranos didn't sing the song as rehearsed, it was ignored because the budget would not allow rerecording."[5]

With more than six decades of experience as a gospel singer and traveling evangelist, Caesar has witnessed, contributed to, and benefited from some of the major transformations within the Christian music industry. Thus, tracing the arc of her career provides significant insight into a variety of issues, including but not limited to the growing impact of funk and soul music on the gospel sound, the efforts of major white Christian labels to claim a bigger share of the black gospel market, the rise of Nashville as an important geographical center of the black gospel industry, and the struggle of African American religious artists to address some of the major political and social problems affecting their local communities and the larger world. As one of the gospel industry's most popular performers, Caesar used her platform to advance the art form and build what religious studies scholar Cheryl Sanders calls "prophetic community": the "exercising of one's individual gifts of ministry and leadership toward the end of empowering congregations to hear the voice of God and speak the word of God in conversation with the deepest concerns of the people and communities one is called to serve."[6]

In explaining her political activism, particularly her decision to run for a seat on the city council in her hometown of Durham, North Carolina, in 1987, Caesar noted, "I not only care about what happens inside the church; I'm equally concerned about what happens in society at large. In my opinion, if the church doesn't influence society, it has failed to live out God's commission."[7] With this goal in mind, Caesar campaigned on a platform emphasizing full employment, quality housing for low-income residents, improvements to the downtown area without sacrificing the needs of the black poor, environmental protections, and quality public schools. As Caesar ventured into new territory in her public life, her campaign was hardly surprising to gospel fans and industry insiders who had followed her career. The socially engaged artist had never shied away from political issues and themes in her music, as Cheryl Gilkes perceptively notes in her analysis:

> Not only does Shirley Caesar make beautiful music, for which she reaps accolades and awards, but also her music, much of which she composes, provides an important narrative or "thick description" of the situations of black people in America and a prophetic critique of the social conditions that challenge black and poor people. Alongside of this description and critique, Shirley Caesar also challenges black people's treatment of one another, particularly across class lines; in the process she illustrates the complexities and complications of class and family issues among black people. Throughout her career, her music has proclaimed God's option for the poor and qualifies as a liberationist discourse.[8]

Caesar provided a model for other women navigating the complex gender politics of both the music industry and the African American church. Her public persona ranged from pious woman mindful of the gender proscriptions of her Holiness background to civic-minded activist committed to improving the lives of the most disadvantaged, particularly those from her hometown of Durham. In her interviews, which in the early part of her career often focused on her single status (Caesar did not marry until her late thirties), she presented herself as somewhat of a traditionalist on gender issues. "I don't consider myself a liberated woman," the singer told an *Ebony* reporter in 1977. "If I had a man, I would be dependent on him." In that same interview, however, she shared with readers her deep love for her work, her financial autonomy, her extensive community involvement, and her general contentment with her single status.[9] Though she distanced herself from certain labels—as did many other African American women at the time—she was very much in control of her personal and professional life.[10] To prove this point and perhaps provide a visual counterpoint to a few of Caesar's statements, *Ebony* included an image of Caesar confidently occupying the driver's seat of her custom-made tour bus, which she occasionally drove when on the road with her band. Self-made and self-fashioned, Caesar demanded that her art and her life be understood on no one's terms but her own. This was about control, but it was also about self-preservation.

The Parable of My Being: Coming of Age in Durham

"The course of my life cannot be explained in simple human terms," Caesar once wrote. "From the beginning I believe I was destined to fulfill God's purpose and plan for my existence. There is no other explanation. With so much working against me—a semi-invalid mother, a deceased father, low-self-esteem resulting from having been called degrading names as a child, and living in a society plagued by racism, sexism, and segregation—I wasn't supposed to make it." Success, let alone superstardom, was not in the cards—so she assumed. "I should have never escaped the impoverishment that surrounded me. But by God's mercy I did. So here I am still running, still singing, still preaching."[11]

The tenth of twelve children, Shirley Ann Caesar was born in 1938 to James and Hallie Caesar in Durham, North Carolina. The Caesars lived in a modest house on Chautauqua Avenue, located in the city's historic Hayti neighborhood.[12] Southwest of downtown, Hayti was the residential, commercial, and cultural center of black Durham. By the time of Shirley Caesar's birth, Hayti was well known among African Americans not just in North Carolina but throughout the nation. As one historian explains, the district enjoyed a "national reputation as a bustling neighborhood with active black commerce, political activism, higher education, and entertainment. Separated from Durham's downtown by unsightly coal yards and railroad tracks, Hayti's residents met most of their needs along the main thoroughfares of their neighborhood. There black florists, pharmacists, auto mechanics, barbers, dry cleaners, grocers, tailors, restaurateurs, hoteliers, morticians, and other businesses catered to them."[13] Not too far from Hayti, several prominent black businesses, including John Merrick's North Carolina Mutual Insurance Company and Richard Fitzgerald and James Shepard's Mechanics and Farmers Bank, flourished on Parrish Street. With such bustling commercial activity, Durham was regarded by some African Americans as the "Capital of the Black Bourgeoisie." "It is a city of fine homes, exquisite churches, and middle-class respectability," the noted sociologist E. Franklin Frazier opined in his essay for Alain Locke's seminal anthology *The New Negro*. "It is not the place where men write and dream; but a place where black men calculate and work. No longer can men say that the Negro is lazy and shiftless and a consumer. He has gone to work. He is a producer. He is respectable. He has a middle class."[14]

The Bull City most certainly had a visible black middle class; however, the vast majority of African Americans in Durham were working-class people. Like many African Americans in the Hayti district, Shirley Caesar's parents worked as tobacco stemmers at Liggett and Myers. Hallie and Jim Caesar brought with them a fair amount of experience in the tobacco industry. A native of North Wilkesboro, North Carolina, Hallie Caesar had previously worked at R. J. Reynolds in Winston-Salem, where she met her future husband, Jim. The couple fell in love, married in 1923, and relocated to Durham three years later. "I got a job in the tobacco factory," Hallie Caesar remembered, "and worked there for thirteen years full-time. . . . The factories paid a little more here in Durham. When we came here, I thought 8 cents a pound was great, because in Winston we would get 5 cents and 6 cents a pound." Changes in the industry, particularly the phasing out of stemmers, coupled with health issues, compelled Hallie Caesar to leave Liggett in 1939. "When I left the factory, I went home. Raising the children was a full-time job."[15]

Together with her husband, Hallie Caesar instilled within her children the values of hard work and self-respect. The couple also stressed the importance of family and God. "In our family," Shirley Caesar remembered, "attending church was not an option—it was an obligation."[16] The family first belonged to Fisher Memorial United Holy Church and then later joined Mount Calvary Holy Church, which was pastored by Frizelle Yelverton. Under the leadership of Yelverton, young Shirley learned the major tenets of the Mount Calvary Holy Church of America, which on the eve of the Great Depression splintered away from the United Holy Church of America.[17] The Mount Calvary denomination's founder and first bishop was Brumfield Johnson, a North Carolina native who in 1928 held a series of revivals in Winston-Salem. These revivals led to the formation of Mount Calvary Holy Church of America, which had a strong base in North Carolina. Mount Calvary placed heavy emphasis on sanctification, pious living, and Pentecostal Holy Spirit baptism—though it did not promote speaking in tongues as the *only* evidence of spirit indwelling. Such teachings would be an important anchor in the religious life of Shirley Caesar.

Another significant anchor for her was gospel music: "Gospel music has always been a viable part of my life. It was the first music I heard as an infant, and the only music that was sung in our household. My mother could always be heard humming a song of praise or singing a hymn."[18] The Caesar children's love for gospel came not just from their mother but from their father as well. Jim Caesar was one of the most respected gospel singers in North Carolina. He, along with three other workers employed at Liggett and Myers, created the Just Come Four Quartet, a talented group that deepened the local community's appreciation for quartet music. "Quartet singing wasn't too popular when I first came to Durham," Hallie Caesar recalled, "but later on there was a lot of them out there." Among the most popular was the Just Come Four Quartet, which thrived on Jim Caesar's powerful singing. "Throughout the Carolinas and southern states," Shirley Caesar proudly boasted, "he was noted for his anointed and energetic style of singing. . . . I'm told he could electrify and magnetize an audience like no one else could."[19] When not attending Mount Calvary or working at Liggett and Myers, Jim Caesar toured with his group, spreading the gospel and earning additional money to support his large family.

The Caesar family suffered a major blow when Jim died unexpectedly in 1945. "My father's sudden death meant intense economic hardship for the family," Caesar somberly recounted. "My mother, who was a semi-invalid, did the very best to provide for us. Although physically challenged, she was by no means a weak lady. But her handicapped foot made it impossible for her to work in a full-time job. Thankfully, as my brothers and sisters grew older they got jobs to help supplement our income. We struggled but at least we struggled together as a family."[20]

Financial hardships notwithstanding, Caesar excelled in the classroom and thrived in Durham's culturally rich black community. One of her elementary teachers, Charlie T. Roach, remembered Caesar as a stellar student and exceptional leader. "I met Shirley in 1950 when she was 11 years old as my sixth-grade student in a class of 34 at W. G. Pearson Elementary School. She was well-mannered, sweet disposition, charming personality, disciplined, and a pleasure to teach." Years after teaching Caesar, Roach still remembered, quite vividly, her contributions to his class's daily devotion period. "We practiced 15 minutes morning devotion daily before class time. The class rotated leadership alphabetically. The students enjoyed Shirley's leadership so much that they voted her to lead daily. Several teachers from other classes stood at our door in the hallway to hear Shirley sing. . . . They knew she was for real!!!"[21]

School was not the only place where Caesar showed great promise as a vocalist. Heavily involved at Mount Calvary, she participated in the junior choir and worked hard to attract the attention of the congregation: "I made sure my contralto voice was heard loud and clear." On those special occasions when she had a solo, Caesar performed with an intensity that belied her age. "I sang as though my very life depended on the projection of that song."[22] Caesar's talents soon caught the attention of gospel lovers outside her church. With her mother's permission, "Baby Shirley," as she was billed on concert advertisements, started traveling with local ministers and singers, most notably Leroy Johnson and Thelma Bumpass and the Royalettes.

Traveling on the road cut into Caesar's study time, but her grades at Hillside High were strong enough to enroll at nearby North Carolina Central College. Founded in 1909 by Dr. James Edward Shepard, North Carolina Central emerged from its modest beginnings as the National Religious Training School to become one of the shining intellectual gems of the Tar Heel State. Economic hardships plagued the school during its early years, but in 1923 its fortunes improved when it became a state institution and changed its name to Durham State Normal School. Led by Shepard until his death in 1948, the school continued to grow under the leadership of its second president, Dr. Alfonso Elder. Like others from her neighborhood, Caesar looked at the college with great pride and felt it a privilege to attend the historically black institution.

This did not mean that her time at Central was easy. Her family's strained financial situation along with her passion for gospel music compounded the typical challenges of college life. On the eve of her sophomore year, Caesar pondered whether to remain at Central or devote herself fully to pursuing her gospel dreams. As had always been the case for Caesar, her family's limited resources concerned her greatly. "I knew my mother didn't have the money to pay for my tuition or buy my books and beyond that I knew that, given our financial situation, the chance of me completing college was almost nonexistent."[23] Caesar's decision regarding school became a lot easier after she attended a concert in Kinston, where she secured an unconventional audition with Albertina Walker's Caravans.

Sweeping the City: Shirley Caesar and the Caravans

A major force in the gospel world, the Caravans had evolved from their roots in Robert Anderson's Good Shepherd Singers to become one of the industry's most beloved groups. Vocally, the Caravans were in a league of their own. "As an ensemble," Robert Marovich explains, "the Caravans pounced on vocal lines with church-wrecking power and precision, filling each lyric line and the pause between them with intense emotional conviction. Their tight, intense harmonies, dynamic ebbs and flows, and staccato attack of the verses were straight out of the church."[24] The group thrived under the leadership of Albertina Walker, who brought a host of talented singers and musicians to the group: Bessie and Gloria Griffin, Johneron Davis, Cassietta George, Dorothy Norwood, Inez Andrews, James Herndon, James Cleveland, and Shirley Caesar.

An avid fan of the Caravans, Caesar was determined to capture Walker's attention during one of the group's visits to North Carolina. Since she wasn't on the official program, she arranged for someone to request "a solo from Shirley Caesar." When the request was made, Caesar rushed to the stage and delivered a rousing performance that convinced Walker to add the talented youngster to the group.

Caesar's impact on the Caravans was immediate and profound. On such classic tunes as "I Won't Be Back," "No Coward Soldier," "I Feel Good," and "A Place Like That," she mesmerized listeners with her signature contralto, sermonic phrasing, and commanding delivery. Her talent was boundless. Not just an amazing vocalist, Caesar was also a first-rate entertainer who wowed concertgoers with her passionate preaching and dancing. Moving across the stage and down the aisles, Caesar brought the spiritual energy and worship style of her Holiness church to every performance. "I was full of energy in those days. Backstage in the Apollo, I could run all of the way up all of those stairs and in 30 seconds be on the top floor. I was so active." Moreover, Caesar continued, "I was just very, very charismatic."[25]

Caesar loved performing but found the rigors of touring exhausting. "Those years with the Caravans weren't always easy ones. The schedules we kept and the conditions under which we traveled were very trying. We would pack our bags and all six of us would pile into our Cadillac, sometimes traveling all day to get to a concert that night."[26] Caesar also had to battle unwelcomed advances from male suitors, shady concert promoters who failed to pay performers, and racist Jim Crow laws and customs that made travel problematic for African American entertainers. Despite these difficulties, Caesar appreciated her time with the group. "The Caravans were my mentors, my sisters, my friends, and my family. We disagreed some, cried some, laughed a lot, and poured out our hearts on stage and in churches for the glory of God. I learned from them all and believe even today that I sing a little like each of them. I would like to think that I have a little bit of their styles in my music."[27]

Wanting greater control over her time, her art, and her ministry, Caesar left the Caravans in 1966 and embarked on a solo career. "On my own, I now had the flexibility to coordinate the scheduling of my concerts around my revival dates. Having that freedom was liberating. I no longer felt as if I was failing the Lord."[28]

After carefully weighing her options, Caesar signed with the Scepter-owned label House of Beauty Records. As part of HOB's recruiting efforts, the label offered Caesar a $4,000 signing bonus and pledged to do everything to advance her solo career. Under the direction of John Bowden, HOB aspired to increase its share of the gospel market by signing acts like the Five Blind Boys of Alabama, the Gospel Harmonettes, the Swan Silvertones, and Caesar.[29]

My Testimony: Shirley Caesar's Tenure with HOB Records

Departing a group as popular as the Caravans carried certain risks, but Caesar's first solo outing, *I'll Go,* proved she was up to the challenge. Anchored by Caesar's stunning contralto and the powerful background vocals of the Institutional Radio Choir of Brooklyn, the music on *I'll Go* reflected the singer's desire to maintain her Caravans audience as well as to reach new markets. Even though Caesar had been in the gospel industry for nearly a decade, *I'll Go* provided her fans with their first glimpse of the person behind the artist. On "Choose Ye This Day" and the title track, "I'll Go," Caesar recounts her family's history, her childhood years, and her father's death at an early age. In both songs, she establishes herself as a battle-tested believer. Throughout her career, Caesar would recount her family's encounters with death and economic hardship as a way to situate herself within the community of the socially disadvantaged as well as to testify to God's deliverance. Another important hallmark of Caesar's music appears on *I'll Go*: her engagement with larger social issues. "Battle Field" and "Choose Ye This Day" reference the Vietnam War and the civil rights struggle, particularly state-sanctioned violence against African American children in political hotbeds like Birmingham.

And then there was "Rapture," a hypnotizing soul number that showcased Caesar's versatility as a vocalist. Though Caesar was unequivocal in her commitment to singing gospel, her performance on "Rapture" confirmed, for many, her potential for great success if she ever decided to enter the pop world.

While willing to engage contemporary sounds and issues, Caesar remained connected to her past, particularly her North Carolina roots. Perhaps nowhere was this connection more apparent than on the record's most powerful cut, "Don't Be Afraid." Caesar's majestic voice captures the religiosity, human warmth, and intimacy of the black church. It conjures up memories of not just the sounds but also the gestures, sights, and smells of Sunday morning.

To reinforce Caesar's deep connection to the church and her Holiness roots, the cover of *I'll Go* featured a picture of the singer in a choir robe. Eyes closed and hands lifted toward heaven, Caesar positions herself as God's servant rather than gospel music entertainer. The image of Caesar was understated, but the music was certainly not. Well aware of the naysayers who questioned the wisdom of her departure from the Caravans, Caesar was happy with the results of her first album. "To me, it was reaffirmation that God indeed keeps His promises."[30]

Caesar's second outing for HOB, *My Testimony*, was equally impressive. It included sermonettes, up-tempo shout songs, and soul-stirring ballads. Caesar composed seven of the twelve songs on the record, which also featured compositions from Cassietta George and James Cleveland. The highlight of the session was her unforgettable performance on "Tear Your Kingdom Down," a haunting number that bears a striking resemblance to "Don't Be Afraid."[31] Singing with great fervor and conviction, Caesar declares war on the devil in no uncertain terms.

Wanting to build on Caesar's momentum, HOB flooded the gospel market with records and singles from the talented songstress. Within months of the appearance of *My Testimony*, the label released *Jordan River*, a record whose title cut adopted the minimalist but powerful approach of "Tear Your Kingdom Down" and "Don't Be Afraid."

Even greater success followed Caesar in 1969 when she released "Don't Drive Your Mama Away," a brilliant sermonette that combined masterful storytelling with strident class critique. "Don't Drive Your Mama Away" tells the story of a mother who has two sons with radically different life trajectories. One son performs well in school, vows to take care of his mother, and eventually becomes a doctor. The other son underperforms in the classroom as a child, has numerous run-ins with the law, and causes his mother much heartache. True to his childhood promise to provide for his family, the "good son" invites his mother to move in with his wife (a schoolteacher) and children and enjoy the benefits of their stable, upper-middle-class life. However, trouble emerges when the daughter-in-law complains about what she perceives as her mother-in-law's negative influence on the children, particularly her country manners and "bad grammar." Siding with his wife, the son informs his mother of his intention to relocate her to a senior citizens' home. En route to the "old folks home," the family runs into the other son, who expresses dismay at the situation and then offers to bring his mother to his house. Though the living accommodations of the "no-good son" pale in comparison to those of his more accomplished sibling, the mother prefers this arrangement to the other possibility: spending her final days among strangers. The sermonette ends on a somewhat triumphant note as the troubled child—who through this kind gesture has now found redemption—and the grateful mother journey down the road toward their new life together.[32] An instant hit, "Don't Drive Your Mama Away" resonated with thousands of African Americans who appreciated Caesar's deft storytelling, as well as her exploration of the class tensions within black communities. "Don't Drive Your Mama Away" also cemented Caesar's status as one of gospel's premier entertainers.

On the road, Caesar generated even greater buzz with her powerful singing, spirited preaching, and joyful dancing.[33] "I cannot do this dead and dry," Caesar once remarked; "I got to move."[34] And move she did. Her live performances received rave reviews from the nation's leading newspapers. *Washington Post* journalist Hollie West showered the singer with praise after her concert at Constitution Hall. Caesar, West marveled, "has the unusual capacity to transform a concert hall into a church-like setting at a moment's notice. . . . In her piercing contralto voice, she performs with the fervor of an evangelist as she preaches the message of her song." The singer's spitfire vocals, passionate preaching, and boundless energy left West spellbound. "Miss Caesar darts back and forth across a stage with such fury that it seems as if she might fall on her face at any time." Fueling Caesar's fire was not just the Holy Spirit but also the energy of her fans: "People were standing in the aisles, clapping their hands and dancing to her fiery rhythm."[35] A perfectionist who fully recognized that working women and men made up the backbone of her audience, she demanded nothing less than the best from her background singers and musicians. On those rare occasions when they missed a beat or played the wrong note, she'd chastise them with a disapproving glance or comment. Simply put, in terms of sheer energy and exactness, she was the closest thing the gospel world had to soul music's greatest bandleader, James Brown.

Caesar's commitment to her art was evident in the high quality of her live shows and her studio productions. A permanent fixture on gospel radio, Caesar won her first Grammy Award in 1971 for her soul-stirring hit "Put Your Hand in the Hand." A year later, she released *Get Up My Brother*. Visually and sonically, *Get Up My Brother* underscores how the cultural politics of the Black Power movement reached far beyond those who identified or positioned themselves as cultural nationalists. The album's cover featured a beautiful portrait of Caesar fashionably attired in a colorful dress. No longer wearing the drab choir robes of the *I'll Go* era, Caesar had a look that reflected the popular styles of the 1970s. As was the case with many black artists, Caesar seemed to be targeting—or at least acknowledging—the soul brothers and sisters in black America.[36]

To tap into gospel's expanding market, as well as the political energy of the times, Caesar also adopted a more contemporary sound on several of the album's cuts, including the title song. With its soulful mix of organ, guitar, Rhodes piano, and drums, "Get Up My Brother" echoes some of the music found on Pastor T. L. Barrett's 1971 record, *Like a Ship . . . (Without a Sail)*. The song has a strong Chicago soul vibe, as does Caesar's cover of Curtis Mayfield's protest anthem "People Get Ready."

A versatile artist who could change with the times yet maintain her individuality, Caesar willingly moved beyond her comfort zone to embrace new sounds, techniques, and marketing strategies. At the same time, she refused to abandon her older fans who didn't like their gospel "too worldly." In addition to the more soulful songs, *Get Up My Brother* featured two powerful traditional gospel cuts: "Teach Me Master" and "Nobody but You Lord."

This balancing act continued over the next several years with the release of *The Invitation, Be Careful of the Stones You Throw, Millennial Reign*, and *No Charge*. These four records find Caesar pushing the sonic and lyrical boundaries of gospel. One of her more intriguing turns was her foray into country music, a genre she was quite fond of. "I love listening to country music," she readily admitted. In addition to covering Hank Williams's classic "Be Careful of the Stones You Throw," Caesar scored a major hit with the country song "No Charge," taken from her 1975 album of the same name. "No Charge" relates the story of an exchange between a mother and a son. Written by Harlan Howard and recorded by Melba Montgomery in 1974, the song opens with the narrator describing a scene in which a young boy comes into the kitchen and hands his mother an itemized list of charges for his chores. The enterprising son has a price for everything, from washing the dishes to completing his homework. Taken aback by the son's list, the mother responds with a recounting of her many responsibilities and sacrifices:

> For the nine months I carried you, growing inside me, no charge
> For the nights I sat up with you, doctored you, prayed for you, no charge
> For the time and the tears and the costs through the years, no charge
> *When you add it all up, the full cost of my love is no charge*[37]

Like millions of Americans, Caesar adored Melba Montgomery's version of the song. "It blew me away," she later remembered. "I laid out in the living room on the floor, trying to sing it like a country singer. I couldn't so I just did it my way and it turned out to be the biggest solo record I've ever recorded."[38]

With her incredible range as an artist, Caesar played an important though largely overlooked role in the diversification of the gospel sound during the 1970s. Together with artists like Andraé Crouch, Rance Allen, and the Hawkins Family, Caesar stretched both the lyrical and sonic boundaries of gospel as she not only borrowed from other genres but also addressed larger societal issues.

A New Day: Caesar and Roadshow

Firmly established in her career, Caesar was not afraid to take chances and move in new directions with her sound. Such openness was necessary in an industry where label restructuring, buyouts, and shutdowns could derail the career of even the most successful artists. Few artists understood this more than the business-minded Caesar, who eventually switched from HOB to Roadshow Records: "The year 1975 proved to be a very pivotal one for me. It was the year my recording contract with Hob [HOB] Records ended, and I opted not to re-sign. By my own election, it was almost two years before I finally consented to sign with another label. I needed time to reflect and reevaluate my sense of direction. My primary purpose as a Christian and as a gospel singer has always been to reach as many people as possible with the message of Jesus, regardless of race, gender, demographic location, or socioeconomic status. At Hob Records I didn't feel that purpose was being adequately accomplished."[39]

With the goal of expanding her base, she signed with Roadshow and began preparing for her next record. When Roadshow's president, Fred Frank, and producer Michael Stokes sent Caesar the rhythm tracks to possible songs for her first recording session with the company, the gospel singer assumed she had received the wrong music. "Well, when I got the tape," Caesar recalled, "I said 'wow, this is gutbucket rock and roll! I can't do this.'" Caesar had never been beholden to one particular style, but these tracks were more experimental than her previous material. Losing her fan base and alienating gospel radio program-mers were real possibilities in an industry with many artists who fell victim to the crossover chase. And yet, Caesar recognized the need to grow as an artist. "It was a question of knowing where I'd been and then thinking about where I was going. What was perhaps the most important part of my decision about the album was understanding that I was still singing gospel. There was no question of me suddenly becoming a rock/R&B performer!"[40]

Not everyone was so certain after listening to *First Lady*. The music ranged from the disco-tinged "Just a Talk" to the more traditional "Faded Rose" to her funky cover of Stevie Wonder's "Jesus Children of America." "If someone didn't tell you it was a gospel album or you didn't listen carefully, you would never know," wrote M. J. Musik of the *New York Amsterdam News*. "There's disco in 'Jesus Is Coming' and funk in 'Just a Talk.'" All serious music listeners, he insisted, needed to engage the record. "Whether you like gospel music or not, you'll love Shirley Caesar's latest album."[41] Along with generating strong reviews, the album sold more than 200,000 copies, an impressive mark for a gospel recording.

Enthused about the results, Roadshow devoted tremendous money and time into marketing her follow-up release, *From the Heart*. With direction from her producer Michael Stokes, primarily known for his work with the soul group Enchantment, Caesar sampled broadly from the contemporary music scene. The singer offered a soulful version of Diana Ross's "Reach Out and Touch (Somebody's Hand)," gave a nod to the lush sounds of Philadelphia International with "He's Got a Love," and masterfully rode the funky grooves of "Message to the People" and "Heavenly Father."

The material was strong, but Caesar was never comfortable with Roadshow. In addition to feeling as if some of the music was "overproduced," Caesar found the company's crossover efforts unsuccessful, by which she meant not so much lackluster sales (the album had strong sales) but failure to gain traction in the pop market. Despite the company's business strategy and her new sound, Caesar's audience remained predominantly gospel: "While at Roadshow I learned a valuable lesson. Innovative marketing strategies and extensive advertising campaigns are no guarantee that you will expand your market share, particularly if the market you are trying to penetrate is not ready for what you are trying to present."[42]

New Directions with Word Records

These lessons weighed on Caesar's mind after Roadshow's collapse in 1980 made her one of gospel music's most coveted free agents. Once again, she faced the challenge of deciding which company could best advance her career without compromising the integrity of her musical ministry. Ultimately, she decided on Word Records, the biggest label in the Christian entertainment industry. Founded in the early 1950s by Jarrell McCracken, the Waco, Texas–based company had been instrumental in the growth of contemporary Christian music through its record-of-the-month club, its distribution deals with Light and Solid Rock Records, and its impressive roster of artists, including the platinum-selling star Amy Grant.[43] To diversify its market, the label sought to add established African American artists to its roster. Toward this goal, Word formed a black division and appointed as its head gospel industry veteran James Bullard, who had previously worked with Caesar at Roadshow. Impressed by Bullard's track record, Word had aggressively courted the ambitious executive. "They wanted to know if I could make Word number one in black Gospel music," Bullard remembered. "Stan Moser, along with Roland Lundy, Dan Johnson and others at Word[,] said if I was willing to head the new division, they would make the commitment to back it all the way." Hiring Bullard proved a wise decision as he exceeded the company's expectations: "The first eight months we did what Stan projected for the first three years."[44] One important factor in Bullard's success was the company's new signee, Shirley Caesar.

Not long after Caesar's signing, Word sought the services of Tony Brown, who produced Caesar's first three albums for the label. A native of Greensboro, North Carolina, Brown had traveled with his family's gospel group as a child, singing and playing the piano. Short stints with the Stamps Quartet and the Oak Ridge Boys prepared him for his biggest gig: pianist for Elvis Presley's gospel group the Voice. After Presley's death in 1977, Brown linked up with Emmylou Harris as he sharpened his musical skills.

Working out of Nashville's legendary Quadrafonic Sound Studios, located in the heart of Music Row, Brown and Caesar blended their distinctive musical talents to create a satisfying mix of New South gospel. The end result was one of the best records of Caesar's career: *Rejoice*, which was released on Word's subsidiary imprint Myrrh.

The nine-song set opens with the upbeat "Whisper a Prayer," a Caesar-penned tune whose hard-knocking groove draws from country, R&B, and disco. There's a hunger, a palpable urgency, in Caesar's singing—something one might not necessarily expect in a seasoned veteran who had been on the top of the charts for more than twenty years. Her intensity continues on Aaron Wilburn's "Satan, You're a Liar," a striking tune featuring clashing guitars, drums, and keyboards. Infused with the rhythms of southern rock and the melodrama of country pop, "Satan" pushes Caesar out of her vocal comfort zone.

If you were combing through Caesar's discography for evidence of her musical range, then "Satan" would probably be among your first choices. Not too far behind would be another tune on *Rejoice*: Caesar's cover of Bob Dylan's "Gotta Serve Somebody." Offering her traditional serving of spitfire extemporizations and nuanced phrasing, Caesar exhorts her listeners to come to the side of the Lord.

Later on the record, Caesar rips through "It's in the Book," a bouncy number from the songwriting team of J. L. Wallace, Ken Bell, and Terry Skinner. A dance tune immersed in disco beats, hillbilly rhythms, and light funk, "It's in the Book" lays to rest any doubts about the musical chemistry between Caesar and her Nashville rhythm section. The arrangements are complex, soulful, and swinging. As the drummer and bassist lay down the pulsating groove, Caesar's voice functions as an additional percussive instrument, injecting the song with greater rhythmic complexity.

Caesar's debut for Word was a triumph both for the artist and for the record company. Released in late 1980, *Rejoice* netted impressive sales in the gospel market and had a strong presence on Christian radio. The forty-two-year-old Caesar remained one of the most innovative artists in gospel. Her rendezvous with Nashville country was as bold and fresh as the gospel-funk hybrids emerging from the Clark Sisters and the Winans.

Impressed by Caesar's ability to adapt to the changing times, music journalists gave her Word material extremely high marks. In his enthusiastic review of 1983's *Jesus, I Love Calling Your Name*, Richard Harrington hailed Caesar as "one of the great black singers of our time." Throughout the album, Harrington marveled, "her singing is superb, riding freely over thumping bass lines and earthy choruses alike. Caesar can twist, compress or enhance a lyric a dozen ways without abandoning her central message of affirmation, strength, and enduring faith."[45]

Caesar's first three albums for Myrrh, *Rejoice, Go,* and *Jesus, I Love Calling Your Name*, elicited great excitement among fans anxious to see Caesar perform her new material live. "With the release of each of those albums," Caesar later reflected, "I found myself on the road even more. Pastors, promoters, and organizations from all around the country were constantly calling me and the Caesar Singers to come either for concerts or revivals. We were performing in excess of one hundred and fifty concerts per year."[46]

One admirer of Caesar's soul-inspired gospel was Lou Rawls, who frequently invited her to perform for his United Negro College Fund telethon. No stranger to Caesar's mammoth talent, Rawls had known Caesar since her days with the Caravans and regarded her as one of the most brilliant performers of any genre:

> I mean when this woman comes out to perform, you can feel the electricity in the room. It's like being in one of those old Baptist churches; you know, where the minister shifts gears on you. You see she does that. She does that in her music. . . . The people that have never heard Shirley Caesar and don't know who Shirley Caesar is when they do hear her and see her—they never forget this woman, because this woman strikes you. POW! She hits you right in the heart, because she's sincere and she means what she's doing.[47]

Indeed, Caesar's music connected with people in deep and meaningful ways.

Despite her national profile and extensive tour schedule, Caesar remained firmly grounded in the local politics and cultural activities of her hometown of Durham. Every year, she sponsored the annual Shirley Caesar Evangelistic Crusade, a weeklong event that featured Caesar and other gospel stars. She also hosted a weekly radio show on WSRC that was broadcast throughout the Raleigh-Durham area.

Carving out time to record new material was not easy, but she managed to complete three new albums between 1984 and 1987: *Sailin', Celebration,* and *Christmasing.* Word also released her greatest hits compilation, *Her Very Best.*

FIGURE 7.1 Street sign commemorating Shirley Caesar in Durham, North Carolina. Photo by author.

During this time, Caesar collected three additional Grammy Awards, one for the song "Martin," a tribute to the civil rights leader Dr. Martin Luther King Jr., and two for "Sailin'," her duet with labelmate Al Green. She also returned to college and earned her degree in business administration with a minor in religion from Shaw University in 1984. Though she never doubted the wisdom of her decision to leave North Carolina Central for a career with the Caravans, Caesar felt incomplete without a college degree. Her desire to finish her education was connected to another passion: politics. Talking and singing about the problems of the world were not enough. She wanted to put herself in a position to effect real, structural change in Durham.

Gotta Serve Somebody: Caesar's Civic Activities in Post–Civil Rights Durham

Three years after receiving her bachelor's degree from Shaw, Caesar ran for a seat on Durham's city council. Noting that she wanted to "focus on the needy, not the greedy," she launched a platform centered around fair housing, programs for the elderly, solving the problem of homelessness, and improving the public school system. The singer received endorsements from the Durham Committee on the Affairs of Black People, the People's Alliance, and the Durham Voters Alliance. Despite her lack of formal political experience, Caesar won an at-large seat, adding councilwoman to her long list of achievements. Election day was a surreal experience for the Durham native. "As the numbers were tallied in my favor, I kept hugging my friends, clapping my hands, and jumping up and down. When all of the precinct results were in, I couldn't believe it. I had won! I couldn't believe we had accomplished what the vote was indicating. I had won election in a southern city by 68 percent of the vote. In fact, African Americans filled all three at-large seats on the council."[48]

After her election, Caesar set her sights on ensuring the city's aggressive urban redevelopment plans addressed the concerns and needs of low-income African American families. "My job is to make sure we focus on affordable housing and not try to push the highest priced housing on people who cannot afford it. We are one with the philosophy of growth but not at the expense of our neighborhoods."[49] In her mind, her civic and religious duties were inextricably linked: "I believe in serving God by serving others." More specifically, she had a deep commitment to Durham. "Durham is where it's at," she once told a local reporter; "this is home."[50] Of course, "home" had experienced great change during the post–civil rights period.

Jim Crow segregation had been dismantled, but racial and economic inequality remained a reality for many African Americans in the Bull City. As historian Jean Bradley Anderson notes, "In the waning decades of the century, a confluence of events and trends enormously increased the complexity of social problems in Durham: urban renewal had displaced many poor families and destroyed low-cost housing; the Vietnam War had left many veterans physically or mentally ill, often addicted to alcohol and drugs, and consequently often homeless." Like other cities across the nation, Durham also felt the sting of deindustrialization. According to Anderson, "The decline of traditional blue-collar jobs in tobacco factories and cotton mills as the economy shifted to biomedical and other research left hundreds of workers jobless and unable to fill jobs requiring an educated and skilled workforce."[51] These problems did not escape the notice of Caesar, who through her political and civic activities hoped to transform the city. Her commitment to the less fortunate won her the respect of thousands of local people. "Shirley is a glorious person in our community," raved one Durham resident.[52]

Live . . . in Chicago: The Making of a Gospel Classic and the Rebirth of a Gospel Legend

Even with her growing political commitments, Caesar remained a force in the gospel world. Her 1988 release, *Live . . . in Chicago*, topped the gospel charts from June 18, 1988, to late February 1989. The record featured one of gospel's hottest acts: Milton Brunson and the Thompson Community Singers. A long admirer of the group, Caesar had collaborated with the "Tommies" in the 1970s and renewed her relationship with the choir in 1987, when she returned to Chicago. Instead of working within the confines of the studio, as she had done for much of her tenure with Word, Caesar opted for a live recording at Brunson's Christ Tabernacle Baptist Church. The church was located on North Central Avenue in the heart of a black community on Chicago's west side. If Caesar was looking for an alternative to the controlled, sometimes sterile atmosphere of the studio, Christ Tabernacle, with its deep connection to the surrounding community, was the ideal place.

The live recording provided a much-needed return of sorts for Caesar. Though they hardly qualified as bad records, her last two outings with Word lacked the innovation and fire of her previous material. Creatively, she was at a standstill. And no one recognized this more than Caesar. "Even though I was winning Grammy Awards and Doves and other accolades, I must admit there was a feeling of discontentment in my spirit. I kept remembering the early years of my career when I would sing a capella—songs like 'Peter, Don't Be Afraid,' 'Teach Me Master, Teach Me,' and 'Satan, We're Going to Tear Your Kingdom Down'—and I missed that old traditional gospel sound. And I believed that many of my older listeners did too."[53]

Working with the Thompson Community Singers provided Caesar with the opportunity to reach a younger fan base, as well as to move outside the studio. "I need to get back to my roots," Caesar pleaded with her record company. "Let me record live with a choir, let me minister, let me be me."[54] In Caesar's view, her music with Word had become too slick, too refined, too predictable. "I have got to be free to improvise, to be creative. That is what I do best. Anything that moves me away from that hurts me more than it helps."[55] Though Caesar presented this record as a return to her roots in traditional gospel, this was the sound of black sacred music moving into the twenty-first century.

On the record's first track, "Never," Caesar floats effortlessly through her verses, then powers through the song's chorus. As the singer testifies to God's faithfulness, she tosses out a series of lines familiar to most gospel listeners: "He'll be your friend, when you're friendless, water, when you thirsty, bread, when you're hungry." With ample support from the Tommies, Caesar works the crowd with her fiery extemporizations. "He's a friend," she clarifies to the audience, "a real friend, he'll walk with you, he'll talk with you, he'll live in you, he'll move in you."[56]

Lowering the pace but not the intensity, Caesar segues into "His Blood," a song she dedicates to the victims of AIDS. Perhaps sensing some tension from the audience, she sternly interjects, "You can say whatever you want, that's a mother's son, a father's boy." Her acknowledgment of the disease's devastating impact on the nation and the African American community marked a welcome departure from the black church's general silence.[57] Predicting a medical cure for the disease within a year, the singer presents the AIDS epidemic as connected to larger social issues. Casting her eye on the "brokenness" engulfing the nation, Caesar calls for spiritual renewal within and beyond the church. As Caesar alternates between singing and preaching, sharing biblical stories of Abraham, Ezekiel, and Jesus, the Tommies melodically repeat the song's refrain: "If you come to him and be sincere / His blood can restore your soul."[58]

The need for spiritual renewal is a recurring theme throughout the album, from the inspirational "Yes Lord, Yes," to the bass-heavy "Born Again." Another dominant theme is the promise of a brighter day for those anchored in God and community. On the duet "Things Are Going to Get Better," Caesar and her former Caravans colleague Albertina Walker encourage their listeners to remain steadfast in their faith. More than twenty years had passed since Walker and Caesar sang as members of the Caravans, but their chemistry was still strong.

All of the aforementioned songs were stellar, but none compared in power or appeal to the night's greatest showstopper: "Hold My Mule."

On this eight-minute sermonette, Caesar introduces the audience at Christ Tabernacle to an elderly man named Shouting John. Against the background of piano trills, bluesy guitar notes, and smoldering drums, Caesar walks her audience through the tale of a brewing conflict between an eighty-six-year-old farmer and his church leaders. Early in the sermonette, she vividly describes church leaders' unsuccessful attempts to subdue the elderly man: "The deacons ran and sat him down; he jumped back up. They tried to hold his legs. His hands were going. When they turned the hands loose, the feet were going!" Working her magic on the crowd, Caesar then shouts: "It's just like fire; it's just like fire shut up in my bones."[59]

Weaving class critique into her narrative, she conveys the church leaders' frustration with John's refusal to oblige the church's politics of respectability. "Doesn't he know we don't act like that in our church?" the status conscious deacons query one another. "Doesn't he know we got dignitaries in our church?" Feeling as if the matter had to be handled outside of Sunday service, the clergymen decide to "go out to John's house."[60]

With the crowd under her spell, Caesar gives a play-by-play account of the church leaders' confrontation with John at his home. "When they got out there," Caesar continues, "they found him and a beat-up mule, plowing in the field." What then follows is a spirited exchange between the leaders and John, who recounts what church folk often refer to as "God's favor." In addition to pointing out his ownership of land, he proudly notes his ability to still "harvest my own crop" at his advanced age. He also speaks of a life free from any entanglements with the legal system. "God gave me all of my children," John testifies, but "not one time have I been to the courthouse, not one time have I been to the cemetery."[61] His point is not to position himself as a member of the privileged elite but as a recipient of God's grace.[62]

If their applauses and shouts are any indication, the audience members at Christ Tabernacle identify strongly with John, a "common man" whose faithfulness to God has been well rewarded. Shifting from preacher to songstress, Caesar closes her story with an image of John rejecting the orders of the church leaders and "dancing all around his place."

Throughout the country, gospel listeners could not get enough of the tale of Shouting John, an everyday man who finished on top. Here was a character who resonated deeply with churchgoing, working-class folks from the South who like John might have been condemned as unsophisticated or uncouth by members of the religious elite. The triumphant John character also appealed to certain members of the African American laboring class whose life trajectories did not fit neatly into popular tales of urban decay, broken homes, and poverty—women and men who had managed like John (only through the grace of God, in their minds) to avoid the traps and pitfalls of America's criminal justice system. Caesar's "Hold My Mule" resonated with African Americans who looked at their lives in totality and felt they had been shown God's favor.

Ironically, Caesar's celebration of Shouting John, an independent black landowner, coincided with the dramatic decline in the number of African American farmers. The same year Caesar released "Hold My Mule," the North Carolina Association of Black Lawyers filed a complaint against the Farmers Home Administration (FMHA) alleging discrimination against African American farmers. In its complaint to the U.S. Commission on Civil Rights, the advocacy group accused the FMHA of racial discrimination: "FMHA's actions have further resulted in a disproportionate number of class members being driven out of farming. Between 1978 and 1982, the total number of black and Indian farmers declined 23.2 percent, compared to 9.8 percent for the white farmers."[63] By 1987, African Americans owned only 2.4 million acres, nearly 10 million less than they did in 1900. Perhaps in Shouting John, African Americans, especially those in the South who had experienced the loss of land or had sold their properties well below their value, found a heroic figure who had managed to maintain one of the race's most treasured yet increasingly elusive assets: land.

Released in the year Caesar celebrated her fiftieth birthday, *Live . . . in Chicago* testified to the enduring power and appeal of her talent. Thanks to the radio hits "Hold My Mule," "Yes Lord, Yes," and "His Blood," *Live . . . in Chicago* dominated the gospel charts for nearly a year. At its peak, according to Caesar, the album was selling on average 25,000 copies a week. In 1989, *Billboard* chose Caesar as its gospel artist of the year and *Live . . . in Chicago* as its gospel record of the year. Caesar's selection was a reflection of the depth of her talent, her commercial appeal, and her singularity as an artist. Here was a musician who had maintained a special place in the hearts of gospel lovers for thirty years—not because of organizational connections or past achievements but because she was still at the forefront of the genre.

Caesar understood and recognized her special gift. "I'm a down-to-earth singer serving a modern God. I'm a southerner, and my roots are in traditional gospel music. I like songs that give a profound message. I'm not saying traditional gospel is the only music. The Lord has all kinds of vehicles to win souls. . . . [And] the Lord is using me in mine."[64]

Notes

1. Shirley Caesar, *Live . . . in Chicago* (Rejoice Records, 1988).

2. Caesar, *Live . . . in Chicago.*

3. Brooksie Eugene Harrington, "Shirley Caesar: A Woman of Words," PhD diss. (Ohio State University, 1992), 82.

4. James Weldon Johnson, *God's Trombones: Seven Negro Sermons in Verse* (New York: Viking Press, 1927), 5.

5. Shirley Caesar, *The Lady, the Melody, and the Word: The Inspirational Story of the First Lady of Gospel* (Nashville: Thomas Nelson, 1998), 93.

6. Cheryl J. Sanders, "Pentecostal Ethics and the Prosperity Gospel: Is There a Prophet in the House?" in *Afro-Pentecostalism: Black Pentecostal and Charismatic Christianity in History and Culture*, edited by Amos Yong and Estrelda Y. Alexander, 141–52 (New York: New York University Press, 2011), 150.

7. Caesar, *Lady, the Melody, and the Word*, 157.

8. Cheryl Townsend Gilkes, "Shirley Caesar and the Souls of Black Folk: Gospel Music as Cultural Narrative and Critique," *African American Pulpit* 6, no. 2 (Spring 2003), 12.

9. "First Lady of Gospel," *Ebony*, September 1977, 98. See also "Gospel Star Shirley Caesar Says Female Pastors Ok!" *New Pittsburgh Courier*, August 10, 1985.

10. For a broader reading on black women and their relationship to feminism, see Patricia Hill Collins, *Black Feminist Thought: Knowledge, Consciousness, and the Politics of Empowerment*, 2nd ed. (New York: Routledge, 1991); Katie Cannon, *Black Womanist Ethics* (Atlanta: Scholars Press, 1988); bell hooks, *Ain't I a Woman? Black Women and Feminism* (Boston: South End Press, 1981); Gloria T. Hull, Patricia Bell Scott, and Barbara Smith, *All the Women Are White, All the Blacks Are Men, but Some of Us Are Brave: Black Women's Studies* (New York: Feminist Press, 1982); Beverly Guy-Sheftall, ed., *Words of Fire: An Anthology of African-American Feminist Thought* (New York: New Press, 1995); and Valethia Watkins, "New Directions in Black Women's Studies," in *The African American Studies Reader*, edited by Nathaniel Norment Jr., (Durham: Carolina Academic Press, 2006), 229–40.

11. Caesar, *Lady, the Melody, and the Word*, 10.

12. Booker T. Washington, "Durham, North Carolina, a City of Negro Enterprises," *Independent* 70 (March 30, 1911): 642–50; Leslie Brown, *Upbuilding Black Durham: Gender, Class, and Black Community Development in the Jim Crow South* (Chapel Hill: University of North Carolina Press, 2009); E. Franklin Frazier, "Durham, Capital of the Black Middle Class," in *The New Negro: An Interpretation*, edited by Alain Locke (New York: Arno Press, 1968), 333–40; Walter B. Weare, *Black Business in the New South: A Social History of the NC Mutual Life Insurance Company* (Durham: Duke University Press, 1993).

13. W. Fitzhugh Brundage, *Southern Past: A Clash of Race and Memory* (Cambridge, MA: Harvard University Press, 2005), 234.

14. Frazier, "Durham, Capital of the Black Middle Class," 333.

15. Interview with Hallie Caesar by Glenn Hinson, May 21, 1979 (H-0194), in the Southern Oral History Program Collection, Series H: Piedmont Industrialization (04007H), Southern Historical Collection, Wilson Library, University of North Carolina at Chapel Hill.

16. Caesar, *Lady, the Melody, and the Word*, 34.

17. See William C. Turner, "An East Coast Celebration of Azusa: Theological Implications," *Journal of Pentecostal Theology* 16, no. 1 (2007), 32–45; and William C. Turner, *The United Holy Church of America: A Study in Black Holiness-Pentecostalism* (Piscataway, NJ: Gorgias Press, 2006).

18. Caesar, *Lady, the Melody, and the Word*, 33.

19. Ibid., 33.

20. Ibid., 18.

21. Charlie T. Roach, box 231, Southern Oral History Program Collection, Southern Historical Collection, Wilson Library, University of North Carolina, Chapel Hill.

22. Caesar, *Lady, the Melody, and the Word*, 35.

23. Ibid., 62.

24. Robert M. Marovich, *A City Called Heaven: Chicago and the Birth of Gospel Music* (Urbana: University of Illinois Press, 2015), 234.

25. Bob Darden, "Shirley Caesar: Singing Evangelist," *Rejoice!*, Summer 1990, 9.

26. Caesar, *Lady, the Melody, and the Word*, 73.

27. Ibid., 81.

28. Ibid., 80.

29. "HOB Doubled '66, Billing Promotion, New Acts," *Billboard*, January 20, 1968.

30. Caesar, *Lady, the Melody, and the Word*, 93.

31. Shirley Caesar, *My Testimony* (HOB Records, 1968).

32. Shirley Caesar, *Stranger on the Road* (HOB Records, 1968).

33. "Gospel Singer Performs before SRO Audiences," *New Journal and Guide*, July 20, 1968.

34. Eleanor Blair, "Shirley Caesar Teaches Gospel in a Running Sermon of Songs," *New York Times*, July 31, 1972.

35. Hollie West, "Church-Like Concert by Shirley Caesar," *Washington Post*, September 8, 1969, B6.

36. See S. Craig Watkins, "Black Is Beautiful and It's Bound to Sell: Nationalist Desire and the Production of Black Popular Culture," in *Is It Nation Time? Contemporary Essays on Black Power and Black Nationalism,* edited by Eddie S. Glaude Jr. (Chicago: University of Chicago Press, 2002), 189–214; and William L. Van Deburg, *New Day in Babylon: The Black Power Movement and American Culture, 1965–1975* (Chicago: University of Chicago Press, 1992).

37. Shirley Caesar, *No Charge* (HOB Records, 1975).

38. Darden, "Shirley Caesar," 8.

39. Darden, 8.

40. David Nathan, "First Lady of Gospel: Shirley Caesar," *Blues and Soul*, January 17, 1978, https://www.rocksbackpages.com/Library/Article/shirley-caesar-the-first-lady-of-gospel.

41. M. J. Musik, "Record Ratings," *New York Amsterdam News*, September 17, 1977.

42. Caesar, *Lady, the Melody, and the Word*, 120.

43. Larry Eskridge, *God's Forever Family: The Jesus People Movement in America* (New York: Oxford University Press, 2013), 231–35.

44. "Executive Spotlight: James Bullard, Word Records," *Totally Gospel*, November 1986, 11.

45. Richard Harrington, "Hail to Shirley Caesar," *Washington Post*, February 18, 1983.

46. Caesar, *Lady, the Melody, and the Word*, 142–43.

47. Quoted in B. Harrington, "Shirley Caesar," 43–44.

48. Caesar, *Lady, the Melody, and the Word*, 155.

49. "Shirley Caesar: Putting the Gospel Truth into Politics," *Ebony*, December 1988, 70.

50. Shirley Caesar interview, WTVD Videotape Collection, 1976–1992, VT-4929/166, Special Collections, Wilson Library, University of North Carolina, Chapel Hill.

51. Jean Bradley Anderson, *Durham County: A History of Durham County, North Carolina* (Durham: Duke University Press, 2011), 422.

52. Shirley Caesar interview, WTVD Videotape Collection.

53. Caesar, *Lady, the Melody, and the Word*, 144–45.

54. Ibid., 147.

55. Ibid., 148.

56. Caesar, *Live . . . in Chicago*.

57. Cathy J. Cohen, *Boundaries of Blackness: AIDS and the Breakdown of Black Politics* (Chicago: University of Chicago Press, 1999); Angelique Harris, *AIDS, Sexuality, and the Black Church: Making the Wounded Whole* (New York: Peter Lang, 2010).

58. Caesar, *Live . . . in Chicago*.

59. Ibid.

60. Ibid.

61. Ibid.

62. This performance is an excellent case of how Caesar used the sermonette to connect with audiences. Once again, the work of Brooksie Harrington is insightful: "By presenting a subject in story form, her listener becomes emotionally involved just as they become physically and emotionally involved with her music. Somehow Caesar has perfected her verbal artistry to the point that whichever mode of performance she calls upon, she entreats her audience to become a part of that performance. She appeals to their emotional interests by 'putting it right down front where they can get it.' She also chooses themes, motifs, and plots that most people can identify with and appreciate." Harrington, "Shirley Caesar," 118.

63. Sinclair Ward, "FMHA Policies Harm Minorities, Group Says," *Washington Post*, November 27, 1987.

64. Geoffrey Himes, "Shout It! Gospel According to Shirley Caesar," *Washington Post*, April 3, 1987.

8

Let the Church Sing "Freedom"

BERNICE JOHNSON REAGON

From *Black Music Research Journal* 7 (1987): 105–118

From 1955 to 1965 the equilibrium of American society was racked by waves of social and political protest. Afro-Americans engaging in massive civil disobedience served notice on the nation and the world that they would no longer tolerate the abuses of American racism. The civil rights movement heralded a new era in the Afro-American struggle for equality.

The movement spread throughout the South, greatly accelerated by the entrance of Afro-American college students who, setting their studies aside, served as organizers and workers in segregated rural and urban communities. They received support from local leaders who listened to them, housed them, and fed them. Sharecroppers, ministers, hairdressers, restaurant owners, independent business people, and teachers were the first to try to register to vote, to apply for a job, or to use a public facility previously reserved for whites.

The response was swift and brutal: economic reprisals, jailings, beatings, and killings. Nonetheless, the movement grew, pulling recruits from all segments of the Afro-American community. The issue of systemized and social racism was placed on the American agenda, and individuals and organizations made the choice to join in supporting a growing and activist Afro-American community. The mobilization of this movement led to assaults against an entrenched system under a generalized concept of freedom and resulted in changes in legal, political, and social processes. Reaching deeper than these sometimes cosmetic changes was the transformation wrought in Afro-America that directly related to the actual waging of the struggle. Of significant importance was the altered stance within a collective community. An overt platform underlining a new agenda for action, visibility, and leadership emerged based on the longheld, often submerged or sublimated sense of worth: the view that within the Afro-American community, America had its richest treasurers of moral and human spirit; and the feeling that white was not only not right for Afro-Americans, but that it was also extremely crippling for whites.

Music has always been integral to the Afro-American struggle for freedom. The music culture of the civil rights movement was shaped by its central participants: Afro-American Southerners steeped in oral tradition. The freedom songs—while later captured on tape, sheet music, and commercial recordings—truly came to life, were developed, and were used within the context of the Afro-American tradition. The power of the songs came from the linking of traditional oral expression to the everyday experiences of the movement. Charles Sherrod, field secretary of the Student Nonviolent Coordinating Committee (SNCC), bears witness to how music galvanized the first mass meeting held in Albany, Georgia, in November 1961, into a moral force of reckoning:

> The church was packed before eight o'clock. People were everywhere in the aisles, sitting and standing in the choir stands, hanging over the railing of the balcony, sitting in trees outside the window. . . . When the last speaker among the students, Bertha Gober, had finished, there was nothing left to say. Tears filled the eyes of hard, grown men who had seen with their own eyes merciless atrocities committed. . . . And when we rose to sing "We Shall Overcome," nobody could imagine what kept the church on four corners. . . . I threw my head back and sang with my whole body (Charles Sherrod, quoted in Zinn 1964, 128–129).

Most of the singing of the civil rights movement was congregational; it was sung unrehearsed in the tradition of the Afro-American folk church. This style has its own parameters for defining the range and use of the vocal instruments and its own rules for determining roles for all singers within the group.

The core song repertoire of the civil rights movement was formed from the reservoir of Afro-American traditional song, performed in the older style of singing. This music base was expanded to include most of the popular Afro-American music forms and singing techniques of the period. From this reservoir, activist songleaders made a new music for a changed time. Lyrics were transformed, traditional melodies were adapted, and procedures associated with old forms were blended with new forms to create freedom songs capable of expressing the force and intent of the movement.

Early in the development of each local civil rights movement campaign, strong songleaders emerged spontaneously and came together to form core songleading units. In Montgomery, Alabama, it was the Montgomery Gospel Trio. In the Nashville, Tennessee, sit-ins, it was four young men, students at the American Baptist Theological Seminary, known as the Nashville Quartet. Out of the Freedom Rides and other activities sponsored by the Congress of Racial Equality came the CORE Singers. From the Albany, Georgia, Movement came the original Freedom Singers, followed by a second group of Freedom Singers and, briefly, the Freedom Voices, made up of field secretaries for SNCC. In Mississippi, SNCC field secretaries Willie Peacock, Sam Block, Hollis Watkins, and Fannie Lou Hamer were widely known for their courage, their organizing abilities, and their power as songleaders. From Birmingham came the Alabama Christian Movement Choir, led by Carlton Reese. Activities in Selma and Chicago brought together Jimmy Collier and the Movement Singers. Out of the pressures and needs involved in maintaining group unity on the community level, while working under conditions of intense hostility and physical threat, the sit-in movement developed its own culture, and music was its mainstay.

During the early sit-ins, music was not usually a part of the actual demonstrations. Sit-in leaders wanted to avoid being charged with rowdiness or uncouth behavior. Most demonstrations were carried out in silence.

The songs of this period came out of the group meetings, rallies, and workshop sessions, while silent marches continued throughout the early months of the movement. Still, John Lewis, Nashville, Tennessee, sit-in leader and later chairman of SNCC, explains why, even then, singing sustained marching:

> At the rallies and meetings we sang. One of the earliest songs I remember very well that became very popular was "Amen."
>
> > Amen Amen Amen Amen Amen
> > Freedom Freedom Freedom Freedom Freedom
>
> This song represented the coming together, you really felt it—it was like you were part of the crusade, a holy crusade. You felt uplifted and involved in a great battle and a great struggle. We had hundreds and thousands of students from the different colleges and universities around Nashville gathering downtown in a Black Baptist church. That particular song . . . became the heart of the Nashville movement (Lewis 1974).

There is a close correlation between the changes that songs underwent during the Nashville movement—the most highly organized of the sit-ins—and the changes that were heard during the Montgomery bus boycott. "Amen," a traditional Afro-American sacred chant with a one-word lyric, was musically simple, though each succeeding refrain was triggered and refreshed with a new lead-line:

> Everybody say
> > Amen Amen Amen Amen Amen
> Let the Church say
> > Amen Amen Amen Amen Amen
> Let the Deacons say
> > Amen Amen Amen Amen Amen

The power of this traditional song came from the richness of Afro-American harmonic techniques and improvisation in choral singing. Within the Nashville setting, it gained a new force by being wedded to a dynamic social upheaval. A simple word change from "Amen" to "Freedom" made it a musical statement of the ultimate national goal of the student activists. In Montgomery the changing of words in the song "Old Time Religion" to "We Are Marching on to Victory," which occurred after leaders had been arraigned by the local law officials, can be equated with the singing of "Amen" in Nashville after the return to the church from a round of sit-ins (Maund 1956). In both cases the activists were returning to a haven after a confrontation with the system they were seeking to change. Again and again, it was to the church that they came for physical protection and spiritual nurturing—the very structure developed by the Afro-American community for the survival of its people. The church provided the structure and guidance for calling the community together; it trained the singers to sing the old songs and gave them permission to create new ones; it sometimes produced real leaders, in its ministers, deacons, and church mothers, who met the challenges and worked to address issues of crisis and everyday survival as they arose. Thus, when the question was put to the churches in local communities, often the doors were opened and the movement had a home, a nurturing ground in which to grow and mature.

The mass meeting provides the most concrete mode of cultural expression from which to view the ways in which the church provided both tradition and room to absorb the changes needed to accommodate the experiences of the new activist community. The following is an examination of a mass meeting with particular concern for the role of song and songleaders in the gathering.

In the fall of 1963 in Greenwood, Mississippi, a meeting was called together by veteran organizer Willie Peacock, a native of Columbus, Mississippi, who had been warned not to return to his community because of his organizing activity. The term "veteran" is appropriately applied to an organizer of Peacock's caliber, not because of his years in the field but because of the intensity of his work over a short period of time. In 1961 Mississippi was targeted for organizing by the Student Nonviolent Coordinating Committee. Peacock, often teamed with Sam Block, was one of the most gifted of the students who left schools, homes, and safety to throw their lives and pit their skills against a system that promised no compassion and no change. By the fall of 1963 Medgar Evers (NAACP State President) had been murdered by Byron De La Beckwith, a quarter of a million people had marched on Washington, and groups of organizers had been sent to communities throughout the state of Mississippi to work on a mock election designed to demonstrate that the state was indeed keeping thousands of Afro-American people from registering and voting. Consequently, on this fall evening a few people gathered in a church. Calling them together was one whom they had trained in the church to sing, to organize, and to commit his life to the opportunity for change that had been too long in coming.

Willie Peacock opened the mass meeting by referring to Mrs. Fannie Lou Hamer, the speaker of the evening. (It is significant that the meeting was being directed by leaders of the community, not necessarily officers of the church: the church served as host, and the central address did not come from the traditional spiritual leader, the minister.) The speaker, Fannie Lou Hamer, was a spiritual leader and a member of the church. Her status as leader came from the experiences she had endured as one of the first Mississippians to try to register and vote. While in most congregations, women were allowed in the pulpit on the traditional Women's Day program, it was not unusual to find a woman in the pulpit of a Baptist congregation during the movement. Peacock ended his reference to Mrs. Fannie Lou Hamer as a great speaker by stating that she was also a great singer and asked that she lead in "This Little Light of Mine." Immediately, the powerful contralto voice of Fannie Lou Hamer filled the room. Before she completed the first two phrases of the song, "This little light of mine, I'm gonna let it shine," she was joined by others in the congregation. The song continued for a few minutes, with new lines signaling each new statement of the cycle.

> Jesus gave it me
> Everywhere I go
> Shine, Shine, Shine
> All in the Jail House
> This Little Light of Mine.

The song swelled as it continued, and one could sense the energy level of the congregation being stirred as the last sung line was covered by a rich sprinkling of "Amens" coming from all sections of the room.

Willie Peacock introduced the next singer as a singer in the struggle from Danville, Virginia, and Knoxville, Tennessee. Matthew Jones led "Keep Your Eyes on the Prize, Hold On," a spiritual he reshaped into a local statement by changing the standard verses.

> Greenwood people bowed in jail
> Got no money to go their bail.
> Keep your eyes on the prize,
> Hold on, hold on, hold on.
> Keep your eyes on the prize, hold on.

This Greenwood-people verse is of course the reworking of the "Paul and Silas bound in jail" verse. This locally inspired substitution continued throughout the song.

Greenwood began to shout.
Jail door opened, and they walked out.

Ain't but one thing we did wrong.
Stayed in this wilderness a day too long.

Ain't but one thing a man can stand
Is that chain of hand to hand.

Chief Larry ain't got no sense.
Fighting nonviolence with violence.

"Ain't but one thing we done wrong" and the "only thing a man can stand" were not lyrics unique to Greenwood or to the song raised by Jones, but were favored lines used in numerous songs throughout local campaigns wherever they could be placed in the structure of a song. These verses were stock verses that every competent songleader had to have in order to function effectively in a mass meeting.

The mass meeting moved at an informal pace with Peacock deciding how to develop the evening as he went along. He asked Jones for another song, this time Jones sang "We Shall Not Be Moved."

We shall not, we shall not be moved.
We shall not, we shall not be moved.
Just like a tree, planted by the water,
We shall not be moved.

Again, before the first phrase was completed, the entire congregation joined in. One could soon distinguish voices and their places in the songs as the song service progressed. Fannie Lou Hamer's voice moved quickly into the background on the alto line, and a high soprano voice could be heard above the other voices throughout the meeting. Peacock carried the tenor line, while a bass worked the bottom. Tight, clear harmony could not be discerned because every sound and texture space between the strongly identified chord and harmony lines seemed worked over for variant lines by the congregation. Volume levels were also not at all matched; one heard the soft subtle voices as distinctly as the loud powerful ones.

One verse that had a Mississippi focus flipped the song around for more than the usual line:

Governor Johnson, we shall not be moved.
Governor Johnson, we shall not be moved.

Governor Johnson, he shall be removed.
Just like a pail of garbage in the alley,
He shall be removed!

Jones began this verse in the traditional way with "we shall not be moved." After the "Governor Johnson" line, a number of singers began reworking the lyrics on the second line so that one heard two lines: "we shall not be moved" and "he shall be removed." By the tag line, the lyrics were "just like a pail of garbage in the alley, he shall be removed!" This new shift became a way of handling negative images that one did not want to stand "like a tree planted by the waters," and it was introduced to a new audience even as they sang the song. On this recording one can experience the congregational learning process in operation as the singers discovered something new being added and made the adjustment to the new lyric line. This change is important in view of the fact that this mass meeting revolved around the struggle for the right to vote, an issue for which the governor of Mississippi expressed no support.

As soon as "We Shall Not Be Moved" was released by the congregation, Fannie Lou Hammer raised "Go Tell It on the Mountain." There was no introduction to this song; it seemed to spring out of a readiness in the singers; there was a feeling that the meeting had officially begun and had developed its own spiritual power and pace. Again, with "Go Tell It on the Mountain," the singers borrowed from a spiritual; this time a song more widely known as a Christmas carol was adapted to the needs of the movement.

Go tell it on the mountain,
Over the hills, and everywhere.
Go tell it on the mountain
That Jesus Christ is born.

"That Jesus Christ is born" became "to let my people go."

He made me a watchman
Upon the city walls.
And if I am a Christian,
I am the least of all.

"When I was a seeker/I sought both night and day/I asked the Lord to help me/ And he showed me the way" was dropped for a stock movement verse:

Paul and Silas began to shout.
Jail door opened, and they walked out.

Mrs. Hamer also used verses more associated with the spiritual "Wade in the Water" and continued building the song:

Who's that yonder dressed in black?
Must be the hypocrites farming in back.

> Who's that yonder dressed in red?
> Must be the children that Moses led.

This last verse had special meaning during the movement, because the director of the SNCC Mississippi Project was none other than a man named Robert Paris Moses. Fannie Lou Hamer had a powerful way of articulating that this was surely a sign from God that it was time for Mississippi Negroes to move.

The last verse of this performance was a traditional verse; another performance would bring another rendering and combining of traditional, stock, and locally influenced verses. The last verse was:

> Had a little book that was gave to me,
> Every page spelled victory.

After each verse the congregation exploded in song and power. When the pace had rested, Peacock asked if there was a need for more singing—adding that, "I could sing all night"—and introduced the first speaker.

Dick Frye was a white worker from California who was working in the mock election and who had been arrested and beaten on the day of the meeting. His talk was a straightforward narrative describing the work of the mock election as well as the arrest the night before of several workers including himself. He described the beating that took place as he left a courthouse to attempt to get bonds so that those still in jail could be released. Those gathered heard a justification for a mock election set up to prove that Afro-Americans would vote if they could.

When Frye finished, Willie Peacock stated, "Just like Frye said, we got to 'wade in the water.' You might have to take over the courthouse." This interpretation of the spiritual[1] was used often. The concept being that "troubled water" was powerful water. The spiritual promised troubled water.

> Wade in the water,
> Wade in the water, children.
> Wade in the water.
> God's gonna trouble the water.

The metaphor of water as troubled water being an element of change becomes in this song a way to urge people to turn in the direction of their fear, and that when they move in the direction from whence comes their trouble, there is the promise of relief in God-troubled-water. After additional statements that started with what "we might have to do," including the threat of violence if the federal government was not forthcoming in response to results of the mock election, Fannie Lou Hamer led right into the song with verses like:

> Some say Peter, some say Paul.
> There ain' but the one God made us all.

You can hinder me here.
You can hinder me there.
But the Lord in Heaven
Gon' hear my prayer.

Without a break Willie Peacock led a stirring rendition of "Come Bah Yah."
"Come Bah Yah," as led by Peacock, blends several stages of the song's evolution. During slavery, "Come By Here" was sung as a spiritual. It was taken
to Liberia, West Africa, where the pronunciation of words already shaped by
Afro-Americans in the United States was further altered by the tonal linguistic
culture. The Africanized version was re-imported and popularized as "Cum Bah
Yah." Although sung in the same mass meeting as "Go Tell It on the Mountain"
and "Wade in the Water" and by the same group of singers, the shift in lead
from Hamer to Peacock resulted in a shift in harmonization and vocal textures.
The core group of songleaders moved into a smoother, more Western classical
choral statement with the tight harmony found in arranged spirituals ("Voices
of the Civil Rights Movement" 1980). Out of the warming of the singing of the
song, Peacock spoke about the speaker of the evening:

> In the spirit of that song—it tells about the suffering that the one who is about
> to speak has undergone, from time to time, from 1962 up until the present
> day. The person who was one of the first to go down and attempt to register
> to vote in Ruleville, Mississippi. At a time when Greenwood was scared to
> show its face, back in '62, this lady of whom I speak received tremendous
> harassment, shot at many times, and yet she keeps praying that prayer which
> the song carries—Fannie Lou Hamer.

Fannie Lou Hamer, a master of the Afro-American spoken word tradition,
held forth, weaving a powerful oration, blending the scriptures with her testimony, and calling to those gathered for company, criticizing those not ready to
take the opportunity.

After Mrs. Hamer's speech, an elder offered the following testimony:

> I have been! I passed! I have boys and girls unless you old people leave Jeff
> Davis—This is a new time, This is a new world. My text is to go to the court-
> house and keep on going.

Out of his statement Fannie Lou Hamer led into "Have You Got Good Religion? Certainly Lord":

> Have you got good religion? Certainly Lord.
> Have you got good religion? Certainly Lord.
> Have you got good religion? Certainly Lord,
> Certainly, certainly, certainly, Lord.

In song, the questions continued, moving into the issues of the movement:

Do you hate segregation?

Do you want your freedom?

Have you been to the courthouse?

Did you try to vote?

Do you love everybody?

With the last verse Mrs. Hamer released the power of her lead, but before the song ended another voice came in with a verse that further localized the statement: "Will you tell Martha Lamb?" (Lamb was the registrar whom people had to face when they went to the courthouse.)

This practice of a song that first seems to be ending being picked up by a new leader is very common within the songleader tradition. However, in this case the new leader began her new line in the wrong key. And Hamer, again within the tradition, rescued the situation by covering the wayward leader with a superior line, clarifying the key, and stabilizing the singing. Hamer continued the singing, but this time it was "Woke Up This Morning with My Mind Stayed on Freedom."

I woke up this morning with my mind stayed on freedom.
I woke up this morning with my mind stayed on freedom.
I woke up this morning with my mind stayed on freedom.
Hallelu, hallelu, hallelujah.

Walking and talking with my mind . . .

Singing and praying with my mind . . .

This gospel song was brought into the freedom song repertoire during the Freedom Rides when the Freedom Riders were jailed in Mississippi in 1961. It had been a popular quartet song entitled "Woke Up This Morning with My Mind Stayed on Jesus." A Rev. Osby of Aurora, Illinois, is credited with revamping the text in the Hinds County jail. Mrs. Hamer's singing of the song is very much in the same mode as it was throughout the South in the freedom version. Before the civil rights movement, quartet songs with a bridge were almost never done as congregational songs. One would have vigorous participatory support, but tightly harmonized bridges were not congregationalized. It was very common to find congregations in mass meetings moving effectively through these kinds of changes. In this song Mrs. Hamer makes the change with "I'm gonna," moving into a kind of vamp on eight repetitions of "walk, walk, walk, walk"; then in a chord change up a fifth to eight repetitions of "talk," bringing the bridge to an end with "oh———walk walk" into "cause it ain' no harm to keep your mind," opening up the next verse.

As soon as the song was finished, Peacock asked Matthew Jones to sing one of his compositions. Jones began by telling the story of a G.I. from Danville, Virginia, stationed at Fort Bragg who, responding to the brutality with which the law officials met demonstrators in his hometown, decided that when he went home, he was going to demonstrate wearing his uniform. Jones spent time sharing a cell with the soldier and wrote "Demonstrating G.I."

> I'm a demonstrating G.I. from Fort Bragg.
> The way they treat my people makes me mad.
> You know that I couldn't sit still,
> Because my home town is in Danville.

Jones sang this song in a calypso ballad style, accompanied by handclapping and footpatting from the congregation. In the second chorus, he was joined by a few straggling voices. When he came out of the McNamara verse, he asked people to join in and the congregation responded:

> I'm a demonstrating G.I. from Fort Bragg.
> The way they treat my people makes me mad.
> You know that I, I couldn't sit still,
> Because my home is in Danville.
>
> I came home one Friday night.
> I saw my sister fighting for her rights.
> I said, "Keep on, Sis, and I'll be back
> Standing tall, in my boots so black."
>
> Sitting in camp I read the paper.
> I said to my sargeant, "I'll see you later."
> I caught a bus and came on home.
> "I told you, Sis, you wouldn't be alone."
>
> I got arrested on Sunday eve.
> The policemen said, "You've been overseas,
> But don't you forget one simple fact,
> That your skin is still black."
>
> Secretary of Defense McNamara
> Said, "Come on boy, what's the matter?"
> I don't care if you fight for freedom,
> But please take off that uniform.

Out of this singing of the song about a companion community engaged in struggle, Jones introduced and sang another song—a ballad documenting the assassination of Medgar Evers who was killed in Mississippi in 1963 at the time of the Danville campaign. The congregation joined in very quickly in the chorus, cast in a Western hymnlike setting reminiscent of the "Ballad of Jessie

James." This meeting was full of people who knew and respected Medgar Evers. They had lived with his work as state president of the NAACP and had very recently lived through his death. As the song continued, the room seemed to become softly washed in its sound. When the song was over, Peacock quietly said, "Let us stand and sing our closing song." Without another cue, Fannie Lou Hamer's voice once again raised the song that had become the signal song of the movement: "We shall overcome/We are not afraid/God is on our side/ We'll walk hand in hand." The meeting was closed in song and prayer ("Mass Meeting" 1963, Tape N33).

The Greenville mass meeting was just one of thousands held during the organizing days of the movement that stretched from Montgomery to the Poor Peoples Campaign in 1968. As it is in most cases, the role of congregational song was crucial; clearly, on this fall evening in 1963 more than sixty percent of the time was devoted to songs. In most of these mass meetings, all songs were to some extent derived from church-based literature. Exceptions occurred in cases where guests offered solos or where, in the case of a Jackson, Mississippi, meeting, the street-based freedom song repertoire was used. The last song of this meeting, "We Shall Overcome," is again a song of the Afro-American congregational-style church. The introduction of this traditional song into the growing repertoire of freedom songs was in part due to the presence of Guy Carawan from the Highlander Folk Center in Mount Eagle, Tennessee, in the Nashville sit-in movement. This song had been brought to Highlander during the 1940s by white tobacco workers on strike at the American Tobacco Company in Charleston, South Carolina. The striking workers, at Highlander for a workshop in union organizing, reportedly told Zilphia Horton, then Highlander's director of music and the wife of director and founder Miles Horton, that this was a song sung by Afro-American members of the union local on the picket line. Horton added the song to her workshop repertoire. She taught it to Peter Seeger in 1947, and it was published in a People's Song Bulletin in 1949. Guy Carawan sang it as one of the songs shared in mass meetings and workshops with the Nashville students who led the sit-ins in that community in 1960 (Reagon 1975, 64–89).

But Nashville students were not the first movement activists to hear the song. Guy Carawan recounted an incident at a Highlander workshop in 1959, attended by people from Montgomery, where the song was pressed into service:

It's amazing what strength this song has. It's just unbelievable sometimes how it can bring people together. One night in 1959, a group of about 60 of us had assembled at the Highlander School. It was the end of a workshop, and we were having punch and cake and seeing a movie. The local police and sheriff burst in. You see, Tennessee officials were always trying to break up the school—they considered it subversive—and a couple of years later they succeeded. Well, for an hour and a half they forced the people—some of them students—to sit in the dark while they went through rooms and searched suitcases and bags. Somebody started to hum "We Shall Overcome" and someone else took it up. Then from a Negro girl—a high school student (Mary Ethel Dozier) from Montgomery, Alabama—a new verse came into being. Sitting there in the dark, this girl began to sing, "We are not afraid, we are not afraid today" (Lowen 1965, 2–8).

From workshops at Highlander and rallies or sit-in activities, "We Shall Overcome" traveled to Shaw University in Raleigh, North Carolina, where over two hundred sit-in leaders met, on April 15–17, 1961, with members of the Southern Christian Leadership Conference (SCLC). At the end of the first evening, Guy Carawan began to lead songs. When "We Shall Overcome" began, everybody stood and joined hands, and from that point on it was the signal song of the movement (Carawan 1974).

> We shall overcome.
> We shall overcome.
> We shall overcome someday.
> Oh, deep in my heart, I do believe
> We shall overcome someday

Of this song, Reverend Wyatt T. Walker, second Executive Director of SCLC, wrote:

> One cannot describe the vitality and emotion this hymn evokes across the Southland. I have heard it sung in great meetings with a thousand voices singing as one. I've heard a half a dozen sing it softly behind the bars of the Hinds County prison in Mississippi. I heard old women singing it on the way to work in Albany, Georgia. I've heard the students singing it as they were being dragged away to jail. It generates power that is indescribable. It manifests a rich legacy of music literature that serves to keep body and soul together for that better day which is not far off (Carawan and Carawan 1963, 11).

The civil rights movement was a "borning" struggle heralding a new period of activism for its time. New ground was broken and prepared, and a foundation was laid that would make it possible for ever-widening segments of society to discover ways in which unacceptable conditions of life could be changed. These methods included organized action against oppression, disenfranchisement, and exploitation. Such action would begin to create a climate that would nurture a standard of life based on equality of opportunity and human dignity. And the cultural and moral underpinning was there—a foundation laid by the Afro-American church, certainly also created for the crucial purpose of struggle; and the church was indeed a freedom singing church.

Note

1. "Wade in the Water" is often associated, in the black oral tradition, with Harriet Tubman, a conductor on the underground railway during slavery.

References

Carawan, Guy. 1974. Interview with the author, July 6.

Carawan, Guy, and Candy Carawan. 1963. *We shall overcome.* New York: Oak Publications.

Lewis, John. 1974. Interview with the author, November.

Lowen, Irving. 1965. We shall overcome, origin of the rights song. *The Sunday Star*, July 11:2–8.

Mass Meeting, Greenwood, Mississippi. 1963. Moses Moon Collection, Program in Black American Culture Archive, National Museum of American History, Smithsonian Institution, Washington, D.C. Tape recordings.

Maund, Alfred. 1956. Around the U.S.A. *The Nation*, March 3.

Reagon, Bernice Johnson. 1975. *Songs of the Civil Rights Movement 1955–1964*: A study in culture history. Ph.D. diss., Howard University.

Voices of the civil rights movement black American freedom songs, 1955–1965. 1980. Washington, D.C.: Smithsonian Institution Collection of Recordings.

Zinn, Howard. 1964. *SNCC: The new abolitionist.* Boston: Beacon Press.

9

After the Golden Age

Negotiating Perspective

EILEEN M. HAYES

From *Songs in Black and Lavender: Race, Sexual Politics,*
and Women's Music, by Eileen M. Hayes (2010)

This is another day! Are its eyes blurred with maudlin grief for any wasted
past? A thousand thousand failures shall not daunt! Let dust clasp dust, death,
death; I am alive!
—Don Marquis

According to both movement founders and scholars, women's music experienced its golden age from the early 1970s to the mid-to-late 1980s, a period that
roughly coincides with the heyday of the women's movement, 1969–1984.[1] As
liberal feminism became more institutionalized, explicit antifeminism emerged
in the late 1970s as a major foundation of the ultraconservative New Right; the
election of President Ronald Reagan reflected the influence of that countermove-
ment.[2] The halcyon days of the women's movement gave way to a period of abey-
ance or suspended activity. Scholars point out that it is possible for members of
social movements to feel they are still a part of those movements, even during
periods of individual or collective inactivity.

The suggestion of endism implied in this chapter's title is appropriate for
a number of reasons. By 1990 one of the early signposts that the women's
music movement was in a state of flux was the demise of most of the women's
music recording and distribution companies that had sustained the women's
music network during the 1970s. Recording companies like Olivia Records
(1973–1989); Redwood Records, founded in 1972 by singer and peace activist
Holly Near; and Women's Wax Works, founded by Alix Dobkin, had ceased
operation by the late 1980s. During the same period, the number of independent women's music distribution companies, including Women's Revolutions
Per Minute, shrank from sixty to only a few, the best known being Ladyslipper
and Goldenrod.[3]

Another signpost was that musicians who performed at women's music festivals early in their careers—white rockers Melissa Etheridge and Michelle Shocked, and black neo-folk-rocker Tracy Chapman among them—became mainstream sensations and, to the disappointment of many fans, did not credit the community that gave them their start.[4] In the end, women's music as a lesbian feminist project did not change the mainstream industry as some of its proponents had hoped. Many women, however, were provided with hands-on experience in lighting design, sound engineering, performance, and concert production. Countless more women, mostly lesbians, benefited from the *communitas* and feminist esprit de corps that women's music concerts and, later, festivals inspired.

Given these signs of decline, a question sounds throughout this book with ostinato-like frequency: How can black women's collective musical experience be integrated into an examination of women's music without positioning their participation as supplemental to a narrative in progress, or even tangential to an era that has been memorialized by cultural insiders and scholars alike?[5] It is tricky to suggest that an era is over and at the same time argue not only that its activities are ongoing but that they matter, yet this is the work I carry out here.

Constructs of golden ages are as interesting for what they tell us about the designators of such eras and the modes of discourse through which such pronouncements are made as they are for the periods they characterize. Refuting suggestions that women's music has lost its relevance or that it is dead, veteran musicians and cultural insiders, black and white, have marked the end of an era in particular ways while at the same time continuing to perform at festivals. *Radical Harmonies,* an award-winning film by ethnomusicologist Boden Sandstrom and director Dee Mosbacher, is a highly visible example of the framing of women's music as an era in the past. The film, situated as a retrospective, is described as a history of a movement that paved the way for today's new wave of musicians in rock.[6] It consists of interviews with prominent musicians, festival producers, and heads of the former women's record labels interspersed with performance footage. In part because of its medium, celebratory tone, and rockist frame, Sandstrom and Mosbacher's film will dictate the way women's music is perceived for decades to come. *Radical Harmonies* subsumes the literature on the topic, which to date consists of several dissertations, articles scattered through the literature of various disciplines, this study, and Bonnie Morris's *Eden Built by Eves.* Morris, a women's historian by training, is well known in the festival community as both a performer and a chronicler of women's music festival history. By her own admission, Morris's book is a "soaring tribute" to women's music festivals and not a scholarly examination, a fact that does not detract from its insights. At the same time, it is unfortunate that Morris counterposes her book against an alternative she describes as a "dry scholarship of festival culture."[7] I would have liked to have read her version of the latter, certain that had she eschewed positivist historical description and problematized issues of women's historiography, the final product would have been anything but dry.

That cultural insiders would frame women's music is both strategic and preemptive. Veteran black producer Linda Tillery describes herself as the "queen mother" to women's music. For some, this description constitutes a rhetorical maneuver by which the esteemed musician attempts to deflect the tendency of women fans to consider her a love interest or sex object.[8] For others, the appellation of "queen mother" recalls the term's honorific association in some African cultures. Holly Near, the well-known white peace activist and singer/songwriter, describes the "women's music era" as a phenomenon of the 1970s and 1980s. No matter how the pie of periodicity is sliced, it becomes clear that time has passed and that lesbian feminism and society as a whole has been affected, a phenomenon that recalls the title of Cris Williamson's *Changer and the Changed*.[9] Cultural insiders have been inspired to put their own spin on the history of an alternative industry that was poised to "change women and music forever."[10]

This chapter explores the effects of the passage of time on the women's music scene. Drawing primarily on interviews with "first-generation" black women musicians, I consider how musicians' lives and attitudes have changed over time, their responses to the ethos of cultural feminism, and how we can most appropriately conceptualize the differences in perspective between the scene's first generation of black musicians and more recent arrivals. After analyzing certain common features in how first-generation musicians conceptualize their multifaceted identities as musicians, feminists, black women, and in some cases lesbians, I conclude the chapter with a consideration of strategic silences and the politics of sexual identity disclosure.

Nostalgia and Hope

The focus on endism calls forth the circulation of nostalgia that accompanies the closure of various projects or perceived ends of eras. This structure of feeling pervades not only recent writings about women's music but also classic rhythm and blues.[11] Ironically, champions of periodization in black music studies often decry the end of a genre while acknowledging or participating simultaneously in its perpetuation. What helps interpret this phenomenon is the suggestion that nostalgia is a cultural practice, not a given content. Its forms, meanings, and effects shift with the context, writes Kathleen Stewart, and one's point of view depends on one's position in the present.[12]

Insiders to women's music also participate in this selective reframing of the past, invoking a discourse of nostalgia, referring to "passed torches" or to the vast numbers of (white) "graying heads" at festivals. The ever-increasing numbers of recreational vehicles in a landscape where tents once predominated, as well as comments that "the music isn't the same as it used to be," or "festivals aren't as political as they were in the past," dramatize nostalgia's role as an "essential, narrative, function of language."[13] Musicians in particular prefaced stories of festival history with "back in the day," a phrase that at one point circulated in African American communities almost exclusively but is now ubiquitous. If the comments of my undergraduate students are any indication, there is little cross-generational agreement as to the temporal dimensions of "the day," meaning whether it was decades or months ago.

Phase one of my research, which was comprised of interviews with musicians of the first generation, was characterized by the selective framing of the past I have described. Conversations I had with black festigoers, both during and after phase one, gave voice to the hope for the future incorporation of more black musicians into the women's music fold.[14] A black woman engineer from West Virginia put it aptly, "Ten years from now, we could have a whole slew of artists in the mainstream." As an African American researcher talking with other black women, I interpreted this point of view as a racialized hope for inclusion. Yet, more than ten years have passed since that declaration, and the interlocutor's hope of witnessing an exponential increase in black lesbian artists in the mainstream has not come to pass. The career trajectory of a Tracy Chapman indicates that it may not be possible or even desirable for black woman artists to maintain a presence in both camps, by which I mean the pop music industry and the alternative social space of women's music based in lesbian separatism.

Within women's music festival culture, temporality is marked by the distance from one memorable event (whether pleasant or rancour filled) to the next. Paradoxically, however, black musicians seemed little inclined to revisit the bad "good ole days," preferring to focus on the present. I spoke about this reluctance with Judy Dlugacz, who in 1973 founded the women's music recording company Olivia. Dlugacz referred to the activities of Olivia during the early period as "a great experiment." She elaborated: "We made incredible music and we put it out there. And we cared about each other and wanted it to work, and the truth is, we couldn't really pull it off." As she articulated later, Olivia made "real attempts" to record diverse music and artists of various ethnicities, but "the economics" weren't in their favor. "The reasons are many," Dlugacz said, "but the main one is that there were not very many women of color out of the closet in the mid-seventies, and so while the R&B [Linda Tillery] and jazz records [Mary Watkins] sold well for an independent label (over ten thousand copies), there was not enough to sustain the economics of the record company." Returning to the reluctance of some musicians to talk about past incidents, she elaborated: "Do we want to be disappointed in each other? Do we want to say 'somebody hurt me'? It's not as though anybody meant to hurt anybody. It's just—what are you going to do?—it didn't work . . . That's why I would say people don't want to talk about it. That would be it."[15] For the reasons Dlugacz describes, part of what I experienced in conversation with "first-generation" musicians (an analytical category I will detail momentarily) was long pauses when I followed certain paths of inquiry. Perhaps some of the reticence alluded to by Dlugacz can also be explained by what a small world women's music is. Although some black women artists have since moved on, many are still performing and enjoy working relationships, if not friendships, with other musicians and festival producers on the circuit. Dlugacz's allusion to the selective lens of memory is compatible with my own interests, for it is not my intent to present a seamless narrative of women's music festival history, a titillating exposé, or a longitudinal ethnographic account of any one festival; rather, the essays of this book are conceived as a contemplation on race and the politics of sexual identity in the women's music festival community.

The Changers and the Changed

Generational fissures figure prominently in public and private debates about the future of the (black) race, feminism, black feminism, and lesbian feminism. How can we reconcile the continued involvement of veteran musicians, some of whom are now in their late fifties or older, with the contributions of musicians who comprise a much younger cohort? This book posits the involvement of two generations of musicians in women's music, a perspective that applies to the white musicians in this arena as well.[16] Indeed, age is a less productive mode of categorization than the distinctive features separating the periods in which musicians came of political age. Both cohorts have exhibited a wide range of musical sensibilities over time and have advocated for themselves as blacks, women, and, in applicable instances, lesbians. The task is to reconcile the involvement of all these musicians with the changing manifestations of racism and the evolution of sexual identity politics from the mid-1970s to the second decade of the twenty-first century.

Musicians who readily identified with the modes of feminist thought exhibited in the political legacy represented by Bernice Johnson Reagon and Sweet Honey in the Rock (SHIR) comprise the "first" generation of musicians. Under Reagon's direction, SHIR brought a civil-rights-protest-era-inflected music and sensibility, as well as a history of radical women's politics, to the women's music scene. Although there is an age difference between Reagon, Linda Tillery, and singer/songwriter Deidre McCalla, for example, within this framework they are all members of the first generation. In an observation into which one can insert politics and musical style, Nancy Whittier writes, "At some point, separate micro-cohorts cohere into a distinct political generation when the similarities among them outweigh their differences."[17] A newer cohort of musicians negotiates feminism and lesbian feminist identities with the advent of queer nation politics emerging in the early 1990s—hence, singer/songwriter/guitarist Doria Roberts's appeal to a constituency that is very different from that of the first generation.

The generational mode of analysis has a practical use. Thinking along the lines I suggest can help temper the propensity of middle-aged adults to despair at the ways members of the next generation "do politics" and, for that matter, music. At the same time, it helps members of the next generation understand the considerable investment of members of a prior generation who, still active, also responded to the complexities of their time.[18] The first and second generations of black women musicians in women's music made commitments to the women's movement, to feminism, and to lesbian feminism at different times and therefore exhibit different frames of reference. In the field of identity politics, coming to terms with the understandings of differently positioned subjects is crucial.

The newer cohort of black musicians, some of whom incorporate sampling into their musical compositions, pay tribute periodically to members of an earlier generation of central figures in women's music, black and white. Nedra Johnson's rendition of Maxine Feldman's "Amazon Woman Rise," originally written in the 1970s, is an example. The tribute to Feldman and to "Amazon history" became a tradition wherein each year musicians performed the song at the opening ceremony of the Michigan festival.[19] I asked Nedra Johnson to talk about what the song meant to her. Her response indicates the appreciation of one generation of black women musicians and feminist activists for paths forged by women of an earlier generation. She speaks to a discourse in which women's music is projected into the past as a sonic reverberation of lesbian feminism and to the importance of contextualizing the contributions of radical feminism to the women's movement:

> Yeah, she [Maxine Feldman] called me crying and was like, "Thanks for not forgetting me." I was like, "Are you kidding? I hear this song every year. We definitely haven't forgotten."
>
> This is where I hear the younger folks being like "old school, lesbian, folk music, blah blah," but I have my own opinion on that. I am like, "This is gangsta. It's not radical?" It's not radical because she did it thirty years ago. It wouldn't be radical to do that today, because young folks are doing more crazy things and they are like, "Look, I'm out; I've always been out of the closet," and they take that for granted. It is great that people can be like that, but it is disappointing, because it's like they think they are Christopher Columbus or something—like they discovered America and didn't nobody live there before.
>
> [Along another line,] I remember twenty years ago, I had her [Alix Dobkin's] card, and it said "International Lesbian Folk Singer." It was dangerous to have a business card that said "lesbian" on it. It might not seem all that deep now.[20]

Johnson critiques the tendency of a newer generation of queer-identified consumers to distance themselves from the music, if not the politics, represented by white musicians Cris Williamson, Margie Adam, Holly Near, Meg Christian, Alix Dobkin, and Maxine Feldman. Ironically, many middle-aged music consumers also both claim and distance themselves from the era evoked by the names of these musicians.

In recent years, black women within and beyond the academy have engaged in an intergenerational exchange of thinking about black feminist identity. These conversations have taken place over coffee, at kitchen tables, in scholarly journals, and in cars while hip-hop music plays at high decibels. Proponents from various camps, discrete and overlapping, maintain that young people—women in particular—care little about inroads into black liberatory struggle or feminism made by members of a generation before them. My conversation with Malika, twenty-five, belies this suggestion. Here, the musician talks generally about the debt her generation owes the preceding one in terms of black feminist activism, lesbian feminism, and so on:

> First of all, I think that the younger generation are really perceived as taking a lot for granted. I think that this might be true, but on the other hand, all the fighting [the older generation did] was so we could take these things for granted. I mean—not to say we should take things for granted—but so we don't have to think about stuff. The idea was to remove discrimination as much as possible so the next generation wouldn't have to deal with it. So now we're not dealing with it as much, so we are just kind of carefree and very loud about our sexuality, which makes the older generation very annoyed, because they are like, "We fought, and all you guys are doing is just throwing parties." But the freedom that they granted us by the work that they did was so that we could throw parties out in the open, and celebrate our music. It's kinda like how—I had a friend whose landlady was annoyed because we weren't going to gay churches, because they had fought for that, when the reality is that they fought to give us the option of going to gay churches. It's like the black college situation. It makes me mad that more of us are not going and that they are closing, but the reality of it is that the civil rights movement was about us being able to go to school wherever we wanted. That's what is happening, so I think you definitely lose some culture from that, but you know, things move on—even when sometimes they probably shouldn't.[21]

Implicit in the observations of both Johnson and Malika is that social movements are not static; nor, over the long haul, are they propagated by the same activist leaders. These understandings can be missed in modes of analyses that pit generation against generation, as the next generation sets its priorities and puts its own spin on the legacy it has been bequeathed. This is as true for the radical women's movement as it is for black liberatory struggle in its current manifestations. In an observation that has relevance for women's music festival culture, Whittier rightly suggests that differences between feminist generations result in generational politics that are more relevant to the resulting debates and shifts within the women's movement than to young women's decisions to become feminists in the first place. In putting conflicts between generations of participants in the women's movement in context, she prosaically says something that others have said more plainly: "A movement remains alive as long as there is struggle over its collective identity, or as long as calling oneself or one's organization 'feminist' means something."[22] These are issues that resonate with insiders to women's music.

"But I Never Believed That": Reactions to the Musical Underneath of Cultural Feminism

Given that women's music festivals continue to this day and that consumers purchase CDs and attend concerts by the musicians discussed in this book, it makes sense for me to clarify more precisely what has ended with the passing of the genre's golden age, unpeeling some of the layers to examine the ideologies of cultural feminism that held sway in women's music during the mid-1970s.

Cultural feminism has been defined as "the ideology of a female nature or female essence reappropriated by feminists themselves in an effort to revalidate undervalued female attributes."[23] Although cultural feminism in its early manifestations was by no means homogenous, its ideals were rooted in essentialist notions about gender, sexuality, politics, and, in this case, music. The latter is a complex that, in mapping essentialized notions of sexual difference onto inanimate objects, can be described as an excess of lesbian feminism that emerged during this time period. Among the manifestations of cultural feminism in women's music were the idea that musical instruments had gender associations (e.g., tubas are coded male whereas harps are coded female), the notion that lesbian separatism was the only viable way for women to achieve autonomy and liberation, and the conviction that gender and sexuality were the epistemological centers of lesbian feminism.

When I broached these issues in conversation with musicians, many of their responses indicated that they never subscribed to these ideas in the first place—hence the title of this section. Musician Vicki Randle addresses the impact of the ideas about instrumentation on musicians: "Instead of defining women's music in the obvious, confrontive and controversial way—as music by lesbians for lesbians, which would have been the most honest at the time—the spokeswomen for this movement tried to sidestep this overt declaration by attempting instead to define what 'female-oriented' and 'male-oriented' music was."[24] While the prescriptive notions Randle mentions were broad enough to include (acoustic) guitarists under the rubric of acceptable musical acts, musical genres adopted by women of color, which often incorporated a wider range of musical styles, such as jazz and funk, as well as instrumentation—horns, for example—were deemed to fall outside of the boundaries of "women's music." Implicitly, according to the logic of this tenet, it was easier to determine the women-identifiedness of a song with lyrics than it was to assess the same of a composition for instruments only. This presented problems for some black women musicians. Composer Mary Watkins, who recorded with Olivia Records (*Something Moving*) at the end of the 1970s, put it this way: "What is women's music? If that's all they're looking for [meaning women-identified lyrics] in women's music, then I guess it [my music] doesn't have anything to do with women's music."[25] Crediting Linda Tillery for the observation that follows, she continued, underscoring the fact that a reified musical structure does not have a gender identity: "I'm telling you, 'a triad is a triad.'" Later, Watkins said:

> I'm an American composer, an African American composer. Anytime I have the opportunity to express the soul of the African American people, I'm going to do that. I love classical music, and I also love the music of my people. I understand where it comes from. I am not bound by a combination of instruments . . . if you want to use strings, use them. I'm saying this because there is a history of "this is what you should use" in women's music. I don't have much patience with it—with women's music or whatever that is. I'm not invalidating the need for an identity, but I don't take well to being dictated to. You don't win popularity contests that way.

Yet, I might add, Watkins is highly esteemed and popular on the festival circuit.

Essentialist perceptions of the sort I have outlined, however short-lived they were and however embarrassing they are now, had long-lasting effects. Another musician, Tara Jenkins, a pianist, addresses attitudes of exclusivity that she perceived in the women's music community: "I could never do music just for lesbians. They reminded me of kittens huddled together, clinging to each other, and anybody who didn't fit their idea of what lesbian feminist was—they were out. This turned me off. Someone decides what femininity is—soft, nurturing—and what's female—usually white, by the way. I saw that they were not particularly supportive."[26]

One of the areas in which black musicians experienced nonsupport initially was when their music was performed as a reflection of their religious heritage. For many white women, feminist spirituality encompassed revisiting patriarchal constructions of Christianity and emphasizing goddess culture, a construct that critics such as Audre Lorde faulted for its racially exclusionary framework.

Conflict within women's music festival culture arose when white members of the festival gospel chorus changed male pronouns to female ones. Melanie DeMore explains:

> Because, you know, we're going to do music which is very African American–identified. I like to include in my shows spirituals and things like that, and the thing is that as an African American woman, I cannot ignore the spiritual influence of my people. So when I do the gospel choir at Michigan, I tell them from the jump [from the start], "If you have a problem with the word 'God' and 'his' and all this other stuff, this is not the group for you to be in, because I refuse to diminish this music because it may feel politically incorrect to you. Get over it. If you don't like it, don't sing in the chorus." So I try to pick music that is universal. I tell them that this is the music that has literally saved my people, and I am not going to change it to make it politically more comfortable for you.[27]

Echoing or rather foreshadowing DeMore's warning to the Michigan festival's gospel choir, the 1992 program booklet describes the choir, led by Linda Tillery: "The repertoire will draw from spirituals and gospel standards and the workshop will include a discussion of the cultural roots of gospel. The music will be sung *exactly* as it is written (no gender substitution of pronouns or names)."[28]

In a separate conversation, musician Sandra Washington elaborated on the point made by Tillery and DeMore. Although recordings of the Washington Sisters, produced by white musician Teresa Trull, do not evidence the performance of songs in idioms typically considered black, the duo fused awareness of their African American heritage into their act by singing "Lift Every Voice and Sing" at festivals: "I'm not going to sing 'she is my Saviour' at one of my concerts. We do let them know that it's not negotiable with us. People have said to us, 'How can you sing this, because it's so patriarchal?' I've heard all this. But we sing this because it has meaning for us. We say it so that people are educated about why we perform it. Hopefully people will be prevented from trying to 'educate' us afterwards."[29]

The one black festigoer I met who had participated in Michigan's gospel chorus said that the fact that musicians such as Linda Tillery and Melanie DeMore had the musical authority to caution choir members against changing the pronouns meant a lot. The examples musicians offered are within an arguably Protestant frame, and not within the context of Yoruba traditional religious practices that some African American festigoers and musicians have introduced to the women's music festival scene. Although beyond the scope of this book, it is worth interrogating the operations of class, generation, region, religion, and musical genre in festival programming by women of color. Some of the excesses of lesbian feminism can also be identified in the expectations some white feminists had of black women in the earlier years of the movement. Jenkins offers the following:

> I hate to say this, but . . . some of it had to do with racism—race . . . people get in their minds what represents what and that's that. You are worthy of acknowledgment as an African American as long as you are accusing them of being racist, lecturing them . . . on their case, making an obvious and distinct difference between what they are and you are. You are supposed to be black—angry, expressing the anger—you grew up underprivileged . . . they [whites] are going to guilt-trip. That is not the way for me to grow and become who I am. I'm not going to say that there isn't somebody who should be doing that—it's just not me. Don't let people get away with shit and be disrespectful. I want to expand. To me, a lot of that bogs you down. It leads to high blood pressure.[30]

Musicians also revealed the cognitive tensions they experienced in earlier years when women's music festivals encouraged more stage performances by amateur musicians, many of whom were not very good. Speaking on the down low, a veteran black musician said that what bothered her most was the lack of musical and performance standards fostered by the women's music community in those years: "The difference," she said, is that "the black women musicians can *play*."[31] White women's music founder Sue Fink underscores at least part of that sentiment: "In many ways I'm disappointed that we don't have a more educated audience to tell the difference between something which is really musically and lyrically art versus something that is just fun entertainment . . . I just feel that if you're going to do something, do it with art. And there's so much that isn't."[32]

Jenkins and Fink were responding to part of the ethos of early 1970s lesbian feminist culture about which Lillian Faderman comments: "At the first National Women's Music Festival in Champaign, Illinois, in 1974, singers who appeared too professional, like stars, got a cold reception. The audience wanted to see their own declassed, unslick image onstage . . . In fact, 'professionalism' of any kind was considered undesirable hierarchical behavior: It represented artificial and destructive categories, barriers set up by the patriarchy that limited the possibilities of women 'creating a vision together.'"[33] Drumming workshops and the occasional guitar workshop notwithstanding, there are fewer opportunities today for the truly novice amateur to take to the stage at women's music festivals.

Time Passages

Many changes have taken place since the early and mid-1990s, when I conducted interviews with first-generation musicians; some of these transformations are more difficult than others for festigoers to accept. Veteran Linda Tillery comments on how her relationship to such audience expectations has changed: "We also change with time. And what we look for as expressions of gratitude and admiration becomes real different. I am in a period now where what I want is to see clearly what my goals are in life for the next, say, 20 years. I know how I want to live my life, and I know what I need to do in order to live it that way. It certainly doesn't include gratuitous sexual admiration, as in former years. So, as we change, our audiences change as well."[34]

At the time of our interview, Tillery had launched Linda Tillery and the Cultural Heritage Choir (CHC), an all-women's a cappella group that specialized in what one member called "African American roots music." While the all-female ensemble was popular on the women's music circuit, several years later Tillery reconfigured the ensemble to include two male members. Explaining that she wanted to "do something new," the CHC did not often perform at women's music festivals in that configuration again.

Still other changes have ensued over the years. That certain audience favorites such as Casselberry and DuPreé and the Washington Sisters had stopped performing on the circuit by the time I began my round of interviews is testimony that career paths vary, especially in music scenes beyond the big tent of the popular music industry. Composer Rachel Bagby and dub-poetry artist Lillian Allen, though still active in other creative ventures, are no longer involved, and singer/songwriter Regina Wells now devotes her energies to the women's drumming circuit, regarded by many as an offshoot of the women's music movement. The career trajectories of musicians worldwide exhibit ups and downs over the decades: A beloved artist falls upon hard times financially, and the women's music community responds with a fund-raiser; capping off an illustrious career in music and activism, Bernice Johnson Reagon retired in 2004 from SHIR, the ensemble she founded thirty years ago, and has moved on to other projects. (The elder Reagon still makes appearances with daughter Toshi Reagon and her band, Big Lovely.)[35]

Few of us have exactly the same interests as we did a decade or two ago, and, as the careers of numerous artists indicate, it is natural for performers to at some point decide to come off the road.[36] In contrast, there is something to be said for the longevity of certain artists; many continue to reinvent themselves and expand their consumer base. It is enough that many of these musicians took to festival stages during critical and formative years of the women's music festival scene. In fact, given a mainstream popular music industry characterized by a fixation on youth, women's music is remarkable for the number of middle-aged women performers it has supported—and continues to support, even after the demise of the women's music recording industry.

Musicians who have contributed to this project include headliner and solo performers, such as Deidre McCalla, as well as members of bands (referred to as "sidemen") or ensembles, such as Bernice Brooks. While soloists or leaders of ensembles are well known to audience members, musicians who figure only as members of ensembles often are not. Many of the performers listed in this book's "Dreamgirls" section maintain significant musical careers beyond the women's music festival circuit; after all, festivals are held typically from May to September only, and artists have to make a living. Some, like Rhonda Benin (CHC) and Emma Jean Foster (former member of CHC), both of whom came into the circuit in the 1990s, enjoyed careers as professional musicians before their paths intersected with the women's music scene.

My use of the term *professional* indicates a high level of musicianship and not necessarily a devotion to the craft full-time; it is true, however, that most of those who are active on the scene make their livings, full-time, as musicians. For some, like veteran Linda Tillery, this means maintaining a career that includes conducting workshops on African American music, producing the albums of other artists, and performing both with the ensemble she founded and with others. Pianist and composer Mary Watkins is the recipient of numerous awards for composition; she recently completed a concert piece titled "Queen Clara," and her latest CD, *Who Has Not Been Touched,* was released in 2004. Musician Vicki Randle was the first and only female member of the Prime Time band, led by Kevin Eubanks. Tillery, Watkins, and Randle have worked with some of the finest musicians in the business. Drumming masters Ubaka Hill and Afia Walking Tree head drumming institutes, offering workshops at women's drumming camps, and at festivals. Judith Casselberry performs with her own band, J.U.C.A., and as a member of Toshi Reagon's Big Lovely.

First-Generation Commonalities

Three salient points emerge from interviews conducted with first-generation musicians. First, in light of the African American feminist legacy that preceded them, it makes sense that members of the first generation, when asked about their identities as musicians, emphasized the totality of their persons as blacks, women, and, in many cases, lesbians. Although it seems almost redundant for me to linger here, we are reminded that historically there have been—and still are—strong cultural expectations that black lesbians and gays express allegiance to one identity over another, meaning the African American community or the (white) gay and lesbian community. Therefore, that narrators consider their identities in terms of race, gender, and sexual orientation as integrated is critically important. Musician Judith Casselberry put it best when she described her identities as a "package deal."[37]

Second, the rhetoric and focus of musicians in women's music suggest that many black musicians have felt compelled to advocate for a heightened awareness of African American culture in these contexts. They have done this through their music, insights they have shared from the stage, and the work they do in festival organizations behind the scenes. This heightened sense of black consciousness might seem paradoxical, given that some artists, such as the Washington Sisters and Vicki Randle, report being reared in environments that were not necessarily or typically black-identified. The trope of returning home to one's roots in terms of music, later rather than sooner, is recurrent also in narratives that appear in the promotional material of Randle and singer/songwriter Laura Love, both of whom discuss their black identity and biracial heritage.[38]

Third, in spite of their contributions to lesbian feminism through performance, and in ways that might not be appreciated by those who came of political age in the aftermath of the emergence of queer nation, performers revealed that they wished to be regarded as musicians first.[39] These revelations were often tacit. This does not mean that performers resist representation as activists, feminists, lesbians, or anything else; it only suggests that although some of these women enjoy iconic status in women's music, they are aware of the complex social fabric in which their positionalities are read. Musicians pursue careers in multiple contexts—on the folk music scene; in creative music circles; and in jazz, film, and gospel music. Given the intricate set of circumstances faced by members of their political generation, it is understandable that they have chosen not to privilege sexual identity in their music—or even in speech about music. First-generation musicians continue to appeal to the lesbian consumer base of women's music festivals while nurturing careers that are more inclusive in terms of audiences across gender, race, and sexual orientation.

Out and About

Based in Los Angeles, Out and About is the name of a special events planning company for lesbians of color. I use the phrase to draw attention to two related issues: my use of the word *lesbian* instead of *queer,* and nuances of sexual identity disclosure. Although my decision to use *lesbian* rather than *queer* puts me at odds with self-identified queer theorists, activists, and other scholars who, in part because of their own backgrounds, apply the term with greater frequency, it is consonant with the preference of the majority of women I interviewed for this book and with the labels adopted by the National Black Justice Coalition (NBJC).[40] My decision not to use the two words interchangeably is made with deliberation and provides a strong counterpoint to those who are concerned with text-based studies, whose context for scholarship, along with, perhaps, their own political commitments, inspires them to use the word *queer* with greater frequency.[41]

The second issue pertains to sexual identity disclosure. During my research, star-struck festival attendees voiced surprise that musicians who seemed quite "out" within the festival environment were not out in the same way under all circumstances. While outness as a lesbian might characterize the choices made by some of the better-known musicians and comediennes associated with women's music (such as white musicians Alix Dobkin, Cris Williamson, and Diane Davidson, and comedienne Kate Clinton), the same is not a given in terms of black performers. Several black lesbian musicians granted me interviews with the caveat that I neither disclose their sexual identities nor reveal their names in publications issuing from my research. Emphasizing the need for her lesbian identity to remain undisclosed, a violinist explained she had "to make a living," and that since she gigged also for musical theater and symphony orchestras, she had to "keep her reputation intact." Moreover, her first love was contemporary, experimental music, but like so many musicians, she had to meet her financial responsibilities: "I want to play what I feel. I don't want to play Bach right now. I don't want to play Andrew Lloyd Weber, but I've got to do that to pay the mortgage. So what's happening now is that I'm prostituting my music—that's what I have to do."[42]

The circumstances this violinist outlines have been discussed by scholars who have suggested that sexual identity disclosure is situational and may emerge over time.[43] This is particularly true in terms of those from or relating to African American communities. Patricia Collins writes that members of the black LGBT community seem "less likely than their White counterparts to be openly gay or to consider themselves completely out of the closet."[44] Of course, the operative word in Collins's observation is "completely."

Interviews revealed that black women organizers of women's music festivals and, in some cases, second-generation musicians think strategically about sexual identity disclosure. Consider Tanya Ray, a festival organizer who articulates the parameters that she and other black lesbians from her region must take into consideration in regard to "coming out": "When we talked about trying to bring in more musicians of color, we quickly realized that a lot of women did not identify themselves as lesbian because—especially here—there's a stigma attached to being black and lesbian in our city [Midwest location]. Most of the women I know in the city are not out in that sense." Here, I interjected a reality check intended to help us move forward: "Right, well, not just in your city, but in a lot of places." Tanya replied, "Okay, sometimes it feels like the rest of the world is proud and gay and we're, like, scared." Recalling Sherrie Tucker's discussion of black women subjects who "don't come out," the contrast between the shortsightedness of some who maintain that everyone should be out all the time and the organizer's reticence was familiar but nonetheless moving. Tanya continued:

TR: Like, you meet women and you know they're gay. "Girl, where you work at?" They won't even tell you where they work for fear that it will get back to their workplaces. It's a phenomenal thing. It was very different in Chicago. There, it was like, "Okay, I'm out and gay—deal with it." . . . The people I associated with—we were out. Not that we were, like, "Hey, how you doin'—I'm a lesbian"—but it was much more free than it is here.

EH: Yeah, Chicago is, what—the third largest city in the U.S?

TR: Yeah, that's part of it. There was no fear of someone finding out I'm a lesbian at work [in Chicago], but here, there is the fear that "I may get fired," or "I'll be ostracized—whatever—kicked out the church."

EH: And do you think that works for gay men the same way it works for lesbians?

TR: No, I think it's much more difficult for us.

EH: I do, too.

TR: Every black church I've ever been in, has a gay musician—I mean, flaming, and no one says anything. I think it's much more difficult for us.[45]

Monica Falls, a second-generation musician in her twenties who works full-time as a middle-school teacher illustrates some of the tensions that even black women of the second generation experience in regard to being out at the workplace:

I am also considered "out" as far as that, even though that is kind of tough at my job, because it can be dangerous. When you are working with kids, people have a lot of misinformation. I ended up on the second page of the metro section in the [newspaper] holding a bullhorn at the black gay Pride march. I was pretty much out at the school at that point. I was really scared about it, honestly, even though [name of city] public schools protect—under their laws they can't discriminate based on sexual orientation. But I know that when they want to get rid of you, they can. I was afraid that parents were going to call and that there would be this really big backlash, but there really wasn't. The kids teased me, which was kind of funny, once I stopped being traumatized and afraid. I guess once you're out, you're out, and you can't really go back in. So there was no point in my being afraid, but I think that's just part of living in this society.[46]

Although the theory the festival organizer and musician articulate has circulated in African American communities for many years, it is rare that the insights of black lesbians and gays are reflected in the ethnographic literature. If blacks and Latinos experience instances of everyday racism, then it is also true that gays and lesbians of color are subject to everyday homophobia, whether or not they are out.[47] The risk of this exposure is something the women of this study have contemplated.

In contrast to the well-considered responses of some lesbians to questions about sexual identity disclosure, replies of some straight women did not always reveal a high degree of forethought. The black leader of a popular percussion ensemble, for example, said she was unaware that white lesbians comprised the majority of the ensemble's audiences at women's music festivals. I was not quite sure how to process this level of what could only be termed denial. In contrast, Chandra Foley, a straight musician in another ensemble, was up-front about her degree of (dis)comfort in women-identified space. Describing her first experience attending a women's music concert, she said, "I saw all these white lesbians—and left the concert! . . . Homophobia runs high in the black community." Interestingly, Chandra explains or links her individual response to a generalization about African Americans. I asked her to elaborate on how she felt about the women's music scene initially, since before joining the band she had no previous experience in the women's community.

CF: Strange. Uncomfortable initially. Eventually, I was able to look at it from a music side instead of from a homophobic side.
EH: So you think of yourself as being pretty homophobic at the beginning?
CF: Real [homophobic]. I never made any bones about it . . . the girls helped me through it. We used to sit down and talk about it—about being straight and being gay. But I found it to be uncomfortable.[48]

The separate cases of straight women coming into their identities as the Other in this lesbian-dominated world provide a glimpse into the journey some must take in order to function successfully in this field.

In this chapter, I asked musicians to think back and blackward—in other words, to share their reactions to the musical manifestation of cultural feminism in the early years of women's music. I offered a conceptual framework that responds to the passing of the golden age with a mode of analysis that accommodates the ongoing presence of two black feminist generations in women's music. The efforts of musicians to intervene in their own representations figure prominently in the way we are to understand this musical scene. Framing the chapters that follow in this way was a necessary undertaking, given the ongoing prominence of the first generation of musicians in women's music and the nostalgia that permeated the festival circuit during the early phase of my research. Chapter 4 takes up the prequel to these issues—that is, the roots of black women's collective and individual participation in the women's music festival circuit.

Notes

1. Nancy Whittier, *Feminist Generations: The Persistence of the Radical Women's Movement* (Philadelphia: Temple University Press, 1995), 57.

2. Verta Taylor and Leila J. Rupp, "Women's Culture and Lesbian Feminist Activism: A Reconsideration of Cultural Feminism," *Signs* 19, no. 1 (1993), 38.

3. In 1989 Olivia ceased operations as a record label and morphed into a more lucrative lesbian-oriented travel and cruise company. For more information on Goldenrod and Ladyslipper, see www.goldenrod.com/custom/herstory.htm and www.Ladyslipper.org, respectively.

4. African American neo-folksinger Tracy Chapman performed at Sisterfire in 1984 and at the Michigan festival in 1986 and 1987. In an interview with Bonnie Morris, white women's music founder Margie Adam says that not everyone expected these artists to look back and thank them, herself included. See Bonnie J. Morris, *Eden Built by Eves: The Culture of Women's Music Festivals* (New York: Alyson Books, 1999), 105.

5. This is a concern that also resonates for Sherrie Tucker in her study of all-girl swing bands of the 1940s. See Tucker, "Introduction," *Swing Shift: "All-Girl" Bands of the 1940s* (Durham, N.C.: Duke University Press, 2000).

6. *Radical Harmonies,* directed by Dee Mosbacher; coproduced by Margie Adam, June Millington, Boden Sandstrom (San Jose, Calif.: Wolfe Video, 2004). See Eileen Hayes, "Radical Harmonies" (film review), *Ethnomusicology* 48, no. 2 (2004): 312–14.

7. Morris, *Eden Built by Eves,* xiii. One of the most important and early dissertations on women's music is Cynthia Lont, *Between Rock and a Hard Place: A Model of Subcultural Persistence and Women's Music,* PhD diss., University of Iowa, 1984.

8. Linda Tillery invokes the term "queen mother" in Morris, *Eden Built by Eves,* 108.

9. Cris Williamson, *Changer and the Changed,* Olivia Records, 1975, reissued by Wolf Moon Records, 1993.

10. "*Radical Harmonies,*" Woman Vision, http://www.womanvision.org/radical-harmonies.html, accessed June 29, 2009.

11. See Nelson George, *The Death of Rhythm and Blues* (New York: Pantheon Books, 1988); Brian Ward, *Just My Soul Responding: Rhythm and Blues, Black Consciousness, and Race Relations* (Berkeley: University of California Press, 1998); and Michael Eric Dyson, *Race Rules: Navigating the Color Line* (New York: Random House, 1996).

12. Kathleen Stewart, "Nostalgia—A Polemic," *Cultural Anthropology* 3, no. 3 (1988): 227–41.

13. Ibid., 227.

14. The year 1997 marked the end of phase one of my research.

15. Telephone interview with Judy Dlugacz, president of Olivia Records, November 19, 2005. Dlugacz was twenty years old when she and nine other women borrowed four thousand dollars and formed Olivia Records. During its twenty years of operation, Olivia produced more than forty albums and sold more than one million records. National Women's Music Festival, program booklet, 1992, 8.

16. In suggesting that there are two different political generations in women's music, I am following the lead of sociologist Nancy Whittier, who in *Feminist Generations* uses political generations as an organizational framework in her study of radical feminists in Columbus, Ohio.

17. Whittier, *Feminist Generations,* 81.

18. For treatment of intergenerational viewpoints about black feminism, see Joan Morgan, *When Chickenheads Come Home to Roost: My Life as a Hip-Hop Feminist* (New York: Simon and Schuster, 1999).

19. Johnson figures as a member of the next generation. The song "Amazon Woman Rise" appears on *Nedra,* Big Mouth Girl Records, 2005. For an in-depth discussion of women's spirituality and the emergence of the opening ceremony, see Boden Sandstrom, "Performance, Ritual, and Negotiation of Identity in the Michigan Womyn's Music Festival," PhD diss., University of Maryland, 2002.

20. Telephone interview with Nedra Johnson, July 26, 2006.

21. Telephone interview with Malika, September 14, 2005.

22. Whittier, *Feminist Generations,* 4, 18.

23. Linda Alcoff, "Cultural Feminism versus Post-Structuralism: The Identity Crisis in Feminist Theory," *Signs* 13, no. 3 (1988): 408.

24. Vicki Randle, quoted in Laura Post, *Backstage Pass: Interviews with Women in Music* (Norwich, Vt.: New Victoria), 1997.

25. Interview with Mary Watkins, Oakland, California, November 27, 1995. *Something Moving,* Olivia Records, 1978. For a discussion of Watkins's music and career beyond her involvement in women's music, see Helen Walker-Hill, *From Spirituals to Symphonies: African-American Women Composers and Their Music* (Westport, Conn.: Greenwood Press, 2002).

26. Interview with Tara Jenkins, musician, 1995.

27. Interview with Melanie DeMore, November 23, 1995.

28. Michigan Womyn's Music Festival, program booklet, 1992, 22.

29. Telephone interview with Sandra Washington, December 3, 1995. Washington presents her comments in present tense, even though by the time of our interview, the Washington Sisters had ceased performing on the women's music festival circuit. More recent footage of a Washington Sisters performance, filmed at a concert held for the making of the documentary, appears in *Radical Harmonies.*

30. Jenkins interview.

31. In African American speech communities, "down low" means that the information or behavior is considered off the record, a secret, or confidential.

32. Sue Fink, quoted in Morris, *Eden Built by Eves,* 15. The statement is also found in "Sue Fink interviewed by Toni Armstrong Jr.," in Julia Penelope and Susan Wolfe, *Lesbian Culture: An Anthology* (Freedom, Calif.: Crossing Press, 1993), 396.

33. Lillian Faderman, cited in Morris, *Eden Built by Eves,* 29 and 30. The passage is taken from Lillian Faderman, *Odd Girls and Twilight Lovers* (New York: Penguin, 1991), 222.

34. Tillery, quoted in Morris, *Eden Built by Eves,* 108.

35. Eileen M. Hayes, "Not Your Mother's Racial Uplift: Sweet Honey in the Rock, Journey, and Representation: Sweet Honey in the Rock: Raise Your Voice," in *Women and Music: A Journal of Gender and Culture* 10 (Winter 2006): 71–79.

36. White musician and women's music founder Margie Adam recounts taking a hiatus from women's music in 1984 and returning in 1991. Upon her return, she found that women were no longer as turned on politically as they had been. As she recounts to Bonnie Morris, "As a political activist who had stepped back in, it seemed to me that lesbians had taken their feminist energies into the gay male political arena to work on AIDS. I'm sure they expected to feminize the men. But I feel that an unintended consequence is that it shifted the energy of radical feminists away from the ongoing struggle for women's liberation in this country and around the world." Adam, quoted in Morris, *Eden Built by Eves,* 104. Adam's observation is borne out by numerous scholars.

37. Telephone interview with Judith Casselberry, January 10, 1996. The tension that attends being asked to rank or prioritize one's identities is captured by Gregory Connerly in "Are You Black First or Are You Queer?" in *The Greatest Taboo: Homosexuality in Black Communities,* ed. Delroy Constantine-Simms (Los Angeles: Alyson Books, 2000).

38. See www.lauralove.net and www.vickirandle.com. Some of the black musicians who identify as biracial seem to have made conscious attempts to assert their black identity through the crafting of their biographical narrative.

39. Musicologist and jazz studies scholar Sherrie Tucker experienced a similar "quietness" in regard to an avowed lesbian identity on the part of members of all-swing girl bands of the 1940s. See her "When Subjects Don't Come Out," in *Queer Episodes in Music and Modern Identity,* ed. Sophie Fuller and Lloyd Whitesell (Urbana: University of Illinois Press, 2000).

40. The NBJC is a national advocacy civil rights organization dedicated to "empowering Black same-gender-loving, lesbian, gay, bisexual, and transgendered people" based in Washington, DC. See http://www.nbjcoalition.org/about, accessed June 2, 2009. Likewise, the National Black Lesbian Conference, sponsored by the Zuna Institute, a national advocacy organization for black lesbians, has not changed its name to reference queer identities. See http://www.zunainstitute.org, accessed June 2, 2009.

41. Addressing the gap between queer theory and lesbian and gay studies, Ellen Lewin and William Leap also discuss the use of identity labels in *Out in Theory: The Emergence of Lesbian and Gay Anthropology* (Urbana: University of Illinois Press, 2002), 6–10. I am cognizant that my decision to use the word *lesbian* instead of *queer* might lessen my cache in some queer studies circles, both black and white.

42. A male colleague referred to a musician who takes up casual work of this sort as a "gig rat"; women I spoke with used other terms that were even less complimentary.

43. See Eve Sedgwick's influential "Epistemology of the Closet," in *The Lesbian and Gay Studies Reader,* ed. Henry Abelove, Michèle Aina Barale, and David M. Halperin (New York: Routledge, 1993).

44. Patricia Hill Collins, *Black Sexual Politics: African Americans, Gender, and the New Racism* (New York: Routledge, 2004). Collins cites writer Keith Boykin in supporting this perspective.

45. Interview with Tanya Ray, organizer, 2006.

46. Interview with Monica Falls, musician, 2005.

47. Patricia Hill Collins, *Fighting Words: Black Women and the Search for Justice* (Minneapolis: University of Minnesota Press, 1998), 38.

48. Interview with Chandra Foley, musician, 1995.

10

The Development of the Rap Music Tradition

CHERYL L. KEYES

From *Rap Music and Street Consciousness*, by Cheryl L. Keyes (2004)

The previous chapter revealed that the concept of rappin can be traced from African bardic traditions to black oral expressive forms of the South and their transformation in the urban North. Although the pretext for rap is embedded in past oral traditions, its development as a discernible musical genre began in the 1970s during the wake of the Civil Rights and Black Nationalist movements of the 1960s. New social policies fostered by the Civil Rights Act of 1964 and Affirmative Action, implemented by the Department of Health, Education, and Welfare in 1967, helped to propel African Americans into full participation in various areas of mainstream American society that were formerly closed to them. But in spite of these political measures, some sectors of the African American community grew pessimistic when these policies made little impact on black Americans in the ghetto, where living conditions steadily worsened, youth gangs multiplied at alarming proportions, and drugs ravaged the communities. The new political incentives brought about by legislation and policy did, however, affect blacks in the music industry positively, fostering a new atmosphere of artistic freedom and a more powerful platform from which to reach a much wider audience. And those who reached the hallowed halls of the industry took the opportunity to give voice to those still struggling in the ghetto and to those who made it out. As Nelson George eloquently states, "The struggle to overcome overt apartheid of America had given blacks an energy, a motivating dream, that inspired the music's makers" (1988b:147).

Black popular music of the 1970s tended to reflect African Americans' split reactions to integration. Some artists made conscious aesthetic choices to launch black musical styles further into mainstream acceptance, while others struggled to keep the music "real" in allegiance to a disenchanted black public. Rap music developed in the United States in complex relation to diverse factors that include geopolitics, shifts in the music industry and the music of the streets, and changes in federal government policies. In response to these factors, inner-city youths—DJs, MCs, graffiti writers, and b-boys and b-girls—forged an arts movement that evolved in the streets called hip-hop. A closer look at the interdependent relationship between musical change and sociocultural factors sheds much light on the maturation of rap.

Musical and Social Change

The 1970s ushered in a new era of black popular music in the United States. Drawing from and expanding on musical concepts associated with past styles of jazz, blues, gospel, rhythm and blues, black rock 'n' roll, and soul, black artists created new and diverse forms of contemporary black popular music (Maultsby 1979:BM10). The three most distinct black popular styles of the 1970s were funk, disco, and rap. Funk and disco were catalysts in the developmental stages of rap as a musical genre.

Funk was a term brought to musical prominence in the title of a jazz tune called "Funky Butt" by a New Orleans jazz cornetist, Buddy Bolden, around the 1900s. In 1953 the term was employed by the hard bop pianist Horace Silver to define "the return to the evocative feeling and expressiveness of traditional blues" as captured in his "Opus de Funk" (Shaw 1986:257). Funk in the jazz culture of the 1950s was a style countering "the coldness, complexity, and intellectualism introduced into the music by Bop, Cool, West Coast, and Third Stream jazz" (257). By the late 1960s, the term was reformulated by the soul singer James Brown to denote an earthy and gritty sonority characterized specifically by Brown's preachy vocal style and his horn and rhythm section's interlocking rhythmic "grooves."[1]

Brown's funk style was recycled later in the music of Sly and the Family Stone and Kool and the Gang, who produced "Thank You (Falettinme Be Mice Elf Agin)" (1970) and "Funky Stuff" (1973), respectively. The style was further advanced by Larry Graham (the former bass player of Sly and the Family Stone) with Graham Central Station and George Clinton of Parliament-Funkadelic. Both Graham's and Clinton's songs were party-oriented, but they differed in many ways.

Clinton, who coined the term "P-Funk," or pure/uncut funk, viewed his music as a way to induce a relaxed mood in his listeners. In establishing this mood, Clinton manipulated varied sound effects produced on the synthesizer and dictated to his audience via an accompanying rappin monologue loosely chanted over music how to be and feel "cool." James Brown's stylistic influence on P-Funk is most prevalent via Parliament-Funkadelic's horn section, which was comprised chiefly of Brown's former instrumentalists. However, in discussing what he contends was the underlying essence of funk, Clinton states, "'We [Parliament] realized that blues was the key to that music. We just speeded blues up and called it "funk" 'cause we knew it was a bad word to a lot of people'" (quoted in Reid 1993:45).[2] Underscoring the P-Funk vision, Clinton expanded on Sly Stone's soul-punk attire and added special effects. He augmented Parliament-Funkadelic's extravagant galactic-centered live shows with the landing of a spaceship called the Mothership. Another trademark of Clinton's image is the popularization of the funk sign—a clenched fist with a raised forefinger and pinky (a salute appropriated by hiphop's godfather Afrika Bambaataa and his Zulu Nation).

In contrast, Larry Graham's "churchy" music used a Hammond B-3 organ (commonly used in black gospel music) and gospel-based vocals. More importantly, Graham's music was dominated by his playing style: his pulling, thumping, and slapping the bass guitar strings, "which became the trademark for defining the funk style" (Maultsby 1979:BM22).

In contrast, the historical precedent for 1970s disco music was the work of the African American artist Barry White and the musical production of Philadelphia International Records, a black-owned company started by Kenny Gamble and Leon Huff.[3] Tunes by White and his forty-piece Love Unlimited Orchestra, such as "Love's Theme" (1974) and MFSB's "TSOP" (The Sound of Philadelphia, 1974), the original theme for the syndicated television dance program "Soul Train," are typical of this music. The musical basis of disco was an orchestral arrangement over a rhythm section, soul vocals, and an underlying bass-drum rhythm that accented all four beats subdivided by the hi-hat cymbal beats. The role of the disc jockey in disco foreshadowed the same in rap: "disco gave prominence to the record producer and the disc jockey—the former for his skill in manipulating the new sophisticated recording technology, and the latter for his ability to use changes in tempo, volume, and mood to manipulate dancers on the floor" (Shaw 1986:251).

By the mid-1970s, European producers, including Pete Bellotte and Giorgio Moroder, entered the disco scene and modified it with female soloists, an eighth-note bass line figure that outlined the notes of a chord, and a shift in tempo from a moderate to a faster beat. Nelson George contends,

> Disco movers and shakers were not record executives but club deejays. Most were gay men with a singular attitude toward American culture, black as well as white. They elevated female vocalists like [Donna] Summer, Gloria Gaynor, Diana Ross, Loleatta Holloway, Melba Moore, and Grace Jones to diva status, while black male singers were essentially shunned. Funk, which in the late-70s was enjoying great popularity in the South and Midwest, was rarely on their playlists. It was too raw and unsophisticated, and one thing dear to the hearts of disco fans, gay and straight, was feeling a pseudosophistication. (George 1988b:154)

"In the quest for commercial success, creativity had given way to formula, and the very excitement and challenge for which the music makers had long striven began to fade" (Joe 1980:31). As a result of being farther removed from its cultural base, 1970s disco became distorted, altered, and less dynamic. It was recognized as "a white, middle-class, youth-to-middle age phenomenon" (Shaw 1986:250).

Black musicians like George Clinton responded to the disco commercial fever by signifyin on its tempo à la funk style, which was the aim of Funkadelic's signature song, "One Nation Under a Groove" (1978). Carl "Butch" Small explains, "'One Nation' was a snub at disco. You know how we were used to hearing the 'lily white' disco with heavy percussion. I did so many sessions in the disco era. During the disco era I worked from sunup to sundown. 'One Nation' was conceived with a tempo like 120 beats per minute. Yeah, a disco dance tempo, but it was black rhythm" (Small interview). A similar radical reaction toward disco occurred among black youth, particularly those in New York City. Bill Adler, an independent rap music publicist and critic, observed:

> In New York City in the mid-70s, the dominant black popular music was disco as it was every place else. The difference about New York was that kids were funk fiends who weren't getting their vitamins from disco music. It was "too nervous," in their terminology, which meant too fast. It was too gay. It was something, but it just didn't move them, and so they were thrown back into their own resources, and what happened was that they started to . . . play a lot of James Brown. . . . His old records were . . . staples, and Kool and the Gang, and heavy funk like that developed. I mean, part of it just had to do with there being a lot of neighborhood parks in New York City . . . and what kind of music was played in those parks by the disc jockeys there. (Adler interview)

While the commercialization of disco did indeed make an impact on the redirection of black popular music in the United States, some have argued that rap music was a consequence of geopolitical factors idiosyncratic to New York, particularly the Bronx. Drawing from the works of Mollenkopf (1983), Walkowitz (1990), and Mollenkopf and Castells (1991), the rap music scholar Tricia Rose points out how postindustrial conditions, such as the replacement of industrial factories with information service corporations and the changes in the federal governmental policies, reshaped the economic structures of cities like New York during the 1970s (1994:27–34). For instance, the dwindling federal funding for the arts had a profound effect on extracurricular school programs for inner-city youth and the public school system's arts programs as well. At the National Endowment for the Arts (NEA) conference in Chicago on April 14, 1994, the author Thulani Davis delivered the keynote address, "The Artist in Society." Davis stated that the days of classroom instruction in music have been replaced by "street arts like rap . . . those little instruments we once learned to play in the classroom, those [days] are gone." This statement fueled a discussion among audience members about the "demise of black music"; the majority of the audience concurred that the lack of funding for the arts in public schools was a major contributor to rap's evolution. In the face of decreased financial support for New York City's public school music programs, particularly the instrumental music curriculum, inner-city youth reacted creatively by relying on their own voices, launching the resurgence of street-corner a cappella singing and popularizing the human beat box (vocal rhythmic simulation of a drum). They also became more interested in musical technology ushered in by disco from turntables to synthesizers.

In addition to the changes in federal education policy, radical changes in housing had a profound effect by institutionalizing poverty and distilling the concentration of the mostly black and Latino underclass into condensed pockets of the urban environment. In New York City, as throughout the country, "deep social service cuts were part of a larger trend in unequal wealth distribution and were accompanied by a housing crisis" (Rose 1994:28). The housing crisis negatively impacted people of color, who comprised more than half of the inner city's working class and underclass. In *Organizing the South Bronx* (1995), the urban crusader Jim Rooney notes that prior to the 1960s, public housing was basically for those who were temporarily "down on their luck" and not for "long term welfare families and unwed mothers." But by the 1960s, "this concept had been discarded, and admission policies were changed to allow welfare recipients into the structures. Thereafter, public housing came to be seen as the shelter of last resort, as a permanent home for the underclass rather than a temporary refuge for 'respectable families'" (1995:46).

By the 1970s, most of the federal monies allocated for inner-city housing were transferred to upscale suburbia and funneled into housing construction there. In the phenomenon known as "white flight," these areas had now become a refuge for whites fleeing the poorly neglected inner cities that had an increasing black and Latino underclass. The disproportionate distribution of monies to build suburbs rather than rebuild the inner city divided the races, causing people of color throughout the nation's urban centers to be segregated and ghettoized. Thus, "modest blocks were bulldozed flat in the name of social progress, and the promise of these high-rise projects [in the inner city] rapidly soured" (Rooney 1995:46).

New York City Gang Culture

Numerous U.S. cities were impacted by similar policy initiatives similar to those affecting New York City. Among those areas profoundly disturbed by the unstable economy in New York was the Bronx, whose decline began rapidly after World War II. Jim Rooney identifies two primary culprits in the disintegration of the Bronx: postwar federal housing and highway initiatives (1995:43). These factors are also catalytic to the evolution of hip-hop culture and music.

In discussing the geopolitics of the region in the 1950s, the rap music journalist Steven Hager writes, "the Bronx was known as the borough of apartment buildings where rent controls . . . were usually kept in the family, handed down" (1984:1). After New York's park commissioner, Robert Moses, ordered that the Cross Bronx Expressway be built through the Bronx in 1959, "the middle-class Italian, German, Irish, and Jewish neighborhoods disappeared overnight. Impoverished black and Hispanic families, who dominated the southern end of the borough, drifted north. Along with the poor came their perennial problems: crime, drug addiction, [and] unemployment" (2–3). Rooney notes that while the Cross Bronx Expressway enabled some people to move to the suburbs and still retain their jobs in the city, "this gargantuan expressway disrupted neighborhoods and destroy[ed] viable parts of the South Bronx. The expressway became the de facto northern border of the South Bronx" (Rooney 1995:59). As a result, property owners sold apartments at lower rates to avaricious landlords, who neglected apartment upkeep yet charged exorbitant rent. Black and Latino residents were forced to live in dilapidated, rodent-infested housing. Exacerbating matters, some landlords devised lucrative schemes to evade taxes by hiring stooges to force residents out by burning down the apartments so they could receive insurance payoffs (Henry Chalfant, personal communication, Manhattan, June 23, 1993). Between 1970 and 1975, there were 68,456 fires in the Bronx—more than thirty-three each night (Rooney 1995:56).[4]

As conditions worsened, crime escalated. Some youths formed neighborhood groups or gangs to police their apartments, projects, streets, and neighborhoods from outside invaders. As soon as one gang formed, others formed in response, eventually leading to fierce territorial rivalry (see the video documentary *Flyin' Cut Sleeves*, 1993). By the 1960s the South Bronx was regarded as a leading headquarters of street gang violence. Numerous brutal gang encounters, particularly around intraterritorial rivalries and sexual assault of female victims by male gang members, were common headlines in local newspapers, as were rapes, murders, and, as one writer recalls, "unspeakable rites of passage" (Hager 1984:5–11). By 1973 statistics revealed that New York City gangs totalled 315 with over nineteen thousand members (George 1992:11), though toward the end of that year gang activity slowly dissipated in part because of a peace meeting between rival gangs in the Bronx. According to *Flyin' Cut Sleeves*, this gang truce was initiated by the Ghetto Brothers, a nonviolent gang, after the death of one of their members, Cornell "Black Benji" Benjamin, who was fatally wounded while trying to stop a fight among rivals of the Seven Mortals, Black Spades, and Mongols gangs.

Other factors that ultimately led to the collapse of street gangs included homicide among gang members, maternal responsibilities of female gang members, and the introduction of heroin. The following best summarizes the disintegration of New York City street gangs as recalled by one member: "'Some gangs got into drugs. Other gangs got wiped out by other gangs. Others got so big that members didn't want to be involved no more. Girls got tired [and] wanted to have children. Plus times were changin'" (Bambaataa quoted in Hager 1984:10).[5]

In the wake of street gang violence, Afrika Bambaataa, deemed the "Godfather of Hip-Hop," asserted his concept of youth solidarity by rechanneling violent competition into artistic contests. Prior to his vision, like many youth in the Bronx, Bambaataa had been a member of the notorious street gang Black Spades. When the Spades established a division in his neighborhood in 1969, Bambaataa had joined them because "'it was all part of growing up in the southeast Bronx'" (quoted in Hager 1984:73).

By the early 1970s Bambaataa had slowly retreated from the Spades by following his passion for DJing at local venues. In an effort to curtail violence, he drifted toward religious and political organizations, including the Nation of Islam (NOI), that deterred street youth from gang activity. He explains his attraction to Islam and its influence in his life: "'What got me excited first was when James Brown came out with "Say it Loud, I'm Black and I'm Proud." . . . I decided to get into the Nation of Islam. It put a change on me. It got me to respect people even though they might not like us because we [were] Muslims. The Nation of Islam was doing things that America had been trying to [do] for a while—taking people from the streets like junkies and prostitutes and cleaning them up. Rehabilitating them like the jail system wasn't doing'" (quoted in Toop 2000:59). Through the teachings and philosophy of the NOI, Bambaataa envisioned a way to terminate street violence in the Bronx River housing project. In 1973 he formed a nonviolent organization called the Youth Organization, which he eventually renamed Zulu Nation. The Zulu Nation is "a huge young adult and youth organization which incorporates people that are into breakdancing, DJing, and graffiti. I had them to battle against each other in a nonviolent way, like rapper against rapper rather than knife against knife" (Bambaataa interview). The creative forces of this youth community, who shared a common historical and political space, were realized via the unification of spiritual, psychological, and linguistic factors.

The Zulu Nation's idea was inspired by the 1964 British film *Zulu*, starring Michael Caine and directed by Cy Endfield. In an interview conducted by the hip-hop critic David Toop (2000), Bambaataa recalls:

"The Zulu Nation. I got the idea [from] . . . this movie called *Zulu* which featured Michael Caine. They [the Zulus) were proud warriors and . . . fighting very well against bullets, canons and stuff. They fought like warriors for a land which was theirs. . . . And then, as the years went by, through all the civil rights movement, human rights, Vietnam war, and all the folk and rock that was happening—all the change of '60s that was happening to the whole world—it just stayed with me to have some type of group like that." (quoted in Toop 2000:57)

Years after seeing the film, Bambaataa visited Africa, where his idea of nation was solidified. Bambaataa's metamorphosis continued as he rejected Western influences and Judeo-Christianity. He believed that Christianity contributed to the acceptance of black cultural stereotypes: "'black was evil, and turn the other cheek...'" (quoted in Toop 2000:57). His religious passion for Islam shaped his perception of the Civil Rights movement and the Nation of Islam. The former seemed passive to him: "'So Martin Luther King was the thing that was happening because he was fighting for civil rights, but Malcolm X was more on the aggressive side. Myself, I was more on the Malcolm X way of thinking'" (quoted in Toop 2000:57).

Following in the tradition of the Nation of Islam, he rejected his anglicized name—"I never speak of my real name, 'cuz I don't consider it my real name anyway" (Bambaataa interview)—and adopted the name Afrika Bambaataa in honor of the legendary African Zulu warrior, whose name means "affectionate leader." Despite his rejection of the nonviolent tactics of Martin Luther King, he cites as influences a wide range of the viewpoints represented by black leaders: "'I always had an understanding of teachers such as the Honorable Elijah Muhammad and Minister Louis Farrakhan and in the '60s watching the Black Panthers, Martin Luther King and the rest of our great leaders that were doing a strong knowledge thing. . . . So by pulling all factions together, we made this whole cultural movement called Hip-Hop'" (quoted in Webb 1992:56).

According to Bambaataa, the word "hip-hop" can be traced to Lovebug Starski, a South Bronx disc jockey. He indicated that at Starski's parties, the DJ would always say, "hip hop you don't stop that makes your body rock." "So I just coined a word myself and started using the word 'hip-hop' to name this type of culture, and then it caught on" (Bambaataa interview). Bambaataa's concept of hip-hop encompassed urban street expressions and embodied a street attitude through gestures, language, and stylized dress associated with street culture.

Hip-hop, as well as the Zulu Nation, was not conceived as an ethnically homogeneous expression or unit comprised solely of and for African Americans. During its early development, many hip-hop innovators were of African Caribbean and Latino (mainly Puerto Rican) descent. DJs like Kool "DJ" Herc, Bambaataa, and Grandmaster Flash were African Caribbean, and Charlie Chase, who deejayed for the Cold Crush Brothers, was Puerto Rican (see Toop 2000; Hebdige 1987; Flores 2000). Graffiti artists were ethnically diverse overall, but Puerto Rican hip-hoppers dominated in breakdancing, while African Americans and African Caribbeans mainly performed as DJs and MCs. It is this cultural intersection of African diasporic blending that ultimately provided the basis for a hip-hop aesthetic.

Full discussion of all the artistic expression encompassed by the youth arts mass movement known as hip-hop and led by Afrika Bambaataa is beyond the scope of this book. The following section will focus primarily on the development of two aspects of this artistic movement—DJing and MCing—which, as a consequence of geopolitics, gang violence, and the commercialization of disco music, became hip-hop's driving force.

From Kingston to the Bronx: The Rise of the Street DJ

Gang activity affected not only the outdoor environs but also the club scene in which hip-hop music was performed. One of the major problems partygoers consistently encountered at the clubs was gang violence. The violence ultimately led to the temporary suspension of DJ performances at local clubs, particularly in areas like the South Bronx, where club gang violence predominated. As one jockey recalls, "'it got too dangerous for people to go to discos'" (quoted in Hager 1984:32). As a result, a few of the South Bronx jockeys like Kool "DJ" Herc and Afrika Bambaataa took their talent to settings remote from neighborhood clubs, such as local parks. These itinerant disc jockeys' mastery on the turntables made them instant heroes in their respective communities. Such itinerant disc jockeys became known in the hip-hop community as street or mobile DJs, as opposed to those who performed in clubs or on the radio. These DJs played an important role in the growing influence of rap music.

Mobile disc jockeys drew their inheritance from radio disc jockeys. A number of DJs and MCs interviewed stated that they took their initial inspiration from and patterned themselves after New York radio personalities such as Frankie Crocker, Gary Byrd, Hank Spann, and others. In exploring the link between radio DJs and mobile DJs, it is apparent that the street DJs, similar to radio jockeys, speak to their audiences in a stylized manner and make an art of dovetailing one record into another. In the early days, street DJs also incorporated sound techniques popularized by radio jockeys, such as "talking through" and "riding gain" in performances. But when I asked them about the roots of the street DJ, they would continually assert that rap music evolved also from toasting. When I asked whether they were referring to toast narratives like "The Signifying Monkey" and "Dolemite," though they knew of these toasts, they cited a different toast tradition known as Jamaican rhymes. One rap artists stated, "we had a lot of toasters coming out of Kingston" (Carson interview).

The link between the Bronx and Kingston is substantial, though in general it has been unmentioned or simply glossed over in previous works on rap music and hip-hop culture. Toasting and DJing were initially employed simultaneously in the Jamaican tradition. The model for this combination can be traced to Kingston and the development of sound system or dancehall culture.

During the 1930s, swing bands dominated the music scene in Kingston, Jamaica. Most of the bands' repertory consisted of American-style music performed primarily in local clubs and rented-out lodges called dancehalls. By the end of World War II, the swing band scene waned. At this time, in desperate need of labor in order to rebuild, Britain passed the British Nationality Act of 1948, conferring citizenship to subjects of the Commonwealth in the West Indies.[6] In discussing the demise of the swing band scene in Kingston, the dancehall scholar Norman C. Stolzoff notes, "Because Britain was in need of massive rebuilding after World War II, the British government turned to the colonies as a source of cheap labor. Given this open-door policy, Jamaicans and other West Indians left home 'seeking greener pastures.' . . . Among them were a significant fraction of Jamaica's trained [swing] musicians" (2000:41). DJs in search of musical alternatives were hired merely to spin records at dancehall parties. With the booming DJ culture came powerful amplifiers or sound systems. According to Stolzoff, the prototype of the dancehall sound system was the PA (public address) system first rented-out and used at political rallies in Jamaica. He credits Hedley Jones, however, as a builder of the first sound system. From an interview with Bunny "the Mighty Burner" Goodison, Stolzoff determines that "from its genesis as a PA system for political rallies, the sound system went on to become the basis of an enterprising dancehall scene" (42).

The new dancehall scene became a phenomenon among Kingston's black working class. Because Jamaica's radio airwaves were dominated by black popular music or rhythm and blues during the 1950s, DJs often spun U.S. imports on their record players. The dancehall scene expanded to outdoor contexts. As one patron described, "'you just pay a sound system man about three or five pounds, as [was] the case in them day. Bring his equipment stick it up on the sidewalk, or inna the yard, and bring in the boxes of beer and thing, and you have a dance and make some money'" (quoted in Stolzoff 2000:42 [bracketed note in original]). The Jamaican producer Junior Lincoln observed, "'A sound system is just like what you call a disco. But the only thing is, it is not as sophisticated as a disco set. The amplifiers are huge, well now amplifiers are as big as 2,000 watts. They emphasise a lot on the bass. And they play sometimes twenty or twenty-four inch speakers. So it really thump, y'know. The bass line is really heavy. You've never heard anything so heavy in all your life'" (quoted in Hebdige 1987:63).

Setting the criterion for who ranks the best in the world of the DJ, Jamaican DJs led the way in using massive sound systems to "try and 'blow' the other off the stage with rawer and rougher sounds" (Hebdige 1987:63). Signifying on their unique skills, sound system DJs created catchy names for themselves and their two-to-three-man crews, such as Duke Reid's Trojan, Sir Coxsone's Downbeat, and Tom Wong, also known as Tom the Great Sebastian, who was Chinese Jamaican. Count Matchukie, a major innovator in the dancehall sound system scene, is considered an originator and master performer of toasting. Matchukie, who once deejayed with Sir Coxsone, recited his rhymes in Jamaican Patois, formal English, and even Spanish to show off his versatility at the microphone. The famous U-Roy was one of a number of other DJs who advanced toasting in their performances.

By the late 1950s, Jamaican DJs shifted their musical taste from American popular music to something uniquely Jamaican. Prince Buster, a sound system DJ, provided this transition. At the time, the Jamaican popular music scene turned toward its own musical resources in the invention of "ska," a forerunner of rocksteady, reggae, and dancehall. Unlike rhythm and blues, in which the rhythmic accents occurred on beats 2 and 4, the rhythmic accents in ska fall on the "and" of beats 1, 2, 3, and 4. Ska makes use of the saxophone and trombone as well. Jamaican-owned and -operated recording studios, including Ken Khouri's Federal Records (founded in 1954) and Edward Seaga's West Indies Records (founded in 1958) produced a number of ska recordings.[7] Ska artists include the Skatalites, the Vikings, Prince Buster, and Justin Hines and the Dominoes. Ska was soon replaced by a slower and more bassy sound called "rocksteady." Unlike ska, rocksteady made little or no use of horns. Alton Ellis, Delray Wilson, and the Vendors rank among the top rocksteady performers in Jamaica.

Alongside ska, several changes took place in Jamaica during the 1960s: the proliferation of the Rastafari movement; the change in political power; and the maturation and globalization of Jamaica's popular musical culture (through the reggae music of Bob Marley and the Wailers). These musical and sociopolitical tides were most evident with Jamaica's youth culture. Dancehall or sound system culture remained closely linked to Jamaica's working class. Soon it would be emblematic of a thriving youth culture, known as "rude boys" or "rudies."

Rudies hung out on Kingston's ghetto street corners. Disenchanted with Jamaica's economy, rudies sported handguns and knives and donned certain clothes: "very short green serge trousers, leather or gangster-style suit jackets, and . . . shades" (Hebdige 1987:72). Caught between the political rivalry of Michael Manley's People's National Party (PNP) and Edward Seaga's Jamaica Labour Party (JLP), rudies fell into youth gangs divided along political lines and recruited by constituents of each party to instigate political resistance. By 1966 political gang warfare escalated. "Gang warfare, political violence between supporters of the PNP and JLP, and clashes between gangs and security forces began in February and March 1966 and continued, except for certain pauses, until after 22 February, the polling day of the 1967 General Election" (Lacey 1977:87). Toward the end of the 1960s, the economic situation worsened in Jamaica, creating growing disenchantment among the poor toward outsiders, particularly British and U.S. businesses in Jamaica. Among the most notorious riots in Jamaica's political history were the Rodney Riots of October 1968, named after Walter Rodney, the alleged conspirator behind the formation of political youth gangs or posses. "The city of Kingston was divided like a checkerboard into political garrisons controlled by the gangs under the patronage of party leadership" (Stolzoff 2000:84).[8]

Gang attacks ensued, spilling into the dancehall scene. When the gang's rudies invaded the dancehalls, DJs retreated from the dancehall scenes to the recording studio. By the late 1960s, a studio-produced form of Jamaican pop called "dubs" emerged. While mixing tracks for Sir Coxsone, the sound engineer Osbourne "King Tubby" Ruddock accidentally stumbled across a way to fade out the vocal and instrumental parts on the two-track recording machine. "He began fading out the instrumental track, to make sure that the vocals sounded right. . . . So instead of mixing the specials in the usual way, he cut back and forth between the vocal and instrumental tracks and played with the bass and treble knobs until he changed the original tapes into something else entirely" (Hebdige 1987:83). The technique of fading certain parts in and out or altering them in creating several varied cuts from the original resulted in dub versions. Alongside King Tubby's invention of the dub concept came "riddims." Riddims are rhythmic reggae grooves consisting of a distinct reggae-style bass line. Leroy Sibbles, the bassist for the Heptones, is acknowledged as a creator of several bass riddims. The riddims grooves Sibbles helped create include "Full Up," "Satta Massagana," "Declaration of Rights," "No Man Is an Island," "Ten to One," "Things a Come to Bump," "Sweet Talking," "Freedom Blues" or "MPLA," "School Riddims," "Book of Rules," "Midnight," "Love I Can Feel," "In Cold Blood," and "Baby Why" (Chang and Chen 1998:77). Riddims become a trademark of reggae and reggae dancehall.

In the past, DJs toasted over live music. The 1970s ushered in toasting over recorded or dub versions called "talk overs." U-Roy, mentioned previously for his influence in toasting, is the person most often credited as the "grandfather" of the contemporary DJ phenomenon. Among his contenders include Big Youth, I-Roy, Linton Kwesi Johnson, and Mutabaruka.

Undoubtedly the talk overs and the sound system concept had a direct impact on musical production throughout the West Indies and eventually the United States through West Indian immigrants. Thus it is not surprising that the three recognized innovators of rap music—Kool "DJ" Herc, Afrika Bambaataa, and Grandmaster Flash—are of West Indian heritage. Their parents were among the many who emigrated from the West Indies to the United States during the 1960s. Although West Indians had migrated to the United States before 1960, a large influx of West Indians occurred after the termination of Britain's Commonwealth Immigrants Act in 1962 and the independence of Jamaica and Trinidad and Tobago from England in 1962, followed by Guyana and Barbados in 1966. Accordingly, West Indians comprised one-third of Caribbean immigrants living in the United States in the 1960s. According to the economist Ransford W. Palmer, the majority came from Jamaica. "The U.S. Census [also] reported 171,525 immigrants from the West Indies in New York City [which] represented 73 percent of all West Indian immigrants in the United States, 48 percent of whom arrived between 1965 and 1970" (1995:20).

With a large concentration of West Indians in New York City, the musical scene would soon be altered. In an effort to create contexts similar to Jamaican dancehall culture, U.S. street DJs followed suit, creating outdoor discotheques in local parks. The rap music artist The Real Roxanne said, "People used to do jams [parties] outside in the schoolyard or handball court. Someone used to bring their two turntables out and plug it into the lamp post outside and that's how they got their power. People would listen and dance to the music out in the streets" (The Real Roxanne interview).

Street DJs were well known in their own boroughs and were supported by local followers. Popular jockeys included Pete "DJ" Jones of the Bronx and Grandmaster Flowers and Maboya of Brooklyn. They occasionally spoke to their audiences in a legato-mellow style reminiscent of early African American radio disc jockeys of the 1950s and 1960s. According to DJ Hollywood of Harlem, New York, street DJs, like Jamaican DJs, were evaluated on the size and sound of their sound systems and their loudness rather than their technical abilities to spin or rap to a crowd in the early 1970s: "Pete 'DJ' Jones, Flowers and Maboya, they weren't microphone DJs, they were DJs that just had big big sound systems and big equipment; and this is what people were into at that particular time. Who had the biggest one, who had the biggest sound. So when I looked back at the concept of what was happening, I said to myself, 'I wanted to be the best'" (DJ Hollywood interview). Although many street DJs were males, there was a noted female from Brooklyn by the name of Lady J. The music promoter Dennis Shaw recognized Lady J as a pioneer and credits her as "very unique for her time. She was a forerunner of lady DJs, who was very adept at mixing" (Shaw interview).

The most innovative of the mobile disc jockeys was the Jamaican-born Clive Campbell, known as Kool "DJ" Herc, whose mixing technique immensely influenced the future direction and production of rap music. Herc emigrated to the Bronx from Kingston, Jamaica, in 1967, when he was only twelve years old.

By 1972, Herc began DJing throughout the Bronx, though his approach to this form contrasted with that of the U.S. jockeys. Instead of simply dovetailing one record after another and talking intermittently to the crowd, Herc recited rhymes over the microphone while mixing. In mixing, the DJ places a disc on each of two turntables and attempts to match their speed with a pitch control device on the turntable system. With the use of an audio-mixer, which sits between the turntables, and its cross-fader lever, a DJ can smoothly shift from one turntable to the next. Simultaneously, Herc also added electronic sound effects—"echoing and reverbing back and forth between the vocal and instrument track; [while manipulating] the treble and bass knobs" (Hebdige 1987:83).

Herc tailored his DJing style after the dub music jockeys of Jamaica by mixing musical fragments referred to by street jockeys as "breaks" or "breakbeats"[9] from various recordings to create an entirely new soundtrack. Afrika Bambaataa recalls in an interview that Herc "'knew that a lot of American blacks were not getting into reggae. He took the same thing that the deejays [were] doing—toasting—and did it with American records . . . He would call out the names of people who were at the party, just like the microphone personalities who deejayed back in Jamaica'" (quoted in Chang and Chen 1998:72). Bambaataa recalls how Herc "'took the music of Mandrill, like "Fencewalk," certain disco records that had funky percussion breaks like The Incredible Bongo Band [a Jamaican disco group] when they came out with "Apache" and he just kept that beat going. It might be that certain part of the record that everybody waits for—they just let their inner self go and get wild. The next thing you know the singer comes back in and you'd be mad'" (quoted in Toop 2000:60). The "certain part of the record that everybody waited for" consisted of an African Latin percussion soundtrack—congas and timbales—called the "break" section. In addition, as Herc went back and forth between breaks and the microphone, his MC, Coke La Rock, continued giving props to various members of Herc's crew. Indeed, Herc's DJ parties fostered an atmosphere of hip-hop arts with his accompanying breakdancers or b-boys, known as the Nigger Twins.

Because of his enormous sound system, Kool Herc could be heard performing at a distance throughout the Bronx. His mixing concept inspired many itinerant jockeys in the Bronx, including Afrika Bambaataa, who eventually perfected this technique. The rap music producer Larry Smith contends that Afrika Bambaataa possessed the most incredible ear for finding beats from all over and using all genres of music in his mixes, a talent that earned him the title "Master of Records" (Smith interview). The "breaks" that contained these beats represented a variety of musical styles, ranging from soul, funk, and disco to commercial jingles and television themes. Most of Bambaataa's favorite break-beat records—including "Funky Drummer" by James Brown, "Take Me to the Mardi Gras" by Bob James, "Think" by Lynn Collins, and "Dance to the Drummer's Beat" by the Herman Kelly Band—have gone on to become the foundation for numerous hip-hop tracks (Fernando 1994:54). L Ju, an admirer of Bambaataa, also notes, "'he blended tracks from Germany, Jamaica, the Philippines, Cali[fornia] and the South Bronx into a beautiful collage called hip-hop jams in the park and created a movement that turned into a world-wide musical and cultural revolution, as well as a billion dollar industry. His parties lifted the dancer into a spiritual state of euphoria based on his overstanding of vibrations, rhythms, cadence, tone, melody and mood'" (quoted in Emery 1998:26).

Another Bronx disc jockey influenced by Kool "DJ" Herc was Joseph Sadler, better known as Grandmaster Flash. Flash began his career as a DJ for neighborhood block parties, but he realized his skills were limited because of his mixing board. Flash felt intimidated by Kool Herc's huge sound system and enormous volume, even though he later discerned that Herc had less than perfect mixing skills.

> "With the monstrous power he had he couldn't mix too well. He was playing little breaks but it would sound so sloppy. I noticed that the mixer he was using was a GLI 3800. It was a very popular mixer at that time. It's a scarcity today but it's still one of the best mixers GLI ever made. At the time he wasn't using no cueing. In other words, the hole was there for a headphone to go in but I remember he never had headphones over his ears. All of a sudden, Herc had headphones but I guess he was so used to dropping the needle down by eyesight and trying to mix it that from the audio part of it he couldn't get into it too well." (quoted in Toop 2000:62)

Flash began going to discotheques to observe other jockeys in performance. At a Manhattan disco club, he met Pete "DJ" Jones. Though Jones performed for a conservative audience, Flash noticed that Jones was more accurate in mixing records than Kool Herc. Also, Jones was known for his extended play concept. Commenting on "the way Pete would connect the records," Flash says, "some of the DJs I used to watch [back then] used to let the record play all the way to the end then play the next one with the gap in between. I found it quite amazing that Pete kept the record going, going, going, all night long. That's how he acquired the name Pete 'With the Funky Beat DJ' Jones" (Grandmaster Flash interview). In addition, Jones had a switch on the system that allowed him to hear what was playing on one turntable before playing it aloud. Grandmaster Flash, a student of electronics, later invented an apparatus allowing him to cue up a record while the other is played through the speakers. He accomplished this with an external amplifier, headphones (later a one-ear headphone), and a single-pole, double-throw switch, which he glued to his audio-mixer. Through experimenting with this apparatus, Flash pioneered two turntable techniques popularly known as "backspinning" and "phasing."

Backspinning, which requires having a copy of the same record on two turntables, is executed by rotating one record counterclockwise to the desired beat then rotating the second record counterclockwise to the same musical phrase, creating a loop-like effect. In phasing (also known as "punch-phrasing"), the DJ accents a short phrase of a recording during the playing of a second record by manipulating the turntable's cross-fader. This technique is somewhat similar to the previously discussed "riding gain" technique employed by black radio jockey personalities of the 1950s, but phasing is done with two turntables. While

Flash perfected his inventions, other disc jockeys experimented with new mixing concepts.

Grand Wizard Theodore from the Bronx, a protégé of Grandmaster Flash, is credited with inventing another mixing technique called "scratching," moving a record back and forth in a rhythmic manner while the tone arm's needle remains in the groove of the record, producing a scratching sound. Although in 1978 Theodore was only thirteen years old, the youngest of the hip-hop DJs at the time, he was considered one of the few who could mix records with skill comparable to that of Flash.

New York DJs like Davy DMX and Grandmixer D.ST perfected Theodore's scratching invention. Grandmixer D.ST is responsible for popularizing scratching as a primary musical feature in the hit single "Rockit" (1983) by Herbie Hancock.[10] Other noted New York street DJs of the time who used various mixing innovations were Junebug, Charlie Chase, Sweet G, Jazzy Jay, Disco Wiz, Disco King Mario, DJ Tex, Afrika Islam, Smokey, Kurtis Blow, DJ Hollywood, the Whiz Kid, and the female DJ RD Smiley.[11] As the mostly male DJ circuit expanded, some jockeys underwent apprenticeship with other better-known

FIGURE 10.1 Hip-Hop veteran MC Grandmaster Caz of the Cold Crush Brothers (front, center), along with colleagues, including Afrika Islam and Lovebug Starski (3d and 4th from the left), at the 18th Annual Universal Zulu Nation Anniversary held at The Muse, New York, 1992. (Photo by the author)

DJs. This usually took the form of an exchange wherein the apprentice disassembled the mentor's sound equipment after performances and in turn received personalized professional advice about the art of DJing. The master-student relationships that developed are often indicated by "surrogate father-and-son" titles. For instance, DJ Afrika Islam is considered the Son of Bambaataa; Joseph "Run" Simmons of Run-D.M.C. is considered the Son of Kurtis Blow; and DJ Funkmaster Flex is recognized as the Son of DJ Chuck Chillout. Since mixing records had become an art in itself, some DJs felt the need for MCs. The next section explores the context in which this merge took place, eventually setting the stage for the rhymin MC.

The Rhymin MC and the Emergence of a Rap Music Genre

By the mid-1970s gang-related violence had declined in many areas of New York City, including the Bronx. In response to this change, a few neighborhood clubs reopened their doors, while others remained ambivalent about hiring street DJs because of potential gang violence. As one club owner observed, "club owners didn't like little young kids from the streets" (Abbatiello interview). Nevertheless, a few clubs, including the Dixie Club, Club 371 of the Bronx, and Harlem World of Manhattan, remained common venues for hip-hop music. Some clubs promoted this music in a series of one-night acts called "one-nighters." One club owner explained this trend pioneered by promoters:

> rap music must have been in the streets for about three or four years. The year that I went over there [it] was just startin' to get the attention of promoters' eyes—street promoters. What they were doing with these popular people ... they were puttin' them up in one-nighters. ... What they would do was they would hire ten of them [DJs], rent out a ballroom that held three or four thousand people, throw in a sound system, and give everybody ten dollars apiece and charge like seven, eight, or ten dollars at the door, and they would make a fortune. ... The promoters were making so much money they had to start giving them something. (Abbatiello interview)

The most important street music club was Disco Fever in the South Bronx, which began as an anonymous neighborhood bar. By 1976, Sal Abbatiello had acquired it as a gift from his father. He converted the bar, often referred to as "The Fever," into a dance club, and promoted street music on an every-night-of-the-week basis, rather than the usual one night of the week. Abbatiello's club featured a different DJ each night: "Eddie Cheeba was on Sundays, Lovebug Starski on Monday nights, Flash on Tuesdays, DJ Hollywood on Wednesdays, and Sweet G and Junebug, the house DJs, on Thursdays, Fridays and Saturdays" (Abbatiello interview). Because the club catered strictly to DJs and their music,

FIGURE 10.2 Sal Abbatiello, owner of Disco Fever, Bronx, New York, 1996. (Photo by the author)

Disco Fever became the hottest hip-hop dance club in New York well as a main attraction for music business entrepreneurs, leading the South Bronx to surface as a major creative center of rap music.[12]

Since playing records on turntables had become an art as well as a business, some jockeys felt the need for MCs. For example, with the hiring of Clark Kent, Jay Cee, and Pebblee-Poo,[13] Herc became the leader of the Herculords. At many of his DJ performances, Bambaataa was also accompanied by three MCs, Cowboy (not Cowboy of the Furious Five), Mr. Biggs, and Queen Kenya. The MC talked intermittently, using phrases like "get up" and "jam to the beat" to motivate the audience to dance while the DJ mixed records. The MC rapped to excite the crowd and engage them in call and response. The DJ spun the records and "played that certain part of the record and made the crowd . . . wild" (Bambaataa interview). The MC could compensate for any musical beat lapse or gaps that sometimes occurred during the DJ's mix. Flowers's MC, Sidley B, was adept at doing so, recalls Carson: "Flowers used to play with Sidley B. He [Sidley] built them [the crowd]. He helped make it go up, the excitement. It was a great timing job . . . between the DJ and whoever was vocalizing on it like Sidley B" (Shaw and Carson interview).

With the popularity of the group Grandmaster Flash and the Three MCs, the rhymin MC emerged as a distinct and primary feature. As one observer explains, "Flash was a great DJ, but his MCs were so different from the other MCs" (Abbatiello interview). Instead of simply talking intermittently to the dancing crowd while the DJ spun records, each of Flash's MCs executed their phrases in a rhyming and rhythmic fashion. Flash notes, "Melvin Glover had . . . a scholastic-type style. . . . Danny could say rhymes from now to doomsday. . . . There's some that can't really catch on when the music's being phased in and out to the beat. Cowboy, he was superb at it. As far as that 'Ho,' 'Clap your hands to the beat' and 'Say oh yeah,' I'd have to give him credit for being one of the creators of that" (quoted in Toop 2000:72).

The Three MCs popularized the concept of "trading phrases," the exchange of phrases between MCs as illustrated in example 10.1 by The Furious Five. They

EXAMPLE 10.1 Trading phrases; "Freedom," performed by Grandmaster Flash and the Furious Five (1979).

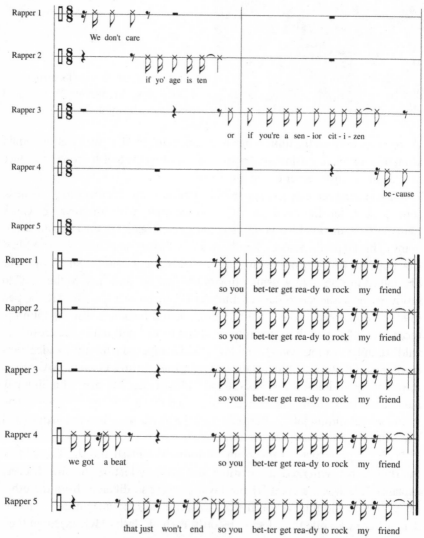

also introduced a percussive style of talk, giving rise to what rap artists call a "party-style" rap. This style features phrases in rhyme, rhythmic chanting, and synchronous timing with the disc jockey, all of which provided the underpinnings of rap as a distinct music genre.

The most acclaimed MC of the party style was DJ Hollywood of Harlem. Although little footage of DJ Hollywood's live performances at The Fever exists, he was nonetheless regarded by almost all the "rappin deejays" and their followers as a trailblazer ("Rap Records" 1980:57). As one critic remembered, "Hollywood can shut people up. After Hollywood, a lot of people won't grab a microphone. They can't say rhymes because he's so witty . . . he's so . . . he's rhythmic. He's everything. He's rap music" (Smith interview). Abbatiello remembered, "I searched all over for the most popular guy. His name was Hollywood. He was the best rapper. He was the greatest . . . the fastest. He was the only rapper I ever saw get applause" (Abbatiello interview).

FIGURE 10.3 The legendary DJ Hollywood with the author, Harlem, 1986. (Photo by the author)

As the reputations of Grandmaster Flash and The Three MCs and Hollywood spread throughout the Bronx, other DJs began using MCs in a similar manner. Street DJs, for example, featured two or more MCs who called themselves "crews," among them Cheeba Crew, Fantastic 5 MCs, The Mercedes Ladies, and The Malachi Crew. Meanwhile, other jockeys, including Eddie Cheeba, Sweet G, Lovebug Starski, Busy Bee of the Bronx, and Kurtis Blow of Harlem, tried their hands at rappin in the party style popularized by The Three MCs.

By 1979 the rhymin MC and DJ concept had become the norm throughout New York City. The symbiotic relationship they established became the model for rap music and would soon be introduced to audiences outside of the South Bronx by two routes: the promotion of rap music in Manhattan, particularly its DJs at Manhattan's mainstream disco clubs, and the commercial recording of Sugarhill Gang's "Rapper's Delight" by the successful independent record company, Sugar Hill Records. By the early 1980s, clubs in lower Manhattan, like The Roxy (a former skating rink) and Negril, began catering solely to a hip-hop clientele. Additionally, street DJs had evolved as popular acts in the disco club circuits among Manhattan's mostly white clientele. One person who was responsible for exposing hip-hop music in the Manhattan area was Kool Lady Blue of London, England. She was initially sent to New York City to operate Malcolm McLaren's World's End punk clothing store for one year. After witnessing the burgeoning hip-hop scene in the Bronx, Kool Lady Blue began promoting hip-hop arts at The Roxy and Negril. Several celebrities visited these clubs, and some of them, like Herbie Hancock, eventually collaborated with artists such as Grandmixer D.ST.

Other music observers from the Manhattan area in turn began to frequent the Bronx. Prominent entrepreneurs like the British punk promotor Malcolm McLaren, the soon-to-be Tommy Boy Records rap mogul Tom Silverman, and Arthur Baker, the owner of Shakedown Sound Studio, frequented Afrika Bambaataa's DJ battles and performances in the Bronx and noticed the musical diversity of his record repertory. Bambaataa recalled, "'First Malcolm McLaren came, 'cause he said, "There's this Black kid playin' all this rock and other types of music to a Black and Spanish audience." . . . He invited me to come play at the Ritz with [his group] Bow Wow Wow. So when I came and did this show, I brought everybody together like Rock Steady [breakdancers] and all the groups We went to the Danceteria and got too big for that until finally the Roxy became our home'" (quoted in George 1993:50).

In *Billboard*, a music trade magazine deemed as the bible of the music industry, Radcliffe Joe and Nelson George used the term "rapping deejay" to describe the result of the merge of the rhymin MC and the street DJ. They noticed that the change in disco "fostered the growth in the popularity of the rapping deejay; and [as a consequence], a number of recordings by rapping deejays are beginning to have an impact on the soul and disco charts of various music publications" (Joe and George 1979:4). "Rapper's Delight" bombarded the airwaves in October 1979. Considered by critics as the first successful commercial rap music recording by any record company, this song initiated an avalanche of similar recordings by makeshift independent record companies and eventually by major labels.

The musical fusion of Jamaican dancehall and African American–based funk music and the verbal art performance of both cultures contributes to the distinctiveness of rap music. Other factors, such as geopolitics, street gang culture, and lack of monies allocated to New York public schools, further fueled a response among inner-city youth like Afrika Bambaataa, whose creative insight laid the foundation for the arts movement known as hip-hop. The next chapter covers the commercialization of hip-hop music, its explosion in the musical mainstream, and the various street music promotion tactics employed in making rap a vital genre of popular music in the late twentieth century.

Notes

1. Several of Brown's songs bore the word "funk" in their titles, including "Ain't It Funky Now" (1969), "Funky Drummer" (1970), "Funky President" (1974), and "It's Too Funky in Here" (1979).

2. Robert Farris Thompson traces the etymology of "funk" to the Ki-Kongo word *lu-fuki*, translated as "bad body odor." He also finds that "funk" is interpreted among the Cajun in Louisiana as *fumet*, meaning the aroma of food and wine in French. He contends that the Ki-Kongo word is closer in form and meaning to praising someone for the integrity of their art, for having "worked out" to achieve their aims. Although Thompson states that the Kongo finds positive energy in funkiness, particularly the smell of a hardworking elder as good luck, in jazz/black English earthiness, the word denotes a return to fundamentals. See Thompson, *Flash of the Spirit: African and Afro-American Art and Philosophy* (New York: Vintage, 1983).

3. According to the popular music critic Radcliffe A. Joe, "disco" originated from the French word *discotheque*. In the pre–World War II era, the operator of a Parisian bar catering to jazz enthusiasts is said to have used the name "La discotheque" for his establishment. Hence, during and after the war the discotheque concept remained affiliated with Parisian bars that incorporated live and recorded jazz performances. Although the French coined the word, it appears they did not apply it until much later to the concept of dancing in a commercial club to recorded music. Early "discotheque" club owners include Jean Castel, Paul Pacine, and Regina Zylberberg. After Chubby Checker introduced the Twist in the United States in the 1960s, the dance was appropriated in Paris, where discotheques replaced jazz with rhythm and blues. Joe argues that the United States simply borrowed the term rather than the concept of the French. Particularly during the 1970s, disco in the United States centered around the record-spinning DJ and the musical production processes associated with the disco sound (Joe, *The Business of Disco* [New York: Billboard Books/WatsonGuptil, 1980], 1). Since making people dance was central to disco, the seven-inch disc was replaced with the twelve-inch, doubling the playing time of a song. Another objective of the twelve-inch disc was to create added space to "enhance and prolong the pulsating tempo of the rhythm and percussions breaks [sections]" for a dance/disco audience (63). The twelve-inch disc concept is credited to Tom Moulton.

4. Some of these fires were actually started by tenants. Disgusted with deteriorating conditions, they hoped that burning their apartments would create government-subsidized opportunities to relocate to new public housing projects and receive up to three thousand dollars for the losses (Jim Rooney, *Organizing the South Bronx* [Albany: State University of New York Press, 1995], 56).

5. With the use of live footage, the documentary *Flyin' Cut Sleeves* (1993) best presents the galvanization of black and Puerto Rican residents. The film indicates that when gang activity eventually subsided in the South Bronx, it was succeeded by positive changes, including the fight for Puerto Rico's independence by both black and Puerto Rican residents.

6. For further information about Afro-Caribbean migration to the United Kingdom, see Mel E. Thompson, "Forty-and-One Years On: An Overview of Afro-Caribbean Migration to the United Kingdom," in *In Search of a Better Life: Perspectives on Migration from the Caribbean*, Ed. Ransford W. Palmer (New York: Praeger, 1990), 39–70.

7. Edward Seaga is worth mentioning because of his political triumph as prime minister of the Jamaica Labour Party in 1980 and his importance as a catalyst in the redefinition of reggae dancehall during this time. Seaga, a Lebanese Jamaican who attained a bachelor's degree in anthropology from Harvard, conducted research on Jamaican folk music, such as Pocomania and Kumina church music.

8. For further information on the PNP and JLP, see Obika Gray, *Radicalism and Social Change in Jamaica, 1960–1972* (Knoxville: University of Tennessee Press, 1991) and Franklin W. Knight, *The Caribbean: The Genesis of a Fragmented Nationalism* (Chapel Hill: University of North Carolina Press, 1990).

9. While Joe finds that disco's twelve-inch disc sensation "enhanced and prolonged the pulsating tempo of the rhythm and percussions breaks," street jockeys used "breaks" in a similar fashion to refer to a percussion vamp section comprised of the timbales, congas, and bongos (1980:63). One of Herc's favorite breaks was "Apache" by the Incredible Bongo Band. By the mid-1980s, breaks or break beats were simply musical motifs from past pre-recorded hits used in a rap music mix.

10. Scratching has exploded into a complex craft. See Doc Rice, "The Language of Scratching," *Rap Pages,* September 1998, p.30, on various terminologies used in the contemporary scene.

11. In the 1980s, hip-hop DJing, considered primarily a male-dominated craft, expanded to include female artists such as DJ Jazzy Joyce (who studied with Whiz Kid), DJ La Spank, Cocoa Chanel, and Latoya "Spinderella" Hanson (the original DJ for Salt-N-Pepa).

12. Several rap music artists were discovered at Disco Fever, including The Fat Boys, Run-D.M.C., Whodini, The Treacherous Three, Dr. Jeckyll and Mr. Hyde, Grandmaster Flash and the Furious Five, and Kurtis Blow. On April 4, 1986, Disco Fever was forced to close because of a cabaret license violation. Sal Abbatiello started another dance club, The Devil's Nest, in the Bronx. It caters mainly to a teenage Latino clientele and plays Latin popular music, including rap and salsa.

13. I was a panelist for the Rap Music: The Blame or the Burden conference, which was held January 29, 1993, at Medgar Evers College in Brooklyn. Among the panelists was Kool "DJ" Herc, who interjected that a female MC, Pebblee-Poo, also performed with the Herculords.

11

Hip-Hop Soul Divas and Rap Music

Critiquing the Love That Hate Produced

GWENDOLYN POUGH

From *Black Women and Music: More than the Blues,* edited by
Eileen M. Hayes and Linda F. Williams (2007)

As Fanon says, "Today, I believe in the possibility of love, that is why I endeavor
to trace its imperfections, its perversions." Dialogue makes love possible. I
want to think critically about intellectual partnership, about the ways black
women and men resist by creating a world where we can talk with one another,
where we can work together.
—bell hooks, "Feminism as a Persistent Critique of History: What's Love Got
   to Do With It?"

In her article "Love as the Practice of Freedom," bell hooks discusses the need
for an "ethic of love" in the fight against oppression.[1] For hooks, love has liberating potential and can free us from oppression and exploitation. She believes
that until we revere love's place in struggles for liberation, we will continue to
be stuck in an "ethic of domination."[2] I believe that Hip-Hop culture and rap
music provide a starting place for us to begin talking about and implementing
an "ethic of love," love meant to liberate. The dialogue that bell hooks believes
makes love possible is the kind of dialogue that I am searching for, a dialogue
that will extend the possibilities of bringing wreck to a project capable of com-
bating racism, sexism, and homophobia. Black feminist criticism, if it goes
beyond admonishing rap for its sexist and misogynist lyrics, can aid in starting
the dialogue. As third-wave Hip-Hop feminists such as Joan Morgan and Eisa
Davis remind us, there is a public dialogue between male and female rappers
and between Black men and women. Therefore, rap music and Hip-Hop culture
can be used as a springboard for various kinds of conversations and actions.
Feminism needs to change its focus in order to take full advantage of the possibilities in rap music. Instead of admonishing rappers, it is time to do something
that will evoke change. Here I probe the public dialogue about love found in

rap songs; furthermore, I challenge Black feminism to interrogate rap as a site for political change.

How is love expressed in the Hip-Hop community? And what kind of love is this? My aim here is to look at love and Hip-Hop as a place to further the dialogue between Black men and women and create a space for more progressive conversations about gender and sexuality. My aim is also to look at the ways this dialogue can be used to bring wreck and help us reconsider some longstanding notions about gender and sexuality.[3]

My Need for Love and Hip-Hop

I remember the first time I heard LL Cool J's soulful rap ballad "I Need Love" (1987). While it was the first rap love song I had ever heard, it will not be the last. Rap and rap artists' never-ending quest to "keep it real" is not limited to the struggles on American streets. Some rappers show a dedication to exploring aspects of love, the struggles of building and maintaining intimate relationships between Black men and women, and maintaining a public dialogue about love, life, and relationships. The beginnings of this public dialogue can be seen in the love raps of the 1960s made famous by Isaac Hayes, Barry White, and Millie Jackson. As William Eric Perkins notes, these love raps were essentially monologues, recorded over a simple melody, that spoke to matters of the heart. Millie Jackson, thought of today as the mother of women rappers, got her start in this genre by recording love raps from a female perspective.[4]

Her raps were often X-rated and she held her own in duets with Isaac Hayes.[5] Talking about love and romance over melodious beats is nothing particularly new in the world of Black music. Black men and women have before and after the 1960s publicly hammered out their differences through song. In the blues tradition of Black music, Angela Davis finds that the mother of the blues, Gertrude "Ma" Rainey, participated in the call-and-response tradition in that many of her songs about love and sex were meant to be responses to the songs of male country blues singers.[6]

In rap, this dialogue can be viewed in the answer/"dis" raps of the 1980s, which gave rise to the women rap stars Roxanne Shante and Salt-N-Pepa.[7] These women paved the way for other women rappers by recording very successful songs that were responses to the hit records of men who were their contemporaries. Shante gave the woman pursued in UTFO's "Roxanne, Roxanne" a voice and ultimately let it be known that women would no longer suffer insults and degradation in silence.

Salt-N-Pepa's "Showstopper" was a direct refutation to Doug E. Fresh and Slick Rick's "The Show," a song in which women are portrayed as objects of conquest. As I argue in the first chapter of my book, some have described the process of shedding light on the things Blacks have had to do to obtain and maintain a presence in the larger public sphere as bringing wreck. *Wreck* is a Hip-Hop term that connotes fighting, recreation, skill, boasting, or violence. Some would argue that the response or talking-back element of "Showstopper" is an example of bringing wreck that appears to be reactionary and therefore limiting. I argue, however, that at that particular moment in Hip-Hop, when female voices were few and far between, the response or answer raps performed by Roxanne Shante and Salt-N-Pepa added a missing part of the conversation. By adding this part, they paved the way for the women who would later initiate their own conversations. Songs such as TLC's "Scrubs," Destiny's Child's "Bills, Bills, Bills," Alicia Keys's "Woman's Worth," and Lauryn Hill's "Doo Wop: That Thing" represent contemporary initiations of the conversation about men, women, and relationships. The public dialogue between men and women can also be seen in contemporary elements of Hip-Hop culture and rap songs.[8] The dialogue surfaces when observing the construction of male and female gender identities and sexualities as well as expressions of love. And although love in the traditional romantic sense is not the first thing to come to mind when one thinks of Hip-Hop culture and rap music, it is important to note that the Hip-Hop generation does talk about and express love. While it may be a different manner of expression than the love that is found in the romantic melodies of the 1960s and 1970s, with their sweet harmonies and equally sweet lyrics—more in line, perhaps, with the rugged and raw sex-filled lyrics such as those performed by contemporary crooners such as Ginuwine, Blackstreet, and B2K—it is still a form of love.

The need for Black men and women to take these private issues into the public sphere is not a new phenomenon. The legacy of racism in the United States made it impossible for Blacks to obtain the luxury of a clearly defined public/private split. The public discussions about love, sex, and identity found in the lyrics of Hip-Hop soul divas and rap artists bring wreck and flip the script on Habermas's notions of the public/private split and identity formation.[9] The necessities that Habermas says are taken care of in the private sphere are the very necessities Black people have been fighting for in the public sphere. These necessities also become a site of public struggle for Black men and women. The issue of identity formation, which is not a concern of Habermas, also becomes a matter for public debate for Blacks participating in the public sphere. Blacks in America have constantly struggled against stereotypes and tried to define themselves against labels put forth by American racism. In fact, the quest for self-definition, self-actualization, and self-determination has been a guiding theme in classical and modern Black nationalism. These themes all lead back to Black Americans' determination to define themselves in the absence of a clearly located homeland. For all of these reasons, then, the struggle for identity becomes a matter of public debate.[10] By using rap lyrics about love, sex, and identity to have an effect on public debate and at the same time shape the subjectivity of listeners and performers, the Hip-Hop generation sheds new light on the possibilities of the public sphere.

Tricia Rose notes four dominant themes in the works of Black women rappers: "heterosexual courtship, the importance of the female voice, and mastery in women's rap and black female public displays of physical and sexual freedom."[11] While men rap artists cannot claim rapping about heterosexual courtship as a dominant theme, the release of "I Need Love" (1987) and other rap love songs crooned by Black men suggest that when the rapper is a man, the discourse about relationships, courtship, and love is predominantly, if not exclusively, heterosexual. Hip-Hop, just like the larger society, is guilty of heterosexism and homophobia. With the exception of rapper Queen Pen, whose duet with Me'Shell NdegéOcello, "Girlfriend," deals with a woman pursuing another woman, rappers have yet to expand the discourse beyond male-female courtship.

Queen Pen's "Girlfriend," unlike the ballads of the Hip-Hop soul divas, which offer strictly heterosexual tales of love and relationships, tells the story of a very confident woman who will woo a woman right off the arm of a man. "Girlfriend," while it was never released as a single, became popular in various clubs in New York and Florida. Making the song was very much a political act with personal implications. Realizing that women rappers have constantly had their sexual orientation called into question because of various reasons too ridiculous to name, Queen Pen decided to record "Girlfriend" on her debut album in order to squelch rumors about her sexuality before they even got started.[12] However, she has yet to officially come out. She simply says, "I'm black. I'm a female rapper. I couldn't even go out of my way to pick up another form of discrimination. People are waiting for this hip-hop Ellen to come out of the closet. I'd rather be a mystery for a minute."[13] Thus her political act loses some of its momentum. While she is clearly the first rapper to rap about a homosexual experience, she waffles on completing her stance.

The lyrics of "Girlfriend" are very similar to the boastful lyrics found in the raps of men. The woman in the song raps about having a lot of bitches that all want her and how her sex is good enough to pull someone out of the closet. She brags that she has women leaving their men and giving her their phone numbers.[14] While Queen Pen's lyrics are boastful, derogatory toward women, and objectifying in some of the same kinds of ways found in the lyrics of men, they break free of the heterosexist hold currently on Hip-Hop culture and rap music by recognizing that same-sex courtship exists in society. As Queen Pen asks in a *New York Times* interview, "Why shouldn't urban lesbians go to a club and hear their own thing?"[15] Perhaps one day more rappers will take a stance similar to Queen Pen's and expand the definition of love to include same-sex relationships.

Even if rap has not reached a stage where it is ready to critique its heterosexism, it is particularly fertile ground for observations and conversations about male-female relationships and the fight against sexism. Rap music can be viewed as a dialogue—between rappers and a racist society, between male rappers and female rappers, and between rappers and the consumer—and the dialogue on love and relationships between the sexes is a productive location for inquiry.[16]

As a woman born in 1970—I was nine years old when the first rap record, the Sugar Hill Gang's "Rapper's Delight," hit the airwaves—I pretty much grew up on rap music. Reading Tricia Rose's discussion of the evolution of Hip-Hop culture through the changes in clothing commodified by rappers and Hip-Hop audiences reminds me of my own evolution from a teenage b-girl in Lee jeans, Adidas sneakers with fat laces, LeTigre shirts, gold chunk jewelry, and a gold tooth to a college freshman in leather jacket, baggy jeans, sweat hood, and fake Louis Vuitton. My relationship with Hip-Hop changed when I stopped consuming the female identities put forth by men rappers. Once willing to be LL Cool J's "Around the Way Girl" (1989), I took issue with the very notion of Apache's "Gangsta Bitch" (1992). Today, while I still consume the music, I have begun to question the lyrics and constructed identities.

Like many of the academics and Black popular critics writing about rap, I have a love for Hip-Hop culture and rap music. This love at one time stopped me from writing about rap, but now it prompts me to critique and explore rap in more meaningful ways. I am no longer the teenage girl who spent Friday nights listening to Mr. Magic's "Rap Attack" and writing rhymes, Saturdays reading her mama's Harlequin or Silhouette romance novels, and Sundays writing rhymes and short stories. Now I am *all grown up*, and although I still listen to rap music and read a romance novel every time I get a chance, Black feminist and womanist theories and politics inform my listening and reading. When I think about the definition of a womanist—"committed to the survival of a whole people, male and female"—I cannot help but wonder how that kind of commitment can be achieved, or even if it can be achieved, in rap.[17] Frantz Fanon's and bell hooks's hope for the possibility of love, quoted in the epigraph to this chapter, urges me to look for it in Hip-Hop. June Jordan's poignant question, "Where is the love?" haunts me. In her article of the same title, Jordan discusses the need for a "self-love" and "self-respect" that would create and foster the ability to love and respect others. She writes, "I am talking about love, about a steady-state of deep caring and respect for every other human being, a love that can only derive from a secure and positive self-love."[18]

As I think about Hip-Hop and the images of "niggas" and "bitches" that inhibit this kind of "self-love" and "self-respect," I am faced with questions concerning the forming of a subject that cannot only survive but must become a political subject—someone who can evoke change in the larger public and disrupt oppressive constructs. All of these issues inform my critique of Hip-Hop.

I am concerned particularly with rap and the love that hate produced—the love that is fostered by a racist and sexist society. This is the kind of love that grows in spite of oppression but holds unique characteristics because of it. In many ways it is a continuation of the way Black men and women were forced to express love during slavery and segregation.

It is common knowledge that during slavery Black people were not allowed to love one another freely. Family members could be taken away at any moment. African American historian Lerone Bennett notes in his book *The Shaping of Black America*:

> Slave marriages had no standing in law; the slave father could not protect his wife and children and the planter could separate slave families at his convenience. This had at least three devastating results. First of all, the imposed pattern of mating limited the effectiveness of the slave family and had a sharp impact on slave morale. Second, it isolated the black woman and exposed her to the scorn of her peers and the violence of white women. Third, it sowed the seeds of sexual discord in the black community.[19]

Lerone Bennett's work is thought provoking because it recognizes the influence that the enslaved past has had on the way Black men and women relate to one another in the present. It is fascinating to me that they continued to build family units even as they were torn apart, and they went looking for lost family members as soon as they were free to do so. Black people found ways to love each other and be together during the era of slavery despite separations and sales of partners. During the days of segregation and Jim Crow, Black people, especially Black parents, had to practice tough love in order to ensure that loved ones would live to see another day and not become the victims of Klan violence.

While strands of these kinds of love persist and the Hip-Hop generation has the legacy of African American history to build on, it also has its own demons. As Kevin Powell writes in *Keepin' It Real: Post-MTV Reflections on Race, Sex, and Politics*, the Hip-Hop generation, plagued by AIDS, drugs, guns, gangs, unemployment, and a lack of educational opportunities, faces more obstacles in their quest to love than other generations.[20] Powell offers the acknowledgment that life for young Black Americans is different, and the very nature of relationships within Hip-Hop culture is necessarily going to represent both the historical struggle and the unique aspects of the Hip-Hop generation. What continues to fascinate me is that in spite of all the historical baggage and contemporary struggles, these young Black people are still trying to find ways to love, just as their ancestors did.

A new direction for Black feminism would aid in the critique and exploration of the dialogue across the sexes. Black feminists such as dream hampton, Tara Roberts, Joan Morgan, and Eisa Davis have begun to explore the relationship between love and Hip-Hop. Joan Morgan maintains in *When Chickenheads Come Home to Roost: My Life as a Hip-Hop Feminist,* "Any feminism that fails to acknowledge that black folks in 90's America are living and trying to love in a war zone is useless to our struggle against sexism. Though it is often portrayed as part of the problem, rap music is essential to that struggle because it takes us straight to the front lines of the battlefield."[21] Rap music and Hip-Hop culture in general, along with Black feminism as an activist project, can be a part of the solution. It is not just about counting the "bitches" and "hoes" in each rap song. It is about exploring the nature of Black male and female relationships. These new Black feminists acknowledge that sexism exists in rap music. But they also recognize that sexism exists in America. Tricia Rose and other Black critics of popular culture argue that rap music and Black popular culture are not produced in a cultural and political vacuum. The systems of oppression that plague the larger public sphere plague Black public spheres as well.

Michele Wallace and bell hooks examine the larger society's role in Hip-Hop's sexism and encourage Black women to speak out against sexism in rap. The new Black feminists, however, are looking for ways to speak out while starting a dialogue right on the "front lines of the battlefield." In "Some Implications of Womanist Theory," Sherley Anne Williams notes that womanist inquiry assumes a proficiency in talking about men and that this assumption is necessary because stereotyped and negative images of Black women offer only part of the story. In order to get the full story, we have to be able to acknowledge and interrogate what Black men are saying about themselves.[22] While Williams is looking at the potential of womanism for examining the work of Black men writers, she offers a useful lens for understanding Black men rappers as well. Some of the questions that form my analysis of Black men rappers are, What are they saying about themselves? What kind of lover is described in the Hip-Hop love song? What is the potential for meaningful and productive dialogue found in the lyrics? What are the implications of a real and continued dialogue in this new direction? What impact do the songs of these men rappers have on the songs of Black women rappers? How have women rappers begun to internalize the images put forth by the men? How do all of these songs impact other young Black women? What is its political and rhetorical relevance? What happens when we really begin to critique and explore the love that hate produced?

Hip-Hop Meets R&B

My reason for using Hip-Hop soul divas' lyrics is threefold. First, the blending of Hip-Hop and R&B has added a new dimension to rap, which is already noted for the way it makes connections with and takes from other forms of Black music via sampling.[23] Thus the Hip-Hop soul diva is helping rap evolve to yet another level of crossover appeal. Second, the Hip-Hop soul diva has changed the nature of the rap love song. We can now hear a soulful singing voice on many rap love songs. During the time of LL Cool J's "I Need Love," this use of R&B singing was not as prevalent as it is today. Third, the love songs on the albums of Hip-Hop soul divas open up the floor for questions about love, thus providing a starting point for dialogue between the sexes.

Hip-Hop soul has opened the largely masculine discursive space of Hip-Hop culture to include more women. In fact, there are now more recorded women Hip-Hop soul artists than there are recorded women rap artists. It has always been a struggle for women to disrupt the masculine space of Hip-Hop, but the success of Hip-Hop soul offers more possibilities for women's voices and issues to be heard. Rap magazine writer Dimitry Leger notes that the "singing sisters" of Hip-Hop soul use the gained space to sing about their lives as members of the Hip-Hop generation. These women come from all regions of the country in which Hip-Hop has a presence, and their music reflects that regional influence with shades of hard-core reality.[24]

The release of Michel'le's 1989 self-titled album marks the beginning of a new era: that of the Hip-Hop soul diva who skillfully blends R&B soul melodies with gritty urban beats. While many credit Mary J. Blige and Puff Daddy with the creation of Hip-Hop soul—Mary J. Blige's *What's the 411?* was the first complete album with R&B lyrics over Hip-Hop beats throughout the entire album—her predecessor, Michel'le, shares some of the credit. Her career makes evident key elements of what constitutes a Hip-Hop soul diva. And her career and work helped lay the foundation for Mary J. Blige's success. The criteria include the backing of a male rapper entourage, a rap record label, and the influence of male producers largely known for their work in the field of rap. In Michel'le's case, the entourage included her labelmates Niggas with Attitudes (N.W.A.); they appear in her videos and set up the Hip-Hop soul diva as queen bee surrounded by a hive of men rappers. The record label for Michel'le's first album was the late Eazy E's Ruthless Records. The male influence is Dr. Dre, the producer of her album, and he can be heard rapping and talking throughout the various numbers. Indeed, the fact that her album was financed by Eazy E, a known womanizer with seven children by six different women who is now deceased due to complications from AIDS, and produced by Dr. Dre, who attacked rap video hostess Dee Barnes and was rumored to be the cause of Michel'le performing at concerts with black eyes, calls forth many questions about the way a woman rises to the top of a male-dominated field such as rap. Michel'le's on-again, off-again career is also a testament to how hard it can be.

The acclaimed queen of Hip-Hop soul, Mary J. Blige, started out with a slew of male rappers and singers as part of her entourage but has since gotten rid of the men who surrounded her early in her career. Perhaps this is why her career has outlasted Michel'le's. Many of Blige's early songs and remixes feature men rappers, not women rappers. Her first label, Uptown Records, started as a largely rap label but found more success with Hip-Hop soul acts such as Jodeci and herself. In fact, Blige, like Jodeci, got her start singing backup for Uptown rap artist Father MC. The producer of her first two double platinum albums, *What's the 411?* and *My Life*, Sean "Puffy" Combs, got his start at Uptown and now has his own rap label, Bad Boy Records. Puffy, like Dr. Dre on Michel'le's album, can be heard talking throughout Blige's entire album, and he and his Bad Boy rappers are in many of the videos from the *My Life* album. Former Bad Boy rappers such as Craig Mack and the late Biggie Smalls rapped on many of Mary J. Blige's early remixes.

Similar to Michel'le, Blige's career reveals how a dominant male influence can sometimes overshadow the accomplishments of women in the world of Hip-Hop. Numerous magazine articles about Blige mention Combs's role in shaping, molding, and creating her, as if she were a lump of clay and not an extraordinarily talented woman. There is also evidence of mental if not physical abuse. In several interviews Blige talks about getting rid of all the negative people and negative influences around her because the men she was working with made her feel bad about herself.[25] "I had a lot of people around me who were trying to hurt me—who were able to hurt me because I couldn't see that I meant something. Now my family is more involved in my career. There's nothing but love surrounding me. I don't allow anything else."[26] She also says that "when you love people, you don't wanna let them go because you love them. It's hard to let them go—family members, boyfriends, girlfriends—but you just gotta because if you keep them around, they'll drain you and try to hold you back. You gotta cut them off, because it's important. I'm important to me now."[27] Mary J. Blige started out as the classic ghetto girl with an attitude. She has evolved into a spiritual person who values herself and her life more than the things she almost let destroy her, namely, men and drugs. She speaks so openly and honestly about the things she believes that she has become a voice for young women in the Hip-Hop generation.

Mary J. Blige has undeniable talent, as Joan Morgan notes in her interview with her, "Hail Mary." Blige offers a different kind of blues that caters to a Hip-Hop generation devastated by crack, AIDS, and Black-on-Black violence. Her voice offers the reality of a ghetto that is simultaneously beautiful and ugly. And Blige can be credited with bringing the entire Hip-Hop generation back to R&B.[28] Even renowned Hip-Hop activist Sister Souljah recognizes Blige's talent and what she brings to the Hip-Hop community. Sister Souljah credits Blige for the issues she brings to public attention about the state of Black communities in her lyrics and notes that Blige brings to light the real implications of our future if we continue to lose sight of love and family. Although Sister Souljah states that Mary J. Blige is not a revolutionary in the tradition of Harriet Tubman or Angela Davis, she notes that Blige has managed to accomplish in her music what other divas have not: She stayed true to herself. She sang in her own rough voice and opened up her own bruised heart to the world. "She pronounced her words in unashamed Black English and she danced her un-choreographed unladylike steps with class."[29]

Mary J. Blige represents the average Black woman from the projects who shared her message with the world through song, managed to get her voice heard, and in doing so brought wreck to the glamorous notions and stereotypes of the recording industry. She also helped make it possible for other young Black women to share their voices. Blige has basically paved the way for other Hip-Hop soul divas such as Sisters with Voices (SWV), Xscape, Total, Adina Howard, Monifah, and Faith Evans. And she offers many women born and raised on Hip-Hop a representation of Black womanhood they can relate to. Former Uptown president Andre Harrell sums her up best when he says that "her interpretation of soul has given women in the inner-city pride. She took the girl from around the way and made her something cool to be."[30]

Mary J. Blige's music becomes the outlet of expression for many of the wants and needs of young Black women. Michael Eric Dyson aptly notes the strength of Blige's voice and music in relation to Hip-Hop culture when he compares her to Aretha Franklin. While Blige represents the gritty explicitness of Hip-Hop culture, Dyson finds that Blige and Franklin are saying similar things in different ways. "Blige's hip-hop soul feminism seeks 'real love.' But it remakes edifying love confessions into gut-wrenching pleas of faithfulness," he notes. "It makes self-love the basis of loving others. And it bitterly, defiantly refuses to accept sexual infidelity."[31] In interview after interview Blige offers advice on relationships and love to her fans. She stresses the importance of self-love and of staying away from abusive relationships: "I believe in love. I believe good relationships do exist, but you've got to have a love affair with yourself first and really know yourself from the inside out before you can have a good relationship with a man or anyone else."[32] It is as if through her music and her interviews, especially the later ones, Blige is trying to heal a generation and open them up for the possibilities of love.

There is really no other artist to use as a guide when coming up with questions about love that are relevant for the Hip-Hop generation. No other soul artist has had such an enormous impact on the Hip-Hop generation. Blige's Hip-Hop understanding of the yearning for love can clearly be seen in her first two albums. In her songs "Real Love" and "Be Happy," we get a glimpse of what the Hip-Hop soul diva is looking for in a mate. In "Real Love," Blige sings about wanting a lover who will satisfy her every need and give her inspiration and real love.[33] In "Be Happy," she questions how she can love anyone else without loving herself enough to leave when things are not going right in the relationship. She sings about finding a love that belongs only to her and being happy.[34] At first glance, Blige's requests seem simple: love and happiness. But anyone familiar with the lyrics of Al Green knows to wait a minute. The questions may appear simple, but can the Hip-Hop lover love? Can he make her happy? The notion of "real love" is not that uncomplicated. What is real love to a Hip-Hop soul diva? What can we find in the lyrics of rap love songs that testify to the fulfillment of every need? Are the love needs expressed by Hip-Hop soul divas different from those of women in mainstream America?

In the introduction to her book *Wild Women Don't Wear No Blues,* Marita Golden notes that Black girls of every class and complexion grow up believing that there are no Prince Charmings in their neighborhoods. Golden questions the possibility of love existing without fairy tales, because in our society the two, fairy tales and love, are so intimately connected.[35] I think it is important to note that society has indeed made fairy tales and love inseparable. And because living in and taking part in mainstream society influences Hip-Hop divas and indeed all Black women, various versions of the fairy tale do exist. The success of novels such as Terry McMillan's *Waiting to Exhale* attests to some Black women's need to find Mr. Right. Assuming that Black women do not believe in and internalize mainstream images of love and romance promotes essentialist notions of Blackness that claim romantic love does not affect or is not important to Black people.[36] An example of a young Black woman's view of the fairy tale comes from Lesley D. Thomas: "I know gangsta bitches that believe in princes and shining armor. Like them, I interpret 'hard-core' as an earned status qualifying Black men to rescue Black women from all this pain and bullshit. The desire to be freed is not a result of being weary and worn. And no, fantasizing as a Black woman is not unrealistic. . . . Hoes, tramps, bitches, whatever, we want our men, at home, being fathers and lovers—not making excuses and angry babies."[37]

Clearly some Black women, to quote Julia Roberts in *Pretty Woman,* "want the fairy tale." It might be a slightly different fairy tale, but it is a fairy tale all the same, with heterosexual relationships, "real" love and happiness, being saved from a life of strife, a man at home being a father and a lover, and living happily ever after. This same need is echoed in the writing of dream hampton, who decided to spell her name in lowercase letters like her feminist role model bell hooks. Like Thomas, hampton envisions a future with a Black man who would marry her and give her beautiful brown babies.[38] The political implications are important to note. Given the lack of clarity on gender roles, these dreams of heterosexual romance hint at a firmly established patriarchy—indeed, what comes to mind are the dreams of the normal bourgeois family described by Habermas, where all the necessities of life are met. However, these descriptions of strong Black male-female relationships also offer possibilities for a united struggle against oppression; a divided house cannot stand, but Black men and women united offers other alternatives. Perhaps a way to use this vision as a base without reinventing the patriarchy would be to do so with what Michele

Wallace calls "black feminism with a nationalist face." Black women and men would need to look at their relationship as working together against oppression and not as men being the head of the family.

With the Hip-Hop soul diva's (and, by extension, Hip-Hop culture's) unique relationship to love in mind, I turn now to the songs of the rapping lovers. What kind of lover do we find in the lyrics of rap love songs? What does the man say about himself? What, finally, is the potential for a meaningful productive dialogue, let alone a relationship with the man we find? What happens when we really begin to critique and explore the love that hate produced?

Critiquing the Love That Hate Produced

Third-wave feminist cultural critic Joan Morgan gives a probing reason for her continuing to listen to and grapple with rap music. She maintains that she exposes herself to the sexism of rappers like Snoop Doggy Dogg and Notorious BIG as a move toward understanding who her brothers really are as people. She listens as a Black woman and a feminist so that she can be clear about what she is dealing with.[39]

I believe that rap love songs can tell us things about what Black men and women of the Hip-Hop generation have to deal with as they seek to build relationships with one another. Two of the songs on the late Biggie Smalls's debut album, *Ready to Die,* can be classified as rap love songs, although they are very different models of love songs.[40] "Me and My Bitch" is an ode to a deceased girlfriend that begins with Sean "Puffy" Combs and an unidentified woman having a discussion. Puffy asks the woman if she would kill for him. The woman hesitates and then responds in the affirmative. He then questions what took her so long to answer, to which she replies she does not know. Puffy then asks, "What the fuck wrong with you bitch?"[41] In the background, Biggie says, "The act of making love, ha ha . . ." Instead of a sung chorus on this cut, there is Puffy and the woman's discussion. At the end of each of Biggie's stanzas we are taken back to the talking couple. It is through the dialogue between lovers that we get our first glimpse of the rapping lover and what kind of lover he wants. "Would you kill for me?" he asks in the first chorus. "Would you ever fuck around on me?" he asks in the second chorus. It would appear that the rapping lover wants a faithful woman who would kill for him.

We get a clearer picture in the lyrics of Biggie Smalls. Is the fairy-tale lover desired by the Hip-Hop soul divas and Black women present here? Biggie lets us know that moonlit strolls are not his thing. And while he admits that he will treat women right if they behave the way he wants them to, he also acknowledges that he will beat them if they do not.[42] And what does Biggie have to say about the possibility for marriage and beautiful brown babies? Biggie asserts that his notion of a wife does not include rings and traditional marriage but involves "main squeeze" status and a set of keys to his home.[43] So what makes this a love song? Besides Biggie paying homage to his "main squeeze" and "best friend," and in spite of the constant repetition of "Just me and my bitch, me and my bitch" throughout the song, the song gives an insightful look at a relationship between a young thug and hustler and his woman, trying to survive in postindustrial New York City—a city with few opportunities for Black people.

However, what really makes the song problematic is that while giving respect to the woman who lost her life because she was murdered in order to get to him, Biggie's "love" for her is defined solely by all the things she did for him and how she made him feel as a man. Undoubtedly it is her love that is the "real" love in this rap love song, a love she dies for. He loves her because she loves him. She helps him in his drug business by bagging up marijuana for him, while he admits he was unfaithful. And he did not have to worry about her telling the authorities about him, because she loved him broke or rich. Even though Biggie raps, "And then we lie together, cry together, I swear to God I hope we fucking die together," he is the one who lives to rap about it, because she is killed by men seeking revenge against him.[44]

We get an even clearer picture of the kind of rapping lover Biggie is in his song "One More Chance," which features his then-estranged wife, Hip-Hop soul diva Faith Evans, singing the background chorus. This song is different from "Me and My Bitch" because of its use of Hip-Hop soul. However, just as in "Me and My Bitch," the woman is doing all the loving. The song starts with Faith singing a remixed version of "Stay with Me" by the 1980s group DeBarge. The chorus is sung in the same melody. This use of the R&B classic is an example of what Russell Potter calls "sonic signifying"—rap's sampling of other Black music forms—and thus sets up a dialogue across generations in Black music. The use of an old-school love song provides familiarity for the listener; it is "repetition with a difference; the same and yet not the same."[45] Sonic signifying helps give the rap love song validity as a love song.

During the chorus Biggie can be heard repeating that he has the good love.[46] But what exactly is his good love? What picture of the rapping lover are we viewing in "One More Chance"? Biggie's lyrics offer some insight. He raps about the many women he has sex with. He raps about how he will essentially have sex with any kind of woman.[47] And he marvels over his own ability to attract and have sex with all these women because he describes himself as Black and ugly and not a heartthrob.[48] He brags about his player skills and his ability to steal another man's girl, because he is both member and president of the players' club.

While his lyrics may be viewed as simply boasting rap, it is important to look at and critique the things he chooses to boast about, his sexual prowess and promiscuity. This is not a stay-at-home, faithful kind of guy. However, what makes this a rap love song is that Biggie uses this boasting as a method to secure female companionship. He is wooing the ladies with promises of all he can do for them. He raps about how wonderful sex with him is and how deep he can go in order for women to have the kind of orgasm that their men cannot give them. He offers cruises, pearls, gator boots, crush linen, Cartier wrist wear with diamonds, luxury cars, diamond necklaces, and cell phones.[49] If fulfilling a woman's every need were based only on material things, Biggie would have been Mr. Wonderful. But somehow I think the love Mary J. Blige sings about is a little deeper than that. Judging Biggie by what he has said about himself in the two songs discussed (he's a womanizing, woman-beating thug who wants a "real bitch" who can take everything he puts out, who would kill and die for him), what does this say or mean to the woman who would love him?

Method Man's Grammy Award–winning "I'll Be There for You/You're All I Need," featuring Mary J. Blige, is perhaps a more hopeful example of love in Hip-Hop. And it offers perhaps a somewhat better picture of the rapping lover. However, Method Man displays more similarities than differences with Biggie. Even though it has been acclaimed as a classic rap love song and has won several music awards—not to mention high praise and accolades from Black women, who cried out, "Finally, a rapper rapping about loving and being with one woman"—"I'll Be There for You/You're All I Need" has room for critique.

Like Biggie's "One More Chance," "I'll Be There for You/ You're All I Need" makes use of sonic signifying by using Marvin Gaye and Tammi Terrell's Motown classic, thus placing Method Man and Blige within a larger tradition of Black love songs and validating "I'll Be There for You/You're All I Need" as a love song.

It also creates a space for dialogue across generations. This dialogue is jokingly hinted at in the Coca-Cola commercial in which an older Black man turns on the Gaye and Terrell version and sits down to enjoy his Coke only to be interrupted by the booming bass of his teenage son upstairs, who is also enjoying a Coke but bopping to the Method Man and Mary J. Blige version of the song. The possibility for dialogue is stifled, however, when the angry father bangs on the ceiling with a broom as if to say, "Turn down that noise." The Coca-Cola commercial sets the scene for possible conversations between younger and older generations, and sonic signifying is the rapper's first move toward such a dialogue.

I will focus on the Puff Daddy razor mix here because it has a hypnotizing rap beat and a longer second stanza by Method Man. I believe that while this is truly a sweet and gripping urban love song, it does not quite fill the model of what the Hip-Hop soul divas and many Black women are looking for. As with Biggie's "Me and My Bitch," we get the sense that the love expressed in "I'll Be There for You" is more a description of her love, and he loves her because she loves him. For example, Method Man raps about her making him feel like some-body even before he became a star and notes that he loves her because she did so. He makes it known that because she was with him through the bad times, she has shown herself to be real and true. He also warns her not to give her sex away and to keep her vagina tight for him.[50] The love that is "real" to the rapping lover in this song is the same kind of put-up-with-everything love expressed in "Me and My Bitch." And interestingly enough, a sample from Biggie's "Me and My Bitch" is used as a second chorus in the song. In addition to Mary J. Blige singing the Motown classic, we have Biggie's lyrics: "lie together, cry together, I swear to God I hope we fucking die together." As an answer to that, we have Mary J. Blige's soulful lyrics, "I'll sacrifice for you, dedicate my life to you." We get the sense that, like Biggie's bitch, she is the one who gives the ultimate love, sacrificing her life for him.

Again, if we keep in mind the questions about love and the fairy-tale-like qualifications that were discussed earlier, Method Man shares a lot of answers with Biggie. In response to the husband question, he too makes it clear that rings and traditional wedding vows are not for him.[51] But in his favor, at least he professes to always be there for his woman and not go out tricking like Biggie. But just like Biggie in response to the romance question, Method Man lets us know that hugs, kisses, Valentine cards, and birthday wishes are romantic crap that he and his woman are far above.[52] I find it interesting that Method Man's rap ends with a request for her to show her love.

While the two express similar views on marriage and romance, they differ in matters of fidelity. Method Man feels that he does not have to shop around because he already has the best. And although they both express unromantic pet names for their women—Biggie's "bitch" and Method Man's "shorty," "boo," and "you my nigga"—Method Man's pet names show much more love. It is a high form of respect—"giving props"—to say "you my nigga" or "that's my nigga" in most Hip-Hop communities. And Method Man, unlike Biggie, expresses some elements of his love in the song—his mad love that he intends to share only with her.[53] One gets the feeling that this love goes deeper than the physical. As if to show this mad love, the video for "I'll Be There for You" shows Method Man getting evil looks from his girlfriend's mother, being hassled on the streets of New York, running from the cops, and a host of other things just to bring her a box of tampons. In the male mind that might just be the highest form of love. The possibility for a love that somewhat resembles what the Hip-Hop soul diva is looking for seems attainable with the man we find in Method Man's song. Maybe that is why "Real Love" songstress Mary J. Blige is singing the chorus.

Lil' Kim and Foxy Brown

The conversation in rap is complicated even more when we take the work of women rappers Foxy Brown (Inga Marchand) and Lil' Kim (Kimberly Jones) into consideration. Their songs work as a direct response to the lyrics of the men.

They take on many of the characteristics that men rappers put forth. Lil' Kim becomes the bitch Biggie raps about. In fact, as the title of her song suggests, she is the "Queen Bitch." And the lyrics remind listeners that she will indeed "stay dat bitch." She has no plans of changing. It is clear that like Biggie's lost love, who would kill to save her lover's life, Lil' Kim would readily kill for her man. Some feel that the reclamation of the word *bitch,* like the reclamation of the word *nigger* or *nigga,* is an empowering act. Indeed, listening to the lyrics of Lil' Kim as she forcefully raps, "I'ma stay dat bitch" exudes a certain sense of power. She comes off as a woman in control—assertive and sexually assured. She is tough, not someone to mess with. She re-creates herself as the bad Black momma from 1970s blaxploitation flicks. Not only is she sexy but she is tough; she will kill you if she has to.

In other songs, Lil' Kim exhibits the same tough but sexy image. She raps about her sexual exploits. And like many of the men rappers, she uses boasting as a method. She raps explicitly about her sexual exploits and the things she is willing to do in order to be sexually satisfied. However, Lil' Kim is not about sex for the sake of sex alone. She reminds listeners that she likes to be compensated by her lover with money, jewelry, designer clothing, furs, and expensive cars. In her song "We Don't Need It," Lil' Kim raps about her desire for good sex, her irritation with men who cum too fast, and her ability to masturbate and please herself if the man is not giving her what she needs.[54] Lil' Kim's songs offer a woman who knows what she wants sexually—to experience pleasure and to cum—even if she has to satisfy herself.

The public image that Lil' Kim grants the listeners is of a strong, self-assured woman who knows what she wants and knows how to get it. That image also seemingly falls in line with the image of a woman that the rappers discussed earlier want. What is interesting in the case of Lil' Kim is that she has constructed dual and conflicting public images: the sexy, self-assured rapper that surfaces in her music and the vulnerable girl with low self-esteem that surfaces in her magazine interviews. Her parents spilt up when she was young, and her mother left her with an abusive father. She left home as a teenager and used men to support her. She has mentioned in interviews that she grew up thinking that she was not pretty. While she now believes she is beautiful because she has a beautiful heart, she still slips into self-consciousness about her looks: "But, like Halle Berry, Salli Richardson, Stacy Dash, Jada Pinkett Smith? I used to wish I looked like them motherfuckers!"[55]

The fact that each of these actresses is fair-skinned and has what is called in Black colloquial expression "good hair" should not be dismissed when thinking about Lil' Kim's desire to look like them. In fact, some might think that she has taken her desire to look like light-skinned, straight-haired Black women to another extreme, with her blonde wigs and blue contacts. She also notes that "when I was young, I didn't feel like I got enough attention."[56] Because she left home when she was fifteen years old, Lil' Kim learned the art of tricking at a young age in order to keep a roof over her head. She talks about living with a man for eight months the first time she left home. "I had a Panamanian boyfriend. I thought he was just so cute. He had a lot of money because he was illegally involved. He was taking care of me and I was living with him."[57] Any critique of Lil' Kim, her sexualized image, and her explicit lyrics must take both of her public images into consideration. The things that come out in her interviews about her abusive father, relying on men for food and shelter, and not feeling pretty complicate our understanding of the things she says on wax and require that we look at her in a more critically engaged way.

Similarly, Foxy Brown expresses tough and sexy lyrics. Like Lil' Kim and Biggie's bitch, Foxy helps her man with his drug business. Like Lil' Kim and Biggie's bitch, she would kill and die for her niggas. In "Holy Matrimony," she raps about being married to her male crew, the Firm, and being willing to lie and die for them.[58] Foxy Brown and Lil' Kim fit very well into the image of Biggie's dearly departed bitch. But they appear to be bitches with agency. Foxy Brown, like Lil' Kim, is very expressive about her sexuality and very boastful about her sexual exploits. In "Get You Home," she lets men know exactly where to kiss her and how to get her excited sexually.[59] She boasts that she has no problem getting her "swerve on." Both of these women combine sex and materialism in their lyrics. Sex and money constitute the good life. Indeed, the woman they construct would be more than happy with the man Biggie constructs in "One More Chance."

Like Lil' Kim, the public images that Foxy Brown puts out are dual and conflicting. In addition to the self-assured sexy rapper, in interviews we get the vulnerable Black girl with low self-esteem, a darker sister who did not feel pretty growing up. However, that is where the similarities between Foxy Brown and Lil' Kim end. Foxy Brown lived a fairly pampered life compared to Lil' Kim's homelessness, abusive father, and having to use men to keep a roof over her head. While her parents also split when she was young, Foxy Brown grew up having her wants and needs taken care of by her family. She did not have to trick to earn a living. There was no physical abuse in her family. She remembers, "In our family, we said 'I love you' every night."[60]

Even though she felt nothing but love in her mother's home, she yearned for her father. His absence influenced her relationships with men: "I thought it was normal for a guy to mistreat me. My father wasn't there to show me the right way."[61] She also grew up not feeling pretty because of her complexion: "My number one insecurity is being a dark female. If you take any beautiful dark-skinned sister nowadays, guys are like, 'Oh she's beautiful.' But back in the day, it was not the cool thing. That was just something I had to get over, because for a while I couldn't stand myself."[62] The estranged relationships with their fathers, ill-fated relationships with other Black men, and uncertainty of self-worth are things that Lil' Kim and Foxy Brown have in common. Their stories fit a lot of young women coming of age in an era of Hip-Hop, though to some extent these are age-old problems for Black girls. We could no doubt find some connections and similarities between their stories and the stories of the girls in the hood discussed earlier. And like the girls in the hood, Lil' Kim's and Foxy Brown's stories beckon Black feminism to find more meaningful ways to intervene in the lives of young Black women.

Ultimately, behind the sex and glamour of their songs and public personas we see the public dialogue about love and relationships in Hip-Hop coming full circle. Just as the men rappers can be read in response to the Hip-Hop soul diva, Lil' Kim and Foxy Brown can be read in response to the men rappers. And while there were some questions about the men rappers presenting what the Hip-Hop soul diva wants, the same cannot be said of these women rappers. The representations of Black womanhood put forth by men rappers are internalized and surface in ways some view as problematic. The questions about Lil' Kim and Foxy Brown being too sexy, too raunchy, too pornographic, and so on have been addressed in every Black popular magazine currently in print. Along with these questions go the charges that Lil' Kim and Foxy Brown are puppets, victims of their male crews—the late Biggie Smalls, Junior M.A.F.I.A., and Puff Daddy in Lil' Kim's case and Jay-Z, Nas, AZ, and Cormega in Foxy Brown's case. Some feel that because Biggie wrote some of Lil' Kim's lyrics and Jay-Z and Nas penned some of Foxy Brown's hits, these women are not legitimate rappers; their use of the word *bitch* in their lyrics is not an empowering act because a man wrote the lyrics, and they are not exploiting their own sexuality but are being exploited.

Angela Davis discusses this issue of agency and the woman performer in her work on the blues woman. In her discussion of Gertrude "Ma" Rainey and the song "Sweet Rough Man," Davis maintains that although the song was written by a man, Rainey's enthusiastic rendition rescued the issue of men's violence against women from the private sphere and gave the issue prominence as a public discourse.[63] For Davis, the issue is not who wrote the song but how the women blues artists used them to bring women's issues into the public sphere. Even the blues woman's sexually frank lyrics are read as women taking control and having a stance that spoke to their freedom as sexual beings. Another example of the way a woman performer exhibits her own sense of agency when performing songs that were written by men can be seen in Aretha Franklin's "Respect." Otis Redding may have written the lyrics, but no one is going to question Franklin's strong presence or her agency when she sings the lyrics. She performs the lyrics so forcefully that the song has become an anthem for women's liberation.

Therefore, rather than belabor the question of who is exploiting whom, I would like to look at all of the lyrics discussed as a fertile ground for dialogue and communication aimed at evoking change—at how the conflicting public images of Foxy Brown and Lil' Kim can be used to bring wreck and help destroy existing notions and stereotypes about Black womanhood and help improve the lives of young Black women. Joan Morgan notes in her article "The Bad Girls of Hip-Hop" that when Hip-Hop is truly significant and meaningful, it gives us images of Blackness that we refuse to see and dares us to get mad enough to do something about them.[64] What the conflicting images of Lil' Kim and Foxy Brown represent is clear if we choose to see it. They have based their womanhood and sexuality on the images that men rappers rapped about, just as I tried to be LL Cool J's "Around the Way Girl" many years ago. With no real constructive conversations going on about sex, Black female identity, and the shaping of public gendered subjects outside of the academy, their lyrics and images are inevitable. As Morgan notes, the "success of these baby girls speaks volumes about the myth shrouding feminism, sex, and black female identity."[65] The success of Lil' Kim and Foxy Brown is a direct result of a Black community consumed with saving the male and not about the problem facing young Black women. Very few people, Morgan points out, are aware of or alarmed by the fact that Black girls growing up in America's inner cities, surrounded by violence and materialism, will suffer their own pathologies. She notes that Black women die disproportionately of AIDS, cancer, and drugs, that the female prison population is exploding, and that teenage pregnancy rates have skyrocketed for Black women. And she asks a very important question: "Is it really surprising that some female MCs (like their male counterparts) would decide to get paid by glamorizing that reality?"[66]

We are constantly bombarded with discourse about the situation of young Black men in America. And while that is a legitimate and worthwhile cause for concern, few are noticing that young Black women are living and trying to grow in the same oppressive environments as these young Black men. If the Black man is endangered, what about the Black woman? No one stops to ask. This neglect is the plight of the Black woman. It has been around since the days of the Black power movement and definitely gained momentum with Daniel Patrick Moynihan's 1965 report on the Black family.[67] The stereotype of the strong Black woman, because we refuse to dismantle it, prevents us from seeing the very real danger that young Black women are in.

Lil' Kim's and Foxy Brown's lyrics help bring light to things once ignored. They can also help Black women face and maybe even get rid of some of the myths and stereotypes about Black women's sexuality and Black female identity that have existed in one form or another since the days of slavery and continue to influence the way Black women live their lives and express themselves. The fear of being labeled sexually promiscuous or always sexually available plagues many Black women. It is a legacy passed down from generation to generation. Foxy Brown's and Lil' Kim's acknowledgment that they are sexual beings who enjoy sex, and lots of it, is hard to face when one is taught to be ashamed of such desire.

What these rappers offer is the opportunity to embrace the sexuality of the self. Their boldness does exhibit a kind of freedom. Ironically, it is this same freedom that exposes the myths surrounding feminism. Morgan suggests that "their success drives home some difficult truths. The freedom earned from feminist struggle is often a double-edged sword. Now that women are no longer restricted to the boundaries of gender expectations, there will be those who choose to empower themselves by making some less-than-womanist choices— and they are free to do so."[68] While I take issue with Morgan on the exact extent to which women have broken the boundaries, I do acknowledge the fact that women have far more choices today than they did thirty years ago.

I contend that the sexually explicit lyrics of these women rappers offer Black women a chance to face old demons and not let the stereotypes of slavery inform or control their lives. After years of Black women being read as supersexual— or asexual, in the case of the mammy stereotype—the lyrics of these women rappers offer Black women a chance to be proud of, and indeed flaunt, their sexuality. And after the images of the Black bitch that have stifled assertiveness in Black women, it is almost nice to have a line such as "I'ma stay dat bitch." It does create a certain amount of agency.

In an era when men rappers are presenting problematic images of Black womanhood—ones that encourage the kind of "ride or die"/"kill a nigga for my nigga" mentality and an obsessive focus on sex, drugs, and materialism—we cannot simply cast aside artists such as Lil' Kim and Foxy Brown because they are not as positive as we would like them to be. The lifestyles they rap about are a reality for some women, who were never told any different. The images young Black women get from contemporary Hip-Hop culture and rap music tell them that they should be willing to do anything for their men. The "ride or die" chick who will do anything and everything for her man is placed on a Hip-Hop pedestal as the ideal woman. From Ice Cube and Yo-Yo's "Bonnie and Clyde Theme" and "Bonnie & Clyde II" to Jay-Z and Beyonce's "'03 Bonnie & Clyde," rap shows a warped obsession with remixing and remaking the tale of the white criminal couple who went out in a blaze of bullets. At first glance this appears to be just another obsession with gangster culture, but it is much more than that. The obsession with Bonnie and Clyde tells us a lot about the state of Black male-female relationships in America. Nowhere is this more telling than in Ja Rule's "Down Ass Bitch" and "Down 4 U."

The video of Ja Rule's "Down Ass Bitch" is very problematic. It is yet another video all about how women should stand by their men and be down for whatever. His rough voice croons, "Every thug needs a lady. Would you ride for me? Would you die for me?"[69] In the video, Ja Rule and female rapper Charlie

Baltimore remix the Bonnie and Clyde theme with Hip-Hop flavor. They rob the mansion of an unidentified rich person, taking a safe full of diamonds. However, before they can make off with the bag full of diamonds, the alarm sounds and they try to escape. Charlie Baltimore is caught. The cops really want Ja Rule, but she, being a "good bitch" and a "down ass chick," does not snitch. She does the time. We see her in her prison-issue orange jumpsuit. She goes from being scared to running the other women prisoners. She becomes a survivor in jail. We see her pushing around the very women who pushed her around when she first entered the prison. When she is released, presumably years later, Ja Rule picks her up. All is well. The message that this video sends to young women, specifically young Black women, is very troubling because it essentially tells them it is okay to commit crimes for their men. It tells them that even if they spend time in jail, it will pay off in the end when their man picks them up from jail in a luxury car and flies them off to a remote island to lavish them with tropical drinks and beautiful clothes. The video tells young women that the only way to obtain material possessions is to let some man use them to commit crime and then depend on him for their reward.

The fastest-growing prison population in this country is Black women. They are going to jail for things like smuggling drugs largely because of their relationships with men who are involved with criminal activities. The recently pardoned Kemba Smith simply fell in love with the wrong man and was too afraid to leave. She recounts, "At age 24, without so much as a parking ticket on my record, I was sentenced to more than 24 years in prison—without parole. Technically, I was convicted of conspiracy to distribute crack cocaine, but I contend that I went to jail for dating a drug dealer."[70] She was finally pardoned as a last-minute act by President Clinton, but she still feels that justice was not served: "You'd think I'd have been doing cartwheels when I was released. Truthfully, my feelings were in conflict. It was tough to leave behind the incredible women I met in prison—especially since many of them were victims of the same laws that put me away."[71]

Of another woman, who like Kemba Smith (and the others still in jail) did time for drug-related crimes, dream hampton writes that she "used to be so fly, the first girl in Detroit with her own Benz. Candy-apple red and convertible, with customized plates that spelled CASH. She bought red boots to match. . . . She liked to make the trip back then. She could drive all the way without stopping (he never did like to drive long distances), but he'd keep her awake with promises about the next forty years."[72] This woman, like Charlie Baltimore in Ja Rule's video, did not snitch on her man. "She's proud of the fact that she never snitched. Doesn't seem suspicious that he served 18 months, went home, and has forgotten to put money on her books for the past ten years."[73] She brags that "little girls like [Lil'] Kim are rhyming about her life."[74] However, the Black female prison population is rising because of stories like these—because of the messages young women are getting from the videos.

Ja Rule's message to women about being a "down ass chick" would not be so bad if it was the only one. But the message is everywhere, and it is not just coming from men. Women rappers such as Lil' Kim and Foxy Brown also rap about the illegal things they would do for their men. And even though Alicia Keys's video for the hit single "Fallin'" somewhat flips the script on this message by having the woman out of jail and visiting the male inmate, the message of the song is eerily similar to those discussed above. She sings, "I keep on fallin' in and out of love with you. I'll never love no one the way I love you."[75] In the video we see a field of women in prison-issue orange jumpsuits, mostly Black and Latina, singing the lyrics. Instead of falling in and out of love with these men, the young Black women need to love themselves. They need to love themselves enough to recognize that no love is worth going to jail for.

The remix of "Down Ass Bitch," the Inc.'s "Down 4 U," is just as problematic as the first version. It features the entire Inc. roster, Ja Rule, Ashanti, Charlie Baltimore, and Vita. The video is the typical beach-and-yacht party scene of which most rap videos trying to showcase a rich and glamorous lifestyle take advantage. The video has lots of bikinis and objectified women. The video also ironically features a cameo appearance by the contemporary R&B incarnation of Bonnie and Clyde, Whitney Houston and Bobby Brown. There are no robberies and prisons, just lots of fun and frolicking in the sun and lots of people living the glamorous life on the beach. The carefree nature of the video is what makes it even more problematic than the video for "Down Ass Chick." Combined with the lyrics, the video sends a false message to young Black women about love, life, and money.

The down ass chick is both an image and a reality that Black feminism needs to deal with. It has a lot of Black women serving time and countless others taking incredible risks with their lives. It is the inevitable conclusion of a community that does not value Black womanhood. Joan Morgan offers the perceptive observation that Foxy Brown's and Lil' Kim's success reflects Black feminism's failure to teach younger Black women about sex, feminism, and power. For both Morgan and myself, Black feminism needs to be accountable to young Black women, saving their lives and widening their world view and the choices they feel they can make.[76]

In order to accomplish this—in order to reach young Black women—feminism needs to come down from its ivory tower. Young Black women, like it or not, are getting their life lessons from rap music. And because voices like Queen Latifah, Salt-N-Pepa, and Queen Pen are few and far between, it is up to Black feminism to pick up the slack. In short, there are many ways that Black feminism can begin to work with Hip-Hop. The first step is to recognize the tremendous possibilities Hip-Hop culture and rap music have to offer.

Notes

This chapter was originally published as "Hip-Hop Soul Mate? Hip-Hop Soul Divas and Rap Music: Critiquing the Love that Hate Produced," in *Check It While I Wreck It: Black Womanhood, Hip-Hop Culture, and the Public Sphere,* by Gwendolyn D. Pough. Copyright 2004 by Gwendolyn D. Pough. Reprinted with the permission of Northeastern University Press.

1. In addition, bell hooks has written several books on love in a series she calls "the love trilogy": *All About Love: New Visions* (New York: William Morrow, 2000), *Salvation: Black People and Love* (New York: William Morrow, 2001), and *Communion: The Female Search for Love* (New York: William Morrow, 2002).

2. bell hooks, "Love as a Practice of Freedom," in *Outlaw Culture: Resisting Representations,* by bell hooks (New York: Routledge, 1994), 243.

3. As Paul Gilroy argues in "'After the Love Has Gone': Bio-Politics and Etho-Poetics in the Black Public Sphere," there is a lack of substantial analysis in relation to gender and sexuality in the scholarship on rap music, and the phenomenology of musical forms is not critiqued as much as the lyrics and video images are analyzed. He suggests that critics pay more attention to issues of gender and sexuality (in *The Black Public Sphere: A Public Culture Book,* ed. Black Public Sphere Collective [Chicago: University of Chicago Press, 1995], 56). I concur with Gilroy's suggestions for critics of Hip-Hop culture and rap. Both are rich with possibilities and open up spaces from which to interrogate issues of identity.

4. Sprite, known for its Hip-Hop–inspired commercials, had a string of Hip-Hop/kung fu commercials in the late 1990s that highlighted the female legacy in rap. Female MCs who were then new to rap, such as Eve and Mia X, fought men rappers karate-style, and their leader was pioneering female rapper Roxanne Shante. While true Hip-Hop fans appreciated the Sprite commercials paying homage to the legacy of women in rap, the "obey your thirst" drink took things to an entirely different level when they showed who the top leader of the group was in the last segment of the series, when the "Big Momma" ended up being Millie Jackson. Again Sprite's marketing department showed they knew a thing or two about Hip-Hop, particularly women's legacies.

5. William Eric Perkins, "The Rap Attack: An Introduction," in *Droppin' Science: Critical Essays on Rap Music and Hip-Hop Culture,* ed. William Perkins (Philadelphia: Temple University Press, 1996), 4.

6. Angela Davis, *Blues Legacies and Black Feminism: Gertrude "Ma" Rainey, Bessie Smith, and Billie Holiday* (New York: Vintage, 1998), 20.

7. The word *dis* is Hip-Hop terminology for "disrespect." These answer raps penned by women artists turned the dis around when men made records that disrespected women.

8. Hip-Hop culture has also expanded to include elements such as Hip-Hop soul, rapso (rap and calypso), gospel rap, and hip-house.

9. *Flip the script* is Hip-Hop terminology for the act of changing the agenda or evoking a different path than the one already set out.

10. Craig Calhoun notes Habermas's limited view on identity formation in his introduction to *Habermas and the Public Sphere* (Cambridge: Massachusetts Institute of Technology Press, 1996). He notes that Habermas weakens his own theory when he treats identities as if they were fully formed in the private world and equipped for the public realms based on that private formation. Calhoun offers an example from Habermas that contradicts the idea of identity being formed in the private sphere by looking at the way the literary public sphere and fiction enabled discussions about selfhood and subjectivity (35).

11. Tricia Rose, *Black Noise: Rap Music and Black Culture in Contemporary America* (Hanover, N.H.: Wesleyan University Press, 1994), 147.

12. Rappers such as Queen Latifah, MC Lyte, and Da Brat have all been accused of being lesbians because they have hard-core lyrics and rock the crowd better than some men rappers.

13. Laura Jamison, "A Feisty Female Rapper Breaks a Hip-Hop Taboo," *New York Times*, January 18, 1998, B34.

14. Queen Pen, "Girlfriend," *My Melody*, Lil' Man Records, 1997.

15. Jamison, "Feisty Female Rapper."

16. For discussion of the various dialogues in which rap music participates, see Rose, *Black Noise*; Russell Potter, *Spectacular Vernaculars: Hip-Hop and the Politics of Postmodernity* (Albany: State University of New York Press, 1995).

17. Alice Walker, *In Search of Our Mothers' Gardens: Womanist Prose* (New York: Harcourt Brace, 1983).

18. June Jordan, "Where Is the Love?" in *Civil Wars*, by June Jordan (Boston: Beacon, 1981).

19. Lerone Bennett, *The Shaping of Black America: The Struggles and Triumphs of African-Americans, 1619 to the 1990s* (New York: Penguin, 1993), 156.

20. Kevin Powell, *Keepin' It Real: Post-MTV Reflection on Race, Sex, and Politics* (New York: Ballantine, 1997), 6.

21. Joan Morgan, *When Chickenheads Come Home to Roost: My Life as a Hip-Hop Feminist* (New York: Simon and Schuster, 1999), 72.

22. Sherley Anne Williams, "Some Implications of Womanist Theory," in *Within the Circle: An Anthology of African-American Literary Criticism from the Harlem Renaissance to the Present*, ed. Angelyn Mitchell (Durham, N.C.: Duke University Press, 1994), 517.

23. For a discussion of rap music and sampling, see H. Baker, *Black Studies, Rap and the Academy* (Chicago: University of Chicago Press, 1993); N. George, *Hip Hop America* (New York: Viking, 1998); Potter, *Spectacular Vernaculars*; and Rose, *Black Noise*.

24. Dimitry Leger, "Hip-Hop/R&B Divas: The New 411," *Source: Magazine of Hip-Hop Culture and Politics*, July 1995, 43.

25. See K. Chappell, "The New Mary J. Blige Tells How Drugs and Attitude Almost Ruined Her Sizzling Career," *Ebony*, January 1999; J. E. Davis, "Proud Mary," *Honey*, October 2001; dream hampton, "All Woman," *Vibe*, April 1997; C. Hancock Rux, "Mary Full of Grace," *Honey*, Summer 1999; P. Johnson, "Mary J's Moment of Peace," *Essence*, July 1999; Joan Morgan, "What You Never Knew About Mary," *Essence*, November 2001; and Joan Morgan, "Hail Mary," *Essence*, April 1997.

26. Morgan, "Hail Mary," 76.

27. Rux, "Mary Full of Grace," 56.

28. Morgan, "Hail Mary," 76.

29. Sister Souljah, "Mary's World: A Former Public Enemy Follows the Career of the Queen of Hip-Hop Soul," *New Yorker*, October 4, 1999, 58.

30. Johnson, "Mary J's Moment of Peace," 138.

31. Michael Eric Dyson, *Race Rules: Navigating the Color Line* (New York: Vintage, 1997), 130.

32. Morgan, "What You Never Knew about Mary," 135.

33. Mary J. Blige, "Real Love," *What's the 411?* Uptown MCA, 1992.

34. Mary J. Blige, "Be Happy," *My Life*, Uptown MCA, 1994.

35. Marita Golden, introduction to *Wild Women Don't Wear No Blues: Black Women Writers on Love, Men and Sex*, by Marita Golden (New York: Anchor, 1993), xi.

36. I'm thinking specifically of Molefi Asante's notion of Afrocentricity and his discussion of love and romance in the African and African American novel. M. K. Asante, *The Afrocentric Idea* (Philadelphia: Temple University Press, 1987).

37. Lesley D. Thomas, "What's Love Got to Do with Hip-Hop? An Original Screenplay," *Source: Magazine of Hip-Hop Culture and Politics,* February 1994, 54.

38. Cheo Coker, dream hampton, and Tara Roberts, "A Hip-Hop Nation Divided," *Essence,* August 1994, 115.

39. Morgan, *When Chickenheads Come Home to Roost,* 72.

40. The late Christopher Wallace went by several rap names: Notorious BIG, Biggie Smalls, and Big Poppa. For the purpose of this chapter, I will use Biggie Smalls and the shorter Biggie.

41. Notorious BIG, "Me and My Bitch," *Ready to Die,* Bad Boy Records, 1994.

42. Ibid.

43. Ibid.

44. Ibid.

45. Potter, *Spectacular Vernaculars,* 27.

46. Notorious BIG, "One More Chance," *Ready to Die,* Bad Boy Records, 1994.

47. Ibid.

48. Ibid.

49. Ibid.

50. Method Man, "I'll Be There for You / You're All I Need to Get By," *Tical,* Def Jam, 1995.

51. Ibid.

52. Ibid.

53. *Mad* is Hip-Hop terminology for "a lot" or "an enormous amount."

54. Lil' Kim, "We Don't Need It," *Hard Core,* Big Beat/Undeas Recordings, 1996.

55. Robert Marriott, "Blowin' Up," *Vibe,* June/July 2000, 132.

56. Lola Ogunnaike, "Hip-Hop's Glamour Girl," *USA Weekend,* June 28–30, 2002, 4.

57. Jaime Foster Browne, "Lil' Kim," *Pride,* April 2000, 69.

58. Foxy Brown, "(Holy Matrimony) Letter to the Firm," *Ill Na Na,* Def Jam, 1996.

59. Foxy Brown, "Get Me Home," *Ill Na Na,* Def Jam, 1996.

60. Michelle Burford and Chris Farley, "Foxy's Dilemma: Dignity or Dollars?" *Essence,* August 1999, 76.

61. Ibid.

62. Ibid.

63. Davis, *Blues Legacies and Black Feminism,* 32.

64. Joan Morgan, "The Bad Girls of Hip-Hop," *Essence,* March 1997, 134.

65. Ibid., 77.

66. Ibid.

67. Daniel Patrick Moynihan, *The Negro Family: The Case for National Action* (Washington, D.C.: U.S. Department of Labor, 1965).

68. Morgan, "Bad Girls of Hip-Hop," 77.

69. Ja Rule featuring Charlie Baltimore, "Down Ass Bitch," *Pain Is Love,* Universal, 2001.

70. Kemba Smith as told to Stephanie Booth, "Pardon Me," *Honey,* September 2001, 86.

71. Ibid.

72. dream hampton, "Free the Girls; or, Why I Really Don't Believe There's Much of a Future for Hip-Hop, Let Alone Women in Hip Hop," in *Hip Hop Divas,* by Vibe Magazine (New York: Three Rivers, 2001), 2.

73. Ibid.

74. Ibid.

75. Alicia Keys, *Songs in A Minor,* J. Records, 2001.

76. Morgan, "Bad Girls of Hip-Hop," 134.

12

"Young, Scrappy, and Hungry"

Hamilton, Hip Hop, and Race

LOREN KAJIKAWA

From *American Music* 36, no. 4 (Winter 2018): 467–486

Hamilton literally wrote a verse to get him off an island—that's the most hip hop shit ever. He transcends the struggle, and if you look at your favorite rapper, that's most likely what they did.
—Lin-Manuel Miranda[1]

In the period coinciding with the final years of Barack Obama's presidency and the vitriolic 2016 presidential battle between Donald Trump and Hillary Clinton, *Hamilton: An American Musical* became the hottest ticket on Broadway, opened a second production in Chicago, and racked up a plethora of awards and honors.[2] In the midst of a national context charged with race, gender, and class divisions, the musical also became a political symbol. Although some critics have expressed concern that *Hamilton* reinforces a white-centered Founders myth by making George Washington and Thomas Jefferson seem cool to a new generation, more fans seem to have been inspired by the way the production writes women and people of color into the story of Revolutionary War hero and first US treasury secretary Alexander Hamilton.[3] Relying primarily on black and Latinx actors, *Hamilton* has earned praise for its bold reimagining of US history. As Lin-Manuel Miranda, the musical's creator and first to star in its title role, put it: "This is a story about America then, told by America now."[4]

Scholars of US history and politics have shown that throughout American history—from George Washington to Donald Trump—executive power has been linked to the president's role as a symbol of national identity.[5] Although Alexander Hamilton was never president, his status as a Founder who arguably did more than some US presidents to chart the early course of the nation makes him a powerful vehicle for projecting different ideas about the kinds of people who truly embody American values. Through its unconventional casting and by reminding viewers of Hamilton's origins in the Caribbean islands, the musical places marginalized groups at the center of the American experiment. As Elizabeth Craft documents in her contribution to this issue, *Hamilton* manages to appeal to fans from across the political spectrum while claiming "cultural citizenship" for the United States' immigrant and minority communities.[6]

Although most writing about the musical's take on national identity begins with its casting, *Hamilton* has worked even for those fans unable to experience it live. As demand for tickets and the costs associated with traveling to New York City to attend a Broadway production drove prices out of reach for many would-be theatergoers, most fans experienced the musical via its Grammy Award–winning cast recording. Produced with help from the Roots' Questlove (Ahmir Thompson) and Black Thought (Tariq Trotter), the album deftly blends musical theater, hip hop, R&B, and other influences and has been a central but often overlooked aspect of *Hamilton*'s popularity. This article focuses on the music of the musical. In particular, it explores how Miranda's engagement with hip hop's history, culture, and aesthetics contributes meaningfully to his retelling of the Founders story. By examining the cast recording as well as Miranda's public statements about his creative decisions, we can hear how the musical participates in the ongoing struggle to define national identity.[7]

A Hip Hop Musical?

Similar to the way it appeals to fans of different political stripes, *Hamilton* attracts a broad audience with differing musical tastes. Although it has been labeled a "hip hop musical" in numerous reviews and think pieces, Miranda and his team deliberately named the production *Hamilton: An American Musical*.[8] The potential slippage between these two adjectives—"hip hop" (often understood as black and oppositional) and "American" (often assumed to be white and mainstream)—hints at the stakes of the musical's reception. Miranda's writing for the show successfully negotiates this tension, appealing to audiences that do not consider themselves rap music fans while also convincing dedicated hip hop listeners of his sincere engagement with the genre.[9] This achievement is no small feat, given hip hop's "keeping it real" ethos and its fans' willingness to shun works that seem lacking in authenticity. The musical's success with musical theater fans, hip hop aficionados, and a large swath of listeners that fall elsewhere on the spectrum speaks to the extent that hip hop has become an accepted part of mainstream US culture.

One key to *Hamilton*'s far-reaching appeal is the way it employs hip hop techniques without much of the "cultural baggage" associated with the genre.[10] The production avoids elements of mainstream hip hop, such as abundant profanity, explicit sexuality, and conspicuous consumption, that some find objectionable.

Instead of being confronted with what Tricia Rose has called the "gangsta-pimp-ho trinity" of mainstream rap, audiences listen to actors of color sing about a once-forgotten hero of the Revolutionary era.[11]

Miranda's ability to recast hip hop techniques for the Broadway stage, however, is only one part of the story. Although the majority of songs in *Hamilton* feature some form of rapping, Miranda and orchestrator Alex Lacamoire wrote a fair amount of traditionally sung music to give the Founders a distinctly American sound. *Hamilton*'s score evokes gospel for George Washington ("History Has Its Eyes on You"), boogie-woogie for Thomas Jefferson ("What'd I Miss"), and contemporary R&B à la Destiny's Child for Angelica, Eliza, and Peggy ("The Schuyler Sisters"). Narrator and antagonist Aaron Burr's show-stopping number "The Room Where It Happens" features a banjo accompaniment, jaunty syncopations, and blue note embellishments that evoke early jazz.[12] Finally, "Aaron Burr, Sir," "Wait for It," and "Non-Stop" all rely on a prominent 3+3+2 rhythmic foundation common in Jamaican dancehall, as well as in its Puerto Rican cousin reggaeton.[13] Although the music of the cast recording is stylistically and temporally diverse, it consistently draws upon sounds from the black Atlantic to represent its revolutionary heroes.

This array of New World popular music references—much like Andy Blankenbuehler's choreographic decision to draw primarily on African American styles of dance—provides a sonic analogue to *Hamilton*'s casting of black and Latinx actors.[14] In fact, the Founders' polyglot musical diversity sharply contrasts the "white"-sounding music of their British foes. In "Farmer Refuted," for example, Alexander Hamilton debates British loyalist Samuel Seabury, who delivers his counterrevolutionary plea in waltz time over a "Bach-like" harpsichord accompaniment.[15] Miranda musically conveys Hamilton's intellectual superiority by having him rap a sharp counterpoint over Seabury's repeated verses. Thus, the scene pits the stuffy Old World of classical music against a nimbler New World represented by hip hop.[16]

Similarly, in "You'll Be Back" and its two reprisals ("What Comes Next?" and "I Know Him"), King George III delivers his perspective on the revolution as "chiming 60s Brit-pop."[17] Sung with an affected haughtiness by white Broadway star Jonathan Groff, the song brilliantly reimagines the rift between the Colonies and the Crown as a romantic relationship gone awry, returning listeners to the original meaning of the British Invasion.[18] Philip Gentry's observation that King George's "feminine gestures" read as gay adds another layer of signification, juxtaposing an effeminate British identity with the virile, heterosexual Founders.[19] Thus, *Hamilton* sounds a colorized US national identity by playing contemporary popular music—most often hip hop and R&B—against music coded as European and white. Miranda's intergenre approach to composing relies on his audience's familiarity with US popular music but does not require a deep understanding or appreciation of hip hop to convey its fundamental messages.

The stylistic diversity of the cast recording belies frequent characterizations of *Hamilton* as a hip hop musical because not all songs in the production feature rapping or sound like hip hop; many of them do not. In fact, the use of hip hop as an adjective could be read as reductive on the part of journalists and critics were it not for Miranda's persistence in calling attention to the musical's deep engagement with rap. Whether quoting specific lyrics, imitating the style of particular MCs, or making more abstract gestures toward the genre (as in the epigraph to this article, where Miranda claims that Alexander Hamilton's biography is the "most hip-hop shit ever"), the musical contains layers of meaning for hip hop fans to dissect.

Placing these overtures to hip hop and other musical genres in a broader context of intertextuality—a defining feature both of hip hop and of musical theater—is helpful. Musicologist Justin Williams argues that intertextuality is the fundamental element of hip hop culture and that hip hop is distinct for its "*overt* borrowing of preexisting materials to new ends."[20] Throughout rap music history, the most well known and controversial instances of borrowing tend to involve digital sampling, but as Williams explains, there are other ways that musicians draw on preexisting source materials, such as alluding to or verbally quoting the work of other MCs or imitating their delivery and vocal timbre. I have just discussed a few instances of intertextuality with respect to genre (i.e., playing contemporary pop against music that sounds old fashioned or white), and there are other numerous examples of borrowing in *Hamilton* that have been uncovered by fans, cited explicitly in the musical's credits, or acknowledged by Miranda himself in interviews and online forums.[21] *Hamilton* even makes a number of overt references to musical theater itself, from the operettas of Gilbert and Sullivan to the megamusicals of Andrew Lloyd Webber.[22]

Arguably the most important preexisting source from which Miranda borrows, however, is Ron Chernow's now best-selling biography of Alexander Hamilton. Miranda conceived of the musical while reading the book on vacation, and he consulted the historian early and often throughout its development. One can hear numerous echoes of Chernow's work reverberating throughout the musical, such as his conception of Alexander Hamilton as an "immigrant" and his highlighting of Hamilton's final words to his wife, Eliza, before his fatal duel with Aaron Burr: "Best of wives, best of women." Miranda even adopts the narrative structure of Chernow's book, which uses Eliza's life after Alexander's death as a coda.[23] But even as Chernow's work provides the basic structure for the musical's plot, Miranda treats its biographical details as more raw material to be manipulated and combined with his other sources from hip hop and musical theater.

Thus, the popularity of *Hamilton* depends not so much on its historical accuracy as it does on the way that Miranda weaves together a compelling narrative from the threads of his many influences. Just as hip hop's beat makers earn their status by creatively manipulating digital samples, Miranda displays his talents by crafting more than two hours of music from the biography of a "forgotten" Founder and a diverse assortment of popular music references. *Hamilton* might end up increasing a generation's understanding of the American Revolution the same way that dedicated hip hop listeners tend to know more than their nonobsessed peers about 1960s and 1970s jazz and soul records.[24] But the real power of *Hamilton*, like hip hop, is the way it flips its source materials to make something that feels fresh.[25]

Although some audiences interpret *Hamilton* as a sincere paean to the white Founders, others hear Miranda's retelling of Revolutionary history as an act of parody and appropriation. In the same way that Bronx DJs transformed turntables and dusty vinyl records into musical instruments, creating something new that turned passive consumers into active producers, *Hamilton* seizes control of a stale Founders myth to fashion something unexpected and timely. To many people, the musical sounds like an intervention in the present moment not to preserve the status quo but to support some of the most marginalized members of US society.[26] As Oskar Eustis, artistic director of the Public Theater, where *Hamilton* had its off-Broadway debut, put it: "By telling the story of the founding of the country through the eyes of a bastard, immigrant orphan, told entirely by people of color, he is saying, 'This is our country. We get to lay claim to it.'"[27] At a time when musicians Kendrick Lamar and Beyoncé represent the soundtrack of the Black Lives Matter movement, bringing Alexander Hamilton, George Washington, and Thomas Jefferson back to life with hip hop and R&B is a gesture that speaks powerfully to the humanity so long denied to black and brown people, as well as to the exploitative relationship between "civilized" white Founders and their racial others.

Starting from the Bottom

Not all examples of musical borrowing in *Hamilton*, however, are created equal. Although the musical draws liberally from a variety of sources, Miranda's references to hip hop music form an essential part of the cast recording's production and reception. Many times, for example, Miranda has claimed that Alexander Hamilton had much in common with famous rap artists such as Tupac Shakur and Notorious B.I.G. because he also rose from difficult circumstances on the strength of his words.[28] In fact, the world first learned about Miranda's interest in Alexander Hamilton during "An Evening of Poetry, Music, and the Spoken Word," an event hosted by Barack and Michelle Obama at the White

House on May 12, 2009. Performing what eventually would become the show's opening number in front of the president and First Lady, Miranda described Hamilton as "somebody who embodies hip hop." Hamilton, he explained, "was born a penniless orphan in St. Croix of illegitimate birth, became George Washington's right-hand man, became treasury secretary, caught beef with every other founding father, and all on the strength of his writing. I think he embodies the word's ability to make a difference."[29]

This view of Hamilton as a uniquely talented individual who journeys from society's margins to its center parallels not only the rags-to-riches plotline of numerous musicals (e.g., *Annie*, *My Fair Lady*, *Oliver!*, etc.) but also the musical biographies of prominent hip hop artists such as Dr. Dre, Eminem, Jay-Z, and countless others. This "started from the bottom" trope—to invoke a famous line from rapper Drake—permeates the genre, serving as a foundation for its gendered class-based constructions of authenticity.[30] Thus, Miranda's assertion that Hamilton embodies hip hop illuminates how heroic individualism, rugged masculinity, and poetic self-invention underwrite narratives of the nation's birth as well as the musical personas of numerous hip hop stars. Even President Obama, a big fan of the musical, has described Alexander Hamilton as the original "hustler," borrowing a term from hip hop culture to describe someone (almost always a man) who works tirelessly, creatively, and sometimes illegally to elevate his status.[31] Hamilton—like the iconic rappers on which he was based—represents an ideal masculinized subject for the dog-eat-dog world of Revolutionary America–cum–entrepreneurial capitalism.[32]

In this way, *Hamilton* mirrors gendered divisions within mainstream rap music. For Revolutionary War heroes such as Lafayette, Hamilton, and Washington, fast-paced and assertive rapping equals intellect and valor. Female characters such as Eliza and Maria Reynolds, however, are relegated to traditional feminine roles, admiring and/or seducing male counterparts with R&B-style singing. The only exception to this division is Angelica Schuyler, whose rapping in songs like "The Schuyler Sisters" and "Satisfied" evokes strong female MCs such as Queen Latifah and Lauryn Hill, who often challenge sexism and misogyny in their music. But even Angelica eventually retreats to the musical's "separate worlds of love and ritual," where men mostly rap and women mostly sing.[33]

To portray Alexander Hamilton as "young, scrappy, and hungry," Miranda used his knowledge of hip hop style to make Alexander Hamilton *sound* like a uniquely talented individual. Consider, for example, the rap lyrics that Miranda wrote for "My Shot," Alexander Hamilton's first big number. In his long solo verses within the song, Hamilton delivers an onslaught of internal and multiple-word rhymes ("disadvantage," "learned to manage," "gun to brandish," etc.), as well as enjambment, the poetic technique in which phrases cascade over the bar lines in effusive rhythm. As Miranda himself explains, "I wrote Hamilton with very polysyllabic rhymes, like [rappers] Big Pun or Rakim, which showed that he was literally in a different dimension than everyone else. I had to prove that his intellect was to be feared in the room."[34]

This sense that Hamilton is in a "different dimension" is bolstered by the contrast between "My Shot" and the barroom scene that precedes it. In "Aaron Burr, Sir," Hamilton's friends—John Laurens, the Marquis de Lafayette, and Hercules Mulligan—introduce themselves with brief four-measure toasts in braggadocio style. Laurens makes his entrance boasting about shooting members of the British occupying forces. He even refers to the redcoats anachronistically as "cops," suggesting a parallel between the War of Independence with the contemporary struggle against police brutality. This verse might contain the musical's most radical lyric—especially when considering the controversy surrounding songs like N.W.A's "Fuck Tha Police"—but it has garnered hardly any attention from critics and fans.[35] This lack of notice, I argue, has something to do with the brevity of Laurens's verse, which is immediately followed by Lafayette's playful mix of French and English and then by Mulligan's humorous boasting about his sexual prowess. In addition, Laurens's "old school" flow, which consists of even phrases and one-word end rhymes that fall predictably on the fourth beat ("be," "three," "me," and "free"), lends his statement a simplistic nursery-rhyme quality. Thus, the barroom bravado of Laurens, Lafayette, and Mulligan serves as a backdrop for Hamilton's elevated flow and more fully developed ideas, helping to signify his intellect and ambition.

This portrayal of Hamilton as both brash and brilliant taps into a long history of outlaw characters in American popular culture, including Tony Montana in *Scarface* and Michael Corleone (and his father, Vito) in *The Godfather*, both of which have been adopted by rappers.[36] Two of *Hamilton's* most obvious references to iconic hip hop songs draw directly on this outsider trope. In "My Shot" Hamilton describes himself as "only nineteen but my mind is older," a quotation of Mobb Deep's classic 1995 song "Shook Ones, Pt. 2."[37] In the original context of "Shook Ones," these lyrics comment on the harsh environment of the Queensbridge housing projects, where "only the strong survive" and children must mature quickly or fall victim to the streets.[38] Miranda's borrowing of this line equates the struggle of inner-city youth with biographer Ron Chernow's description of Alexander Hamilton as a remarkably strong individual who overcame poverty, abandonment, and the death of his mother at an early age.[39]

The other reference, which is easily recognizable even to casual rap fans, is the song "Ten Duel Commandments." Inspired directly by Notorious B.I.G.'s "Ten Crack Commandments," Miranda borrows the distinctive countdown that begins each song ("1, 2, 3, 4, 5, 6, 7, 8, 9").[40] Similarly, the lyrics to each song consist of a number-by-number elaboration on the respective rules of dueling and drug dealing—two social rituals in which men negotiate their reputations through a mastery of violence. The parallels in this case of borrowing are striking and loaded with irony. As Miranda himself explains, "I came up with the idea of doing 'Ten Duel Commandments' because 'Ten Crack Commandments' is a how-to guide for illegal activity in the 90s. And this is a how-to guide for illegal activities in the 1790s."[41] Thus, by highlighting the way illicit activities were a part of the world of white Founding Fathers and setting their exploits to a popular rap song, Miranda suggests that Hamilton, Burr, and others who took part in duels exist on a comparable moral plane with present-day drug dealers laboring in the underground economy. And in complementary fashion, Miranda's prominent use of Notorious B.I.G.'s famous song about the unofficial rules of street-level drug dealing smuggles some of the most marginalized members of contemporary US society into the heart of the Founders' mythology.

Indeed, if there is an overriding message embedded in *Hamilton* for hip hop listeners, it is this familiar trope: rappers and the personas they create are nothing less than a reflection of fundamental American ideals. The hip hop gangsta—like the Mafia don before him—is an embodiment of American enterprise. Like Alexander Hamilton and the Marquis de Lafayette, they find a way to get the job done. They get rich, or they die trying.[42] And in their quest to survive the system, they—perhaps inadvertently—reproduce it.

For these reasons, political scientist Lester Spence characterizes gangsta rap as a quintessentially neoliberal subgenre because it functions as an allegory for how black people, whom the white Founders actually regarded as unable to meet the demands of democratic citizenship, might be redeemable as capitalist subjects after all.[43] By placing such a great emphasis on the entrepreneurial spirit of individual actors, hip hop music helps to foster a "parallel public" that reproduces rather than critiques neoliberalism, an ideology that acknowledges diversity as a social good while deploying meritocratic arguments to justify ongoing material inequalities.[44] Through its many intertextual references to hip hop, *Hamilton* suggests that the Founders and famous rappers are cut from the same enterprising cloth.

Race over Class

Another way that *Hamilton*'s use of rap mirrors neoliberal ideology can be found in its deployment of race to trump issues of class. In "Cabinet Battle #1," for example, Jefferson and Hamilton square off against one another in a debate over Hamilton's plan to use the newly created national bank to pay off the wartime debts of individual states. In this rap battle, Hamilton rebuts Jefferson's arguments by pivoting from his economic plan to the issue of slavery:

> A civics lesson from a slaver, hey neighbor
> Your debts are paid 'cause you don't pay for labor
> "We plant seeds in the ground; we create!"
> Yeah, keep ranting; we know who's really doing the planting[45]

In this way, the northern Hamilton uses the specter of slavery to claim the moral high ground over the southern Jefferson. Miranda even wrote a third cabinet battle, eventually cut from the production, in which Hamilton and Jefferson debate the question of slavery itself. In this track, the demo of which was released as a part of *The Hamilton Mixtape*, Hamilton launches yet another personal attack against Jefferson, calling out his enslaved concubine Sally Hemings by name and warning that outlawing slavery would impede Jefferson's ability to secure female companionship.[46]

The musical's repeated jabs at Jefferson, including his elaborate staircase entry at the beginning of the second act, seem to justify the concerns of some historians who worry that Miranda only invokes slavery when it makes his lead character look good.[47] In contrast to this moral posturing, historian Edward Baptist has shown that northerners from Hamilton's Federalist Party also profited handsomely from American slavery. In the early 1800s the Wall Street system engineered by Alexander Hamilton provided the credit necessary to expand slavery into its most brutal phase. As cotton production expanded into the Louisiana territories and began to propel the US economy into the modern industrial era, tens of thousands of enslaved blacks were sold from tobacco plantations in the North, forced on a grueling march hundreds of miles south, and imprisoned within a tortuous system of labor exploitation.[48] In the musical, however, the architect of the financial system that enabled this brutally efficient system by connecting it to the global economy is celebrated by Miranda as a champion of the people.[49]

Thus, *Hamilton*'s celebration of racial diversity without concern for economic justice reflects current tensions in politics and in popular culture. If the musical's borrowing from hip hop enables it to press for a more racially diverse sense of cultural citizenship, then it also reproduces some of the genre's own political contradictions. Mainstream rappers today celebrate black wealth, but they tend to avoid critiquing the economic system that makes it difficult for more of their peers to rise up. Jay-Z, who went from selling crack cocaine on New York City street corners to having prime seats at Barack Obama's 2009 presidential inauguration, portrays himself as an extraordinary individual who, like former President Obama, beat the odds to succeed. His story—like those of numerous other rappers—redeems blackness for capitalism and promises that anybody can make it to the top of American society if they possess the talent and will to do so. Similarly, *Hamilton*'s retelling of the Founders' story—like the Chernow biography on which it is based—casts its main character as an exceptional individual who through hard work and innate genius helps to found a nation. In this way, *Hamilton* performs the cultural work of neoliberalism by representing a United States where all are welcome to participate and all are individually responsible for their achievements, as well as for their failures.

Hamilton in the Age of Obama

To further demonstrate how *Hamilton* sounds national identity through its intertextual relationship with hip hop, it is instructive to examine former president Barack Obama's relationship to the genre. The way that many fans react to *Hamilton*'s colorization of US history—the sense that it is *claiming* the United States for previously marginalized groups—parallels the excitement and sense of change embodied by the election of the first black president, and it seems appropriate for *Hamilton* to have achieved widespread fame in the last years of the Obama presidency. Just as the musical seems to advance a broader conception of national identity, the election of the United States' first black president appeared to many as a sign that the United States had entered a more inclusive phase of its history.[50] As political scientist Joseph Lowndes explains, Barack Obama's mixed-race heritage, which he made a central focus of his writings and campaign speeches, symbolized for many the possibility of overcoming the nation's painful racial divisions.[51]

Obama's success at inspiring his followers, however, did not come directly from his DNA but from the way he performed inclusiveness throughout his campaign. American studies scholar Michael Jeffries explores the importance of Obama's ability to "code switch" and how his situational authenticity—the way he easily adapts to the norms and conventions of different contexts—mirrors evolving standards of authenticity in hip hop.[52] Jeffries explains that Obama's effortless switching between black vernacular and standard English mirrors the rise of hip hop celebrities such as Jay-Z who cultivate images of themselves as street smart, world-traveling businessmen as comfortable in the boardroom as they are in the inner-city neighborhoods where they were raised. During his 2008 campaign, Obama relied on strategic references to hip hop and R&B, allowing him to appeal to young voters without alienating members of the civil rights generation, an approach Dana Gorzelany-Mostak aptly describes as "keeping it real (respectable)."[53]

In similar fashion, Miranda's success at bringing hip hop and musical theater together, gaining the trust and support of prominent rap artists, and expanding his career and personal brand into the wider world of the entertainment industry places him in the company of Barack Obama and Jay-Z, both of whom also appear to move effortlessly across the social spectrum. Since the success of *Hamilton*, Miranda's own code-switching talents, which he has acknowledged self-reflexively in multiple interviews, have allowed him to move from Broadway celebrity to the film industry, writing and performing music for the Disney hit *Moana*, as well as to more mainstream hip hop and R&B with *The Hamilton Mixtape*.[54] In public life, Miranda can collaborate with rap superstar Nas or fluently discuss classic tracks from hip hop's golden age with *New York Times* music critic Jon Caramanica.[55] But he is also at ease speaking with NPR's Terry Gross about *The Little Mermaid* and other animated Disney musical films on which he was raised.[56] Miranda, much like Jay-Z and Obama, seems to exist within a more recent paradigm of hip hop authenticity that is defined not by essential ties to particular neighborhoods, unassailable street credibility, or revolutionary politics but instead by the ability to exercise power across diverse platforms.

These parallels between Obama and Miranda are more than coincidental. As has already been mentioned, the song that would become the musical's opening number first debuted at the White House, and the Obamas were among some of the earliest and biggest celebrities to attend and praise the Broadway production. In March 2016, in the midst of Hamilton mania, Miranda and the cast visited the White House for a series of performances and events. In addition to performing selections from the musical for the soon-to-be-former president and First Lady, including a poignant rendition of "One Last Time"—the song in which George Washington announces that he is leaving office—Obama took time to sit down for an interview with Miranda and participate in a Rose Garden freestyle session.[57]

In a broad sense, Obama and Miranda's use of hip hop to make a powerful symbolic connection with marginalized populations reflects the neoliberal legacy of the 1980s. The same Reagan-era moves toward privatization, defunding the public sector, and mass incarceration that helped shape the rap music that Miranda draws on in *Hamilton* also, to a large degree, set limits on Obama's presidency. As Erik Nielsen and Travis Gosa point out in their introduction to *The Hip Hop & Obama Reader,* mainstream hip hop's current celebrations of wealth and entrepreneurial spirit are easily legible against the former president's own narrative of individual success.[58] Obama's story, *Hamilton*'s story, and contemporary mainstream rap all feature powerful symbols of blackness that substitute celebrations of achievement for more difficult discussions about the ongoing legacy of racial discrimination.

Hamilton in the Age of Trump

Due in part to these prominent themes of individual effort and bootstrap success, *Hamilton* has been embraced not just by supporters of President Obama and 2016 Democratic candidate Hillary Clinton, but also by some conservative Republicans. The PBS documentary *Hamilton's America* features interviews with House Speaker Paul Ryan and other prominent Republicans who also express enthusiasm for the show. As Elizabeth Craft explains, *Hamilton* transcends traditional party divisions in part because its plot and the Founders' myth on which it is based remain open to multiple readings and interpretations along both conservative and liberal lines.[59] Whereas liberal fans can celebrate the musical for placing immigrants and people of color in leadership roles and at the center of the nation's history, conservative fans can read *Hamilton* as endorsing the position that anybody can rise up in the United States as long as they are willing to work hard.

Thus, *Hamilton*'s politics depend upon who is watching and listening. In Craft's formulation, there is not a singular *Hamilton* but instead multiple *Hamiltons*.[60] In a world where people increasingly get their news from highly polarized sources and interpret the same facts in dramatically different ways, this multivalence of meanings should come as no surprise. However, such multiplicity does not mean that *Hamilton*'s politics are without limit. In fact, both liberal and conservative praise for the musical tends to center around a common acceptance of diversity as good. *Hamilton*'s broad appeal reflects the way that the concept of "racial diversity" has become malleable enough to serve multiple political agendas.

This neoliberal consensus on diversity, implicit in the broad acceptance of *Hamilton*'s casting and hip hop–influenced score, helps to explain more recent developments in the musical's history. In November 2016, days after Donald Trump defeated Hillary Clinton in the US presidential election, *Hamilton* made political headlines when then vice president–elect Mike Pence attended an evening performance. During the curtain call, Brandon Victor Dixon, the actor playing the role of Aaron Burr, delivered a message to Pence from the stage of the Richard Rodgers Theater: "We, sir, we are the diverse America who are alarmed and anxious that your new administration will not protect us—our planet, our children, our parents—or defend us and uphold our inalienable rights, sir. But we truly hope that this show has inspired you to uphold our American values and to work on behalf of all of us. All of us. Again, we truly thank you for sharing this show, this wonderful American story told by a diverse group of men [and] women of different colors, creeds, and orientations."[61] Speaking on behalf of the cast, Dixon expressed anxiety about the incoming administration's commitment to "all of us," implying the most vulnerable members of US society, such as racial and religious minorities, LGBTQ people, immigrants, and women.[62] While many members of the theater audience cheered this call to lead on behalf of all Americans, then president-elect Donald Trump took to Twitter not to defend his commitment to diversity and inclusion but to demand an apology for the harassment that Pence allegedly endured. Trump tweeted, "Our wonderful future V.P. Mike Pence was harassed last night at the theater by the cast of Hamilton, cameras blazing. This should not happen!"[63] And "the Theater must always be a safe and special place. The cast of Hamilton was very rude last night to a very good man, Mike Pence. Apologize!"[64]

For some observers, Dixon's speech and Trump's angry response may have been just another minor spectacle in the twenty-four-hour news cycle. But it was one that underscores how *Hamilton*'s musical celebration of diversity contrasts with Trump-style nationalism. In fact, a study published in *The Nation* magazine argues that fears about diversity drove many voters to favor Trump. Drawing on survey data, authors Sean McElwee and Jason McDaniel conclude that feelings about racial identity and tolerance of diversity are more salient predictors of voting patterns than socioeconomic status, and they found that whites with the most negative attitudes toward diversity were most likely to vote Trump.[65] In fact, the term "diversity" itself, which white supremacists mistakenly interpret as a euphemism for "white genocide," has become a favorite target of right-wing nationalists.[66]

Trump's hostility toward *Hamilton*, which he has refused to see and has maligned as "overrated," can be interpreted as a symbolic rejection of racial diversity. Because the genre of hip hop remains so thoroughly coded as black, Trump's tweets against the musical—much like his inauguration planner's statement that Kanye West was not being invited to perform at the "typically and traditionally American" inauguration festivities—match well with a campaign and presidency defined by the controversial support of white nationalist and alt-right groups.[67] In their quest to reassert white hegemony, such groups have explicitly broken with the neoliberal consensus that values ethnic diversity and integrated global markets, and they have seen in Trump a president who will limit immigration and defend white supremacy.

This political shift brought a renewed sense of urgency to *Hamilton*. Although one initially might have seen the musical as a victory lap for the Obama presidency, the postelection climate endowed *Hamilton* with an aura of increased militancy. Without the cover of multiculturalism promised by Barack Obama's presidency or Hillary Clinton's unsuccessful bid for the Oval Office, the dissonance between *Hamilton*'s sounding of American identity and the Trump White House's picture of it increased dramatically. Thus, it is not surprising that the 2016 presidential election marked a pivotal moment in *Hamilton*'s reception history. For many, Miranda's colorized Founders story seemed to contradict Trump's backward-looking campaign slogan, "Make America Great Again," which idealizes the United States' white Christian past, suggesting that perhaps America was better before civil rights were extended to blacks, gays, and women or before mass immigration from Asia and Latin America transformed the demographics of the country. Likewise, Miranda's support for Hillary Clinton's campaign seemed natural and expected. Her slogan "Stronger Together" appeared to undercut the nativist tone of Trump's campaign and strike a chord with a Democratic coalition that depends on young people, people of color, unmarried women, and LGBTQ people.

This politicization of diversity underscores the way *Hamilton* participates in the struggle to define US national identity. Although mainstream hip hop continues to be coded as a black genre, one of Miranda's achievements in *Hamilton* is to open up a space on Broadway that illuminates the shared struggle of black and brown people. In fact, *Hamilton* suggests some important parallels between his hip hop idols and the Latinx immigrants around which he was raised. Miranda recalls that he learned from Chernow's book that Hamilton was actually born in Nevis and raised in St. Croix before migrating to the United States. After reading about Hamilton's early life, he remembers, "I was like, 'I know this guy.' I've met so many versions of this guy, and it's the guy who comes to this country and is like, 'I am going to work six jobs if you're only working one.'"[68]

One of the most often cited refrains from the musical comes from "The Battle of Yorktown," when Hamilton and Lafayette are reunited on the battlefield and exclaim, "Immigrants, we get the job done."[69] By highlighting both Hamilton's and Lafayette's status as immigrants, the musical suggests other forms of hustle. Hamilton's drive to succeed is compared not only to aspiring hip hop artists "writing their way out" of the projects but also to migrant workers, documented and undocumented, who cross the border in search of a better life for their families. In this way, Miranda's blending of hip hop and Horatio Alger harks back to the diverse roots of hip hop itself, where Puerto Rican, African American, and Jamaican youths, among others, came together in the South Bronx to create something positive in the midst of urban decay.[70] Miranda makes this connection explicit in one of his *Genius* annotations: "I wanted to outline the improbability of this situation. This is the story of hip-hop. It's Tupac's image of the rose that grew out of some concrete. It's Richard Pryor growing up in a brothel, to being one of the greatest comedic geniuses of our time. Real genius, like Hamiltonian genius, will survive its circumstances. This type of genius is simply undeniable. And it's an immigrant story, too, which reminded me of my father, who came here at 18 from Puerto Rico, not speaking a word of English and selling newspapers."[71]

Despite its revolutionary subject matter, a number of questions remain about the musical's inclusivity. For example, what roles might Native American actors or actresses play in *Hamilton*, and what might be the implications of such casting choices? Historian Rachel Herrmann has noted that Philip Schuyler (Alexander Hamilton's father-in-law) had several dealings with Native Americans while working as New York's state surveyor general: "Schuyler became interested in canal construction north and west of Albany in the 1790s. He built up lands at Saratoga (now Schuylerville) and 'Cortlandt Manor,' inherited from his parents and his uncle. He also acquired thousands of acres in the Mohawk Valley. This territorial acquisition continued because New York State had taken the land of the Iroquois—at Fort Herkimer in 1785, at Fort Schuyler in 1788, and at Albany in 1789—despite the fact that some Iroquois, particularly the Oneidas, fought for the Americans in the war."[72] In other words, much of the Schuyler family's wealth—a subject central to the musical's plot—came from the appropriation of Native lands. Although *Hamilton* makes slavery a central issue in its retelling of the Founders' myth, similar attention is not paid to the violence of settler colonialism. In fact, the musical's unconventional casting has been limited mainly to actors who identify as black and/or Latinx, and one could argue that even a musical that casts the descendants of slaves as white Founders might be participating in other forms of exclusion.[73]

It is not surprising that *Hamilton*'s feel-good celebration of diversity has limits, especially when it comes from a theater charging upward of $400 per ticket. With its focus on the exceptional genius of its star character, *Hamilton*—much like many examples in mainstream rap music—reinforces neoliberal attitudes toward social inequality. Barack Obama's improbable path to the presidency as a symbol of black-white reconciliation, Jay-Z's miraculous survival of inner-city projects and rise as a musical star and businessman, Alexander Hamilton's humble beginnings as an immigrant outsider who writes his way to prominence and helps found a nation, and Lin-Manuel Miranda's own personal narrative as the MacArthur "Genius" Grant–winning son of Puerto Rican migrants all represent stories about great men whose innate talents led to upward mobility and acclaim. As the United States continues to shred its social safety net and reward corporations and wealthy individuals with tax breaks, *Hamilton*'s complicity with neoliberal politics of individual responsibility merits greater discussion and debate.

Although these and other political contradictions remain unresolved, *Hamilton*'s engagement with hip hop's history, culture, and aesthetics forms an undeniable part of the musical's appeal. *Hamilton* deserves to be called a "hip hop musical" not simply because its black and Latinx actors rap on the Broadway stage but because of the production's rich and overt intertextuality. Adopting hip hop's fundamental commitment to musical borrowing, *Hamilton* sounds national identity through the racialized matrix of American popular music. The musical and its cast recording represent a potent example of how politics and popular culture can inform one another and how the combination of musical theater and hip hop can serve as a mirror and also, perhaps, as an inspiration for political struggle. Miranda's use of hip hop as a lingua franca for the entire production is fundamental to *Hamilton*'s political thrust, sounding out the distance between the United States' ideals of liberty and justice for all and its ongoing realities.

Notes

1. Lin-Manuel Miranda as quoted in Alex Beggs, "Read Lin-Manuel Miranda's Genius Annotations for 'Hamilton,'" *Vanity Fair*, November 2, 2015, https://www.vanityfair.com /culture/2015/11/hamilton-lyrics-genius-lin-manuel-miranda (accessed April 15, 2018).

2. Just to name a few examples, in 2016 *Hamilton* won eleven Tony Awards, including best musical, and it also received a Grammy Award for best musical theater recording. Creator

Lin-Manuel Miranda received the Pulitzer Prize for drama, as well as a prestigious MacArthur "Genius" Fellowship.

3. In a well-publicized piece on *Hamilton,* historian Lyra Monteiro accused Miranda of reinforcing the white Founders' narrative at the expense of lesser known stories about the lives of people of color living in Revolutionary era America. See Lyra D. Monteiro, "Race-Conscious Casting and the Erasure of the Black Past in Lin-Manuel Miranda's *Hamilton,*" *Public Historian* 38, no. 1 (February 2016): 90.

4. As quoted in Edward Delman, "How Lin-Manuel Miranda Shapes History," *Atlantic,* September 29, 2015, https://www.theatlantic.com/entertainment/archive/2015/09/lin-manuel -miranda-hamilton/408019/ (accessed April 15, 2018).

5. See Joanne B. Freeman, *Affairs of Honor: National Politics in the New Republic* (New Haven, CT: Yale University Press, 2001); Stephen Skowronek, *The Politics Presidents Make: Leadership from John Adams to George Bush* (Cambridge, MA: Belknap Press, 1993); Sidney Milkis and Michael Nelson, *The American Presidency: Origins and Development of the US Presidency, 1776–2007,* 5th ed. (Washington, DC: CQ Press, 2008).

6. See Elizabeth Craft, "Headfirst into an Abyss: The Politics and Political Reception of *Hamilton,*" in this issue.

7. Charles Hiroshi Garrett, *Struggling to Define a Nation: American Music and the Twentieth Century* (Berkeley: University of California Press, 2008).

8. This approach, which seems to target the broadest possible audience, echoes the marketing strategy for Lin-Manuel Miranda's first Broadway success, *In the Heights.* See Elizabeth Craft, "'Is This What It Takes Just to Make It to Broadway?!': Marketing *In the Heights* in the Twenty-First Century," *Studies in Musical Theater* 5, no. 1 (2011): 56.

9. Fans of the musical include hip hop royalty, such as Jay-Z, Nas, and Queen Latifah, as well as those one would not normally expect to be associated with the genre, such as former vice president Dick Cheney, Mitt Romney, and Julia Roberts.

10. Asked whether or not his first Broadway production, *In the Heights,* which also featured rapping, could appeal to a broad audience, Miranda explained, "The fun is bringing people along for the ride without any of the cultural baggage that may go along with hip-hop music." Misha Berson, "Salsa and Rap Musical *In the Heights*—Coming to 5th Avenue—Lifted Creator to Early Stardom," *Seattle Times,* September 23, 2010, http://www.seattletimes.com/entertainment /salsa-and-rap-musical-in-the-heights-8212-coming-to-5th-avenue-8212-lifted-creator-to -early-stardom/ (accessed April 15, 2018).

11. For a discussion of problematic caricatures of black life in mainstream rap music, see Tricia Rose, *The Hip Hop Wars: What We Talk About When We Talk About Hip Hop and Why It Matters* (New York: Basic Civitas, 2008).

12. According to *Hamilton*'s music director, Alex Lacamoire, "The Room Where It Happens" evokes John Kander and Fred Ebb's style of Broadway musical writing (think *Chicago* or *Cabaret*). See Lin-Manuel Miranda and Jeremy McCarter, *Hamilton: The Revolution* (New York: Grand Central Publishing, 2016), 184.

13. The 3+3+2 pattern has become common in popular music both inside the United States and around the globe. The most famous contemporary example coinciding with *Hamilton*'s popularity is Luis Fonsi and Daddy Yankee's 2017 megahit, "Despacito," which has Puerto Rican origins but global reach, climbing to the number-one chart position in dozens of countries. For more on this phenomenon, see Wayne Marshall, "Everything You Wanted to Know About 'Despacito,'" *Vulture,* August 22, 2017, http://www.vulture.com/2017/08 /everything-you-ever-wanted-to-know-about-despacito.html (accessed April 15, 2018).

14. See Anne Searcy, "Bringing Dance Back to the Center in *Hamilton,*" in this issue.

15. Miranda describes this number as "getting my Bach on." See William Robin, "'Hamilton' Is Known for Its Music, but What Did Alexander Hamilton Listen To?," *New York Times*, August 11, 2017, https://www.nytimes.com/2017/08/11/arts/music/hamilton-music-lin-manuel-miranda-los-angeles.html?_r=1 (accessed April 15, 2018).

16. As Elissa Harbert notes, in dramatic representations of colonial America, "it's often in the music for British or British loyalist characters that we see the most signifiers of European music." By contrast, "the patriot side very often will be represented by very up-to-date popular musical styles." As quoted in ibid.

17. Jody Rosen, "The American Revolutionary," *New York Times Magazine*, July 8, 2015, https://www.nytimes.com/interactive/2015/07/08/t-magazine/hamilton-lin-manuel-miranda-roots-sondheim.html (accessed April 15, 2018). "You'll Be Back" also has been described as a "Carnaby Street breakup song not unlike 'With a Little Help from My Friends.'" Jesse Green, "Lin Manuel Miranda's 'Hamilton' Is Worth Way More Than $10," *Vulture*, February 17, 2015, http://www.vulture.com/2015/02/theater-review-lin-manuel-mirandas-hamilton.html (accessed April 15, 2018).

18. As Justin Williams points out, this musical juxtaposition also plays upon hip hop's concern with "authenticity" vis-à-vis the pop mainstream. See Williams, "'We Get the Job Done': Immigrant Discourse and Mixtape Authenticity in *The Hamilton Mixtape*," in this issue.

19. Philip Gentry, "*Hamilton*'s Ghosts," *American Music* 35, no. 2 (2017): 271–80.

20. Justin Williams, *Rhymin' & Stealin': Musical Borrowing in Hip Hop* (Ann Arbor: University of Michigan Press, 2012), 1–2.

21. The most comprehensive collection of such intertextual references can probably be found on the music site Genius.com, a lyrics website featuring user-created annotations of songs, including many by Miranda himself.

22. For example, in "Right Hand Man," George Washington's rhythmic delivery and alliterative rhyme scheme sample "The Modern Major General" from Gilbert and Sullivan's *Pirates of Penzance*. In similar fashion, the steamy "No to This," which details Hamilton's affair with Maria Reynolds and his blackmail by her husband, ends with an interpolation of the title phrase "Nobody Needs to Know" from the musical *The Last Five Years*. These borrowings constitute a nod and wink to musical theater fans while also reflecting a more general hip hop approach to composition.

23. Ron Chernow, *Alexander Hamilton* (New York: Penguin Books, 2004).

24. Some of the most prominent musical references in *Hamilton* are credited in the musical's playbill, meaning that permissions were secured from copyright holders. Although Miranda probably did not need to do so and could have claimed "fair use," some observers believe that Miranda obtained permissions out of respect, acknowledging the importance of hip hop music and showing a sense of solidarity with rap artists who must routinely clear their samples. See Larry Iser, "'Hamilton' Part II—Why Lin-Manuel Miranda Didn't Really Need to Clear the Music," *Forbes*, June 27, 2016, https://www.forbes.com/sites/legalentertainment/2016/06/27/hamilton-part-ii-why-lin-manuel-miranda-didnt-really-need-to-clear-the-music/#13edc0b945d5 (accessed April 15, 2018).

25. Or as Miranda put it, he wanted "to eliminate any distance between a contemporary audience and this story." Edward Delman, "How Lin-Manuel Miranda Shapes History," *Atlantic*, September 29, 2015, https://www.theatlantic.com/entertainment/archive/2015/09/lin-manuel-miranda-hamilton/408019/ (accessed April 15, 2018).

26. Elissa Harbert locates *Hamilton* in a tradition of "history musicals" and notes that a shared feature of this genre is the way that historical plots become "vehicles for cultural commentary relevant to the present day." See "*Hamilton* and History Musicals" in this issue.

27. Rebecca Mead, "All About the Hamiltons," *New Yorker*, February 9, 2015, http://www
.newyorker.com/magazine/2015/02/09/hamiltons (accessed April 15, 2018).

28. Miranda makes such claims numerous times in his annotations about Hamilton on
the Genius.com website, https://genius.com/artists/Lin-manuel-miranda (accessed April 15,
2018).

29. https://www.youtube.com/watch?v=WNFf7nMIGnE (accessed April 15, 2018).

30. Drake, "Started from the Bottom," *AAC File* (Cash Money Records, 2013).

31. *Hamilton's America*, directed by Alex Horwitz, television documentary (Arlington,
VA: PBS, 2016).

32. In this way, Hamilton mirrors gendered divisions within mainstream rap music.
For Revolutionary War heroes, such as Lafayette, Hamilton, and Washington, fast-paced
and assertive rapping equals intellect and valor. Female characters, such as Eliza and Maria
Reynolds, however, are relegated to traditional feminine roles, admiring and/or seducing
male counterparts with R&B-style singing. The only exception to this division is Angelica
Schuyler, whose rapping in songs like "The Schuyler Sisters" and "Satisfied" evokes strong
female MCs like Queen Latifah, who often challenged sexism and misogyny in her music.

33. Gentry, "*Hamilton*'s Ghosts."

34. Beggs, "Read Lin-Manuel Miranda's Genius Annotations."

35. For more on N.W.A's song, see Chris Moore, "'Fuck Tha Police': N.W.A's Most Coura-
geous Song Is Still as Relevant as Ever," *Mass Appeal*, August 14, 2015, https://massappeal
.com/fuck-tha-police-nwa-most-courageous-song-is-still-as-relevant-as-ever/ (accessed
April 15, 2018).

36. These underdog characters tend to be working-class immigrant men. Finding themselves denied legitimate paths to power, they resort to criminal violence in order to achieve
the American dream. Robin Kelley explains the appeal and symbolic power of such outlaw
types in his classic essay on gangsta rap. Robin D. G. Kelley, *Race Rebels: Culture, Politics,
and the Black Working Class* (New York: Free Press, 1994), 183–227.

37. Mobb Deep, "Shook Ones, Pt. 2," *The Infamous* (RCA Records 07863 66480-1, 1995).

38. Mobb Deep, "Survival of the Fittest," *The Infamous* (RCA Records 07863 66480-1,
1995).

39. Chernow, *Alexander Hamilton*.

40. Notorious B.I.G., "Ten Crack Commandments," *Life after Death* (Bad Boy Entertainment 78612-73011-1, 1997). Notorious B.I.G's version features the voice of rapper Chuck D
via a sample taken from Public Enemy's "Shut 'Em Down." In *Hamilton*, cast members sing
an imitation of the iconic countdown.

41. Beggs, "Lin-Manuel Miranda's Genius Annotations."

42. 50 Cent, *Get Rich, or Die Tryin'* (Shady Aftermath 0694935442, 2003).

43. Lester Spence, *Stare in the Darkness: The Limits of Hip-Hop and Black Politics* (Minneapolis: University of Minnesota Press, 2011), 19–54.

44. Ibid., 8–9.

45. Lin-Manuel Miranda, "Cabinet Battle #1," *Hamilton: An American Musical—Original
Broadway Cast Recording* (Atlantic Records 551093-2, 2015).

46. Various, "Cabinet Battle #3 Demo," *The Hamilton Mixtape* (Atlantic Records 551092-2,
2016).

47. Anne Searcy provides a brilliant reading of how "What'd I Miss" draws on Broadway
iconography to critique Jefferson as a slaveholder, concluding that "the choreography is a
much harsher judge of Jefferson's character than the music or lyrics." See "Bringing Dance
Back to the Center in *Hamilton*," in this issue. For historians' concerns about the musical's
selective references to slavery, see Monteiro, "Race-Conscious Casting," 95.

48. Edward Baptist, *The Half Has Never Been Told: Slavery and the Birth of American Capitalism* (New York: Basic Books, 2014), 1–38.

49. As some scholars have noted, the 2016 election year, which was animated by populist politics on both the Left (Bernie Sanders) and Right (Donald Trump), seemed like an "odd moment for the public to embrace an unabashed elitist who liked big banks, mistrusted the masses and at one point called for a monarchal presidency and a Senate that served for life." Sean Wilentz, as quoted in Jennifer Schuessler, "'Hamilton' and History: Are They in Sync?," *New York Times*, April 10, 2016, https://www.nytimes.com/2016/04/11/theater/hamilton-and -history-are-they-in-sync.html?emc=eta1 (accessed April 15, 2018).

50. For an example of such claims, see Daniel Schorr, "A New, 'Post-Racial' Political Era in America," *NPR's All Things Considered*, January 28, 2009, https://www.npr.org/templates /story/story.php?storyId=18489466 (accessed April 15, 2018). For a study refuting this idea, see Michael Tesler and David O. Sears, *Obama's Race: The 2008 Election and the Dream of a Post-Racial America* (Chicago: University of Chicago Press, 2010).

51. Joseph Lowndes, "Barack Obama's Body: The Presidency, the Body Politic, and the Contest over American National Identity," *Polity* 45, no. 4 (2013): 469–98.

52. Michael P. Jeffries, "The King's English: Obama, Jay-Z, and the Science of Code Switch-ing," in *The Hip Hop & Obama Reader*, ed. Travis Gosa and Erik Nielson (New York: Oxford University Press, 2015), 243–61.

53. Dana Gorzelany-Mostak, "Keeping It Real (Respectable) in 2008: Barack Obama's Music Strategy and the Formation of Presidential Identity," *Journal of the Society for American Music* 10, no. 2 (2016): 113–48.

54. "Lin-Manuel Miranda on Disney, Mixtapes and Why He Won't Try to Top 'Hamil-ton,'" *Fresh Air* with Terry Gross, January 3, 2017, https://www.npr.org/2017/01/03/507470975 /lin-manuel-miranda-on-disney-mixtapes-and-why-he-wont-try-to-top-hamilton (accessed April 15, 2018); Brian Hiatt, "'Hamilton': Meet the Man behind Broadway's Hip-Hop Mas-terpiece," *Rolling Stone*, September 29, 2015, http://www.rollingstone.com/culture/features /hamilton-meet-the-man-behind-broadways-hip-hop-masterpiece-20150929 (accessed April 15, 2018); Justin Williams, "'We Get the Job Done': Immigrant Discourse and Mixtape Authenticity in *The Hamilton Mixtape*," in this issue.

55. For the collaboration with Nas, listen to the track "Wrote My Way Out" on *The Ham-ilton Mixtape*. See also Jon Caramanica, "Lin-Manuel Miranda Discusses How Hip Hop Influenced Him and 'Hamilton,'" *New York Times*, September 25, 2015, https://artsbeat.blogs .nytimes.com/2015/09/25/lin-manuel-miranda-discusses-how-hip-hop-influenced-him-and -hamilton/?mcubz=0 (accessed April 15, 2018).

56. *Fresh Air with Terry Gross*, January 3, 2017.

57. The recording of the freestyle session—in which Obama held up cue cards with words that Miranda had to incorporate into his improvised rap—went viral, and footage from their interview was used for the PBS documentary *Hamilton's America*. Daniel Victor, "Lin-Manuel Miranda 'Hamilton' Creator, Freestyles for Obama," *New York Times*, March 15, 2016, https:// www.nytimes.com/2016/03/16/arts/lin-manuel-miranda-hamilton-creator-freestyles-for -obama.html?mcubz=0&_r=0 (accessed April 15, 2018).

58. Travis Gosa and Erik Nielson, "Introduction: The State of Hip Hop in the Age of Obama," in *The Hip Hop & Obama Reader*, ed. Travis Gosa and Erik Nielson (New York: Oxford University Press, 2015), 8–11.

59. Craft, "Headfirst."

60. Ibid. Elissa Harbert also notes how the Revolutionary Era's rich history and noncon-troversial symbolism in US history appeals to people on both sides of the aisle in her work

on the reception of another Broadway musical, *1776*. See "'Ever to the Right'? The Political Life of *1776* in the Nixon Era," *American Music* 35, no. 2 (2017): 237–70.

61. Video of the speech is widely available online. See also "'Hamilton' Had Some Unscripted Lines for Pence. Trump Wasn't Happy," *New York Times*, November 19, 2016, https://www.nytimes.com/2016/11/19/us/mike-pence-hamilton.html?_r=0 (accessed April 15, 2018).

62. Dixon's statement was actually a collaborative effort written in consultation with the show's creator, Lin-Manuel Miranda, its director, Thomas Kail, and its producer, Jeffrey Sellers.

63. Online at https://twitter.com/realDonaldTrump/status/799972624713420804 (accessed April 15, 2018).

64. https://twitter.com/realDonaldTrump/status/799974635274194947 (accessed April 15, 2018).

65. Sean McElwee and Jason McDaniel, "Fear of Diversity Made People More Likely to Vote for Trump," *Nation*, March 14, 2017, https://www.thenation.com/article/fear-of-diversity-made-people-more-likely-to-vote-trump/ (accessed April 15, 2018).

66. Just days before McElwee and McDaniel published their research in *The Nation*, Representative Steve King (R-Iowa) tweeted a controversial message sympathizing with xenophobic politicians in the Netherlands, exclaiming, "We can't restore our civilization with somebody else's babies." Two weeks later, alt-right website Breitbart ran a story suggesting that ethnic diversity "is bad for social cohesion." Although the headline portrays diversity as negative, the article cites a study showing social cohesion to be extremely high in Sweden despite increasing levels of diversity. Virginia Hale, "Study Finds Diversity Bad for Social Cohesion," Breitbart, May 29, 2017, http://www.breitbart.com/london/2017/05/29/study-ethnic-diversity-bad-sweden/ (accessed April 15, 2018).

67. Helena Andrews-Dyer, "Kanye West Not 'Traditionally American' Enough to Perform at Trump Inauguration, Hints Organizer," *Chicago Tribune*, January 19, 2017, http://www.chicagotribune.com/entertainment/music/ct-kanye-west-trump-inauguration-20170119-story.html (accessed April 15, 2018).

68. Edward Delman, "How Lin-Manuel Miranda Shapes History," *Atlantic*, September 29, 2015, https://www.theatlantic.com/entertainment/archive/2015/09/lin-manuel-miranda-hamilton/408019/ (accessed April 15, 2018).

69. This line from the song was also sampled to create a new song of the same name on *The Hamilton Mixtape*. See Williams, "'We Get the Job Done': Immigrant Discourse and Mixtape Authenticity in *The Hamilton Mixtape*," in this issue.

70. Jeff Chang, *Can't Stop, Won't Stop: A History of the Hip Hop Generation* (New York: St. Martin's Press, 2005).

71. Beggs, "Lin-Manuel Miranda's Genius Annotations."

72. Rachel Herrmann, "'Daddy' Schuyler, Hamilton, and the Dakota Access Pipeline," *Junto*, November 1, 2016, https://earlyamericanists.com/2016/11/01/daddy-schuyler-hamilton-and-the-dakota-access-pipelinaccessed April 15, 2018).

73. Despite claims by Miranda and others that the cast reflects the demographic diversity of America today, similar questions could be asked about Asian American participation. With the exception of Phillipa Soo, no Asian American actors or actresses occupy prominent roles in *Hamilton*'s original production and cast recording. Beginning with the musical's second touring company in 2018, however, the roles of Alexander Hamilton, Eliza Schuyler, and George Washington were performed by Asian American actors Joseph Morales, Shoba Narayan, and Marcus Choi, respectively.

Original Publications

George, Nelson. *Where Did Our Love Go? The Rise and Fall of the Motown Sound.* University of Illinois Press, 2007.

Goins, Wayne Everett. *Blues All Day Long: The Jimmy Rogers Story.* University of Illinois Press, 2014.

Harold, Claudrena N. *When Sunday Comes: Gospel Music in the Soul and Hip-Hop Eras.* University of Illinois Press, 2020.

Hayes, Eileen M. *Songs in Black and Lavender: Race, Sexual Politics, and Women's Music.* University of Illinois Press, 2010.

Hayes, Eileen M., and Linda F. Williams, eds. *Black Women and Music: More than the Blues.* University of Illinois Press, 2007.

Kajikawa, Loren. "'Young, Scrappy, and Hungry': *Hamilton*, Hip Hop, and Race." *American Music* 36, no. 4 (Winter 2018): 467–486.

Kelley, Robin D. G. "New Monastery: Monk and the Jazz Avant-Garde." *Black Music Research Journal* 19, no. 2 (Autumn 1999): 135–168.

Kernodle, Tammy L. "Black Women Working Together: Jazz, Gender, and the Politics of Validation." *Black Music Research Journal* 34, no. 1 (Spring): 27–55.

Keyes, Cheryl L. *Rap Music and Street Consciousness.* University of Illinois Press, 2004.

Reagon, Bernice Johnson. "Let the Church Sing 'Freedom.'" *Black Music Research Journal* 7 (1987): 105–118.

Tucker, Mark. "The Genesis of *Black, Brown and Beige.*" *Black Music Research Journal* 13, no. 2 (Autumn 1993): 67–86.

Tucker, Sherrie. "Nobody's Sweethearts: Gender, Race, Jazz, and the Darlings of Rhythm." *American Music* 16, no. 3 (Autumn 1998): 255–288.

Contributors

NELSON GEORGE is an author and filmmaker whose books include *Where Did Our Love Go? The Rise and Fall of the Motown Sound* and *Hip Hop America*.

WAYNE EVERETT GOINS is university distinguished professor of music and the director of jazz studies in the School of Music, Theater, and Dance at Kansas State University. Goins authored *Blues All Day Long: The Jimmy Rogers Story*, which was named "Blues Biography of the Year" by *Living Blues* magazine in July 2015. Goins is working on a biography of legendary blues musician Taj Mahal.

CLAUDRENA N. HAROLD is a professor of history and African American studies at the University of Virginia. She is the author of *New Negro Politics in the Jim Crow South* and *When Sunday Comes: Gospel Music in the Soul and Hip-Hop Eras*.

EILEEN M. HAYES is dean of the College of Arts and Communication at the University of Wisconsin–Whitewater and the author of *Songs in Black and Lavender: Race, Sexual Politics, and Women's Music*.

LOREN KAJIKAWA is associate professor of musicology at the George Washington University's Corcoran School of the Arts and Design. He is the author of *Sounding Race in Rap Songs*.

ROBIN D. G. KELLEY is distinguished professor and Gary B. Nash endowed chair in U. S. history at the University of California, Los Angeles. His many books include *Thelonious Monk: The Life and Times of an American Original*.

TAMMY L. KERNODLE researches and teaches in the areas of gender studies in music, and African American music (popular and classical). She is the author of *Soul on Soul: The Life and Music of Mary Lou Williams*. Her work appears in a number of journals, anthologies, and edited volumes. She is currently university distinguished professor at Miami University in Oxford, OH.

CHERYL L. KEYES is a professor of ethnomusicology, global jazz studies, and African American studies and the chair of African American studies at the University of California, Los Angeles. Keyes conducted extensive research and fieldwork on rap music and hip-hop culture in Detroit, London, Los Angeles, New York City, and Mali throughout the 1980s and '90s. Her book *Rap Music and Street Consciousness* is recognized as one of ". . . the first book-length hip-hop ethnographies and musicological histories of rap."

GWENDOLYN D. POUGH is dean's professor of the humanities and professor of women's and gender studies at Syracuse University. Her books include *Check It While I Wreck It: Black Womanhood, Hip-Hop Culture, and the Public Sphere* and *Home Girls Make Some Noise! Hip Hop Feminism Anthology*.

BERNICE JOHNSON REAGON is professor emeritus of history at American University. A member of the original SNCC (Student Non-Violent Coordinating Committee) Freedom Singers, she founded the internationally renowned African American women's a cappella ensemble Sweet Honey in the Rock. Her books include *Wade in the Water: African American Sacred Music Traditions*.

MARK TUCKER (1954–2000), a professor at Columbia University from 1987 to 1997 and the College of William and Mary until 2000, was a master teacher, scholar, and performer of classic jazz. He was the author of *Ellington: The Early Years* and *The Duke Ellington Reader*.

SHERRIE TUCKER is a professor of American studies at the University of Kansas. She is the author of *Dance Floor Democracy: The Social Geography of Memory at the Hollywood Canteen, Swing Shift: "All-Girl" Bands of the 1940s*, and co-editor with Nichole T. Rustin of *Big Ears: Listening for Gender in Jazz Studies*.

Index

Mills, Florence, 69
Mills, Irving, 72–73
Mingus, Charles, 114, 120, 121, 123, 132, 134
Minnie, Memphis, 29, 31
Miracles, the, 146, 158, 160
Miranda, Lin-Manuel: annotations on
    Genius.com site, 283, 286n21, 287n28;
    awards for, 284, 285n2; code switching by,
    279–80; on contemporary relevance of
    Hamilton, 274, 286n25; Dixon's statement
    to Pence, 289n62; on "Farmer Refuted,"
    286n15; freestyle session with Obama, 280,
    288n57; on Hamilton, 270, 273, 275, 283; on
    In the Heights, 285n10; hip-hop techniques
    used by, 271–73, 285n10; intertextuality
    and, 286n21, 286n24; on "My Shot," 275–76;
    support for Clinton campaign, 282. See
    also *Hamilton: An American Musical*
"Miss D. D." (Williams), 103
"Misterioso" (Monk), 126
Mitchell, Jimmy, 103–4
mixing records, techniques, 236–38
Moana (film), 279
Modern Jazz Quartet, The, 107, 117
Moncur, Grachan, III, 120
Monifah, 254
Monk, Nellie, 123
Monk, Thelonious, 5–6, 106, 107, 113–38;
    acclaim, 113–14, 118, 129; Black masculin-
    ity and, 117–18; Coltrane and, 116, 126, 127,
    138n1; compositional style, 124, 128–31;
    criticism, 113–14, 118, 124, 128, 129; at Five
    Spot, 116, 127, 138n1; image of, as politically
    disinterested, 120, 122–24; at Jazz Gallery,
    131, 139n8; recording contracts, 114, 124;
    sidemen, 124, 127, 134–35. See also avant-
    garde jazz
Monk, Thelonious, influence of, 124, 128–37,
    139n3; arrangements performed by other
    musicians, 119–20, 133–35, 136, 139n9; on
    Coltrane, 118, 135; on Dolphy, 120, 135–37,
    139n9; on Lacy and Rudd, 117, 118, 120, 122,
    131–35
Monk, Thelonious, performance style, 115–16,
    124, 139n2, 139n5; chord voicings, 125–26;
    dances while performing, 116–17, 126, 130;
    freeing effect, 126–27, 133–34, 137; improvi-
    sation and, 126–27, 130, 131, 132–33, 134–35;
    New Music and, 125; Taylor on, 128–31;
    tonality use, 115, 117–18, 125, 126, 128–29
"Monk, Bunk, and Vice Versa" (Mingus), 120
"Monk and the Nun" (Coleman), 120
"Monk in Wonderland" (Moncur III), 120

Monk-Rouse-Ore/Gales-Dunlop/Riley quar-
    tet, 114, 122, 127
"Monk's Mood" (Monk), 132, 136
Monroe, Al, 54
Monson, Ingrid, 64n35, 123
Montgomery, Melba, 175
Montgomery Gospel Trio, 189
"Mood Indigo" (Ellington), 67
Moore, Warren, 161
"More Love" (Robinson), 159
Morgan, Joan, 245, 250–51, 253, 256, 263–64,
    266
Morgenstern, Dan, 128
Moroder, Giorgio, 224
Morris, Bonnie, 203–4, 219n4
Morse, David, 162
Mosbacher, Dee, 203
Moser, Stan, 177–78
Moses, Robert (New York park commis-
    sioner), 227
Moses, Robert Paris (SNCC Mississippi direc-
    tor), 195
Motor Town Revue (Motown Revue), 146
Motown label, 7, 146–62; as Black-owned,
    147–50; competitiveness at, 155–57; expan-
    sion of premises, 151; orders policy, 157–58;
    organized crime rumors, 151–52; Robinson
    with, 146, 148, 149, 152, 155, 156, 158–62; Vee
    Jay and, 147–48; whites in operations of,
    147, 150–51; writer-producers scrutinized
    by, 155–56; Young on, 154–55. See also
    Gordy, Berry, Jr.; Robinson, Smokey
Mount Calvary Holy Church of America,
    169, 170
Movement Singers, 190
Moynihan, Daniel Patrick, 263
Mr. Biggs (MC), 239
MTV, 9
Murray, Sunny, 122
"Muscadine Wine" (Rogers), 15–16
musical elements: atonality, 116, 125, 128–29,
    132; chord progressions/changes, 30, 45,
    115, 125, 132, 136, 139n5; chord voicings,
    125–26, 135, 139n5; gendered coding of,
    117–18, 139n2, 209–10; in *Hamilton,* 271–72,
    285n13, 286nn15–16, 286n24; harmolodic
    theory, 132, 133–34; syncopation, 37, 117;
    tempo, 79, 100–101, 117, 134, 137, 224, 225;
    3+3+2 rhythm, 272, 285n13; time signa-
    tures, 134, 135, 272. See also arrangements;
    composition; rhythm; tonality
musical skill, gender and, 43–46, 47–49, 52,
    64n28, 87, 212; masculinity associations,

Paul, Clarence, 149, 156
Payne, Odie, 28
Peacock, Willie, 190, 191, 195–97
Pebblee-Poo, 239, 244n13
Pence, Mike, 281–82, 289n61–62
"People Get Ready" (Mayfield), 175
performance style: of Bambaataa, 235; of Caesar, 165, 174, 187n62; of the Darlings, 38, 45; of Headhunters, 27; of Monk, 116–17, 124, 130; of Sweethearts, 45. *See also* improvisation; Monk, Thelonious, performance style
Perkins, William Eric, 246
Perry, Julia, 4
"Peter, Don't Be Afraid" (Caesar), 182
P-funk (term), 223
Philadelphia International Records, 224
Philharmonic Hall, 102
Phillips, Sam, 146
piano, left hand use in, 126, 139n6. *See also* Monk, Thelonious
Pittsburgh Jazz Festival (1964), 5, 101, 104–7, 110n14
"Played Twice" (Monk), 132, 137
Point of Departure (Hill), 137
police brutality, 123
political generations, 206, 219n16
Pollack, Ed, 151
Pontiflet, Theodore, 123
Porgy and Bess (Gershwin), 82n6
post-racialism, 10
Potter, Russell, 257
Powell, Bud, 93, 126
Powell, Buttercup, 93
Powell, Kevin, 250
Prairie View Co-Eds, 38–39
"Praise the Lord" (Liston), 103–4, 106, 107
"Praying Slave Lady" (Caesar), 165
Presley, Elvis, 146, 178
Price, Lloyd, 146
Priestley, Brian, 72
prison population, 265–66
Pryor, Snooky, 12, 18, 19
public/private spheres, 247
Puerto Rico, 229, 244n5
Puff Daddy, 252, 253, 256, 262
"Put Your Hand in the Hand" (Caesar), 174

"Queen Bitch" (Lil' Kim), 260
"Queen Clara" (Watkins), 214
Queen Kenya (MC), 239
Queen Latifah, 268n12, 275, 285n9
Queen Pen, 248
queer (term), 215–16
Questlove (Ahmir Thompson), 271

race: "all-girl" bands and, 40, 64n28; in jazz history, research deficit, 64n35; Monk's image as avoidant of race politics, 120, 122–24; musical skill and, 60–61, 212; race consciousness, 71, 73
race records, 13, 145, 147
racial identity: as voting pattern predictor, 282; women's music movement and, 214–15, 216–18
"Racial Prejudice in Jazz" panel, 139n4
racism, 121, 247; in jazz and jazz criticism, 128, 129–30, 139n7; white feminism and, 212
Radical Harmonies (film), 203
radio, 19, 29, 55, 179, 231
rags-to-riches stories, 275
Rainey, Gertrude "Ma," 38, 108, 246, 262
"Raise Four" (Monk), 126
Randle, Vicki, 209–10, 214
rap music, 9, 222–43, 267n3; DJing and, 230–38; ethic of love and, 245; gang culture and, 226–30; love song lyrics in, 246, 247–49, 251, 256–66; musical and social change in development of, 223–26; "rapping deejays," 242–43; "rapping" scriptural lyrics in "Praise the Lord," 104; rhymin MCs and, 238–43, 244n13. *See also* disc jockeys (DJs); hip-hop music; women rappers
"Rapper's Delight" (Sugarhill Gang), 242, 243
"Rapture" (Caesar), 173
Rawls, Lou, 179
Ray, Carline, 108–9
Ray, Tanya, 216
R&B singing, 251–52
RCA label, 145, 146
"Reach Out and Touch (Somebody's Hand)" (Ross, covered by Caesar), 177
reading music, 46
Ready to Die (Biggie Smalls), 256
Reagon, Bernice Johnson, 206, 213
Reagon, Toshi, 213, 214
"Real Love" (Blige), 254, 259
recordings: lack of all-girl bands, 39, 40, 64n28; Monk's recording contracts, 114, 124; of Rogers, 13–19, 26; "Soundies," 39, 64n28; studio *vs.* live performance, 182; underground recording scene on Maxwell Street, 13
record labels, 3–4, 9, 145–46; antiracist artists silenced by, 121; Black-owned, 147–50, 224; Caesar's signings with, 165–66, 172–80, 182; hip-hop music, 242; "indies," 146; Jamaican-owned and operated, 232; Sunnyland Slim's influence, 19–20, 25–26, 27–28; women's music movement and, 202, 205,

Music in American Life

The University of Illinois Press
is a founding member of the
Association of University Presses.

University of Illinois Press
1325 South Oak Street
Champaign, IL 61820-6903
www.press.uillinois.edu